Walking in the Light of His Word

Daily Scripture Reflections

REV. JOSEPH D. CREEDON

Walking in the Light of His Word:
Daily Scripture Reflections
Copyright © 2022 Rev. Joseph D. Creedon

Produced and printed by Stillwater River Publications.
All rights reserved. Written and produced in the
United States of America. This book may not be reproduced
or sold in any form without the expressed, written
permission of the author(s) and publisher.

Visit our website at
www.StillwaterPress.com
for more information.

First Stillwater River Publications Edition

ISBN: 978-1-955123-81-5

Library of Congress Control Number: 2022902526

1 2 3 4 5 6 7 8 9 10

Written by Rev. Joseph D. Creedon
Cover photograph *Sunrise at Point Judith Light* by Jay Swoboda
Cover & interior book design by Matthew St. Jean
Published by Stillwater River Publications,
Pawtucket, RI, USA.

The views and opinions expressed
in this book are solely those of the author(s)
and do not necessarily reflect the views
and opinions of the publisher.

*To the good people of Christ the King Parish
who nourished me for 31 wonderful years.*

Contents

Acknowledgements	vii
Advent	1
Christmas – Epiphany	35
Holy Season of Lent	55
The Triduum	104
Easter – Pentecost	108
Holy Trinity – Corpus Christi	163
Ordinary Time	169
Holy Days, Solemnities and Major Feast Days	445
Lectio Divina	472

Acknowledgements

As always, Sallie Sirhal edited my manuscript with her usual precision and attention to detail. Jack Lavin, good friend and fellow priest, read the manuscript and offered both grammatical and theological clarifications. Since the writing of these reflections took place over the span of almost a year and a half, some stories were repeated. Jack found them all. At least I hope he did. Jay Swoboda was once again kind enough to let me use one of his photos for the cover.

I just finished my last reflection. This project has taken me the better part of a year and a half. It is not yet finished. Now comes the difficult part. Now I have to patiently, prayerfully, and critically evaluate what I have written. The rough draft is the easy part; the finished product is the more difficult part, but you cannot have one without the other. I made a conscious decision at the beginning of this writing that I would write in the first person plural. I did so because I wanted to create the sense that whoever follows these reflections does not travel alone. We may never meet each other in person, yet we can journey together. We share the common story of salvation, but still believe that God speaks to each of us differently. When we meet, when we share our faith, we need to share what God says to us and through us, and invite others to share their experience of God with us. It is in sharing that we help faith grow, and help "Your Kingdom come" as we pray so often in the Our Father.

A Few Notes on How to Use These Reflections

The Catholic liturgical calendar can be confusing. Many parishes used to give out calendars provided by a local funeral home, but in the digital age that custom is slowly dying. There are Ordos for each diocese, which clearly state what readings are assigned to each day, but they are expensive and give more detail than the average person needs. The easiest way to know what the assigned readings are for each day of the year is to go to go to **http://bible.usccb.org**. There you will be able to sign up for the readings to be sent to your email address everyday.

Once you know what the gospel for the day is, I would recommend that you read it carefully and prayerfully. If you have the time, the practice of Lectio Divina will be helpful. (A brief description of this practice is printed on the inside back cover of this book.) Let the scriptures speak to you, and then read my reflection on the daily gospel. Believe that the Holy Spirit will speak to you through the scripture passage, my reflection and your own reflection.

Advent

First Sunday of Advent (A)

> Stay awake, therefore!
> You cannot know the day your Lord is coming.
> "Be sure of this: if the owner of the house knew when the thief
> was coming he would keep a watchful eye
> and not allow his house to be broken into.
> You must be prepared in the same way.
> The Son of Man is coming at the time you least expect."
> Mt 24: 37 – 44

In today's second reading from St. Paul to the Romans, we are invited to cast off our deeds of darkness and put on the armor of light. In the gospel, we are exhorted to be prepared. All of us need an advent in our lives; we need a period of time to rediscover what should be important, a time to wake up before it is too late. We need a time to cast off our deeds of darkness.

Let's face it, we grow complacent in our lives. We settle; we adjust rather than challenge things. We need something to capture our attention; we need a wake-up call.

I love to people watch. I especially like to observe couples in restaurants. Couples seem to fall into two groups. The first group, made up of people who are of a certain age, seem bored. They are mostly silent. I get the feeling he would be more excited watching sports on television, and that she would be more focused if one of the grandchildren came for a visit. It is as if time has robbed them of whatever joy and spontaneity used to be in their relationship. The second group, usually younger, are engaged. Their eyes sparkle; they laugh and playfully touch each other. They are engaged and vibrant. I always wonder if in thirty years they will have moved into the first group? Will they have grown complacent?

How can we let Advent capture our attention and enliven our faith?

First Sunday of Advent (B)

> It is like a man traveling abroad.
> He leaves home and places his servants in charge,
> each with his own work,
> and orders the gatekeeper to be on the watch.
> Watch, therefore;
> you do not know when the Lord of the house is coming,
> whether in the evening, or at midnight,
> or at cockcrow, or in the morning.
> May he not come suddenly and find you sleeping.
> What I say to you, I say to all, "Watch!"
> Mk 13: 33 – 37

We begin a new liturgical year with the First Sunday of Advent. This can be a powerful liturgical season, but we have to work at it. The church calls us to be countercultural during Advent. Our culture does not have time for Advent. There is no time set aside to prepare for Christmas. The stores have been hawking Christmas items since early November.

There is a bumper sticker that says, "Jesus is the reason for the season." Our focus during Advent is twofold. The first focus is on preparing for Jesus coming at the end of time. The second focus is on preparing for Jesus to be born once again in our hearts and lives. This second focus begins on December 17.

If we use Advent to be watchful, then Christmas will be a season and not be crammed into just one day and then discarded. It takes discipline to make room for faith in what is becoming more and more a holiday and less and less a holy day. May we hear John the Baptist cry out, "Prepare the way of the Lord." And live the prayer attributed to St. Richard of Chichester but made famous by the musical Godspell, "Day by day, O Dear Lord, three things I pray: to see thee more clearly, love thee more dearly, follow thee more nearly, day by day."

How can we better respect the gift of Advent?

First Sunday of Advent (C)

> "Be on guard lest your spirits become bloated
> with indulgence and drunkenness and worldly cares.
> The great day will suddenly close in on you like a trap.
> The day I speak of will come upon all who dwell
> on the face of the earth, so be on the watch.
> Pray constantly for the strength to escape
> Whatever is in prospect,
> and to stand secure before the Son of Man."
> Lk 21: 25 – 28, 34 – 36

Let's not become complacent! That should be the battle cry of Advent. Complacency is our greatest enemy. We start off with great motivation, with great ideals, but then reality sets in and we settle.

At the beginning of each new year many of us will feel compelled to make a New Year's Resolution; few of us will succeed.

The season of Advent is a liturgical gift from the church so that we can examine where we have become complacent, or where we have given up. Many of us want to be more familiar with the Bible. We decide to read a bit of scripture every day. Then something happens and that new-found ritual is abandoned. Most of us were once very regular at Sunday Mass. Then the kids were finished with CCD or Religious Education, and we slacked off. Even saying our morning and evening prayers can fall by the wayside. No aspect of our lives is free from complacency. One thing is certain – all of us can be better believers and Advent is a great time to get started on our improvements.

We have more than one thing that needs improvement – where will we start?

Monday of the First Week of Advent

> As Jesus entered Capernaum,
> a centurion approached him with this request:
> "Sir, my serving boy is at home in bed paralyzed,
> suffering painfully."
> He said to him, "I will come and cure him."
> "Sir" the centurion said in reply,
> "I am not worthy to have you under my roof.
> Just give an order and my boy will get better."
> Mt 8: 5 – 11

We experience God through our lives. Who we are determines how we encounter God. This was brought home to me vividly many years ago when I was on a study fellowship in Topeka, Kansas. Right next door to the parish where I was living was an orphanage. The nuns who ran the orphanage would have the children in their care act out Bible passages. They were working on the parable of the Prodigal Son. Everyone was doing fine with one exception, no one wanted to play the role of the loving father. More accurately no one knew how to be the loving father because none of them had experienced a loving father.

The centurion experienced a God of power because he was a man of power.

Women experience God differently than men. Children experience a different kind of God than adults. One experience is not better than another, just different. What we need to do is create room for others to share their experience of God with us.

Such a sharing always leads to a richer experience of God. God will always be bigger than our experiences. As the writer Walter Lippmann reminds us, "When all think alike, no one thinks very much."

Advent is a wonderful time to enlarge our vision of God. How can we do that?

Tuesday of the First Week of Advent

> Jesus rejoiced in the Holy Spirit and said,
> "I give you praise, Father, Lord of heaven and earth,
> for although you have hidden these things
> from the wise and the learned
> you have revealed them to the childlike.
> Yes, Father, such has been your gracious will."
> Lk 10: 21 – 24

Children are innocent. They have not yet learned about hidden agendas or guarded thoughts. What they think is what they say; what they hear is what they believe. They are trusting and unguarded. They have not yet been taught the prejudices and biases of the dominant culture. They are told that God loves them, and they believe it without hesitation.

Then they grow up. Children on the way to adulthood can be cruel and hurtful. They learn to like certain people and avoid other kinds of people. They become surly and moody.

Does it have to be like that? Does the journey to adulthood have to seem like it is all downhill? The answer is "No" because there are some people who become adults without losing their childlike approach to life.

Our creator wants us to grow up and grow out; our creator does not want us to become closed or narrow-minded. Nothing destroys faith like cynicism. God always draws near with open arms; may we always approach him with unguarded hearts.

Where has our faith become hardened by life's negative experiences?

Wednesday of the First Week of Advent

> At that time,
> Jesus walked by the Sea of Galilee,
> went up on the mountain, and sat down there.
> Great crowds came to him,
> having with them the lame, the blind, the deformed, the mute,

and many others.
They placed them at his feet, and he cured them.
The crowds were amazed when they saw the mute speaking,
the deformed made whole,
the lame walking,
and the blind able to see,
and they glorified the God of Israel.
Mt 15: 29 – 37

Today's gospel ends with the multiplication of the loaves and the fish, but it is important to remember how it begins. It begins with brokenness. It begins with wanting to be made whole.

All the brokenness in today's gospel is visible. We can see the deformity, we can see the limping, hear the words not being properly formed, and observe the hesitancy of the blind. Jesus healed the obvious brokenness, but he also healed that which was hidden.

The disciples could not see a solution to how they would feed the crowd, but a little boy taught them to offer what they had so that a solution could be found. Jesus was willing to see the coming hunger, when those around him were blind to it. It was a combination of fear, selfishness, and helplessness that prevented the disciples from daring to find a solution. He made them whole by showing them how to share more generously. Together in love and faith there is nothing we cannot achieve.

What inner brokenness do we need to bring to Jesus for healing?

Thursday of the First Week of Advent

Jesus said to his disciples:
"Not everyone who says to me, 'Lord, Lord,'
will enter the Kingdom of heaven,
but only the one who does the will of my Father in heaven.
Everyone who listens to these words of mine and acts on them
will be like a wise man who built his house on rock.
The rain fell, the floods came,

> and the winds blew and buffeted the house.
> But it did not collapse; it had been set solidly on rock."
> Mt 7: 21, 24 – 27

We are only as strong as the foundation on which we are built. Our values are the foundation of our lives. The challenge is not just to say what our values are but to live those values.

I had a personal experience that brought this point home to me. After my first year of Theology at the American College in Louvain, Belgium, my travel partner and I headed out on our motorcycles to begin our summer. We were going to spend six weeks working in a summer camp, and six weeks travelling around France. We set our sights on riding to Paris the first day, but we got lost and ended up staying in a little village the first night. When I woke up the next morning, I realized that today I would find out who I was, and what I believed. For the first time in my life I would not meet anyone I knew. I was on my own. No peer pressure, no supervision, no agenda. Nothing. I was on my own, just me and my values. I was scared. It turned out I had nothing to fear. My family had given me good values, my schooling had reinforced them, and the seminary strengthened them.

Since that day there has been plenty of rain and wind, and more than a few storms, but I had been solidly set on rock.

What are the true values that guide our life choices?

Friday of the First Week of Advent

> As Jesus passed by, two blind men followed him, crying out,
> "Son of David, have pity on us!"
> When he entered the house,
> the blind men approached him and Jesus said to them,
> "Do you believe that I can do this?"
> "Yes, Lord," they said to him.
> He touched their eyes and said,
> "Let it be done for you according to your faith."
> Mt 9: 27 – 31

My favorite scripture passage is, "Lord, I believe. Help my unbelief." We believe. All of us believe, but there are holes in our belief.

There is a great little story that brings home the fragility of our faith. A man is out hiking on a mountain trail. It is a beautiful day, and nature is alive with beauty. As he rounds one bend on the trail, he stumbles, and begins to fall down the side of the mountain. He reaches out and grabs ahold of a tree branch and momentarily stops his tragic descent. He clings to the branch, but his grip is growing weaker, so he calls out, "Help. Help. Is there anyone up there?" His plea is met with silence so he cries out louder, "Help. Is there anyone up there?" This time he hears a voice that says, "This is your loving God. Trust me. Let go of the branch and fall into my saving hands." The man pauses and then cries out, "Is there anyone else up there?"

There are times when we are all afraid to make the leap of faith!

Where have doubt and fear held us back from living our faith more fully?

Saturday of the First Week of Advent

> Jesus went around to all the towns and villages,
> teaching in their synagogues
> proclaiming the Gospel of the Kingdom,
> and curing every disease and illness.
> At the sight of the crowds, his heart was moved with pity for them
> because they were troubled and abandoned,
> like sheep without a shepherd.
> Mt 9: 35 – 10: 5A, 6 – 8

Jesus was the shepherd for the lost and abandoned, but he needed help. So he gathered the Twelve and gave them power over unclean spirits, but it did not stop there. The Twelve sent out others in their name to give people hope. And it's been going on for more than two thousand years.

That is the power and the mystery of this thing called church. We, the baptized, are gathered together and empowered by the Holy Spirit to create the Kingdom of God. It is a mystery why or how it works, but work it does.

At a micro level the church is the parish. The parish is made up of people, every variety of people. Some are better than others at being Church, but all are called to proclaim the presence of God in our midst. St. Paul tells us we are all in this together. No one is more important than others. We all have gifts, none better than others just different. Theologians call this being together the mystical body of Christ. Most of us just call it my faith family. Together we can change the world.

How can we share our gifts better to build up the church?

Second Sunday of Advent (A)

> When John the Baptizer made his appearance as a preacher
> in the desert of Judea, this was his theme:
> "Reform your lives! The reign of God is at hand."
> It was of him that the prophet Isaiah had spoken when he said:
> "A herald's voice in the desert:
> 'Prepare the way of the Lord,
> make straight his paths.'"
> Mt 3: 1 – 12

I can give you a dozen reasons why we should ignore John the Baptist, and none for why we should listen to him. He was politically incorrect and proud of it. He spoke his truth; he pulled no punches.

In the middle of today's gospel he says to the Pharisees who have come out to receive his baptism, "You brood of vipers! Who told you to flee from the wrath to come? Give some evidence that you mean to reform." Vipers and snakes regularly shed their skin, but that is all that changes. John is not one to sugar coat his message.

Advent calls for real change. Anthony de Mello in *The Heart of the Enlightened* tells a wonderful story about how we are afraid to really change. "After thirty years of watching television, a husband said to his wife, 'Let's do something really exciting tonight.' Instantly she conjured up a vision of a night on the town. 'Great!' she said. 'What shall we do?' 'Well,' he said, 'let's change chairs.'" Advent has to be about more than changing chairs.

What needs to change if we are to truly reform our lives?

Second Sunday of Advent (B)

> As it is written in Isaiah the prophet:
> "Behold, I am sending my messenger ahead of you;
> he will prepare your way.
> A voice of one crying out in the desert:
> 'Prepare the way of the lord,
> make straight his paths.'"
> John the Baptist appeared in the desert
> proclaiming a baptism of repentance for the forgiveness of sins.
> Mk 1: 1 – 8

John the Baptist has always fascinated me. He was an odd stick to put it mildly. I think of him as being a little off. He was a loner, dressed funny, and had a very strange diet. Then there was his message. "Give up your sins. Repent, and turn your lives around." Going around calling people sinners is not a good way to be popular. John knew that, but he did it anyway because that is what God was calling him to do.

Even stranger than his message was its effectiveness. All kinds of people showed up to be baptized by him in the Jordan River. John obviously had a gift. He could call people sinners without being rejected. I wish we had more details about how he went about his ministry. He was able to call people sinners without condemning them to be sinners forever. That must be his gift. One thing is certain, when he called sinners to repent he was talking to everyone. There is a saying that always reminds me of John the Baptist and his ministry. Here it is, "The Church is not a gathering of saints, but rather a gathering of sinners who have not yet given up." That is my kind of church.

Where have we let our sins define who we are?

Second Sunday of Advent (C)

> He went about the entire region of the Jordan
> proclaiming a baptism of repentance
> which led to the forgiveness of sins,
> as is written in the book of the words of Isaiah the prophet:
> "A herald's voice in the desert, crying
> 'Make ready the way of the Lord.
> clear him a straight path.'"
> Lk 3: 1 – 6

There is a straight path in all of our lives. It is the main aisle of our parish church. That straight path is there for us as we begin our journey of faith at baptism. In many churches the baptismal font is right at the beginning of the main aisle as a reminder to always remain on the path that leads us home. At the end of the main aisle is the altar where we encounter Jesus hopefully on a regular basis. If we stay connected to the Eucharist we will stay on the straight path. The main aisle leads to our seat where we listen to the Word of God proclaimed. It is the same aisle that we walk down in order to offer peace to one and other.

If we process down the main aisle of our parish church, we will never be alone. We will always be part of the procession that leads to worship. There will always be obstacles that will try to block our procession. There will always be gaps and bumpy times, but if we can make it to our parish church, with its very straight main aisle, we will never get lost and we will never wander far from Jesus' loving embrace.

What have we let keep us from the main aisle of our parish church?

Monday of the Second Week of Advent

> One day Jesus was teaching,
> Pharisees and teachers of the law,
> who had come from every village of Galilee and Judea and Jerusalem,
> were sitting there,
> and the power of the Lord was with him for healing.

> And some men brought on a stretcher a man who was paralyzed;
> they were trying to bring him in and set him in his presence.
> But not finding a way to bring him in because of the crowd,
> they went up on the roof
> and lowered him on the stretcher through the tiles
> into the middle in front of Jesus.
> When Jesus saw their faith, he said,
> "As for you, your sins are forgiven."
> Lk 5: 17 – 26

This gospel passage is like a precious gem – it sparkles from so many different angles. One angle would be that the Pharisees and the teachers of the law were open to learn from Jesus. That is not how they are usually portrayed. Next would be the role of the friends. They were not going to be frustrated in their desire to get healing for their friend. Not only did they carry him there, hoist him up on the roof, lower him down in front of Jesus, they actually loaned their faith to their friend. Remember Jesus cured the paralyzed man not because of his faith, but because of his friends' faith.

The angle I want to pursue concerns the man who owned the house where Jesus was teaching. Certainly, he wanted the honor of having Jesus in his home, but he got more than he bargained for. He got a hole in his roof. I doubt seriously that the man's friends climbed back up on the roof and reset the tiles. No, they went off to celebrate with their healed friend.

Now the homeowner learned what we all have to learn. When we invite Jesus into our lives, things are going to change. Faith brings with it disruption. Perhaps that is why we are hesitant to go all in with our faith.

If we believed more fully in Jesus as our Lord and Savior, what would be the first thing to change in our lives

Tuesday of the Second Week of Advent

> Jesus said to his disciples:
> "What is your thought on this:

> A man owns a hundred sheep and one of them wanders away;
> will he not leave the ninety-nine out on the hills
> and go in search of the stray?"
> Mt 18: 12 – 14

There is no more popular image of Jesus than the good shepherd. Nevertheless, Jesus is not all that good as a shepherd. First of all, he does not notice that one of his sheep has wandered away. Then once he takes a count, and realizes one is missing, he refuses to cut his losses. He leaves the ninety-nine unattended willing to risk that some could be poached and others could fall prey to predators.

Let's face it, Jesus is not a good shepherd, but he is a great Messiah. Jesus was sent to save us and save us he will. He will never stop searching for us no matter how far we roam away from his way.

There is a story about two monks walking by a river. Floating by them is a bunch of branches with a scorpion on them. One monk reaches out to grab the branches and save the scorpion from drowning. As he does the scorpion stings him. His fellow monk reprimands him saying, "You knew the scorpion was going to sting you. Why did you do it?" His brother monk replied, "It is the nature of the scorpion to sting; it is my nature to save. I won't let his nature change mine." Jesus will not let our inclination to wander change his nature to save.

What is our most serious form of wandering away from the way Jesus taught?

Wednesday of the Second Week of Advent

> Jesus said to the crowds:
> "Come to me, all you who labor and are burdened,
> and I will give you rest.
> Take my yoke upon you and learn from me,
> for I am meek and humble of heart;
> and you will find rest for yourselves.
> For my yoke is easy, and my burden is light"
> Mt 11: 28 – 30

There is gentleness and warmth in this scripture passage. To me it is the ultimate proof that Jesus took on our human condition. He spoke to the crowds from his personal experience. He knew that life can be hectic. He knew that we can get lost in the minutiae of the daily grind because he sometimes got lost in that same minutiae.

Jesus had learned that he needed time away to pray. He needed to reconnect with his father, and that always refreshed him. As odd as this might sound, from time to time, Jesus needed to be reminded that he was not facing the challenges of this world alone. His father, our God, was with him always. It was that, and that alone, that kept Jesus anchored.

Jesus wants to share his discovery with us. That is why he invites us to come to him. He wants us to know that we are never alone. That he is always with us. We have a personal relationship with Jesus. Imagine, having a personal relationship with God. Remember the beautiful words of Pope Francis in *Evangelii Gaudium*, "I invite all Christians, everywhere, at this very moment, to a renewed personal encounter with Jesus Christ, or at least an openness to letting him encounter them; I ask all of you to do this unfailingly each day." (#3)

What is keeping us from renewing our relationship with Jesus?

Thursday of the Second Week of Advent

Jesus said to the crowds:
"Amen, I say to you, among those born of women
there is none greater than John the Baptist;
yet the least in the Kingdom of heaven is greater than he.
Mt 11: 11 – 15

John the Baptist is the man when it comes to Advent. His whole life was an advent experience. First he had to wait to meet the Messiah, and once he had successfully done that, the rest of his life was bringing people to Jesus.

I'm afraid that sometimes we forget that John had trouble figuring out just who the Messiah was.

When Jesus presents himself for baptism by John at the Jordan River, he tries to decline. He protests that he, John, ought to be baptized by Jesus. There may be a bit of revisionist history going on when that gospel story is being told.

We know that earlier in the same chapter of Matthew's gospel from which the above quote is taken that John, in prison, sends his disciples to ask Jesus, "Are you the one who is to come, or should we look for another?"

John the Baptist had to work to find Jesus and so do we. That is why we have this wonderful season of Advent. We have too many false gods and not enough of the true God.

What false god can we shed this Advent?

Friday of the Second Week of Advent

> Jesus said to the crowds:
> "To what shall I compare this generation?
> It is like children who sit in marketplaces and call to one another,
> 'We played a flute for you, but you did not dance,
> we sang a dirge but you did not mourn.'"
> Mt 11: 16 – 19

As today's gospel continues, Jesus points out that the people thought John the Baptist was too severe, and that Jesus was too relaxed. This was Jesus bestowing the fickle finger of fate award that was made popular on the Smothers Brothers' television show of happy memory.

Neither Jesus nor John hired a consultant so as to tailor their message to fit their audience's desires. That is not how it works. Neither God nor one of his messengers fashions the message to fit the audience. No, the audience is challenged to fashion their lives according to the message.

The crowds did not want a savior, or more accurately they wanted a political savior not a religious one. They ignored John because he called them sinners. They ignored Jesus because he wanted them to be more loving, welcoming, and forgiving.

As the old saying goes, "We have been created in the image of God, and we have been returning the favor ever since."

What excuse do we use to ignore the challenges of our faith?

Saturday of the Second Week of Advent

> As they were coming down the mountainside,
> the disciples put this question to Jesus:
> "Why do the scribes claim that Elijah must come first?"
> In reply he said:
> "Elijah is indeed coming, and he will restore everything.
> I assure you, though, that Elijah has already come,
> But they did not recognize him
> and they did to him whatever they pleased.
> Mt 17: 1 – 13

Jesus is saying John the Baptist is the second coming of Elijah. That the prophecy of Elijah's return foretold at the end of the Book of Malachi has been fulfilled. That reminds us of a problem we all must confront – our inability or unwillingness to recognize the many ways that God enters our lives.

Each one of us has a notion of what God looks like, and how God is going to act. However, God will not be crammed into our categories or act out the script we write for him.

We want a God who stays in church and only wants our attention one hour each week. God however comes to us in ways that surprise us. He is in the beauty of a sunset or in the outstretched hand of a beggar. God is there in the smile of a dedicated nurse, and in a mother's frown. A soaring eagle can speak to us of God's grandeur, and the rainbow can speak to us of the covenant God has made with us.

Advent is all about being still and discovering God's presence in our lives.

Where is God speaking to us and we are not listening?

Third Sunday of Advent (A)

> "Why then did you go out – to see a prophet?
> A prophet indeed, and something more!
> It is about this man that Scripture says,
> 'I send my messenger ahead of you
> to prepare your way before you.'
> "I solemnly assure you, history has not known
> a man born of woman greater than John the Baptizer.
> Yet the least born into the Kingdom of God
> is greater than he."
> Mt 11: 2 – 11

My brother, Jerry, when he worked for NASA, had a sign on his wall saying, "When you are up to your neck in alligators, it's hard to remember your job was to drain the moat." In today's gospel, John the Baptist is trying to remember what his job is. He is in prison so he sends his disciples to Jesus asking if he is the Messiah. Jesus tells them, "Go back and report to John what you hear and see: the blind recover their sight, cripples walk, lepers are cured, the deaf hear, dead men are raised to life, and the poor have the good news preached to them." Prison is John's alligators.

Like John, our job is to point out God by the lives we live. We are called to be signs of God's love and presence in the world. We need to ask, do we reveal or conceal God's presence by the lives we live. There will be lots of alligators in our lives; they will distract us from our call to point out God's love and presence. When we get distracted the alligators win; when we stay focused God wins. No matter what is going on in our lives we need to ask, "If not me, then who? If not now, then when?" When we waver, we need to ask the Baptist to be our guide.

What distractions have been winning in our struggle to point out God?

Third Sunday of Advent (B)

> So they said to him,
> "Who are you, so we can give an answer to those who sent us?
> What do you have to say for yourself?"
> He said,
> "I am the voice of one crying out in the desert,
> 'Make straight the way of the Lord.'
> as Isaiah the prophet said."
> Jn 1: 6 – 8, 19 – 28

John the Baptist knew who he was; he knew what he was supposed to do with his life, and he did it. But don't think he came by that knowledge easily.

John had to discover who he was and what his talents were. It was a slow discovery. Like us he learned by trial and error. Right from birth his parents, like all parents, knew he was special; that he was their gift from God.

Even when he had started out baptizing people, he had doubts. When he got to baptize Jesus, he was unsure. Even after he had pointed out Jesus as the Messiah, he was not one hundred percent sure he was doing the right thing. Remember he sent his disciples to Jesus to ask him, "Are you he who is to come, or should we look for another?" And that is just the stuff we know.

He must have been tempted to get more attention for himself. He was probably tempted to see if he could pull off being the Messiah. But he remained true and even gave his life for living out his vocation.

Are we being true to who God wants us to be?

Third Sunday of Advent (C)

> The crowds asked John, "What ought we to do?"
> In reply he said,
> "Let the man with two coats give to him who has none.
> The man who has food should do the same."

> Tax collectors also came to be baptized, and they said to him,
> "Teacher, what are we to do?"
> He answered them,
> "Exact nothing over and above your fixed amount."
> Soldiers likewise asked him,
> "What about us?"
> He told them,
> "Do not bully anyone.
> Denounce no one falsely.
> Be content with your pay."
> Lk 3:10-18 (9)

The thing I always like about this gospel is John has both a generic and a specific recommendation for everyone. We are different; we need to live our faith in different ways. Christianity is not one size fits all.

To the crowds, the community, he reminds them of the need to care for the less fortunate. Make sure everyone has clothes; make sure everyone has food; make sure everyone has the basics. That is why even in our day parishes still have food drives and give out food baskets. Advent is a great time to reflect on how we can be ever more generous to those in need. That will be our generic Advent preparation.

Now we get to the specific application of Advent. Just as the tax collectors and soldiers were given different tasks that were applied to their everyday efforts, so it should be for us. We cannot go out to the desert to ask John, "What about us?" But we can ask him in prayer. We have parts of our lives that need help. How can I be a better mother and wife? How can I be a better husband and father? How can I be more loyal to my friends? Where is my faith calling me to give better witness to what I believe? The more specific our answer, the better the chance that we will be able to make a genuine effort to become better people and better believers this Advent.

What changed behavior will be my gift to Jesus this Christmas?

Monday of the Third Week of Advent

> Jesus said to them in reply,
> "I shall ask you one question, and if you answer it for me,
> then I shall tell you by what authority I do these things.
> Where was John's baptism from?
> Was it of heavenly or of human origin?"
> They discussed this among themselves and said,
> "If we say 'Of heavenly origin,' he will say to us,
> 'Then why did you not believe him?'
> But if we say, 'Of human origin,' we fear the crowd,
> for they all regard John as a prophet."
> So they said to Jesus in reply, "We do not know."
> Mt. 21: 23 – 27

Jesus always seems to get the better of his discussions with the chief priest and the elders. There must have been times when Jesus did not have the right retort; there must have been times too when it was only later that Jesus came up with the best response.

That is what happens with us. Sometimes, but never often enough, when someone tries to trip us up in conversation, we upend him or her. They try to make us look bad, and we turn the tables on them. More often than not it is a day or two later that we come up with what we wished we had said.

The trick is to do it like Jesus does it. He does not gloat; he does not rub in his victory. He is gentle. He defuses the situation and moves on.

With Jesus what was important was to be the Messiah. He was sent to teach, heal, and set the captives free. He was not sent to win arguments. He was sent preach the good news. Jesus would not let himself get distracted from his life's work. We, on the other hand, get distracted more often than not.

What do we let distract us from being better believers?

Tuesday of the Third Week of Advent

> Jesus said to them, "Amen, I say to you,
> Tax collectors and prostitutes
> are entering the Kingdom of God before you.
> When John came to you in the way or righteousness,
> you did not believe him;
> but the tax collectors and prostitutes did.
> Yet even then when you saw that,
> you did not later change your minds and believe him
> Mt 21: 28 – 32

You know you are not having a good day when you come in third right after the tax collectors and prostitutes. But that is precisely where Jesus puts the chief priests and elders of the people.

Jesus is all about forgiveness and mercy. The message of Advent is to change our ways so that we are more ready to greet Jesus at Christmas and at the end of time. What Jesus is saying is that those who were formerly tax collectors and prostitutes are entering the Kingdom of God. They heard John's call to repentance and they had their sins washed away by John in the Jordan River.

The chief priests and elders of the people went out to listen to John. They went to make sure he was being orthodox. They refused or were unable to see their sins. They weren't skimming money off the top to enrich themselves, nor were they selling themselves for profit. They had grown blind to their hypocrisy and legalism.

Unfortunately, it is always easier to see the sins of others than our own sins. Advent is an invitation to look critically at ourselves. That should keep us so busy we won't have time to focus on anyone else's shortcomings.

What sins have we become blind to in our lives?

Wednesday of the Third Week of Advent

> And Jesus said to them in reply,
> "Go and tell John what you have seen and heard:
> the blind regain their sight,
> the lame walk,
> lepers are cleansed,
> the deaf hear, the dead are raised,
> the poor have the good news proclaimed to them.
> And blessed is the one who takes no offense at me."
> Lk 7: 18b – 23

The prophets in the Hebrew Scriptures had given people the signs they should look for to recognize the presence of the Messiah. Jesus knew those signs as did John the Baptist and his disciples. Jesus rattles them off to John's disciples as a refresher course. The blind see, the lame walk, the deaf hear, the dead are raised, and the poor have the good news proclaimed to them.

Jesus believes that actions are more important than words. He just points to his works. He never directly answers John's question. He just points to his deeds.

Maybe all John needed was a little reassurance. Maybe sitting in his prison cell with too much time to think he began to wonder, did I point out the right person as the Messiah? When his disciples returned and told him what Jesus had told them, I'm sure he smiled and thought, "I got it right."

What a great thing to be able to say as your life is coming to an end.

Are we getting our lives right? Are we who God wants us to be?

Thursday of the Third Week of Advent

> What did you go out to see in the desert –
> a reed swayed by the wind?
> What, really, did you go out to see –
> someone dressed luxuriously?

> Remember, those who dress in luxury
> and eat in splendor are to be found in royal palaces.
> Then what did you go out to see – a prophet?
> He is that, I assure you, and something more.
> This is the man of whom Scripture says,
> "I send my messenger ahead of you
> to prepare you way before you."
> Lk 7: 24 – 30

They were fascinated by John the Baptist. He did not fit in and did not want to fit in. He dressed funny; he ate a strange diet to say the least. In order to hear him you had to go out of your way. His message was harsh, but it was true. No one would ever accuse John the Baptist of playing to the crowd. He told people they had wandered from the truth; they had gotten lost in their own folly.

This pithy definition has become an aphorism. "Irish diplomacy is being able to tell someone to go to hell in such a way that he looks forward to the journey." John the Baptist must have been part Irish because he could tell people they were sinners in a way that made them want to change. John got the people started on the road to conversion, and Jesus brought them home. During Advent the Church through the liturgy reminds us that we live in the shadows which the darkness of our sins creates. There is even more darkness than light in nature during Advent. Soon the light of Christ will be born to lead us home. May we walk these last few days of Advent toward the light of God's goodness so that our shadows are behind us rather than ahead of us.

What deed of darkness can we shed before the birth of our Savior?

Friday of the Third Week of Advent

> "He was the lamp, set aflame and burning bright,
> And for a while you exulted willingly in his light.
> Yet I have testimony greater than John's,
> namely, the works the Father has given me to accomplish.
> These very works which I perform

> testify on my behalf
> that the Father has sent me."
> Jn 5: 33 – 36

John has his job to do; Jesus had his to do. God had given them works to accomplish, and they did what they were supposed to do. One of the challenges of Advent is to prayerfully ask God to help us realize what task he has assigned us.

Each person is a unique creation with a specific set of skills. We have to discover our talents and skills, develop them, and finally find the best way to put those talents and skills at the service of God. The only way the Kingdom of God can come to fruition is if each of us finds a way to work together.

John and Jesus were part of a team. John knew his calling was to prepare the way for Jesus; Jesus' calling was to be the Messiah. Teamwork is essential in the Kingdom of God. Bill Belichick, the legendary and quirky coach of the New England Patriots, has created many clichés, but one of my favorites is, "Do your job!" If the eleven players on the field just do their job everything will work out. Discipline is necessary in faith as well as in football. Everyone cannot be a show horse and succeed, but everyone can be a work horse and succeed.

What task has God given us to accomplish?

Fourth Sunday of Advent (A)

> Joseph her husband, an upright man
> unwilling to expose her to the law,
> decided to divorce her quietly.
> Such was his intention when suddenly
> the angel of the Lord appeared in a dream and said to him,
> "Joseph, son of David, have no fear about taking Mary as your wife.
> It is by the Holy Spirit that she has conceived this child.
> She is to have a son and you are to name him Jesus
> because he will save his people from their sins."
> Mt 1: 18 – 24

On this final Sunday of Advent our focus switches from preparing for the second coming of Jesus at the end of time to the birth of Jesus in our time. That is always the tricky part of Advent – we are either looking forward to his second coming or looking back at his first coming. It seems like Advent is either in the past or in the future. Advent, however, has to be in the present so that Jesus can be born in our lives now.

Joseph shows us how to make that happen. Too often we focus only on the yes that Mary gave to the angel. We forget that without Joseph's yes, God's plan would have been frustrated. Just as God needed Joseph to be part of Jesus' birth in time so now God needs our yes for that miracle to continue in time.

The time draws near. Unless we can create room in our hearts and in our lives Jesus will not once again be born to free us from our sins. God needs each and every one of us for Jesus to be fully born in our day.

What yes is God waiting for us to give?

Fourth Sunday of Advent (B)

> The angel went on to say to her:
> "Do not fear, Mary.
> You have found favor with God.
> You shall conceive and bear a son
> And he shall be called Son of the Most High.
> The Lord God will give him the throne of David his father.
> He will rule over the house of Jacob forever
> And his reign will be without end.
> Mary said, "How can this be since I do not know man?"
> Lk 1: 26 – 38

Mary is trying to use logic. She is trying to fit God's plan for her into her categories. As always, God won't fit in our categories. Our categories are too small, too rigid, too fixed. God's ways are not our ways!

Mary finally boils her choice down: do I say yes only to what I can understand, or do I take the leap of faith? Fortunately, she took the leap of faith. She puts herself in God's plan by saying, "Lord, let it be done to me as you say."

God always invites us out of our comfort zone. God sees the more to come in us; too often we want to settle for who we are not who we are called to be. Inertia is unfortunately part of our faith life. Life should not work that way. The quality of our lives is determined by the risks we are willing to take. On our first day of school, we wanted to stay in the safety of our home, but mom would not let us stay home. When we said yes to marriage or to ordination or religious profession there had to be doubt, but we found a way to say yes and our lives changed. When there is a chance for promotion at work, part of us wants to stay where we are, while part of us wants to discover if there is more for us to do. It never ends. The need to surrender to the will of God will be with us until we breathe our last.

Where is God calling us to grow further in our lives of faith?

Fourth Sunday of Advent (C)

> Mary set out, proceeding in haste into the hill country
> to a town of Judah, where she entered
> Zechariah's house and greeted Elizabeth.
> When Elizabeth heard Mary's greeting,
> the baby stirred her womb,
> and Elizabeth was filled with the Holy Spirit,
> and cried out in a loud voice:
> "Blessed are you among women
> and blessed is the fruit of your womb.
> But who am I that the mother of my Lord should come to me?
> Lk 1: 39 – 45

The gospel events get speeded up a bit here. Mary did set out in haste, but there is haste and then there is haste. Gabriel appears to Mary; Mary says "yes"; Mary tells Joseph; he has his doubts; Gabriel appears to Joseph and tells him "It's all right to marry Mary; Joseph says "yes"; word has to get from Zechariah and Elizabeth's home in Judah to Joachim and Ann's home in Nazareth that Elizabeth was pregnant in her old age; now Mary is in a hurry to get to Elizabeth to help her with her pregnancy.

We don't like to think about it, but it was probably a good time for Mary to be out of Nazareth for a while. She is not the first pregnant woman to go visit a relative nor will she be the last. That being said, Mary did have genuine compassion for her and genuinely wanted to be there to help her out. And Elizabeth could be a good sounding board for Mary. Both were experiencing unusual pregnancies and they certainly had a lot to talk about.

Then there's John's hearing Mary's greeting and meeting his cousin for the first time. They would meet again at the Jordan River, but this is where it all began. As we draw near to Christmas it is good that we reflect on just how fully Jesus took on our human condition, aunts, uncles, and all sorts of cousins. There is no being human without having an extended family.

Is our faith strong enough for Jesus to be both human and divine?

December 17

> The book of the genealogy of Jesus Christ,
> Son of David, the son of Abraham…
> Eleazar became the father of Matthan,
> Matthan the father of Jacob,
> Jacob the father of Joseph, the husband of Mary.
> Of her was born Jesus who is called the Christ.
> Mt 1: 1 – 17

Thus we enter into phase two of Advent – preparing to celebrate the birth of Jesus. Thus we have the genealogy from the beginning of Matthew's gospel. Now you know that Jesus' grandfather was Jacob who was married to Rachel who was Jesus' grandmother. We don't think of Jesus' family tree very often. We are usually content to realize that he was a descendant of David because the Messiah had to be from the house of David.

The humanity of Jesus too often gets lost in his divinity. We don't focus on Jesus' humanity enough. Jesus was both human and divine, but we are almost embarrassed by his humanity. We are, I think, afraid that Jesus' humanity will somehow diminish his divinity even though it is a dogma of our faith that Jesus was fully human and fully divine.

The apostles and the early church had trouble believing Jesus was divine. They were well aware of his humanity. They walked with him and ate with him. They saw him get tired and cranky. They saw his temper when he kicked the moneychangers out of the temple. We, on the other hand, have no problem with Jesus' divinity; we have trouble believing he was human. We see the miracles and the Resurrection. We need to embrace both Jesus' humanity and his divinity!

How can Jesus' humanity make us better believers?

December 18

> This is how the birth of Jesus Christ came about.
> When his mother Mary was betrothed to Joseph,
> But before they lived together,
> she was found with child through the Holy Spirit.
> Joseph her husband, since he was a righteous man,
> Yet unwilling to expose her to shame,
> Decided to divorce her quietly.
> Mt 1: 18 – 25

Now we have real humanity. Joseph and Mary are engaged, but not yet married, and Joseph discovers Mary is pregnant. Some problems are ageless.

Joseph decided to break off the engagement. That would be bad for Mary because it would say to her neighbors in her small town that someone other than Joseph must be the father.

When Gabriel appeared to Mary to announce that she was asked to be the Mother of the Messiah, his first words to her were, "Do not be afraid!" Gabriel's first words to Joseph were the same, "Do not be afraid!" Nevertheless, both Mary and Joseph had to be afraid. What the angel was actually saying to them was "do not let fear make your choices" and neither of them did. Mary did not understand fully what God was asking of her, nor did Joseph but both of them were willing to put faith and trust before their fear and understanding. Both took the leap of faith and said yes to God's plan for them. We need to ask both Joseph and Mary to help us make that same leap of faith.

Where are we afraid to say "yes" to God's plan for us?

December 19

> The angel said to him, "Do not be afraid Zechariah,
> Because your prayer has been heard.
> Your wife Elizabeth will bear you a son,
> And you shall name him John…
> He will drink neither wine nor strong drink.
> He will be filled with the Holy Spirit even from his mother's womb,
> And he will turn many of the children of Israel
> to the Lord their God.
> He will go before him in the spirit and power of Elijah
> to turn the hearts of fathers toward children
> and the disobedient to the understanding of the righteous,
> to prepare a people fit for the Lord."
> Lk 1: 5 – 25

Looking back we can see that God had a plan for Zechariah and Elizabeth, just as he had a plan for John the Baptist. God had a plan for Mary and Joseph; he even had a plan for Jesus. It is always easier to see the plan that God has for others; what is much more difficult is to see and embrace the plan that God has for us.

Each one of us is a unique creation. We are a special mix of gifts and talents. Each of us can announce the message of God's love differently. The English word "person" is made up of two Latin words "per" and "sonare." "Per" means through, and "sonare" is the verb to sound. God sounds through each one of us differently because each one of us is uniquely different. Our sins and failings can diminish how God sounds through us. We don't want flat notes or sharp notes. We need to sound together in beautiful harmony. That is when God will be most fully present in our world.

How have we diminished the way God can sound through us?

December 20

> Mary said, "Behold, I am the handmaid of the Lord.
> May it be done to me according to your word."
> Then the angel departed from her.
> Lk 1: 26 – 38

Mary is a believer, the best believer. She was a young girl who had a religious experience that turned her world upside down. Gabriel tells her she has found favor with God. She knows immediately that this favor will change the way people look at her and think about her. She will be from that day forward the girl who got pregnant before she was officially married.

If she heard Gabriel with her mind, she would have said "No." Fortunately, she heard the angel with her heart, so she said "yes." She dithered a bit. She asked her questions and expressed her doubts. But in the end she surrendered her future to God. She said, "Let it be done to me according to your word." She made herself a vessel for God when she embraced the future with an open mind, open arms, and an open heart. May she guide us to do the same.

Where have we not yet fully surrendered to God's plan for us?

December 21

> When Elizabeth heard Mary's greeting,
> the infant leaped in her womb,
> and Elizabeth, filled with the Holy Spirit,
> cried out in a loud voice and said,
> "Most blessed are you among women

> and blessed is the fruit of your womb.
> And how does this happen to me,
> that the mother of my Lord should come to me?"
> Lk 1: 39 – 45

Elizabeth had new life within her; Mary had the same. Each was filled with and by the Holy Spirit. Their exchange gives us the outline of the first prayer most of us ever learned, the Hail Mary. "Hail Mary, full of grace, the Lord is with thee. Blessed art thou among women, and blessed is the fruit of thy womb, Jesus. Holy Mary, mother of God, pray for us sinners, now and at the hour of our death. Amen." Could there be a better prayer or a better person to guide us through the final days of Advent?

Mary is the lynchpin that holds the whole nativity narrative together. We need to see these next few days through her eyes. Our waiting needs to be dynamic. New life is coming. Jesus cannot be born in our world unless he is born in our lives. The Hail Mary and "Come, Lord Jesus, come" are the two prayers that will guide us to the manger.

Have we let the familiarity of the Hail Mary sap its power in our lives?

December 22

> "My soul proclaims the greatness of the Lord…
> He has shown the strength of his arm,
> and has scattered the proud in their conceit.
> He has cast down the mighty from their thrones
> And has lifted up the lowly.
> He has filled the hungry with good things,
> and the rich he has sent away empty.
> He has come to the help of his servant Israel
> for he remembered his promise of mercy,
> the promise he made to our fathers
> to Abraham and his children forever."
> Lk 1: 46 – 56

I liked the old translation better, "My soul magnifies the Lord…" We, like Mary, are called to do more than to proclaim the Lord. We need to magnify him by the lives we live and the choices we make. We have the power to magnify or diminish God. That sounds like a heresy, but I don't believe it is.

Whether we like it or not God is abstract. Jesus took on flesh so that we could be saved, but also so we would have a concrete image of divinity. God was made physically present in our world when Jesus was born in the manger. That presence left us when Jesus ascended into heaven. Yet that does not mean God cannot still be physically present.

Every time we reach out a helping hand, our God takes on flesh. Every time we offer forgiveness or refuse to act out of hatred, our God is present. Tom Kendzia, the music director at my former parish, wrote a beautiful song about this phenomenon, *The Eyes and Hands of Christ*. The refrain says it all, "Where two or three are gathered in my name, love will be found, life will abound. By name we are called, from water we are sent to become the eyes and hands of Christ." That is what Mary did; that is what we are called to imitate.

Do our choices magnify or diminish God's presence in the world?

December 23

> He asked for a tablet and wrote,
> "John is his name,"
> and all were amazed.
> Immediately his mouth was opened, his tongue freed,
> and he spoke blessing God.
> Then fear came upon all their neighbors,
> and all these matters were discussed
> throughout the hill country of Judea.
> All who heard these things took them to heart, saying,
> "What, then, will this child be?"
> For surely the hand of the Lord was with him.
> Lk 1: 57 – 66

All parents look at their newborn children and ask, "What will this child be?" That is what parents do. They look on their children with love and wish only the best for them.

Parenting is godlike. Parents create new life; they nurture life, and they nourish it. Parenting is a tremendous responsibility. There is no training, and there are no instructions to read. Parenting is a learned behavior.

Zechariah and Elizabeth had to learn how to parent John; Joseph and Mary had to learn how to parent Jesus, just as our parents had to learn how to parent us.

As an observer of parenting over the years, I am amazed at how many truly heroic sacrifices parents make for their children. Each phase of development brings its own challenges. But the most difficult thing parents have to do is learn when it is time to let go. To love anyone is to set them free. To anyone who is reading this and is a parent, "Thank you." You have made our world a better place.

Let us pause and thank God for our parents.

December 24

> "And you, O child,
> shall be called the prophet of the Most High
> for you shall go before the Lord
> to prepare a straight path for him.
> Giving his people a knowledge of salvation
> in freedom from their sins.
> All this is the work of the kindness of our God;
> he, the Dayspring, shall visit us with his mercy
> to shine on those who sit in darkness and
> in the shadow of death,
> to guide our feet into the way of peace."
> Lk 1: 67 – 79

There is some darkness in all of us. On the final day of our preparation to receive the light of the world into our hearts we need to take inventory. We need to examine the quality of our Advent preparations. Let us end Advent with an examination of conscience:

- Did we let scripture speak to our hearts?
- Did we spend enough time in prayer?
- Did we find time to share our gifts with those on the margins of life?
- Did we gather prayerfully each evening to light the Advent wreath?
- Did we shop responsibly?
- Did we donate to charity?
- Did we decorate our homes for Advent?
- Did we let early Christmas crowd out Advent?
- Did we try to live in liturgical or secular time?

May we gather all that is darkness in our lives and present it him who comes to set us free.

Christmas – Epiphany

Christmas (A,B,C)

> The angel said to them,
> "Do not be afraid;
> for behold, I proclaim to you good news of great joy
> that will be for all the people.
> For today in the city of David
> a savior has been born for you who is Christ and Lord.
> And this will be a sign for you:
> you will find an infant wrapped in swaddling clothes
> and lying in a manger."
> And suddenly there was a multitude
> of the heavenly host with the angel,
> praising God and saying:
> "Glory to God in the highest
> and on earth peace to those on whom his favor rests."
> Lk 2: 1 – 14

There are three different gospels for Christmas: one for midnight, one for dawn, and one for during the day, but I always use the gospel for midnight Mass, which is what I have done here.

Luke goes to great lengths to anchor Jesus' birth in history. He tells us it took place during the census ordered by Caesar Augustus, while Quirinius was governor of Syria. Luke does not give us a date for Jesus' birth because the celebration of birthdays was not yet a custom. The Church did not celebrate Jesus' birth until sometime in the 4th century. December 25 was picked to offset the pagan celebration of Saturnalia.

The day is not important; the event is. Jesus took on our human condition. As the Bible says, "He pitched his tent among us." Our God loved us so much that he had his son walk among us. As St. Paul tells us, "Have among yourselves the same attitude that is also yours in Christ Jesus, who, though he was in the form of God, did not regard equality with God something to be grasped. Rather, he emptied himself, taking the form of a slave, coming in human likeness and found in human appearance, he humbled himself becoming obedient to death, even death on a cross." (Phil 2: 5 – 8)

The birth of Jesus was and is a gift. Just as he had to empty himself so do we if his gift is to be fully received.

A blessed and holy Christmas to all!

December 26 – The Feast of St. Stephen

> Jesus said to his disciples:
> "Beware of men, for they will hand you over to courts
> and scourge you in their synagogues,
> and you will be led before governors and kings for my sake
> as a witness before them and the pagans.
> When they hand you over,
> Do not worry about how you are to speak
> or what you are to say.
> You will be given at that moment what you are to say.
> For it will not be you who speak
> but the Spirit of the Father speaking through you."
> Mt 10: 17 – 22

The liturgical calendar is a wonderful teacher. You and I would not put the feast of St. Stephen, the first martyr, on the day after Christmas. We would pick a more uplifting feast. But remember yesterday's reflection, Jesus emptied himself, and we are called to do the same. Being a Christian means being willing to give up our lives if we have to.

Today's first reading tells of Stephen's eloquence in preaching the Good News of Jesus to Crete, Alexandria, and the inhabitants of Cilicia and Asia, in other words the entire non-Jewish world. They could not outwit him so they killed him and they piled their cloaks at the feet of a man named Saul.

The day after Christmas is dedicated to conversion that leads to dynamic witnessing. Stephen became of follower of Jesus, then was selected one of the seven deacons. He grew to become a preacher of the Way, and finally embraced martyrdom by saying, "Lord, Jesus receive my spirit." His witness, his life-giving sacrifice turned the heart of Saul, who became Paul and brought the Good News to the Gentiles. Paul in turn gave his life, and the Church began to increase. We are all called to do our part to help the Church reach full stature.

How are we being called to help the Church grow?

December 27 – Feast of St. John – Apostle and Evangelist

At that, Peter and the other disciple started on their way to the tomb.
They were running side by side,
But then the other disciple outran Peter and reached the tomb first.
He did not enter but bent down to peer in,
and saw the wrappings lying on the ground.
Presently, Simon Peter came along behind him
and entered the tomb…
Then the disciple who had arrived first at the tomb went in.
He saw and believed.
Jn 20: 2 -8

John writes about himself and Peter. Discretely he does not use his name; he is simply "the other disciple." The real question is why is this John's feast day?

It is really quite simple. John is the disciple whom Jesus loved. At the Last Supper John was at one side of Jesus and Peter was on the other. We know this from scripture, and not from a painting. Peter was to be the leader of the apostles, but John was to be Jesus's friend. John stayed at the cross to see his friend die. Jesus gave John custody of his mother as he was dying. John was always part of the big three that Jesus took with him when something special was about to happen. The phrase, "Jesus took Peter, James and John…" precedes the Transfiguration, the raising of Jairus' daughter, and the Agony in the Garden.

But most of all John's feast day is on December 27 because of his theology. The Synoptic gospels of Matthew, Mark, and Luke, have us being saved by Jesus' death on the cross. John has us being saved by Jesus' birth. As always, the liturgy is a great teacher.

Jesus can be our friend. Will we let him?

December 28 – Feast of the Holy Innocents

When Herod realized that he had been deceived by the magi,
He became furious.
He ordered the massacre of all the boys in Bethlehem and its vicinity
Two years old and under,
in accordance with the time he had ascertained from the magi.
Then was fulfilled what had been said through Jeremiah the prophet:
A voice was heard in Ramah,
sobbing and loud lamentation;
Rachel weeping for her children,
And she would not be consoled,
Since they were no more.
Mt 2: 13 – 18

And the liturgy keeps on teaching. Herod was not willing to empty himself. He was not going to give up his power. What was he worried about? It would be many years before a child would become king. Nevertheless, Herod became both desperate and cruel.

How could anyone become so depraved that he would order all babies two years old or younger to be slaughtered? How do you slaughter fellow human beings? People seem to find a way.

Think of the culture in which we live. War is just another name for killing fellow human beings. The same is true for abortion and capital punishment. Murders and homicide rates are climbing all the time.

Yet we act as if we are powerless to change these sad events. We are not. War should be a last resort, never the first choice. Capital punishment should be abolished. Adoption should replace abortion, and unrestricted possession of firearms is a foolish distortion of the second amendment. We cannot condemn Herod when we are as guilty as he was.

Where have we been silent in the face of violence?

December 29 – The Fifth Day in the Octave of Christmas

> He came in the Spirit into the Temple;
> And when the parents brought in the child Jesus
> to perform the custom of the law in regard to him,
> he took him into his arms and blessed God, saying:
> "Lord, now let your servant go in peace;
> your word has been fulfilled:
> my own eyes have seen the salvation
> which you prepared in the sight of every people,
> a light to reveal you to the nations
> and the glory of your people Israel."
> Lk 2: 22 – 35

Simeon was an old man. He had poured out his life in loving service of God, and, like all good Jews, he awaited the Messiah. His faith was so great that he could see early on what some would never see. He could look at an eight-day-old infant about to be dedicated as a firstborn son, and thank his God for being true to his promise.

This prayer is known as the Song of Simeon, or more colloquially, as the Nunc Dimitis (now you can dismiss) the first two words of the Latin translation. It is prayer every day in the Liturgy of the Hours as part of evening prayer.

What a beautiful way to end each day by proclaiming that God has revealed himself to us this day. The revelation might be partial, but he has revealed God's footprint and fingerprint.

There is an old saying, "It isn't that God does not visit us; it is that too often we are not at home." By prayer Simeon learned how to stay home so he was ready when his Messiah came to him as a baby. We need to ask Simeon to help us learn how to stay focused.

Where have we missed God's visits to our life?

December 30 – The Sixth Day in the Octave of Christmas

> When they had fulfilled all the prescriptions
> of the Law of the Lord,
> they returned to Galilee
> to the town of Nazareth.
> The child grew and became strong, filled with wisdom;
> and the favor of God was upon him.
> Lk 2: 36 – 40

Now the real work begins. Mary and Joseph had dedicated their firstborn to God, and he was circumcised, and now they went home. We will not hear about them again for twelve years until Jesus stays behind in the temple.

These are the quiet years, but nonetheless filled with meaning. Jesus had to grow up. He had to go to school; he had to learn how to speak. He had to go through all the stages of development that we had to go through. We don't focus on this process enough. Jesus had to experience friendship. There had to be times of joy and sorrow. He had to go through the whole range of emotions. There would be times when he would not do his chores, not finish his supper, and not go to bed when it was time.

We think he must have been the perfect child, but there is no such thing. Being human is a process and no one goes through it smoothly. Mary would comfort him when tears flooded out. Joseph had to teach him how to measure a board and cut it to the correct length.

We know that Joseph and Mary did a good job because their son did ultimately figure out who God wanted him to be.

Who does God want us to be?

December 31 – The Seventh Day in the Octave of Christmas

> In the beginning was the Word,
> and the Word was with God,
> and the Word was God.
> He was in the beginning with God.
> All things came to be through him,
> and without him nothing came to be.
> What came to be through him was life,
> and this life was the light of the human race;
> the light shines in the darkness,
> and the darkness has not overcome it.
> Jn 1: 1 – 8

And so we come to the last day of the secular year, which is not the same thing as the end of the liturgical year. The liturgical year ends with the Feast of Christ the King and begins with the First Sunday of Advent. Tomorrow is New Year's Day. Our faith will always keep us just a bit out of step with the times.

There are two important themes in today's gospel. One is "the Word." John calls Jesus the Word. Our words are supposed to make our God more present in our world. When our words hurt, discriminate, offend, mislead, or insult, we make God less present. We need to use our words better.

The second theme is light and darkness. John tells us that "the light shines in the darkness and the darkness has not overcome it." It has not and it will not. Jesus is the light of the world. Jesus came to take away our darkness, and to save us from our sins. He will not be deterred. At our Baptism we were given a candle that was lit from the Pascal candle and the priest said, "Receive the light of Christ." Then he says to our parents and godparents, "This light is entrusted to you to be kept burning brightly. This child of yours has been enlightened by Christ. She is to walk always as a child of the light. May she keep the flame of faith alive in her heart. When the Lord comes, may she go out to meet him with all the saints in the heavenly kingdom."

Where can our light shine more brightly?

Feast of the Holy Family (A, B, C)

> But after Herod's death, the angel of the Lord appeared
> in a dream to Joseph in Egypt with the command:
> "Get up, take the child and his mother,
> and set out for the land of Israel.
> Those who had designs on the life of the child are dead."
> He got up, took the child and his mother
> and returned to the land of Israel.
> He heard, however, that Archelaus had succeeded
> his father Herod as king of Judea,
> and was afraid to go back there.
> Instead, because of a warning received in a dream,
> Joseph went to the region of Galilee.
> There he settled in a town called Nazareth.
> In this way what was said through the prophets was fulfilled,
> "He shall be called a Nazorean."
> Mt 2: 13 – 15, 19 – 23

As a sociologist would say, "Once the dyad becomes a triad, nothing will ever be the same." Once a husband and wife are blessed with a child nothing will ever be the same. When a couple becomes a family, priorities have to change.

Early on in my priestly ministry, when I was away on a study fellowship, I received a beautiful letter from a new mom. I had presided at her wedding two years earlier. This was her memorable sentence in that letter, "a bit too much mommy, a bit too little wifey, mid-course adjustment needed." They recently celebrated their fortyfifth anniversary so they must have made the necessary adjustments. Every couple needs to make adjustments; Mary and Joseph needed to make adjustments.

The thing that I find interesting about this feast day is that most people don't know what they are celebrating. This is Holy Family Sunday; it is not Perfect Family Sunday. There is no perfect family. Not even one that contains two saints and the Messiah.

Just what is a holy family? It is a family that is focused; a family that is anchored in faith. There are disagreements, but they are amicably resolved. There are hurt feelings, but they are healed. There are burnt meals, disgruntled adolescents, and money and emotional problems. The Holy Family and our holy family are not made holy by the absence of problems but by the way those problems are faced and resolved.

What adjective best describes our family?

January 1 – Mary, The Holy Mother of God

> The Lord blesses you, and keeps you!
> The Lord let his face shine upon you, and be gracious to you!
> The Lord looks upon you kindly and gives you peace!
> Numbers 6: 22 – 27

Today's feast day has had many iterations. Long ago it was the Feast of The Circumcision, then it was the World Day of Peace, and finally it is presented to us as the Feast of Mary, The Holy Mother of God. That being said, it is New Year's Day and that is what most of us are celebrating.

Today we pause and look back at the year that is ending and we look forward to the year that is to come. In the words of Dag Hammarskjold, "For all that has been, Thank You. For all that is to come, yes!"

Some of us cannot wait for this year to end because it was a year filled with more pain and suffering than with joy and success. Others don't want the year to end because it was a year of happiness and fulfillment.

Time is a gift. We are not in charge of time. We need to strive to make the most of the time that God gives us. As Bill Keane, the cartoonist who created Family Circus, said in one of his cartoons, "Yesterday is history. Tomorrow is mystery. Today is a gift of God, which is why we call it the present."

What better way to start the New Year than to make a list of all we have for which we should be grateful?

January 2

> This is the testimony of John.
> When the Jews from Jerusalem sent priests
> and Levites to him to ask him,
> "Who are you?" He admitted and did not deny it.
> But admitted, "I am not the Christ."
> So they asked him, "What are you then? Are you Elijah?"
> And he said, "I am not."
> "Are you the Prophet?" He answered them, "No."
> So they said to him,
> "Who are you so we can give an answer to those who sent us?"
> Jn 1: 19 – 28

Life is all about being able to answer the question, "Who are you?" In order to answer that question we have to be actively engaged in discovering who we are. Not who do we want to be or who do others think we are. But right now, today, who are we? It is more difficult than we think to discover our true identity.

John the Baptist knew who he was so he could honestly answer the priests and Levites. They came with their questions and their answers. They wanted to put him in one of their preconceived boxes. But he did not fit into them. He, as a result of much work and inner struggle, came to know that he was the precursor of the Messiah. Once he knew who he was, he knew how to act.

There is a thing called the poor person's psychological exam. It goes like this: Does who you are determine what you do or does what you do determine who you are? Only one answer leads to the truth. The former leads to the truth, the latter leads to a life of spinning our wheels.

Ask God to give us the insight of his spirit so we can discover who we are and then ask for the courage to live that truth.

January 3

> See what love the Father bestowed on us that
> we may be called the children of God.
> Yet so we are.
> The reason the world does not know us
> is that it did not know him.
> Beloved, we are God's children now;
> what we shall be has not yet been revealed.
> 1 Jn 2: 29 – 3:6

Too often faith and religion seemed to focus on what will be rather than what is. In this understanding, religion is seen as pedaling, "pie in the sky, bye and bye." Our first reading today tells us we are "God's children now." Yesterday we were challenged to find out who we are. Today, St. John gives us the answer.

We are God's children; let's act like it. Not too long ago someone said to me, "You are just like your father!" I don't think they meant it as a compliment, but I took it as one.

What do we know about God? We know God is love! If we are God's children, we need to lead with love. We need to grow in love, each day become more loving. We know that God is forgiving. When we pray the Our Father we say, "Forgive us our sins as we forgive others." I don't know about you, but I have some work to do in this regard. God is a lot more than loving and forgiving and his children need to be a lot more, but loving and forgiving are great places to start, don't you think?

Whom do we need to love more and forgive more generously?

January 4

> The two disciples heard what he said and followed Jesus.
> Jesus turned and saw them following him and said to them,
> "What are you looking for?"
> They said to him, "Rabbi, where are you staying?"

> He said to them, "Come, and you will see."
> Jn 1: 35 – 42

Sometimes translations are not helpful. I suspect that today's scripture quote is one of those times. In today's translation, it appears that John's disciples want Jesus' address so he invites them to follow him home. There has to be more to it than that.

What the disciples are really saying is, "What anchors you?" "What gives you the strength to heal people?" "Why aren't you more like the Messiah we were anticipating?" Jesus understands the deeper level of their question and basically says, "Why don't you come and spend the day with me?" He does not want to tell them the answer to their question; he wants to show them the answer to their question.

Jesus is really not that good at answering questions. Frequently in scripture when Jesus is asked a question he answers with a story. The rich young man asks, "Who is my neighbor?" and Jesus replies, "There was a man going from Jerusalem to Jericho who fell prey to robbers." In place of an answer, we get the story of the Good Samaritan. Like all good teachers, Jesus leads us further than we want to go.

Are we hesitant to spend more time in prayer because we are afraid Jesus will lead us further than we want to go?

January 5

> When Jesus saw Nathanael coming toward him, he remarked:
> "This man is a real Israelite. There is no guile in him."
> "How do you know me?" Nathanael asked him.
> "Before Philip called you," Jesus answered,
> "I saw you under the fig tree."
> "Rabbi," said Nathanael,
> "You are the Son of God; you are the king of Israel."
> Jesus responded,
> "Do you believe just because I told you I saw you under the fig tree?
> You will see much greater things than that."
> Jn 1: 43 – 51

Today's gospel reminds us that faith is a process. Our faith grows; it ebbs and flows. It is not static. Nathanael seems to be a very gifted believer. We are in the very first chapter of John's gospel and he has it all figured out. "Rabbi, you are the Son of God; you are the King of Israel."

Truth is that on this day, when he is called to follow Jesus, all the pieces fit nicely together. There will be days yet to come that will not be so focused. There will be days when he will question if Jesus really is the Son of God or the King of Israel. There would be days when Jesus' lesson for the day will be clear and easily understood; then there will be days when nothing Jesus said made sense.

That does not make Nathanael a bad believer any more than our questions, doubts, and uncertainty make us bad believers. They just make us human believers.

What is important is that our faith does not become static. There will always be more to know about our faith. Our relationship with Jesus must remain a work in process. We need to be thankful on the days, or perhaps just the moments, when our faith is in clear focus, and we need to be hopeful for those times when nothing seems clear.

Where have we allowed our faith to become moribund?

Epiphany of the Lord (A,B,C)

> When Jesus was born in Bethlehem of Judea
> in the days of King Herod,
> behold magi from the east arrived in Jerusalem saying,
> "Where is the newborn king of the Jews?
> We saw his star at its rising and have come to do him homage."
> Mt 2: 1 – 12

It is a shame that this great feast day has lost so much of its importance. Once, it was called Little Christmas, and was the day when believers exchanged gifts. January 6, the twelfth day of Christmas, used to be the end of the Christmas season. We need to let the spirit of this feast invigorate our faith once again.

Today is a day for dreamers and risk-takers, a day for poets and magicians. Epiphany is a day that invites us to lift up our eyes, open our minds, and revel in the signs that God sends to us. In today's gospel, Herod has the power but what good does it do him? The chief priests and the scribes have the knowledge of where the Christ was to be born. However that knowledge did not motivate them to travel to Bethlehem. What good did their knowledge do them? Only the magi bothered to follow the star.

Epiphany always reminds me of this quote of Kent Nerburn's in his book, "Letters to My Son": "If we don't offer ourselves to the unknown, our senses dull. Our world becomes small and we lose our sense of wonder. Our eyes don't lift to the horizon; our ears don't hear the sounds around us. The edge is off our experience, and we spend our days in a routine that is both comfortable and limiting. We wake up one day and find we have lost our dreams to protect our days. ***Don't let yourself become one of these people.***" (bold and italics added)

What lost dreams do we need to recapture in our lives?

Monday after Epiphany

> From that time on Jesus began to proclaim this theme,
> "Reform your lives! The Kingdom of heaven is at hand."
> Jesus toured all of Galilee. He taught in their synagogues,
> proclaimed the good news of the kingdom,
> and cured the people of every disease and illness.
> Mt 4: 13 – 17, 23 – 25

Now that Jesus has been revealed to the non-Jewish world through the wise men, we go right to his public ministry. We know only one thing about Jesus from his circumcision until the beginning of his public life. We know that as an adolescent he became separated from his parents for a few days. I wish we knew more but we don't.

Instead we have Jesus calling on people to reform and embrace the Kingdom. Jesus had his ministry and he worked at it. He went throughout all of Galilee; he taught in their synagogues. He had success and he had failures. People would ask him to stay around and teach them more; other times people would ask him to leave. When he miraculously fed the crowd of five thousand people, they flocked after him. When he sent demons into a herd of swine and they plunged to their death in the sea, they asked him to leave.

Jesus did not worry about his reception; he worried about proclaiming his Father's message. We are all familiar with the saying, "The truth will set you free." But as a very wise man added, "but first it will make you miserable." It is never easy to speak the truth, especially to authority, but that is what Jesus did, and what he calls us to do.

Where have we been too timid speaking our truth to authority?

Tuesday after Epiphany

> By now it was already late
> and his disciples approached him and said,
> "This is a deserted place and it is already very late.
> Dismiss them so that they can go to
> the surrounding farms and villages
> and buy themselves something to eat."
> He said to them in reply,
> "Give them some food yourselves."
> Mk 6: 34 – 44

Recognizing a problem is only half the solution. The disciples, being good managers, saw that feeding the vast crowd was going to be a problem. Jesus did not see a problem but an opportunity. That is why he was such a great teacher. The disciples did not want to solve the problem; they wanted to move it.

Jesus knew that the solution was at hand; all they needed was to trust that God would provide. He asked penetrating questions – "What do we have? And what is the best way to use it?" This story of the multiplication of the loaves appears in all four gospels. John adds a very interesting detail. John says it was a young boy who came forward with the five loaves and the two fish. Why is that an important detail?

Only a child would trust that so little could do so much.

Jesus took what was offered, thanked God for it, and shared with an open heart. In the end, it was the sharing that worked the miracle. When everyone shared what they had there was more than enough for everyone to be satisfied. The gathered assembly had to empty their baskets before they could fill them up with the fragments left over. The real miracle was that people trusted and shared what they had.

Where do we need to be more trusting? How can we more generously share what we have?

Wednesday after Epiphany

> After the five thousand had eaten and were satisfied,
> Jesus made his disciples get into the boat
> and precede him to the other side toward Bethsaida,
> while he dismissed the crowd.
> And when he had taken leave of them,
> he went off to the mountain to pray.
> Mk 6: 45 – 52

"He went off to the mountain to pray." It would be easy to miss this little detail. Jesus was able to do all that he did because he was rooted in prayer. Jesus is always slipping away to pray. Indeed, in his darkest hour, when he was about to be betrayed, he invited Peter, James, and John to pray with him in the garden. Do you remember how that time of prayer ended? "Father, not my will but your will be done."

Jesus prayed throughout his life. He did not pray for God to change his mind; he prayed that he would be able to know what God wanted and be able to embrace God's will. Many of us pray; too few of us are rooted in prayer.

There is a Russian proverb that says, "Most prayer is that two plus two equals 5." We pray when we are in trouble; we pray when someone is sick; we pray when all else fails. I was a campus minister and then pastor of a university parish for almost forty years. Many students would pray that they would pass their exams. I never heard of one student who prayed that God would help them study better. Too often prayer is the last refuge of a scoundrel.

How can we find more time for "real" prayer in our lives?

Thursday after Epiphany

> He came to Nazareth, where he had grown up,
> And went according to his custom
> into the synagogue on the Sabbath day.
> Lk 4: 14 – 22

What happens when we lose our customs? When we lose our customs, we lose our identity. Unless old customs are revered they are not allowed to produce new and better customs.

It was important that Jesus was accustomed to go to the synagogue. He was taught by Joseph and Mary to pray, to read the scriptures, to go to the synagogue, and to obey the laws that helped keep the Sabbath holy.

A very wise, holy, and intelligent philosophy professor of mine was fond of saying, "Religion is caught not taught!" When I taught religion in a Catholic high school immediately following ordination, I used to enjoy parent night. Once I met the parents, I understood their children so much better. I used to tell the principal to schedule parent night the first week of school. That way I could know right from the beginning which students would be a joy and which ones would be a challenge.

The same is true with our children and their faith. Our children catch their faith from us.

Where have we failed to pass on our faith to the next generation? Is it too late to correct the damage?

Friday after Epiphany

> "I do will it. Be made clean."
> And the leprosy left him immediately.

> Then he ordered him not to tell anyone, but
> "Go and show yourself to the priest and offer for your cleansing
> what Moses prescribed; that will be proof for them."
> Lk 5: 12 – 16

What a waste of breath. Imagine telling someone who because of leprosy was ostracized from family and community not to talk about being cured. Imagine someone who had to carry a bell and ring it and announce "Unclean!" if anyone came near; imagine being rid of all those terrible exclusions and not telling anyone. We would want to shout it from the rooftops and that is probably exactly what the leper in today's gospel probably did.

Why then did Jesus tell him not to tell anyone? Because he knew just how quickly things could get out of hand. Jesus went about preaching the good news and working signs and wonders. Scripture tells us when the Messiah comes "the blind will see, the mute will speak, the deaf will hear, the dead will rise, and the poor will have the good news preached to them." If biblical signs are going to work they have to be transparent. The people have to see through them to the greater reality. Jesus knew that too many people would get stuck at the signs and not see through them to the greater reality.

Where is God calling us to see the "more to come" in the people around us?

Saturday after Epiphany

> The one who has the bride is the bridegroom;
> the best man, who stands and listens for him,
> rejoices greatly at the bridegroom's voice.
> So this joy of mine has been made complete.
> He must increase; I must decrease.
> Jn 3: 22 – 30

John knew his place. He knew who he was supposed to be and how he was supposed act. That does not make John the Baptist unique. What makes him unique is he accepted who he was and acted accordingly. John was not the star attraction; he was the supporting cast. For Jesus to be the Messiah John had to bow out of the way. Not an easy thing to do.

Seems to me there are always people who will not accept their proper role. It happens at work, at home, on committees, on teams, and any other place where cooperation is required. I recently came across this quote in a book I was reading. The setting was the world of politics but it is applicable to all group endeavors. A very senior politician was giving some advice to a newly elected member of congress. He said, "Always remember there are show horses and work horses. Be a workhorse!"

When the New England Patriots won their first Super Bowl title against the St. Louis Rams, "the greatest show on turf," they refused to go along with a long- standing custom. They refused to be introduced as individuals; they were introduced as a team. Individuals don't win Super Bowls; teams do! On successful teams every player knows his job and does it.

Where do we need to work at being less me and more we?

Feast of the Baptism of Jesus (A, B, C)

Jesus came from Galilee to John at the Jordan to be baptized by him.
John tried to prevent him saying,
"I need to be baptized by you and yet you are coming to me?"
Jesus said to him in reply,
"Allow it now, for thus it is fitting for us to fulfill all righteousness."
Mt. 3: 13 – 17

Jesus needed to be baptized by John. He did not need to repent; he needed to belong. He was not just going through the motion; he needed affirmation. We need to see today's gospel story through the eyes of Jesus not the eyes of John.

Perspective is indeed everything. The Apostles, the disciples of both Jesus and John, indeed John himself had no trouble believing that Jesus was human. They walked with him, ate with him, saw him get tired, and saw him sleep. The early church had trouble embracing Jesus' divinity not his humanity. We, on the other hand, have no trouble with Jesus' divinity but we tend to deny his humanity. Jesus' baptism only makes sense for his humanity.

Jesus knew the power of ritual; Jesus needed to belong. Jesus got more than he bargained for. Not only did he get a sense of belonging, he was also affirmed in his growing realization that he was the Messiah. Jesus got to hear the voice say, "This is my beloved Son, with whom I am well pleased."

How can we be more affirming of the people with whom we share the gift of life and faith?

Holy Season of Lent

Ash Wednesday

> Jesus said to his disciples:
> "Take care not to perform righteous deeds
> in order that people may see them;
> otherwise, you will have no recompense
> from your heavenly Father."
> Mt. 6: 1 – 6

And so we come to another Lenten opportunity. Will this Lent be different? If so, in what way(s)?

Too often Lent is habitual. We tend to do the same things over and over. We give up drinking, swearing, sweets, or movies. I wonder if God has a good laugh at how we miss the boat every Lent.

Too often we turn Lent into an excuse for losing weight or getting in better shape. Lent too often seems like a second chance at our New Year's resolution. Lent should not be when we give up something but when we take on something.

How about finding 15 minutes a day for prayer time? Giving up 15 minutes of social media does nothing for us in a religious sense unless those 15 minutes are spent prayerfully reading the Bible or letting God speak to us in solitude. Give up sweets if you must but put the money you save to better use by donating to a local soup kitchen.

What are we going to do this Lent that will please God more than ourselves?

Thursday after Ash Wednesday

> Then he said to all,
> "If anyone wishes to come after me, he must deny himself
> and take up his cross and follow me."
> Lk 9: 22 – 25

Too often we choose our crosses. We choose what crosses we are going to carry. But that is not the way it works. That is not what Jesus is asking us to do in today's gospel.

The important crosses are the ones that find us. One such cross is the one called forgiveness. If we choose to carry the forgiveness cross it is usually a reluctant choice. We lay down our conditions. The offending person has to say they are sorry before we forgive. Jesus wants us to forgive without the "I'm sorry" part.

How about the cross called attentiveness. We have to choose to pay attention. Attention requires discipline.

How about the cross of enduring hardship without complaining. Or perhaps we need to work on the cross called service to others, concern for the least among us or visiting the sick. There are many opportunities to take up our crosses and follow Jesus and Lent is a good time to get started.

What cross have we avoided taking up?

Friday after Ash Wednesday

> The disciples of John approached Jesus and said,
> "Why do we and the Pharisees fast much,
> but your disciples do not fast?"

What is it about human nature that has us worry much more about the behavior of others than our own behavior? Maybe it is part of original sin; maybe it is laziness. Whatever its source living by comparison is dangerous and destructive.

The disciples of John should have been wondering if they were fasting for the right reasons. Instead, they were worrying about why Jesus' disciples were not fasting. They were being very non-productive.

We tend to fixate on what others are doing or not doing. Imagine how different the world would be if we would learn to mind our own business?

"Why doesn't the bishop do…? Why don't those parents do…? If only my neighbor would…? If the boss would just…?" If there is an issue or a problem we need to assign ourselves to the solution. If everyone would just do their part, we would all be too busy to complain about others.

Where have we allowed comparisons to taint our worldview?

Saturday after Ash Wednesday

> The Pharisees and their scribes complained to his disciples, saying,
> "Why do you eat and drink with tax collectors and sinners?"
> Jesus said to them in reply,
> "Those who are healthy do not need a physician, but the sick do.
> I have not come to call the righteous to repentance but sinners."
> Lk 5: 27 – 32

Pope Francis is a wonderful reminder of how Jesus wants us to live. Francis is always reaching out to those on the periphery of life. He reaches out to sinners, of course, but he reaches out to those whom the world seems to forget.

He not only speaks out for the dignity of immigrants, he reaches out and treats them with dignity.

Just recently, he turned a Vatican palazzo into a place for the homeless called "Palace of the Poor." Francis has appointed Konrad Cardinal Krajewski as the papal almoner. In that role, he "carries out acts of charity and raises money to fund them." Krajewski says that the pope told him, "You can sell your desk. You don't need it. You need to get out of the Vatican. Don't wait for people to come ringing. You need to go out and look for the poor."

Every diocese and every parish in the world needs to do the same.

Where do we need to extend a helping hand to those in need?

First Sunday of Lent (A)

> Then the devil took him up a very high mountain,
> and showed him all the kingdoms of the world in their magnificence,
> and he said to him, "All these I shall give to you,
> if you will prostrate yourself and worship me."
> Jesus said to him,
> "Get away, Satan!"
> Mt 4: 1 – 11

Ah temptations, they are as ubiquitous as they are personal. The evil one picks the best temptation for the right person in a precise situation. Some of us are easier marks than others.

In his delightful book *Screwtape Letters,* C. S. Lewis has this conversation between the senior devil and a devil in training, "It does not matter how small the sins are provided that their cumulative effect is to edge the man away from the Light and out into the Nothing. Murder is not better than cards if cards can do the trick. Indeed the safest road to Hell is the gradual one – the gentle slope, soft underfoot, without sudden turnings, without milestones, without signposts."

Many years ago I gave a homily about temptation. In it I said, "My problem isn't will power; my problem is won't power." For any of us to make progress with our spiritual lives we need to say no to the temptations that so easily ensnare us. May God give us "won't power" when next we are tempted.

Where do I need to place more trust in God's loving providence when I face temptation?

First Sunday of Lent (B)

> After John's arrest,
> Jesus appeared in Galilee proclaiming God's good news:
> "This is the time of fulfillment.

> The reign of God is at hand!
> Reform your lives and believe the good news."
> Mk 1: 12 – 15

What a great summary of Lent, "Reform your lives and believe the good news!" We are, or should be, in a constant state of reform. One of the frustrating things about our faith is that it is always ongoing. We never get to the goal of our faith.

Many years ago, my moral theology professor mentioned in class that our faith is like climbing a mountain. We look up at a peak and we put all of our energy into climbing to that peak. When we get there, we realize that there was another peak that we could not see before, so we set out once again to climb to that peak. When he said this he smiled and said, "You can see where this is going; there will always be another peak." When I first listened to his wisdom many years ago my first reaction was discouragement followed quickly by a sense of frustration. However the more I thought about it, the more I appreciated his honesty and his wisdom.

All the important tasks in our life are never ending. Learning is ongoing, as are parenting and friendship. Why should faith be any different?

Lent is a time to reform, to re-energize, and to be renewed. Ideally, our faith is not a constantly recurring cycle but rather an always rising spiral that helps us see the more to come in our lives and in the lives of those around us.

What in our lives needs to be reformed this Lent?

First Sunday of Lent (C)

> The devil took him up higher and showed him all the kingdoms
> of the world in an instant. He said to him,
> "I will give you all this power and the glory of these kingdoms;
> the power has been given to me
> and I give it to whomever I wish.
> Prostrate yourself in homage before me, and it shall all be yours."

> In reply, Jesus said to him,
> "Scripture has it,
> 'You shall do homage to the Lord your God;
> him alone shall you adore.'"
> Lk 4: 1 – 13

There is nothing more personal than temptations. We are unique, and our weaknesses are unique. Some people crave power and glory, while others could care less. Some want to be spectacular, while others want to fly under the radar. Some people's downfall is food, while for others it is booze or some other drug. Some people eat too much, while others eat too little.

But amid all these variables there is one constant – the devil hides in the shadows of our lives. He never hides in the light because his lies and deceptions would be easily recognized in the light. The shadows are the perfect milieu for the devil. St. Peter expresses it thus, "Be sober and vigilant. Your opponent the devil is prowling around like a roaring lion looking for someone to devour. Resist him, steadfast in faith, knowing that your fellow believers throughout the world undergo the same sufferings." (1 Pt 5: 8 – 9) The battle between good and evil is ancient; the outcome is still unknown. We are in it together.

If we walk toward the light of God's love each and every day, then the shadows will always be behind us, and the devil will not catch up to us. When we turn our back on the light of God's love, then our shadow is in front of us, and we are walking into the devil's trap. It is all about the light!

What shadows cause us the most harm?

Monday of the First Week of Lent

> Then the righteous will answer him and say,
> "Lord, when did we see you a stranger and welcome you,
> or naked and clothe you?
> When did we see you ill or in prison, and visit you?"
> And the King will say to them in reply.

> "Amen, I say to you, whatever you did for one of these
> least brothers of mine, you did to me."
> Mt. 25: 31 – 46

Matthew gives us the only description of what the last judgment will be like; I wish he had not. Early on in our lives of faith we were introduced to what I call spiritual economics. We are taught to keep score because God keeps score. God, just judge that he is, watches our every move. We get points for the good we do, and we lose points when we sin. We win the game, if when we die, we end up with enough positive points to make it to purgatory, where our friends can pay off our spiritual debt with the prayers they offer for us. Eventually, we make it to heaven. We lose if we end up in Hell for all eternity.

No one will take credit for teaching us this spiritual form of economics, but most of us were taught it and need to unlearn it.

Matthew does not so much unteach our spiritual economics as expand the notion of what counts as good. Most of us count prayers, all kinds of prayers, the rosary, memorized prayers, personal prayers, novenas, and visits to the Blessed Sacrament as our good deeds. Matthew does not mention anything about prayer as increasing our spiritual bank account. Instead he talks about good deeds; he talks about what we have come to call the corporal works of mercy as what counts for salvation. Too bad most of us think of the corporal works of mercy as optional.

What needs to change if those on the periphery are to receive more attention from us?

Tuesday of the First Week of Lent

> This is how you are to pray:
> Our Father who art in heaven, hallowed be thy name
> Thy Kingdom come,
> Thy will be done on earth as it is in heaven.
> Mt 6: 7 – 15

Many years ago, Louis Every wrote a delightful little book on the Our Father. Chapter 1 – Our, Chapter 2 – Father. You get the idea.

Many of us need to review what "our" means when we say the Our Father. Many of us say "our" but we think "my" Father, and that is a bigger deal than we might think.

There is a tendency to privatize our faith and our religion. When we gather to celebrate the sacraments do we gather as a community or as a group of individuals? The correct answer is "as community"; the lived answer is too often "a group of individuals."

When we gather for Eucharist, some people sing, some people don't. Everyone is supposed to sing. If we are a community everyone sings – those with good voices, those with average voices, and those with little or no musical ability. In a community, everyone would sing. Allow me an example. When a family (the original community) gathers to celebrate a birthday, everyone sings "Happy Birthday." No one would think of saying, "I don't have a good voice." Everyone sings because that is what communities do.

When I travel around the country giving Stewardship talks, there are many things I look for at liturgy. Does someone greet me at the door; does everyone join in the singing and responses and what to people say in response to the Prayer of the Faithful. Do they say, "Lord, hear our prayer" or do they say, "Lord, hear our prayers." If they say "prayer" they are a community; if they say "prayers" they are a group of individuals.

God is our Father, Jesus is our brother, and we are supposed to be sisters and brothers to each other. What happened?

Wednesday of the First Week of Lent

While still more people gathered in the crowd Jesus said to them,
"This generation is an evil generation;
it seeks a sign, but no sign will be given it,
except the sign of Jonah.
Just as Jonah became a sign to the Ninevites,
so will the Son of Man be to this generation."
Lk 11: 29 – 32

What good is a sign if we don't know how to read it? Words are signs; we have to learn how to read them. English is a series of agreed upon signs, so is Spanish, Russian, and Greek. We can read English signs, but most of us can't read Russian or Greek signs. For those sign systems, we need translators. Even then we miss some of the meaning because translation is not an exact science.

Have you ever had someone throw you a surprise party? I have and I was surprised. I don't know how they pulled it off. Once the party had begun I realized that there were a lot of clues that I just missed. I was leaving a campus ministry position. It was June; the academic year was over. Nevertheless I kept running into professors and administrators. Someone ever made a fake appointment with me so that I would be in my office that day. I missed all the signs that day. Each new day, God throws us a surprise party. Too often we miss most of his signs.

How many of God's signs are we presently missing?

Thursday of the First Week of Lent

> "Do to others whatever you would have them do to you.
> This is the law and the prophets."
> Mt 7: 7 – 12

The Golden Rule – treat others the way you want to be treated. A simple, common sense rule, which begs the question why is common sense so uncommon?

It seems we like to make things more complicated than they need to be. We buy something online that comes with the warning, "some assembly required." The product arrives and we try to assemble it. It always takes longer than it should take. Nevertheless, most of us persist with the false narrative, "When all else fails, read the instructions." Why don't we read the instructions first?

We don't like to be accused. Yet we insist on accusing others without realizing it. Whether we like it or not, "You never listen to me!" is an accusation.

"Do not accuse and you will not be accused." "Forgive and you will be forgiven." "Give and it will be given unto you."

When I was a high school religion teacher, I learned quickly there are two kinds of questions. Questions that are seeking the truth, and questions that are a stalling tactic. God has figured out the same thing. So most of the time when we ask God, "What should I do?" he knows we are using a stalling tactic.

How can we find the courage to live the way we should be living?

Friday of the First Week of Lent

> Jesus said to his disciples:
> "I tell you, unless your righteousness surpasses that
> of the scribes and Pharisees,
> you will not enter into the Kingdom of heaven.
> Mt 5: 20 – 26

Righteousness is first and foremost an attribute of God. It means ethical conduct. God has to be righteous; we not so much. We are supposed to be righteous, but often we do not live up to the challenge. In the Hebrew scriptures Job is identified as righteous; in the New Testament Joseph is called "just" which I think means the same as righteous.

Jesus points out those who need to improve their righteous behavior. He wants us to be righteous; he will help us be so. Will we invite him more fully into our decision-making?

There is an adjective that best describes each one of us. If you want to have fun with a gathering of friends ask each person to come up with the adjective that best describes each of the others and the adjective that best describes themselves. Then spend some time having people share their opinions. Experience has shown that it is better to do this exercise early in the evening rather than later. A few ground rules may be in order such as the adjective must be positive, and if you don't have something kind to say don't say anything, etc.

What adjective do we think God uses to identify us?

Saturday of the First Week of Lent

> Jesus said to his disciples:
> "You have heard that it was said,
> *You shall love your neighbor and hate your enemy.*
> But I say to you. Love your enemies,
> Pray for those who persecute you,
> that you may be children of your heavenly Father,
> for he makes his sun rise on the bad and the good,
> and causes rain to fall on the just and the unjust."
> Mt 5: 43 – 48

Why can't Jesus leave well enough alone? The world worked perfectly well when we had it divided up between neighbors and enemies, friends and foes. We were nice to our neighbors and hostile with our enemies.

The system worked or at least we convinced ourselves that it worked. In truth, it was a system that had to fail. People change, enemies become friends, friends become enemies. Past behaviors come back to haunt us.

What Jesus is saying is that it takes two to make an enemy. If we can rise above the behavior of others, we determine the choices we make. If we let others control our choices, we put them in charge of our lives. Why would we let someone we neither like nor respect make decisions in our lives? Nevertheless that is precisely what we do when we make someone an enemy. That person then gets to determine our mood, our words, our deeds, and our actions.

Jesus lived what he preached. Hanging on the cross he could have withheld forgiveness and let his executioners win. Instead he said, "Father, forgive them for they do not know what they are doing." In so doing he saved everyone, not just some of the people.

Where are we allowing someone we neither like nor respect to make decisions in our lives?

Second Sunday of Lent (A)

> Jesus took Peter, James, and John his brother,
> and led them up a high mountain by themselves.
> And he was transfigured before them;
> his face shone like the sun
> and his clothes became white as light.
> And behold, Moses and Elijah appeared to them conversing with him.
> Then Peter said to Jesus in reply,
> "Lord, it is good that we are here."
> Mt 17: 1 – 9

Peter, James, and his brother John are sometimes referred to as Jesus' inner circle. When we hear these three mentioned together, we need to pay attention because something important is about to happen. These three are first called out when Jesus raises Jairus' daughter from the dead (Mk 5: 37). Next they are the called upon to witness the transfiguration (Mt 17: 1 – 8, Mk 9: 2 – 8, Lk 9: 28 – 36). And finally, they are invited to participate in the Agony in the Garden of Gethsemane (Mt. 26: 36 – 46, Mk 14: 32 – 42, Lk 22: 40 46, and Jn 18: 1 – 11).

What is important about the Transfiguration? It is a breakthrough moment. Jesus' divinity briefly breaks through his humanity. It was what psychologists call a peak moment. A time when all the pieces fit and life makes sense. A memory to be treasured.

We experience transfigurations throughout our lives. We go to the symphony, we get lost in the music, time melts away, and suddenly we are on our feet applauding the experience. Other times, we go to the symphony and the music is OK but we keep looking at our watch to see when it will be over. We are having lunch with a good friend, the conversation goes deeper than usual, hearts are laid bare, trust is magnified and time is diminished. Two week later we can have lunch with the same friend in the same restaurant with no spark and no new breakthrough or insight. It is just lunch. The same thing can happen with liturgy. Some Sundays it all makes sense and nourishes us; other Sundays we are just getting our ticket punched.

What is the best liturgical experience we have ever had?

Second Sunday of Lent (B)

> He hardly knew what to say,
> for they were all overcome with awe.
> A cloud came, overshadowing them,
> and out of the cloud came a voice,
> "This is my Son, my beloved.
> Listen to him."
> Suddenly, looking around, they no longer saw anyone with them –
> only Jesus.
> Mk 9: 2 – 10

The second Sunday of Lent always features the Transfiguration. Matthew, Mark, and Luke give us three different takes on what happened on that mountain. The accounts are both similar and different, which is true of the various descriptions of any important life-changing event. We are unique, so our experiences are unique. In the end, all that matters is that the experience was life changing.

There are only so many events in life that can be called life changing. The number is not large – two, maybe three, maximum.

For me, studying in Louvain, Belgium, would be one. Ordination would be another, and my time as pastor of Christ the King parish would be the third. What would yours be?

There are many experiences that fashioned who we are – our families, our friends, our travels, etc., but there is a difference between life forming and life changing.

For Peter, James, and John the transfiguration had to be life changing. That is why when coming down the mountain Jesus tells them to keep it to themselves. Live with it for a while, let it mature, let it ripen. When the time is right, you will be able to share it and be thankful for it.

What are the life-changing experiences in our lives?

Second Sunday of Lent (C)

> Suddenly two men were talking with him – Moses and Elijah.
> They appeared in glory and spoke of his passage
> which he was about to fulfill in Jerusalem.
> Peter and those with him had fallen into a deep sleep;
> but awakening, they saw his glory and
> likewise saw the two men who were standing with him.
> When these were leaving, Peter said to Jesus,
> "Master, how good it is for us to be here.
> Let us set up three booths, one for you,
> one for Moses, and one for Elijah."
> Lk 9: 26 – 36

The Second Sunday of Lent always features an account of what we call the Transfiguration. This year we have Luke's account. What can Luke teach us?

We know the event – briefly Jesus' divinity breaks through his humanity – and Peter, James, and John experience the fullness of who Jesus is. Peter's suggestion that they set up three tents highlights a human foible – we want to capture what cannot be captured. The transfiguration was a moment; it was never meant to be a monument. Making it permanent would rob it of all meaning.

It reminds me of a missionary who gave the chief of a village a sundial as a sign of friendship. The chief put the sundial in the middle of the village in a place of honor, and both the missionary and the tribal chief were very pleased. The missionary would visit the village every month or so. On every visit they would gather at the sundial and pray. On one visit to the village the chief was excited to show the priest an improvement they had made for the sundial. When they arrived at the sundial the missionary saw that they had put of roof over it to protect it from the elements. That's what happens when we try to capture God in a hymn, a prayer, a tabernacle, or a church. We cannot capture God!

How have we tried to capture and control God?

Monday of the Second Week of Lent

> Jesus said to his disciples:
> "Be merciful, just as your Father is merciful.
> Stop judging and you will not be judged.
> Stop condemning and you will not be condemned.
> Forgive and you will be forgiven."
> Lk 6: 36 – 38

In 2016, Pope Francis called for a Jubilee Year of Mercy. Luke 6: 36 – 38, today's gospel, was his motivation. Francis explained it this way, "Here, then, is the reason for the Jubilee: because this is the time for mercy. It is the favorable time to heal wounds, a time not to be weary of meeting all those who are waiting to see and to touch with their hands the signs of the closeness of God, a time to offer everyone the way of forgiveness and reconciliation."

Everyone needs forgiveness; all have failed in various degrees. Fortunately, God's forgiveness is always greater than our sinfulness. God never tires of extending his healing forgiveness. The only limit on God's forgiveness is our willingness to share it. Forgiveness is a gift; gifts are meant to be shared.

I remember being shocked when I heard a priest say in a homily, "I have trouble forgiving people who offend me. When I cannot forgive someone then I say to God, 'You forgive them' and maybe someday I will be able to do so myself." I was shocked not because the priest admitted having trouble forgiving some people (I identify with that problem clearly). I was shocked that he thought God should make up for his deficiency, but I'm sure God was not shocked at all.

Where are we presently withholding forgiveness from someone in our lives?

Tuesday of the Second Week of Lent

> Call no one on earth your Father;
> You have but one Father in heaven.
> Do not be called 'Master';

> You have but one master, the Christ.
> The greatest among you must be your servant.
> Whoever exalts himself will be humbled;
> But whoever humbles himself will be exalted.
> Mk 23: 1 – 12

There is a great story about Muhammad Ali, indeed there are many great stories about him. Often referring to himself as "The Greatest," Ali was not afraid to sing his own praises He was known for boasting about his skills before a fight, and for his colorful descriptions and phrases.

There is this story about him when he was on an airplane preparing to go to a fight. The flight attendants had given their pre-flight preamble about seat belts and what to do in the unlikely event of an emergency landing and were going down the aisle to make sure everyone had their seat belt fastened. When the flight attendant got to Muhammad Ali, she asked him to fasten his seat belt. Ali, in characteristic fashion announced that, "Superman don't need no seat belt." The flight attendant without hesitation said, "And Superman don't need no airplane!" Guess who buckled up?

I don't know about you, but I love to see uppity folks put into place so adroitly. There are too many people who think the rules don't apply to them. I love it when they are reminded that no one is above the rules.

When was the last time we were taken down a peg or two?

Wednesday of Second Week of Lent

> But Jesus summoned them and said,
> "You know that the rulers of the Gentiles lord it over them,
> and the great ones make their authority over them felt.
> But it shall not be so among you … Just so,
> the Son of Man did not come to be served but to serve
> and to give his life as a ransom for many.
> Mt 20: 17 – 28

Some people get leadership; others don't. I've worked with people, and I have worked for people. I prefer to work with people. I think that is true of most people no matter where they work, or what they do for a living.

In church circles sometimes the rulers lord it over the folks; sometimes those in charge have a need to make their authority felt. Seems to me it all flows out of a healthy self-image. The healthier the self-image, the more likely a person will be a servant leader. This is true at every level of church service from the pope to the chairperson of the parish activities committee. The more a person clings to a title the less likely it is that person will be a servant leader. People who insist on being called bishop, or father, or music director, or director of religious education, in my experience, are not easy to work with.

Titles tend to get in the way; the same way uniforms can get in the way. Titles and uniforms too often create walls rather than bridges. When I was a college chaplain, I met a man who used to offer workshops on creating a healthy work environment. On the day of the workshop, he and his team would show up and meet the people. There were no titles, the clothing was casual. My friend always said that if within the first thirty minutes of the workshop he could tell who the boss was then the work environment was most unlikely unhealthy.

Where do we hide behind titles and rank rather than letting our abilities speak?

Thursday of the Second Week of Lent

Jesus said to the Pharisees:
"There was a rich man who dressed in purple garments and fine linen
and dined sumptuously each day.
And lying at his door was a poor man named Lazarus,
covered with sores,
who would gladly have eaten his fill of the scraps
that fell from the rich man's table."
Lk 16: 19 – 31

Subtle things can make all the difference. In today's parable Jesus introduces a bit of subtly. Nowhere at any level of society in Jesus' time right up until our time, do the poor have a name and the rich go nameless. Even the rich man knows Lazarus by name. That just doesn't happen.

The poor are nameless; they are faceless. That is just the way the world works. Jesus wants to change that; he wants us to change that.

The name Lazarus means, "God has helped" or "My God is my helper."

One of the tenants of the Storyteller's Creed is that, "all stories are true, some actually happened." This story fits that tenant. There was a seminary where the final examination before ordination had only two questions. The first question was, "How has the resurrection of Jesus changed the way you live?" The second question was, "What is the first name of the cleaning lady in Clark Hall?" The first question was worth 25 points. The second question was worth 75 points. The moral of the story is, "What good is all our theology if it does not lead us to treat people better?"

Where are we guilty of ignoring the service people who are so essential in our lives?

Friday of the Second Week of Lent

> Jesus said to the chief priests and the elders of the people:
> "Hear another parable.
> There was a landowner who planted a vineyard, put a hedge around it,
> Dug a wine press in it and built a tower.
> Then he leased it to tenants and went on a journey.
> When vintage time drew near,
> He sent his servants to the tenants to obtain his produce."
> Mt 21: 33 – 43, 45 – 46

Everything worked out until it was time to pay the rent. We forget that we are renters here on earth; we act as if we own the world. We don't own the world; God owns the world. God gives us the world as a gift; all we have to do is take care of it.

The spirituality of Stewardship teaches that everything we have is a gift from God. Life is a gift, as is our health, our family, our job, our home, and our friends. We don't really own anything.

Perhaps a story will help us to see the world as it is rather than as we want it to be. The story takes place outside a small village in Ireland during a time of economic uncertainty. There was an abandoned farm. The fields were fallow, the stone walls in need of repair, the thatched roof had collapsed, and no crops were planted. A stranger bought the place and began to fix it up. He put a new roof on the house and gave it a fresh coat of whitewash. The walls were fixed, wheat was planted, and there were sheep in the fields. The new owner, however, did not attend church, so the parish priest paid him a visit. He knocked on the door and was invited in for a cup of tea. During the conversation that followed the priest said to the new owner, "I love what you and God have done with the place." The owner took a slow sip of tea and then said to the priest, "Father, do you remember what the place looked like when God had it by himself?"

Where in our lives do we need to be more grateful for all God's gifts?

Saturday of the Second Week of Lent

> While he was still a long way off, his father caught sight of him,
> and was filled with compassion.
> He ran to his son, embraced him, and kissed him.
> His son said to him,
> "Father, I have sinned against heaven and against you;
> I no longer deserve to be called your son."
> But his father ordered his servants, "Quickly, bring
> the finest robe and put it on him, put a ring on his finger
> and sandals on his feet.'"
> Lk 15: 1 – 3, 11 – 32

Today's gospel is the parable of the Prodigal Son, which is possibly the best-known parable in the New Testament. Just about every believer can tell the story without assistance from the Bible. We remember the story because it rings true; we can identify with most of the major characters.

We have been the younger son. We have taken God's gifts and talents and wasted them. We know what it is like to be profligate. Many are the times we have tried to reclaim our lives from the wreckage of our own making, and many are the times we have luxuriated in the warmth of God's inexhaustible forgiveness. Indeed, we have been the younger son.

We have been the older son. We have been filled with misguided rage; we have complained to God about his treating others better than he treats us. We have kept score in our relationships, and have concluded that others get treated better than we. God has presented us with opportunities where we could extend the loving embrace of forgiveness, but we have been lost in the hardness of our hearts. We have sinned with our righteousness. We have been the older son.

The real problem is that too often we have not been the loving father. We have not embraced those who have turned against us. We have been miserly and not lavish with our forgiveness. More often we need to imitate the loving father in this story.

Where can we be more generous with our forgiveness?

Third Sunday of Lent (A)

> At that moment his disciples returned,
> and were amazed that he was talking with a woman.
> But still no one said, "What are you looking for?"
> or "Why are you talking with her?"
> The woman left her water jar
> and went into the town and said to the people,
> "Come and see a man who told me everything I have done.
> Could he possibly be the Christ?"
> Jn 4: 5 – 42

Frequently, a gospel story can only be fully appreciated if we go beyond the first level of the story. The gospel says, "It was about noon." Why would that be important?

No one living in a hot, dry climate would go to get water at noon. The ideal time would be early in the morning or late in the afternoon. Yet here is this woman who comes out at noon to fill her water jug. When we find out about the woman's background, her five husbands, we realize that she was there at noon because she did not want to meet the townsfolk who refer to her as "that woman!" She has a reputation, and that reputation put limits on her activities.

I imagine her heart must have skipped a beat when she saw a man seated at the well. I'm sure her heart was relieved when she saw that the man was not only a stranger, but also a Jew. She did not have to worry about a conversation.

But Jesus did speak to her, and he knew all about her. He knew all about her and yet he spoke with her respectfully. He treated her as the person she could be rather than the person she had become. He approached her with his vision focused on her future not on her past. And it worked.

The woman runs into town. She runs to speak with the people she had learned to avoid. She becomes a disciple. "Could this be the Christ?"

What needs to change so we can become the people God is calling us to be?

Third Sunday of Lent (B)

> In the temple precincts he came upon people
> engaged in selling oxen, sheep and doves,
> and others seated changing coins.
> He made a whip of cords
> and drove them all out of the temple area,
> sheep and oxen alike,
> and knocked over the moneychangers' tables,
> spilling their coins.
> He said to those who were selling doves:
> "Get them out of here!
> Stop turning my Father's house into a marketplace!"
> Jn 2: 19 – 25

I have always had a problem with my temper. It is not as bad as it used to be, but I have to constantly be on guard. I cannot count how many times I have had to confess losing my temper. I remember in grammar school being somewhat relieved that Jesus lost his temper in the temple. I also remember that the nuns went to great lengths to explain that Jesus did not lose his temper in a way that was sinful. I never really got that distinction.

Jesus was appalled by what he saw in the temple, and he lost it. Yet he was in control of his temper. He was able to treat those who were selling doves so that the poor had something to sacrifice differently than the sheep and oxen sellers and the moneychangers. When I lose my temper, I never have control. So maybe the nuns were right.

What we need to focus on is our ability to see what is wrong and to do something about it. Too often, we can see what the problem is, but we convince ourselves that there is nothing we can do about it. Truth is we are powerless only if we allow ourselves to be controlled by what others think. We need to be more courageous when it comes to getting rid of what is wrong in our lives, our families, our churches, and our country.

Where have we been silent in the face of evil?

Third Sunday of Lent (C)

Jesus spoke this parable:
"A man had a fig tree growing in his vineyard,
and he came out looking for fruit on it but did not find any.
He said to the vinedresser, 'Look here!
For three years now I have come in search of fruit on this fig tree
and found none. Cut it down.
Why should it clutter up the ground?'
In answer the man said,
'Sir, leave it another year while I hoe around it
and manure it; then perhaps it will bear fruit.
If not, it shall be cut down.'"
Lk 13: 1 – 9

God is the vinedresser; the vinedresser has endless patience and hope. God not only believes that we can turn our lives around, he gives us endless opportunities to do so.

No matter how many times we fail, our God believes in us. God does not give up on us; we give up on ourselves. Perhaps we don't give up; perhaps we just get comfortable with our sins and give in.

Perhaps no sacrament has changed more in the last fifty years than the sacrament of Reconciliation. We used to call it confession; now we call it Reconciliation. It used to be celebrated more frequently. In the good old days, we used to go to confession weekly, now we go weakly. But there is one thing that has not changed. Most of us confess the same sins over and over again. We examine our conscience, but we seldom discover any new sins. It is almost as if our sins are recorded on a loop. The only thing that changes is the number of times we have committed them. That means we have become comfortable with our sins and failings. Lent is the perfect time to look with fresh eyes on our sins, and to believe that we can repent. We can make progress; we can bear good fruit.

God believes in us. Can we believe in ourselves once again?

Monday of the Third Week of Lent

> Jesus said to the people in the synagogue at Nazareth:
> "Amen, I say to you, no prophet is accepted in his own native place."
> Lk 4: 24 – 30

Jesus goes home and finds out you can't go home. Things change. We like to put people in boxes, and we don't like it when they don't stay in their assigned boxes. We do it all the time.

Many years ago, I was invited to preach at a parish graduation mass for 9th graders. I arrived at the church and went into the sacristy where the nun, who was principal of the school, warmly greeted me. We chatted briefly and we discovered that she had been a teacher at my parish school when I was a student. She said she remembered the Creedon boys; then she asked whatever happened to the short, chubby, shy Creedon boy. She was caught off guard when I said I was doing just fine, and thank you for asking. I was no longer short or chubby and my shy days were a distant memory. But those were the boxes she had assigned to me. The people of Nazareth had Jesus in the box of carpenter and neighborhood boy. They were not ready for him to be an itinerate preacher and miracle worker. He had to outgrow their boxes if he was to become the Messiah.

What boxes do we need to outgrow in order to become the people God is calling us to be?

Tuesday of the Third Week of Lent

> Peter approached Jesus and asked him,
> "Lord, if my brother sins against me, how often must I forgive him?
> As many as seven times?"
> Jesus answered, "I say to you, not seven times but seventy-seven times."
> Mt 18: 21 – 35

For the Hebrews the number "7" represented perfection. Peter did not just pick the number out of a hat. He was asking a serious question. Jesus was trying to teach Peter something about God's forgiveness.

Even a number that represents perfection cannot do justice to God's forgiveness. There is no limit to God's forgiveness. We can be certain of this – we will never exhaust God's forgiveness! The light of God's loving forgiveness will always cast out the shadows created by the darkness of our sinful deeds!

No matter how depraved, how selfish, how jealous, how debauched, or how low we go, God will always forgive us and lift us up again.

We should never count the times we fall down; we should only count the times we fail to get up. God wants us to get up one more time than we fall down. We need to rejoice because our God is the God of second, third, and fourth chances. The real challenge is to live according to his way so that we do not need his forgiveness.

Pick one area of personal darkness, and hand it over to God's light.

Wednesday of Third Week of Lent

> Jesus said to his disciples:
> "Do not think that I have come to abolish the law or the prophets.
> I have come not to abolish but to fulfill."
> Mt 5: 17 – 19

Laws exist for a reason. Sometimes a law can outlive its raison d'etre. When that happens the law needs to be abolished. This fact was brought home to me in a very vivid way when I arrived at the American College in Louvain, Belgium, to begin my theological studies. The year was 1964; the Church was in the midst of the Second Vatican Council. Everything seemed to be up for grabs. Back then the seminary was run by the "rule." Everything from what time you got up in the morning, when you prayed, when you ate, and when Grand Silence began were subject to the "rule." The only problem was there was no "rule." The old "rule" was obsolete, and the faculty were working on the "new rule." The upper classmen were of no help. We first year students would ask them what the "rule" was for such and such and they would say, "If they haven't told then you there is no rule for that. Just do what you think is best." You have no idea how strange that sentence was in the seminary world of the early 1960s. At the first house meeting of the year this "problem" was highlighted. One of the deacons asked why we got up at 5:30 every morning. The rector said, "Philosophy classes start at 8:30 a.m. while Theology classes begin at 9:00 a.m. We get up early for the Philosophy students." The deacon said, "There have not been any Philosophy students here for the past five years." The next day we got up at 6:30 because the valid reason for getting up at 5:30 no longer existed.

Can we think of a few Church laws that need to be done away with because they no longer make sense?

Thursday of the Third Week of Lent

> Jesus was casting out a devil that was mute,
> and when the devil was cast out the dumb man spoke.

> The crowds were amazed at this.
> Some of them said,
> "It is by Beelzebul, the prince of devils, that he casts out devils."
> Others, to test him were demanding a sign from heaven.
> Lk 11: 14 – 23

Over time, belief in the devil or in evil spirits has waned, and that is a shame. There is evil in the world; that is a given. There are evil people in the world. Evil exists.

Oddly, belief in God has also waned. Not as rapidly as belief in the devil, but nevertheless it is happening. God and the devil are really two sides of the same coin. God is the personification of goodness; the devil is the personification of evil. Both God and the devil have to play by the same rules. Neither God nor the devil can enter our lives without an invitation. William Blatty, who wrote The Exorcist, which was later made into a film, respects this truth. If you remember at the beginning of the book the young girl, Regan MacNeil, was playing with a Ouija board, which is an openness to the occult. God and the devil respect our free will. They cannot force us to do anything. We have to give them an opening.

Truth be told, we should be more concerned about being open to God. That is what prayer and the sacraments are all about. We have to call upon God; we have to want God in our lives. If God is in our lives then we need not fear the devil.

Are we more open to God or the devil?

Friday of the Third Week of Lent

> One of the scribes came to Jesus and asked him,
> "Which is the first of all the commandments?"
> Jesus replied, "The first is this:
> Hear, O Israel!
> The Lord our God is Lord alone!
> You shall love the Lord your God with all your heart,
> with all your soul, with all your mind,

> and with all your strength.
> The second is this:
> You shall love your neighbor as yourself.
> There is no other commandment greater than these."
> Mk 12: 28 – 34

Not all questions are created equal. I doubt that today's scribe was really interested in what the greatest commandment was. He probably didn't care if there were a super commandment. What he wanted was to show up Jesus. Any question would have done.

Seekers ask honest questions; phonies don't. Some questions just cannot be answered in a simple fashion. Other questions cannot be answered at all. Jesus' answer was not limited by the narrowness of the scribe. Jesus' answer was for any honest person who happened to be in the crowd. Jesus basically ignored the scribe, or rather gave him the attention he deserved, which was none.

When people ask me, "Do you have a minute?" I always say, "no" because no one ever wants just a minute of my time. A better question would be, "Is now a good time for you to answer a few questions?" "Would you be willing to sit and listen to me while I try to figure out how to deal with a challenge that has come up in my life?"

I find that I respond better to honest questions than I do to camouflage questions.

Where are we guilty of asking God misleading questions?

Saturday of the Third Week of Lent

> "But the tax collector stood off at a distance
> and would not even raise his eyes to heaven
> but beat his breast and prayed,
> 'O God, be merciful to me a sinner.'
> I tell you the latter went home justified, not the former;
> for everyone who exalts himself will be humbled,
> and the one who humbles himself will be exalted."
> Lk 18: 9 – 14

The short version of today's gospel is, "Two men went up to the temple to pray. One did; one didn't." There is more to prayer than going to the temple. Prayer is a dialogue. We speak; God listens. Then we listen and wait for God to speak. Prayer is a two-part deal. Most of us are good at the talking to God part; most of us are deficient in the listening to God part.

Part of the problem is we live in a culture of noise. We are surrounded by noise; we crave it. We have the radio on in the car; the television never gets turned off at home. We have our ear pods, which basically block out stuff we don't want to hear. Silence scares us!

In music the spaces between the notes are as important, if not more important, than the notes themselves. At Mass, the period of silence after the readings is just as important as the readings themselves. Silence can, and will, speak to us if we will just let it.

There is an axiom that says, "Don't ask the question if you are not ready for the answer." The reason most of us don't give time for God to respond to what we say is that we are afraid of what God will say to us.

How can we add more moments of silence in our daily lives? What are we afraid God will say to us?

Fourth Sunday of Lent (A)

> He replied, "If he is a sinner, I do not know.
> One thing I do know is that I was blind and now I see."
> So they said to him,
> "What did he do to you? How did he open your eyes?"
> He answered them,
> "I told you already and you did not listen.
> Why do you want to hear it again?
> Do you want to become his disciples too?"
> Jn 9: 1 – 41

The story of Jesus healing the man born blind on the Sabbath has plenty of twists and turns. There are the rules for the Sabbath. There is the belief that people had infirmities and disabilities because they or someone in their family had sinned. There is the growing partisan divide between those who believed that Jesus was the Messiah and those who did not.

The best thing is not to get lost in the fine details but to celebrate the obvious. Jesus was a caring person; he tried to help whenever he could. And he was not afraid to get down and dirty. Imagine spitting to make mud. Imagine spreading that spittle-mud on someone's eyes. Imagine letting someone put mud on our eyes. Imagine believing that mud could restore eyesight. Imagine what it is like to be blind, to have only fuzzy images in your mind of what reality looks like. Imagine seeing your parents, siblings, friends, home, and self for the first time. Learning how to deal with colors, and day and night. Imagine the whole world miraculously opening before you and people asking you meaningless questions. There is a lot going on in today's gospel.

When we encounter Jesus in any way, our way of seeing others and ourselves should change.

How can we better look on others with love?

Fourth Sunday of Lent (B)

> Yes, God so loved the world that he gave his only Son,
> that whoever believes in him may not die
> but may have eternal life.
> God did not send his Son into the world to condemn the world,
> but that the world might be saved through him.
> Jn 3: 14 – 21

The first verse quoted above is the famous John 3: 16 that is always being held up on signs in the stands at the Super Bowl or in stadia during the World Series. This gospel verse is called the gospel in miniature.

If we tried to distill the New Testament down into one sentence, we could do no better than, "Yes, God so loved the world that he gave his only Son, that whoever believes in him might have eternal life." But isn't that part of the problem? We are not supposed to distill the gospel; we are supposed to fulfill it. We live in a time of the five-second news bite and bumper sticker philosophy. Yet we know we need more than five seconds to express the truth, and it is not possible to fit wisdom and truth on a bumper sticker.

Yes, God loves us, but that love has to be experienced. We have to learn how to revel in God's love expressed in the person of Jesus. Sometimes, I fear, we are too casual with the word love; too easily we say, "I love you" before we are ready to live what that love means. Jesus finally said to us, "I love you" when he hung on the cross. His love had to be expressed in action. The same is true of our love. Each day we need to show God that we love him by the lives we live and the choices we make.

Do our lives proclaim our love of God as well as possible?

Fourth Sunday of Lent (C)

> With that he set off for his father's house.
> While he was still a long way off,
> his father caught sight of him and was deeply moved.
> He ran out to meet him, threw his arms around his neck,
> and kissed him.
> The son said to him,
> "Father, I have sinned against God and against you;
> I no longer deserve to be called your son."
> The father said to his servants. "Quick! bring out the finest robe
> and put it on him;
> put a ring on his finger and shoes on his feet.
> Take the fatted calf and kill it.
> Let us eat and celebrate because this son of mine was dead
> and has come back to life.
> He was lost and is found."
> Then the celebration began.
> Lk 15: 1 – 3, 11 – 32

The parable of the Prodigal Son. Stop now and tell the story from the memory in your heart....

This parable is like a favorite recipe; it has become part of our psyche. There are three main characters – the wandering son, the righteous son, and the father. I don't know about you but I have been the wandering son too often in my life, and I have been the righteous son far too often as well. We have sinned, and we have wanted to punish those who offend us.

What we have not been often enough is the loving, forgiving, father. Let's take a second look at the father. He runs out to welcome back his wandering son. He is anxious to forgive. When we offer forgiveness, we offer it begrudgingly. Our forgiveness is measured; his is lavish. He celebrates with hugs and kisses, rings and robes. The father is fully focused on the future. He wants to concentrate on what will be, not what has been. Our focus is too often stuck on the offense, not the reform. He has to forgive both sons; his forgiveness is unlimited. Our forgiveness is limited. It is more likely to be exhausted than replenished. The Father has a lot to teach us about forgiveness.

Where can our forgiveness be more lavish?

Monday of the Fourth Week of Lent

> Now there was a royal official whose son was in in Capernaum.
> When he heard that Jesus had arrived in Galilee from Judea,
> he went to him and asked him to come down and heal
> his son, who was near death.
> Jn 4: 43 – 54

The royal official was used to being in control. His position gave him power over others. There would be few who would challenge him. People in control, people in charge, get used to being looked up to.

But in today's gospel, the man of power is lost and near panic. His son is sick. We don't know how old the royal official was; we don't know how old his son was. In my imagination the son is young, ten or twelve at the most. The royal official was a young man. Maybe thirty. The story doesn't say, but I imagine he is married and his wife is still alive. She was probably at home with her son while her husband is trying to track down the miracle worker. He's the dreamer; she is the practical one. Do they have other children?

What we don't know about the background is not really that important, but if we fill in what we don't know with our faith imagination then the story can come alive, and it is easier for us to relate to the scriptures.

We frequently don't know what is going on in the lives of those around us. When, and if, we find out, then, and only then, can we better understand their behaviors.

Where can we be more open with the people around us?

Tuesday of the Fourth Week of Lent

>Now there is in Jerusalem at the Sheep Gate
>A pool called in Hebrew Bethesda, with five porticoes.
>In these lay a large number of ill, blind, lame, and crippled.
>One man was there who had been ill for thirty-eight years.
>When Jesus saw him lying there
>and knew that he had been ill for a long time, he said to him,
>"Do you want to get well?"
>Jn 5: 1 – 16

What a strange question to ask a man who has been sick for thirty-eight years. "Do you want to get well?" Doesn't every sick person want to get well? Of course they do. But we need to understand what illness meant in Jesus' time for us to understand his question. In Jesus' time, illness was a sign of sinfulness. People got sick or were blind, lame, or crippled because either they or someone in their family was a sinner. Remember last Sunday's gospel where the question is asked, "Rabbi, who sinned this man or his parents, that he was born blind?" Jesus is trying to get rid of this false notion, but it is slow going to say the least.

So if people believed that disabilities or illness were related to sinful behavior, then the question, "Do you want to get well?" begins to make sense. The question means are you ready to give up your sinful ways? Are you willing to embrace the commandments in your life once again?

All of us are sinful. Many of us struggle with our sinfulness. We confess our sins and make a promise to sin no more. We mean it when we say it; but then along comes temptation, and more often than not, we sin again. Jesus will continue to forgive us, but he will keep asking, "Do you really want to get better?"

What is the most persistent sin in our lives? Do we really want to change that behavior?

Wednesday of the Fourth Week of Lent

Jesus said to the Jews,
"My Father is at work until now,
and I am at work as well."
The reason why the Jews were even more determined to kill him was
that he not only was breaking the sabbath but,
worse still, was speaking of God as his own Father,
thereby making himself God's equal.
Jn 5: 17 – 30

There was a member of the parish who suffered from mental illness. On occasion he would hit me up for money just before Mass was about to begin. He was a nice man, and we got along very well. From time to time he would make an appointment to see me. We had some wonderful conversations. On one such occasion, he stumped me with this question, "Father I hear voices and they call me a schizophrenic; Jesus and many other holy people hear voices and we call them saints. What's the difference?" I forget what answer I gave, but it was clearly insufficient.

Fact of the matter is Jesus made some outrageous claims. He claimed that he could forgive sins. Only God can forgive sins. He claimed that God was his Father. Throughout history a number of people have claimed the same. Only difference was that Jesus was telling the truth. We have the benefit of looking back at Jesus through the lenses of history.

If you ever saw the movie, The Last Temptation of Christ, you might remember a scene at the beginning where Jesus wrestles with who he really is. As I remember that scene, it was almost like Jesus was having a breakdown. Many were offended by that scene, indeed by the whole movie, but I just remember it as portraying honestly the struggle Jesus had to go through to ultimately believe that he was the Messiah. It deepened my love for Jesus. We need to realize that there was more suffering than his death for him to be our Messiah.

How can we deepen our appreciation for the depth of Jesus' love for us?

Thursday of the Fourth Week of Lent

> I came in the name of my Father,
> but you did not accept me;
> yet if another comes in his own name,
> you will accept him.
> How can you believe, when you accept praise from one another
> and do not seek the praise that comes only from God?
> Jn 5: 31 – 37

What role to we let praise have in our lives? To do things to receive praise is to build our lives on quicksand. Praise is good, and we all enjoy praise, and we all need praise, but we should never act for praise. Praise should always be a byproduct.

We need to do things because they are the right thing to do. All of us have found ourselves in conflicted situations. Situations where we know the right thing to do, but we want to explore our options. We hope to find an easier way to do what is right. Sometimes doing right is easy; other times it is very difficult.

It is all about following our conscience. The Second Vatican Council in its decree *Gaudium et Spes* tells us, "In the depths of his conscience, man detects a law which he does not impose upon himself, but which holds him to obedience. Always summoning him to love good and avoid evil, the voice of conscience when necessary speaks to his heart: do this, shun that. For man has in his heart a law written by

God; to obey it is the very dignity of man, according to it he will be judged." (GS # 16)

God's voice speaking to our heart will always lead us to the right thing to do, and that is sufficient praise in itself.

How have we tried to mute the voice of God in our lives?

Friday of the Fourth Week of Lent

> "Yet I did not come on my own,
> But the one who sent me,
> whom you do not know, is true.
> I know him, because I am from him,
> and he sent me."
> So they tried to arrest him,
> But no one laid a hand upon him,
> Because his hour had not yet come.
> Jn 7: 1-2, 10, 25 – 30

Because Jesus took on flesh, and our human condition, he came to realize that it is all about timing. Context and timing determine everything. In music the silence between the notes is as important as the notes themselves. There is a right time to speak, and a right time to be silent. There is a time to act, and a time to hold back.

Jesus knew his hour was coming, but he also knew it had not quite arrived. Too bad the Pharisees and the people did not realize that the timing was wrong. That their efforts to get rid of him were for now doomed to failure.

Sometimes people spend their whole life waiting for the right time to say, "I love you." On other occasions, when constructive criticism is in order, people fall silent because it's not the right time. A friend has had a bit too much to drink, and we want to ask him for his keys, but he might not react well.

Sometimes it is better to act and find out it was the wrong time than to hold back and be too late. The scriptures tell us that Jesus was born "in the fullness of time." Even then it was not the right time for some folks. I guess there is no "fullness of time" for some things. Give it your best attention, pray, and then act or speak, and trust that God will make things right.

There is a big difference between prudence and fear. Where do we need to be more prudent and less fearful?

Saturday of the Fourth Week of Lent

> Nicodemus, one of their members,
> who had come to him earlier, said to them,
> "Does our law condemn a man before it first hears him
> and finds out what he is doing?"
> They answered and said to him,
> "You are not from Galilee also are you?
> Look and see that no prophet arises from Galilee."
> Then each went to his own house.
> Jn 7: 40 – 53

I love the last line of today's gospel passage, "Then each went to his own house." I don't think John was just commenting on where they physically went. I don't even think he was primarily thinking about their geographical location. John, the writer of the Gospel of signs, was alluding to where everyone went mentally.

There was a disagreement. The Pharisees had their view, the guards had their orders, but they had their view as well. Then along comes Nicodemus and says, "I think we need more information. We need to ask Jesus questions and listen to his answers."

When we are faced with disagreements, it is always a good thing to ask for more information and listen to what is being said with as open a mind as possible. (I was going to say with a completely open mind but that might just be impossible given our human condition.)

Some of the Pharisees had probably heard Jesus but many had not. The guards who went out to arrest him had heard him because they say, "Never before has anyone spoken like this man." The guards heard, and their minds were changed.

Nicodemus wants everyone to have the opportunity to hear Jesus, but the Pharisees were afraid, so they temporarily shut down the project.

"Then each went to his own house" today's scripture tells us. That means the Pharisees preserved their opinion without being exposed to more information. Never a good place to be.

Where do we cling to our own opinions rather than search for more information?

Fifth Sunday of Lent (A)

> Having said this, he called out loudly,
> "Lazarus, come out!"
> The dead man came out,
> bound hand and foot with linen strips,
> his face wrapped in a cloth.
> "Untie him," Jesus told them, "and let him go free."
> Jn 11: 1 – 45

Jesus was friendly with Martha, Mary, and Lazarus. He used to visit them and enjoy their hospitality. Martha was a worrier; Mary was more of a free spirit. We do not know much about Lazarus. At the beginning of today's gospel, we are told, "The sisters sent word to Jesus to inform him, 'Lord, the one you love is sick.'" Jesus loved Lazarus; they were friends.

The thing that always amazes me is that Lazarus had to die twice. He had said his good-byes. He had surrendered to God. He was at peace, and Jesus brought him back. I wonder if they ever talked about that. What a fascinating conversation that must have been!

'Untie him, and let him go free." That is what friends do. They set each other free.

We have things that hold us back. Too often we are discouraged by our failures; we are lost in selfishness. When that happens we can count on our friends to set us free, to get us back on track.

Where do we need Jesus to set us free?

Fifth Sunday of Lent (B)

> Philip went to tell Andrew;
> Philip and Andrew in turn came to inform Jesus.
> Jesus answered them:
> "The hour has come for the Son of Man to be glorified.
> I solemnly assure you,
> Unless the grain of wheat falls to the earth and dies,
> It remains just a grain of wheat.
> But if it dies, it produces much fruit."
> Jn 12: 20 – 33

Jesus goes on to teach us, "The man who loves his life loses it, while the man who hates his life in this world preserves it to life eternal." Indeed, one of life's most difficult truths to master.

The world in which we live is constantly reinforcing the message, "Take care of number one." No one has to teach us that we are number one. That is taken for granted. The problem is that repeating a message does not make it true. Taking care of number one only produces a lot of selfish, self-absorbed people.

Our lives are filled with people who put others first; these people have made our world a better place while they made us better people. Parents by definition put their children first. Family functions best when we follow the example set by our parents. Coaches, teammates, and friends are precisely the ones who make time for us so that we can grow and improve.

Here is a wonderful story to make this point. Two brothers are having breakfast; mom is making pancakes. There are two pancakes left on the plate. One is twice the size of the other. Mom knows there is going to be a fight for the bigger one, so she intervenes by saying, "If Jesus were sitting here what would he do?" The older brother says, "He would take the smaller one so his brother could have the bigger one." Mom beams with success until that same brother says to his younger brother, "You be Jesus."

Where do we need to be better at putting the needs of others ahead of our needs?

Fifth Sunday of Lent (C)

> The scribes and Pharisees led a woman forward
> who had been caught in adultery.
> They made her stand there in front of everyone.
> "Teacher," they said to him,
> "This woman has been caught in the act of adultery.
> In the law, Moses ordered such women to be stoned.
> What do you have to say about the case?"
> Jn 8: 1 – 11

Sometimes for fun, I like to rewrite scripture passages to give them an unexpected twist. The rewrite for today's gospel would go like this. When the scribes and Pharisees say, "What do you have to say about the case?" Jesus would pause, frown, and then say, "What did Moses say should happen to the man who must have been caught in adultery with her? And where by the way is he? Your law is obviously incomplete, so leave me alone."

But we have to deal with the real passage not the rewrite. Jesus calms down the crowd by pointing out that everyone has sinned. Each of them has done something that they regret. They could all be made to stand in front of everyone and be shamed. Once confronted with their own dark past, they drift away beginning with the elders.

Once Jesus is alone with the woman, once the group shame has ended, he addresses the woman, "Has no one condemned you?" Once the witnesses are gone, there is no accusation to be made. Notice that Jesus does not forgive her. He merely tells her to be on her way, and to avoid this sin. I wonder how the rest of her life was lived.

Where do we need to point the figure of accusation at ourselves?

Monday of the Fifth Week of Lent

> Then the scribes and the Pharisees brought a woman
> who had been caught in adultery and made her stand in the middle.
> They said to him, "Teacher, this woman was caught
> in the very act of committing adultery.

> Now in the law, Moses commanded us to stone such women.
> So what do you say?"
> Jn 8: 1 – 11

We grow too comfortable with some scripture passages. When this happens we don't notice when something is out of whack. If the woman was caught "in the very act of adultery" then where is the man? Did they just let him walk away? Did the Law of Moses not prescribe some punishment for a man who committed adultery?

The other thing that I want to know is what, if anything, did Jesus write in the dirt? Part of me wants Jesus to walk up to one of the accusers and write that person's sin in the dirt. Then proceed to the next accuser and do the same. That would explain why one by one they walked away. Maybe Jesus did not write anything. Maybe he was just doodling while he came up with an answer to their question.

Whatever he was doing it led to solution. When there was no one to point a finger at her, when all the accusers had left, Jesus could forgive her. Jesus always looks to our future; he never gets lost in the past. What is done is done. It cannot be changed. What can be changed is the future. Knowing that God in his infinite love has forgiven her she is free to learn from her sin and become a better person.

Where do we need to be more forgiving in our lives?

Tuesday of the Fifth Week of Lent

> So Jesus said to them,
> "When you lift up the Son of Man,
> then you will realize that I AM,
> and that I do nothing on my own,
> but say only what the Father taught me.
> The one who sent me is with me.
> He has not left me alone,
> because I always do what is pleasing to him."
> Because he spoke this way, many came to believe in him.
> Jn 8: 21 – 30

In order to fully understand today's gospel passage we will need a Dale Harvey, the rest of the story, moment. Jesus is making a double reference in today's gospel. First he is drawing on Moses' encounter with God in the burning bush. When Moses asks Yahweh for his name this is what is written, "God replied, 'I am who am.' Then he added, 'This is what you are to tell the Israelites: 'I Am sent me to you.'" When Jesus says, "When you lift up the Son of Man, then you will realize that I AM…" Jesus is proclaiming his divinity and his relationship with the Father. It might not be obvious to us, but to his audience it could not have been more clear. That is the first reference point.

The second reference point is just as strong. When the chosen people were on their Exodus journey, they got discouraged, and complained about God abandoning them. As a punishment, God sent seraph serpents among his people. Whoever was bitten would die. The chosen people then realized they had sinned against God and pleaded with Moses to help them. God told Moses to make a bronze serpent, and mount it on a pole, and hold it up for the people to see. Whoever looked at the serpent would get better. So when Jesus says "When you lift up the Son of Man" he is reminding his audience of Moses interceding for them, and by doing so is preparing them for his own crucifixion when he will be lifted up on the cross to save all people from their sin.

When we make the Stations of the Cross, at each station we say, "We adore you and praise you because by your holy cross you have redeemed the world." Today's gospel should help us to say that prayer with more understanding.

What would cause us to believe in Jesus more fully?

Wednesday of the Fifth Week of Lent

> Jesus said to them, "If God were your Father,
> you would love me, for I came from God and am here;
> I did not come on my own, but he sent me."
> Jn 8: 31 – 42

I fear that we so habitually call on "God, our father" that we forget the consequences of that relationship. If God is our father, then Jesus is our brother, and, finally, we are sisters and brothers with each other. We are a family, and that has consequences.

Family is family. Family is a special bond. Family members can have difficulties. Relationships can be weakened, and strained, but, if family is real, that relationship can never be broken. It is the parents who hold our families together.

I know there was nothing I could ever do that would destroy the love my father and mother had for me, and my brothers knew the same. Nothing! I could hurt them, and disappoint them, but their love would always be greater than my misdeeds.

Just so, God is our loving parent, the parish church is our spiritual home, and at the Eucharistic table we are always fed.

If we could just start thinking of our parish communities as our parish family, and really begin to see each other as sisters and brothers, our faith communities would be much stronger and more vibrant places of worship.

What needs to change so that our communities of faith can be transformed into our faith family?

Thursday of the Fifth Week of Lent

>Jesus said to the Jews: "Amen, Amen,
>I say to you, whoever keeps my word will never see death."
>So the Jews said to him, "Now we are sure you are possessed.
>Abraham died, as did the prophets, yet you say,
>'Whoever keeps my word will never see death.'
>Are you greater than our father, Abraham, who died?
>Or the prophets, who died?
>Who do you make yourself out to be?"
>Jn 8: 51 – 59

The fear of dying seems to be universal. We live in a death denying culture. We don't want to grow old. Ponce de Leon never found the fountain of youth, so we keep searching for it.

The aging process sort of sneaks up on us. Many years ago, my parents came to a Sunday Mass at the parish where I was stationed. My father dropped my mother off at the door and then parked the car. As he was walking into church, a young boy saw my father and in a loud said to his mother, "Mommy, Mommy there's Fr. Creedon when he gets old." The mother was horrified, but my parents and I had a good laugh over it.

No one gets out of here alive; we are going to die. We need to live each day to the fullest. We need to embrace the gift called life, and each and every day unwrap that gift and enjoy it fully.

Death is the door to eternal life. Let us live in such a way that when our time comes we will be able to walk through the door of death with all the dignity with which we lived our lives.

How do we want people to remember us once we have passed through the door of death?

Friday of the Fifth Week of Lent

> The Jews picked up rocks to stone Jesus.
> Jesus answered them, "I have shown you many good works from my
> Father
> for which of them are you trying to stone me?"
> The Jews answered him,
> "We are not stoning you for a good work but for blasphemy.
> You, a man, are making yourself God."
> Jn 10: 31 – 42

Jesus was not a mixture of good and bad. Jesus was all good. We are a mixture of good and bad. We are capable of wonderful, tender, kind, and loving actions. Unfortunately, we are also capable of not so wonderful acts of anger, jealousy, selfishness, and violence.

A second grade teacher was trying to teach her students about good and bad behaviors. She told her students that good people were colored green and bad people were colored yellow. She then went around the room and asked her students what color they were. Most said green; a few said yellow. But one boy got it right. He said he would be streaky. We are all streaky.

The challenge is to affirm our good behaviors and reform our bad behaviors. We should never forget that the struggle is more important than the results. As long as we struggle to embrace our good qualities, and reject our evil ones, we are on the right path.

A very good friend of mine, who is now with his God, and with whom I did homily preparation for more than 35 years, was fond of this quotation, "There is a little bit of good in the worst of us, and a little bit of bad in the best of us. So it ill behooves any of us to speak ill of the rest of us."

Where do I need to improve my ability to see the good in others?

Saturday of the Fifth Week of Lent

> Now the Passover of the Jews was near,
> and many went up from the country to Jerusalem
> before Passover to purify themselves.
> They looked for Jesus and said to one another
> as they were in the temple area, "What do you think?
> That he will not come to the feast?"
> Jn 11: 45 – 56

Jesus would not let fear prevent him from doing his Father's will. Yes, the Scribes and the Pharisees were out to get him. Yes, he withdrew to the desert with his disciples. But then not only did he come to the feast; he entered in triumph, which we will celebrate tomorrow.

Jesus overcame his fear; too often we surrender to ours. We learn to settle because we are afraid to change. What happens if we try to change and fail? Yes, my life could be better. Yes, I need to bring up a difficult topic with my spouse or my children, but not now. Now is not the right time. The thing about the "right time" is that it never comes. That is why we settle.

Perhaps that is why the Serenity Prayer is so popular. "God, grant me the serenity to accept the things I cannot change, courage to change the things I can, and the wisdom to know the difference." I think we could all use a dose of courage.

Where do we need the Holy Spirit's gift of courage to make necessary changes in our lives?

Palm Sunday – Procession (A, B, C)

> The crowds preceding him and those following
> kept crying out saying:
> "Hosanna to the Son of David;
> Blessed is he who comes in the name of the Lord;
> Hosanna in the highest."
> And when he entered Jerusalem
> the whole city was shaken and asked, "Who is this?"
> And the crowds replied,
> "This is Jesus the prophet, from Nazareth in Galilee."
> Mt 21: 1 – 11

There is no other liturgy during the liturgical year that has such a dramatic shift of tone than Palm Sunday. The procession gospel, part of which is quoted above, is all about praise and triumph. Jesus allows the spontaneous celebration. He even sends two disciples to get the beasts of burden. The disciples throw their cloaks over them. The people, hoping to keep down the dust from the road, throw down palm branches while crying out "Hosanna to the Son of David." Jesus knew their spirit was fickle. He knew that in just a few days the same people would be crying out, "Crucify Him! Crucify Him!"

The Prophet Jeremiah said it best:

> "More tortuous than all else is the human heart,
> beyond remedy; who can understand it?
> I, the Lord, alone probe the mind and test the heart,
> to reward everyone according to his ways,
> according to the merits of his deeds. (Jer 17: 9)

Our faith is fickle. We can only hope that God will remember when we praise him and choose not to focus on our deeds of darkness.

Palm Sunday – The Passion (A,B,C)

> When it was evening, he reclined at table with the Twelve.
> And while they were eating, he said,
> "Amen. I say to you one of you will betray me."
> Deeply distressed at this,
> they began to say to him one after another,
> "Surely, it is not I, Lord?
> Mt. 26: 14 – 54

We would clearly join our voices to the disciples' chorus, "Surely, it is not I, Lord?" And we would do so without hesitation. But maybe we should hesitate just a bit. Most of us (in truth all of us) have betrayed our Lord; we just don't like to think about it.

Someone once described church this way, "Church is not a gathering of saints, but rather a gathering of sinners who have not yet given up." We are all sinners. Do you remember the consternation Pope Francis caused when he answered a reporter's question, "Who is Jorge Mario Bergoglio?" by saying, "I am a sinner. This is the most accurate definition. It is not a figure of speech, a literary genre. I am a sinner."

He went on to put his quote into context, "I am a sinner, but I trust in the infinite mercy and patience of our Lord, Jesus Christ." We are sinners, but God has not given up on us yet and neither should we.

To sin is one thing; to be defined by our sins is quite another. When we define ourselves by our sins then even God's love cannot save us. We need to own our sinfulness, and then bring our sins to our God asking for his forgiveness. His love and mercy will never abandon us.

Where have we let our sins, faults, and failings define us? Can we trust God to set us free from that incomplete definition?

Monday of Holy Week

> They gave a dinner for him there, and Martha served,
> while Lazarus was one of those reclining at table with him.
> Mary took a liter of costly perfumed oil
> made from genuine aromatic nard
> and anointed the feet of Jesus and dried them with her hair;
> the house was filled with the fragrance of the oil.
> Jn 12: 1 – 11

How did Jesus ever let someone anoint his feet with oil and then dry his feet with her hair? Would you let someone do that? I know it is a cultural thing and a historic thing, but I just cannot imagine letting that happen. Would we let someone wash our hands, or face, or hair? Would we sit still for something like that to happen? I think not.

One of Jesus' attributes that frequently gets overlooked is his gentleness. His ability to let people express themselves in ways that work for them. In Luke's gospel we have the story of the blind man who cried out, "Jesus, Son of David, have pity on me." The disciples try to silence him, but he cries out, "Jesus, Son of David, have pity on me," even louder. Jesus does not try to silence him; Jesus calls him over. (Lk 18: 38 – 40) When one leper returns to thank Jesus for healing him, the scriptures tell us that he threw himself at the feet of Jesus and gave praise. (Lk 17: 11 – 19) He did not tell the man to get up, he merely asked him a question. There are many such examples in scripture.

It takes a special person to let people express themselves in their own way. Remember when at a papal ceremony for participants in the Special Olympics a young girl with Down syndrome got by security? When security moved in to bring the girl back to her mom, Francis invited her to sit with him, and she held his hand while he finished his talk. Special indeed.

Where do we need to relax and be more flexible in inviting people to be more natural with us?

Tuesday of Holy Week

> Simon Peter said to him, "Master, where are you going?"
> Jesus answered him, "Where I am going,
> you cannot follow now, though you will follow later."
> Peter said to him, "Master, why can I not follow you now?
> I will lay down my life for you."
> Jesus answered him, "Will you lay down your life for me?
> Amen, Amen, I say to you, the cock will not crow
> Before you deny me three times."
> Jn 13: 21 – 23, 36 – 38

Peter was indeed an impulsive man. He would frequently speak without thinking about what he was saying. Jesus loved him not in spite of this behavior, but because of it. Jesus always saw the more to come in people; he paid more attention to their future than their past, or even their present. Too often we put people in boxes, and once we have them in there we won't let them out.

I remember very early on in my priestly ministry being given a new assignment to a new parish. I knew the priest whose place I was taking so I gave him a call, and I asked him what my new pastor was like. He said, "I think it would be better if you discover that yourself." It was, I discovered, very good advice.

We are all familiar with the statement, "Your reputation proceeds you." Hopefully we have learned how damaging that statement can be. We use labels for people; labels diminish growth opportunities. Imagine how different our Church would be if we would stop using labels such as progressive, liberal, conservative, or orthodox, and instead just approached each other as fellow Christians and sisters and brothers in the Lord.

How can we let people grow and evolve in their lives?

Wednesday of Holy Week

> He said, "Go into the city to a certain man and tell him,
> The teacher says, 'My appointed time draws near;
> in your house I shall celebrate the Passover with my disciples.'"
> The disciples then did as Jesus had ordered
> and prepared the Passover.
> Mt 26: 14 – 25

Jesus, the teacher, reaches out to one of his students and asks a favor. Teacher is a special title; it is a title of honor. There are teachers and then there are **teachers!** The older we get the more respect we have for the **teachers** in our lives. We are who we are because of the teachers who have formed us. Our first and best teachers are our parents and grandparents. They hold dear the virtues we do not yet know how to embrace. Then come our classroom teachers and our professors who continue the work of our parents. Most of us have two or three, more if we are very fortunate, who stand out among all our teachers. Tim Russet had his Sister Lucille whom he credited with steering him to a career in journalism. Hopefully we all have a Sister Lucille somewhere in our lives. Teachers, the really good teachers, have a way of seeing the future. They focus on who we are becoming not on who we are. That's just what they do. Teachers bring out the best in their students and then they let them go.

All my teachers are now dead. Only a few of them did I thank sufficiently while they were still alive. Now all I can, and do, is pray for them, and trust that one of their unrecognized gifts was the ability to intuit the thankfulness of the students whose lives they fashioned.

Let us think of those special teachers in our lives. If we can thank them, we should. If not, then a prayer of thanksgiving for their presence in our lives will have to suffice.

The Triduum

Day One – Holy Thursday

> So when he had washed their feet
> and put his garments back on and reclined at table again,
> he said to them, "Do you realize what I have done for you?
> You call me 'teacher' and 'master' and rightly so, for indeed I am.
> If I, therefore, the master and the teacher, have washed your feet,
> you ought to wash one another's feet.
> I have given you a model to follow,
> so that as I have done for you, you should also do."
> Jn 13: 1 – 15

The older I get the more I love liturgy, and especially the Eucharist. I don't really know when that love began. I wish I could point to a day, or a celebration that sealed the deal, but I cannot. I began to be fascinated by liturgy when I was in the college seminary. It was before the Second Vatican Council, Mass was still in Latin, but my Latin was improving, and I was able to understand what was happening without following along in my missal. That was the beginning. I did not need the missal. I was able to look up and enter into the action of worship.

Then came the reforms of the Council, and we were invited to be participants and not just observers. That is when the liturgy came alive for me. Then came ordination and the full meaning of the priest as presider at liturgy. Sometime after that, the full power of today's gospel completed my love of liturgy and the Eucharist.

Eucharist must lead to service; service must return to Eucharist. Eucharist is stunted if it does not impel us to serve the needs of those around us. Eucharist that is just vertical, just between Jesus and us, is a pale reality when compared to Eucharist that is vertical and horizontal, Jesus, me, and all my sisters and brothers in the human family. Jesus did indeed give us a model to follow. Unfortunately, sometimes we think we know a better model, and forget to follow the teacher.

Eucharist means "thanksgiving." In the Eucharist we thank God for all his gifts and are reminded that our gifts ought to be shared. Where can we share them better?

Day Two – Good Friday

> After this, aware that everything was not finished,
> in order that the Scripture might be fulfilled,
> Jesus said, "I thirst."
> There was a vessel filled with common wine.
> So they put a sponge soaked in wine on a sprig of hyssop
> and put it up to his mouth.
> When Jesus had taken the wine, he said,
> "It is finished."
> And bowing his head, he handed over his spirit.
> Jn. 18: 1-19, 42

Good Friday would not have happened if Jesus had not taken Peter, James, and his brother, John, with him the night before while he prayed in the Garden of Gethsemane. It was there that Jesus asked this cup to pass him by. He asked, but he concluded, "Not my will but your will be done." So the cup did not pass him by, and he did give up his spirit.

Jesus did not want the cross; he did not want his death on the cross. But that was his father's will, and he embraced that will. How did Jesus do that?

The answer is simple – all those times when Jesus went off to pray; all the times he went to synagogue and listened to the scriptures. He listened to the stories of his ancestors in faith. He knew of Moses embracing the will of God. He knew of Abraham and Sarah embracing that same will. He knew of the prophets who gave their lives to do the will of God. It was not easy for Jesus, but he knew the example of those who went before him, and that paved the way for him.

Good Friday is when we are given the fullest example of doing God's will. Few, if any of us, will be asked to give our lives to fulfill God's will, but all of us are asked to make difficult decisions to let God's will be done.

As the story goes, when we appear before St. Peter he will ask, "Where are your scars?" If we have no scars, he will say, "Was there nothing worth fighting for?"

Jesus had his scars. May today inspire us to have ours!

What is worth fighting for in our lives? How goes the battle?

Day Three – Holy Saturday

> Then the angel said to the women in reply,
> "Do not be afraid!
> I know that you are seeking Jesus, the crucified.
> He is not here, for he has been raised just as he said.
> Come and see the place where he lay.
> Then go quickly and tell his disciples,
> 'He has been raised from the dead.
> And is going before you to Galilee;
> there you will see him.'
> Behold I have told you."
> Mt 28: 1 – 10

They came to see the tomb. They came to pay their respects to the dead. They came to say good-bye to the Master. But they came; they came at dawn. They wanted to begin their grieving.

Then their world was turned upside down. Instead of the darkness of death they were confronted with the light of life. The ground shook; they were afraid. As so often happens in scripture when someone encounters God, or an angel messenger of God, the first words they hear are, "Do not be afraid." They gathered themselves and did what the angel told them. They viewed the empty tomb, and then they left to give the disciples the message to go to Galilee where they will see the Risen Lord. On their way, they were the first to see the Risen One. As they continued on to where the disciples were, their faith grew stronger.

All four Gospels confirm that the first encounters of the empty tomb, and the Risen Jesus are for women, and not men. Jesus clearly counted women among his disciples. In life and now in death, he holds women in esteem.

In Revelation 21: 5, he who is seated on the throne said, "Behold, I make all things new." This is where it all began. Alleluia, He is risen! He is risen indeed!

No reflective question today. Just a pause to thank our God for the gift of faith and redemption.

Easter – Pentecost

Easter Sunday

> When Simon Peter arrived after him,
> he went into the tomb and saw the burial cloths there,
> and the cloth that had covered his head,
> not with the burial cloths but rolled up in a separate place.
> Then the other disciple also went in,
> the one who had arrived at the tomb first,
> and he saw and believed.
> For they did not yet understand the Scripture
> that he had to rise from the dead.
> Jn 20: 1 – 9

I think we need to rediscover the vacillation between belief and doubt that the early Church had with the resurrection of Jesus. Sometimes I think our acceptance of the resurrection is too facile, too easy, and too smooth. That is not how it was in the early church.

Because they wrestled with doubt, their faith grew stronger. Without struggle strength does not happen. Perhaps a story will help. A young boy was walking through the woods when he saw a caterpillar cocoon hanging on a branch. He carefully broke off the branch and brought it home. Up in his room, he turned on his study lamp and examined the cocoon. The walls were vibrating so he knew there was life within. He took out his pocketknife and carefully slit open the cocoon. A butterfly appeared, flapped its wings but could not fly, and it died. He asked his father why, and his father explained that because the butterfly did not struggle to use its wings to break out of its tomb, its wings never grew strong enough to fly. It was being deprived of the struggle that had doomed the caterpillar's full transformation.

Is it any wonder that one of the earliest symbols of the resurrection is the butterfly? Let the struggle begin.

Alleluia, Christ is risen! He is risen indeed!

Monday in the Octave of Easter

> While they were going, some of the guard went into the city
> and told the chief priests all that had happened.
> The chief priests assembled and with the elders and took counsel;
> then they gave a large sum of money to the soldiers,
> telling them. "You are to say, 'His disciples
> came by night and stole him while we were asleep.'
> And if this gets to the ears of the governor,
> we will satisfy him and keep you out of trouble."
> Mt 28: 8 – 15

In the end it all boils down to trust. Who are we going to trust? The soldiers take the word of the people who just told them to lie in the first place. Why would anyone trust a liar? No one should, but many people do.

For Mary and the other woman who went to the tomb it was easier. Jesus told them what to do. It did not make a lot of sense, but it was Jesus so they trusted him. The same was true for Peter and John who raced to the tomb. They trusted Jesus. Why not?

Jesus was the Master; Jesus was the teacher. They knew he was true to what he said. He called them, he taught them. He prayed with, and for them. He made the impossible seem possible. So when their world was spinning, and Jesus told them to go to Galilee, they went to Galilee.

When someone says to me, "Trust me," all I see are red flags. Fortunately, there are many people who never have to ask for trust because their lives give testimony to their trustworthiness.

Trust is a gift we give to others; it can never be earned. But it can be lost.

Let us be thankful this day for all the people we can trust.

Tuesday in the Octave of Easter

> When she had said this, she turned and saw Jesus there,
> but did not know it was Jesus.
> Jesus said to her, "Woman, why are you weeping?"
> She thought it was the gardener and said to him,
> "Sir, if you carried him away,
> tell me where you have laid him,
> and I will take him."
> Jesus said to her, "Mary!"
> She turned to him and said to him in Hebrew, "Raboni,"
> which means Teacher.
> Jn 26: 11 – 18

There is much that is unsaid in this gospel that is very important. Mary is not crying; she is weeping. She is grieving the loss of Jesus, her rabbi, her teacher, but, most importantly, her friend. She was at the tomb early to mourn her friend.

She had kept the Sabbath, and now she was at his tomb.

Jesus was not there. The tomb was empty. She suspects foul play but was only concerned that her friend be buried properly. She thinks the gardener is the culprit. She says if you have taken him just tell me where he is, and I will take care of him.

Then everything changes. Jesus calls her Mary. Now her tears no longer hinder her sight. Now she does not need her sight. She hears his voice and calls him Teacher.

Every believer needs to have a personal relationship with Jesus. No one can borrow a relationship or a friendship. We develop relationships by spending time with the other, by sharing insights and concerns with the other. For relationships to grow we have to commit to them.

What do we need to do if our relationship with Jesus is to grow stronger?

Wednesday in the Octave of Easter

> But they urged him, "Stay with us,
> for it is nearly evening and the day is almost over."
> So he went and stayed with them.
> And it happened that, while he was with them at table,
> he took bread, said the blessing, broke it, and gave it to them.
> With that their eyes were opened and they recognized him,
> But he vanished from their sight.
> Lk 24: 13 – 35

Great story. So much theology; so much humanity. Their day begins with an unlikely story told by some women who were at the tomb and did not find Jesus. Their day ends with an even more unlikely story. The story of the two disciples on the road to Emmaus gives credence to the admonition, "Stay tuned."

I forget where I first read it, but I did read it somewhere. The author said that he always thought of the two disciples as two men, but that is just an assumption. What if they were a couple; a husband and a wife. I'm not sure why, but for me that makes the whole story come alive.

Here is a couple who together followed Jesus. They thought he was the Messiah. That hope crumbled before their eyes on Calvary. They are going home in despair, and they meet a stranger. He explains the scriptures to them, but that does not work. They reach home, and I am sure they just wanted to be alone with each other. But they were not so overwhelmed by their sorrow that they could not see that the stranger needed a place to stay. They put his needs before their own needs. They extended hospitality and were richly rewarded. It was the verbs, the actions that made it happen. He took, blessed, broke, and shared, and their eyes were opened.

Where is our hospitality in need of an upgrade?

Thursday in the Octave of Easter

> "Thus it was written that the Christ would suffer
> and rise from the dead on the third day
> and that repentance, for the forgiveness of sins,
> would be preached in his name to all nations
> beginning from Jerusalem. You are witnesses of these things."
> Lk 24: 35 – 48

We are all witnesses of these things. Jesus has a message for the world, the world of his time and the world of our time. Jesus had to suffer, and he had to die. But he also had to rise and bring forgiveness to the world.

The need for forgiveness is always greater than its supply. The first word of Jesus to his followers when he appears to them after the Resurrection is, "Peace." We are by disposition an anxious and worrying people. We need reassurance; we hunger for peace.

What is this peace that Jesus is offering? Perhaps a story will help. A cruise liner was crossing the ocean and was caught up in a mighty storm. Everyone was confined to quarters. But after a day and a half of confinement one passenger decided to take a look around the ship. All of the corridors had taut ropes for people to hang on to and propel themselves along. The passenger was pulling himself along on one of these ropes when he came to a corner. Around the corner there was a young girl playing a game of Jacks. The passenger said to him, "Why are you playing Jacks? Aren't you afraid?" The young girl stopped bouncing his ball, looked up at the passenger and said, "I'm not afraid because my Daddy is the Captain." That is the peace that Jesus offers to us!

How can we trust more in the providential love that God has for us?

Friday in the Octave of Easter

> Simon Peter said to them, "I am going fishing."
> They said to him, "We also will come with you."

> So they went out and got into the boat,
> but that night they caught nothing.
> Jn 21: 1 – 14

"I'm going fishing" sounds harmless enough, but is it? Not really. Peter is not talking about fishing as a way to pass some time. Remember Peter used to be a fisherman, but he left everything and followed Jesus.

If Peter, James, and John and the others had left everything to follow Jesus, whose boat did they get into that night? You don't just take any boat you want. Someone must have hedged his bet. Someone must have left everything but not sold everything. Was that someone Peter? We don't know.

Now that Jesus was dead, even after encountering the risen Jesus on several occasions, Peter and some of the others were ready to throw in the towel and go back to their old way of life. There is a reason why we have the word "backslider" in the English language, and no one reading this has to go to a dictionary to look up its meaning. We know it all too well.

Perhaps another story will help. A man with a weight problem finally gets his act together. He has a plan, and he sticks to it. He gets down to his goal weight. His family, friends, and co-workers are all super happy for him, and shower him with praise.

Then one day he comes into the office with half an oversized Danish pastry in his hand. A co-worker says to him, "Bill, what happened?" Bill told him that he was coming to work and went past the bakery where he used to indulge. His car windows were down and he could smell all the good things in the bakery. He was tempted but he said to God, "If you want me to have one of those wonderful pastries let there be a parking spot right in front of the bakery." He then looked at his co-worker and said, "Don't you know that on my fifth time around the block, there was a parking spot right in front. God wanted me to have it."

Where have we given up on a dream and gone fishing?

Saturday in the Octave of Easter

> But later, as the Eleven were at table, he appeared to them
> And rebuked them for their unbelief and hardness of heart
> because they had not believed those
> who saw him after he had been raised.
> He said to them,
> "Go into the whole world
> and proclaim the Gospel to every creature."
> Mk 16: 9 – 15

Jesus sends those he has just rebuked for their unbelief and hardness of heart to proclaim the Good News to the world. No one is unworthy of Jesus' love, and forgiveness. He could have seen a bunch of sinners, he could have focused on their failures, but that is not what he did. Instead, he focused on their future and their potential. Jesus has a long history of helping people turn their lives around. He has done it before, and he can do it again with us if we will just let him.

When I was in the college seminary, my spiritual director was a wonderful and holy man. He lived very simply in his third floor rooms in the manor house. He had one piece of furniture that stood out. It was a beautiful grandfather clock. There was only one problem. The clock was broken. It always said it was ten minutes past two. One day, when I was not particularly interested in receiving any spiritual direction, I said to him, "Why don't you get that thing fixed or get rid of it?" He paused and said, "It is right twice a day. I have to know when to look at it." I was not interested in any spiritual direction that day, but I got it anyway. God knows when to look at us. He sees when we do things correctly, and he chooses not to see our mistakes. We need to do that with one another.

Pick out one person whose faults are too obvious to you. See if you can catch that person doing something right.

Second Sunday of Easter (A, B, C) Divine Mercy Sunday

> Jesus came, although the doors were locked,
> and stood in their midst and said, "Peace be with you."
> Then he said to Thomas, "Put your finger here and see my hands,
> and bring your hand and put it into my side,
> and do not be unbelieving, but believe."
> Thomas answered and said to him, "My Lord and my God."
> Jn 20: 19 – 31

Thomas wanted to be a believer, and he clearly stated his terms of belief. He missed Jesus' first appearance in the upper room. The ten told him, "We have seen the Lord." He did not question their belief; he did not try to talk them into not believing. For it to be real for him, he had to experience what they had experienced.

The disciples were afraid; they were locked in the upper room because they were afraid. Was it the same upper room where they had celebrated Passover with Jesus? We don't know. We just know it was a place where they felt safe, or as safe as they were going to feel. Notice that after Jesus appeared their fear did not evaporate. We know this because the gospel says, "Now a week later his disciples were again inside and Thomas was with them. Jesus came, although the doors were locked, and stood in their midst and said, "Peace be with you."

The doors were still locked. One appearance did not cement their faith. Their faith took over somewhere between Easter and Pentecost. Thomas said, "My Lord and my God" that day, but it took him time to live up to and into those words.

Where do we need to grow into the words of faith we too glibly proclaim?

Monday of the Second Week of Easter

> There was a Pharisee named Nicodemus, a ruler of the Jews.
> He came to Jesus at night and said to him,
> "Rabbi, we know that you are a teacher who has come from God
> for no one can do these signs that you are doing

> unless God is with him."
> Jesus answered and said to him, "Amen, amen,
> I say to you unless one is born from above
> he cannot see the Kingdom of God."
> Nicodemus said to him,
> "How can a man once grown old be born again?"
> Jn 3: 1 – 8

Indeed, how can someone be born again once they have grown old? As St. John Cardinal Henry Newman was fond of saying, "To live is to change, and to be perfect is to have changed often." To be born again is just another way of saying to be open to change.

Change is not something to which most people look forward. We are by and large change averse. We have our comfort zone and we cling to it. What we have may not be perfect but at least we have it. If we let go of what we have, what we get may be better but it may be worse. Why risk it?

Most of us are familiar with the old bromide, "How many graduates of Harvard does it take to change a light bulb?" The answer is one. The graduate of Harvard holds on to the light bulb and the world evolves around her. You may not have heard the follow up question. "How many Catholics does it take to change a light bulb?" The answer is "Change? What is that?"

There is an old saying, "ecclesia semper reformanda." "The church is always changing." For a few hundred years before the Second Vatican Council (1962 – 1965) the Catholic Church was rigid and unchanging. St. John XXIII changed all that. It has been more than fifty years since the close of the Council, and as Pope Francis is trying to implement the decrees of that council, there are still some Catholics who are clinging to what was rather than embracing what is, and what is to come.

Where in our faith are we clinging to old ways rather than being open to new ideas?

Tuesday of the Second Week of Easter

> Jesus said to Nicodemus:
> "You must be born from above.
> The wind blows where it wills, and you can hear the sound it makes
> but you do not know where it comes from or where it goes;
> so it is with everyone who is born of the Spirit."
> Nocodemus answered and said to him,
> "How can this happen?"
> Jn 3: 7 – 15

How can this be? That is the question that Mary asked at the Annunciation, and it is the question that Nicodemus asks here. Indeed, it is the question that every believer must ask.

When Jesus called twelve very ordinary people and made them apostles it is not recorded, but certainly they said, "How can this be?" When Jesus told Peter he was a rock and would be the leader of his church, Peter must have said, "How can this happen?" When Paul was knocked off his horse on his way to Damascus to round up those who believed in Jesus, and learned that he too was to be an Apostle, surely he said, "How can this be?"

Throughout the centuries, as Jesus calls ordinary people, very ordinary people, to the waters of Baptism and then gives them a mission and a ministry, each of us should say, "Certainly, he could have chosen better people." We see our ordinariness; Jesus does not. Jesus knows that, as St. Paul has so eloquently stated, "But we hold this treasure in earthen vessels, that the surpassing power may be of God, and not from us." (2 Cor 4: 7) Jesus works through us. He elevates our ordinariness to his service and his power is manifest in our weakness. That is how it can happen. God working through us!

Why are we not better messengers of Jesus' wisdom?

Wednesday of the Second Week of Easter

> God so loved the world that he gave his only-begotten Son,
> so that everyone who believes in him might not perish
> but might have eternal life.
> Jn 3: 16 – 21

How many times have you seen someone at March Madness or the Super Bowl or the World Series holding a sign that said, "John 3: 16"? If you are the curious type, or you really know your bible, you know that today's scripture quote is John 3: 16. This verse is frequently called the gospel in miniature because it pithily states what Jesus is all about – **God sent Jesus to save us.**

A number of years ago in a homily I gave my own rendition of the Gospel in miniature. Here is my version, "Jesus said to everyone he encountered, 'I don't care where you have been, or what you have done. I love you, I forgive you, and I set you free.'" If at the end of each day, we could just review our efforts, embrace where we have failed, and then remember that Jesus loves us, forgives us, and sets us free to be better followers tomorrow, we would be better people, and the world would be a better place. Remember it should never be about what we do for Jesus, but rather about what Jesus does through us.

Where do we need to let Jesus love us, forgive us, and set us free?

Thursday of the Second Week of Easter

> The Father loves the Son and has given everything over to him.
> Whoever believes in the Son has eternal life,
> but whoever disobeys the Son will not see life,
> but the wrath of God remains upon him.
> Jn 3: 31 – 36

In the Hebrew Scriptures there is plenty of talk about the wrath of God. In the New Testament the wrath of God seems to give way to the mercy of God. How did that happen?

The best explanation I ever heard was that God didn't change, rather it is our understanding of God that changed. When I was a boy my father was an imposing figure. In truth, he was an imposing figure throughout his life. As a boy, my father was the disciplinarian. He was the one who handed out the punishments. There was in truth very little wrath in my father, but when I was a boy, I won't say I was afraid of him, but I will say that he was a force with whom I had to recon.

As I grew older, I grew to love him more and more. I saw him in a different light. I respected him. I understood better his principals, his virtues, and his work ethic. When my brothers and I were young, and it was time to be punished for our misdeeds, my father used to say, "This is going to hurt me more than you." As an adult, I realized he was telling the truth.

When I was a boy, God was an exacting judge. As an adult, God has become for me a loving father. God did not change, my understanding of him changed.

Where has a lingering fear of God held us back from a more loving relationship with our Creator?

Friday of the Second Week of Easter

One of his disciples, Andrew, the brother of Simon Peter, said to him,
 "There is a boy here who has five barley loaves and two fish
 but what good are these for so many?"
 Jn 6: 1 – 15

The multiplication of the loaves is a great story. Jesus sees a vast crowd and is moved by compassion to feed them. He asks Philip, "Where can we buy enough food for them to eat?" This is where the little boy enters the story. He must have overheard Jesus ask the question. He wanted to do his part. It would never dawn on a child that a little bit of bread and a couple of fish could not be the answer. But they were his answer. There was a need, and he wanted to help. Like Jesus, he was moved with compassion. He wanted to do his part.

Word of the little boy's gesture must have spread through the crowd. When the others heard what he had done, they followed his example, and began to share what they had with others. When everyone began to put the needs of others before their own needs the problem was solved. Selflessness begets selflessness.

The miracle was not that loaves and fish were multiplied; the miracle was that human hearts were changed. People shared rather than hoarded what they had.

There is a clue at the end of today's gospel that suggests that bread was shared not multiplied. When everyone had eaten they gathered up the fragments and filled twelve baskets. No one carries around an empty basket. The baskets became empty when what they held was shared.

As good stewards, God asks us to share our time, talent, and treasure. How can we do so more generously?

Saturday of the Second Week of Easter

> As evening drew on, the disciples of Jesus came down to the lake.
> They embarked, intending to cross the lake toward Capernaum.
> By this time it was dark, and Jesus had still not joined them;
> moreover with a strong wind blowing,
> the sea was becoming rough.
> Finally, when they had rowed three or four miles,
> they sighted Jesus approaching the boat,
> walking on the water.
> They were frightened, but he told them,
> "It is I; do not be afraid."
> Jn 6: 16 – 21

They truly were fishermen. It was dark, they were rowing against the wind, but everything was fine. They only became afraid when they saw Jesus walking on the water. They, like all of us, were afraid of what they did not understand.

They knew the water, they knew how to fish, and they knew about storms. What they did not know was how someone could walk on water. That is what made them fearful. They had a new reality to deal with, and they were afraid.

When Jesus enters into our lives things are supposed to change. Unfortunately, we have let our encounters with Jesus be defanged. We need to rediscover the fear that is really a sense of awe. Annie Dillard, in her book, Teaching a Stone to Talk, speaks of what we need. "Why do people in church seem like cheerful, brainless tourists on a packaged tour of the Absolute?...Does anyone have the foggiest idea what sort of power we blithely invoke? Or, as I suspect, does no one believe a word of it? The churches are children playing on the floor with their chemistry sets, mixing up a batch of TNT to kill a Sunday morning. It is madness to wear ladies' straw hats and velvet hats to church; we should all be wearing crash helmets. Ushers should issue life preservers and signal flares; they should lash us to the pews. For the sleeping god may wake someday, and take offense, or a waking god may draw us to where we can never return."

Where can we find the courage to experience the fear and awe of God once again?

The Third Sunday of Easter (A)

> And it happened that while they were conversing and debating,
> Jesus himself drew near and walked with them,
> but their eyes were prevented from recognizing him.
> Lk 24: 13 – 35

We have already had the story of the two disciples on the road to Emmaus on the Wednesday of the Octave of Easter; now we have it again. The beauty of this story is there are so many different themes that it can always speak to us in myriad ways.

Today I want to focus on what prevents us from seeing, or hearing, or encountering Jesus. The first reality is obviously that we are too busy. We brag about how many hours we work; some even brag about how long it has been since they had a vacation. We should not brag about these things; we should repent of them. When Jesus walked this earth, he was busy, but he always found the time to pray. He would go off by himself and pray to his Father. We should never be so busy that we don't have time for ourselves or time for prayer and reflection. As Socrates so wisely stated, "The unexamined life is not worth living."

One other reality that prevents us from seeing, or hearing, or encountering Jesus is rigidity. We want to experience God on our terms. But Jesus is always the God of surprises. We need to be ever attentive to God's fingerprints on our lives. As one very holy person once said, "It isn't that God doesn't visit us; it is that too often we are not at home." We need to seek God in unexpected places.

Where are we making it difficult for God to break into our lives?

The Third Sunday of Easter (B)

> While they were still speaking of all this,
> he himself stood in their midst and said to them, "Peace to you."
> In their panic and fright they thought they were seeing a ghost.
> He said to them,
> "Why are you disturbed? Why do such ideas cross your mind?
> Look at my hands and my feet; it is really I.
> Touch me, and see that a ghost does not have flesh and bones as I do."
> Lk 24: 35 – 48

There are times when we just need to hear the words, "Peace be with you." The words are not a magical balm. The words do not bring immediate healing, but they begin the process of healing. In today's gospel, the disciples are a hurting group. Their leader, their teacher, indeed their friend, is dead. Killed in the most humiliating way possible. Now comes word that he is somehow alive. The two disciples who encountered Jesus in the breaking of the bread in Emmaus have returned to Jerusalem to tell their story. Now they had two stories, one told by Mary Magdalene, who had encountered him on the way to his tomb, and one by the two disciples from Emmaus.

They were still trying to accept that the Messiah was dead, and now they are hearing that he is not dead. Their minds were filled with both dread and hope. To which voice would they listen? Which voice would be true?

This is where Jesus enters and says, "Peace to you." They are reassured of Jesus' love; they are reminded that he told them he would never abandon them. They need more. So he gives them more. He tells them they have to get to know him in a new and, if it possible, a better way. He is not who he used to be, but he is not a ghost. He is not a figment of their imagination. He will be present to them for a little while in what we call his glorified body. They need to be open to a new way of experiencing him in their lives.

Are we open to experiencing Jesus in new ways?

Third Sunday of Easter (C)

> When they had eaten their meal, Jesus said to Simon, Peter,
> "Simon, son of John, do you love me more than these?"
> "Yes, Lord," Peter said to him, "you know that I love you."
> At which Jesus said,
> "Feed my lambs."
> A second time he put his question,
> "Simon, son of John, do you love me?"
> "Yes, Lord," Peter said, "you know that I love you."
> Jesus replied, "Tend my sheep."
> A third time Jesus asked him,
> "Simon, son of John, do you love me?"
> Peter was hurt because he had asked a third time,
> "Do you love me?" So he said to him,
> "Lord, you know everything. You know that I love you."
> Jesus told him, "Feed my sheep."
> Jn 21: 1 – 19

Jesus is having a bit of fun with his friend Peter. As far as we know Jesus never brought up either his prediction of Peter's denial or the actual denial. It was still a raw wound; it needed healing. It must have been eating away at Peter.

So now that the apostles were getting used to the idea that the teacher was not dead, that he was risen because he had eaten with them, it was time to take care of some unfinished business.

Peter denied Jesus three times, so Jesus makes him confess his love for him three times. Peter, true to all that we know about him, was true to himself. The irony of being asked three times, "Do you love me?" is missed by him. He gets angry about it. I wonder when the whole event came into focus for Peter. Was it when Jesus smiled at him? Or was it a day or two later?

One thing we know for sure, we know that Peter knew he was forgiven. He knew that Jesus had put his denials in the past, and that Peter needed to do the same. Peter did and became the leader of the early church feeding both the lambs and the sheep.

What sins, what denials of Jesus, do we need to put in the past?

Monday of the Third Week of Easter

> Do not work for food that perishes
> but for the food that endures for eternal life,
> which the Son of Man will give you.
> For on him the Father, God, has set his seal."
> Jn 6: 22 – 29

God has set his seal on Jesus, and on us. The problem is that it is easier to recognize the seal on Jesus than on ourselves. What does it mean for God to set a seal on us?

Think of the seal as God's trademark. No one could look on the Risen Lord and not see God. God, the Creator, sent Jesus, the Redeemer, to save us. Maybe we should think of God's seal as his signature. Great artists sign their masterpieces. They own what they have created. Whenever we enter into a contract, we own the agreement by signing our name. Which means we give our word, and our word is true.

Many of us grew up with the "Good Housekeeping Seal of Approval." The Better Business Bureau and Underwriters Laboratories exist to verify that businesses and products meet the highest standards.

In baptism we are anointed with oil, which sets God's seal on us. We need to remember this, and to live accordingly.

How can we more fully make visible in our lives that we belong to God?

Tuesday of the Third Week of Easter

> So they said to Jesus,
> "Sir, give us this bread always."
> Jesus said to them, "I am the bread of life;
> whoever comes to me will never hunger,
> and whoever believes in me will never thirst."
> Jn 6: 30 – 35

Hunger and thirst are primal appetites. They drive and motivate us. Without consciously thinking about these appetites, they nonetheless occupy quite a bit of our time.

We work so that we can afford to eat and drink. Without food and drink, we cannot survive. Since we live in a land of plenty, we take food and drink for granted.

We don't have many fast days left in our religion. I can remember when there were many more days of fast and abstinence. I never liked them. I liked the discipline that they inspired, but not the reality they brought. Tell me I have to abstain from meat, and all I can think about is a greasy cheeseburger, and I don't even like cheeseburgers. Tell me I have to fast, and I spend most of the day thinking about when I can eat again. It must have something to do with original sin.

What Jesus is saying in today's gospel is that when we put our trust in him, all will be well. When we believe in him, all our needs will be met. It is Jesus who puts our values in right order.

How do we let Jesus feed us?

Wednesday of the Third Week of Easter

> And this is the will of the one who sent me,
> That I should not lose anything of what he gave me,
> but that I should raise it on the last day.
> For this is the will of my Father,
> that everyone who sees the Son and believes in him
> may have eternal life,
> and I shall raise him on the last day.
> Jn 6: 35 – 40

The purpose of life determines what our end game should be! For believers the purpose of life is to make our lives a vibrant expression of our thanks for God's love.

St. Augustine expressed it this way, "Thou hast made us for thyself, O Lord, and our hearts are restless until they rest in thee."

Our lives lived in vibrant thanksgiving are all about finding our way back to God. This becomes a problem when we think we are doing all the work of finding God. The truth is that Jesus seeks us out. He journeys with us. He lifts us up when we are discouraged; he encourages us when downcast. The journey back to our God is easy once we realize we never travel alone. Our God is always with us; his people are on the pilgrimage with us.

Recently, I went to the Holy Land for the first time. On our pilgrimage we said a prayer every morning, "Lord, Jesus Christ, you were a pilgrim in this Holy Land. As we follow in your steps, we ask the grace to keep our eyes on you. Open our hearts that we may find you not only in ancient stones, but in your people and in each other. Let your words be a fire burning within us. Write your Gospel upon our hearts. Give us a spirit of prayer lest we return full of facts, but not of grace and love." If that is how we live then we will be reunited with our God at the end of this pilgrimage called life.

How can we become more aware that we are not traveling alone?

Thursday of the Third Week of Easter

> I am the living bread that came down from heaven
> so that one may eat it and not die.
> I am the living bread that came down from heaven;
> Whoever eats this bread will live forever;
> and the bread that I will give is my flesh for the life of the world.
> Jn 6: 44 – 51

Bread, often called the staff of life, is part of all lives. There are so many varieties of bread. Each culture seems to have its signature bread. There are even religious breads – the bread of the Passover and the bread of the Eucharist.

In today's reading Jesus is talking about the future bread of the Eucharist. The bread that was born when he celebrated his final Passover meal with his Apostles, family, and friends. (DaVinci left out a few people in his painting.) Jesus took the unleavened bread of the Passover, and gave it a new, and fuller meaning. No longer would the bread just represent the bread our ancestors rapidly made before the avenging angel struck down the first born of Egyptians, and God parted the Red Sea. Now the bread would be Jesus, always present to his disciples for ages to come in the form of bread.

We who even now share the Eucharist know its life-giving properties. When we eat the bread with faith, we may one day die physically, but spirituality we will never die. Spiritually we go from knowing Jesus partially in this life to knowing him fully in the Kingdom of his Love.

How can we deepen our love for the Eucharist?

Friday of the Third Week of Easter

> "Just as the living Father sent me
> and I have life because of the Father,
> so also the one who feeds on me will have life because of me.
> This is the bread that came down from heaven.

> Unlike your ancestors who ate and still died,
> whoever eats this bread will live forever."
> Jn 6: 52 – 59

Who is it that gives us life? Some people give life; others diminish it. Almost every one of us, when were growing up, had a friend or friends of whom our parents did not approve. It is part of growing up. Most often their concern was well deserved even if we could not see it at the time.

As we set out on our life journey, we had to learn for ourselves that some people are good for us while others are not. The sad reality is that frequently the people who are not good for us appear to be the most fun people to be with.

Jesus tells his disciples that he has life because of the Father. The Father is good to be with. Then Jesus takes it to the next level. Just as he has life from the Father, so he will pass on that life to those follow him. Jesus gives that life in many ways, but today he reminds us that he gives us his life in the Eucharist. It is life giving to gather with our sisters and brothers, share the stories of our faith history, offer bread and wine in thanksgiving, receive the bread of life and the cup of blessing, and be sent out to make the world a better place.

How can we make the Eucharist the center of our lives once again?

Saturday of the Third Week of Easter

> As a result of this,
> many of his disciples returned to their former way of life
> and no longer walked with him.
> Jesus said to the Twelve, "Do you also want to leave?"
> Simon Peter answered him, "Master, to whom shall we go?
> You have the words of eternal life.
> We have come to believe
> and are convinced that you are the Holy One of God."
> Jn 6: 60 – 69

No one, not even God, can force us to believe. Faith is a gift that God gives to everyone. Some open the gift and develop it while others never seem to get the gift of faith unpacked. Then there are those who lose the gift of faith, or just throw it away.

Faith has to be freely chosen. The church, or our parents, or the nuns, or the brothers, or priests may from time to time try to force faith on us, but that is a waste of time. All they can do is to force someone to go through the motions of faith. Sometimes we don't need an outside force to make us go through the motions of faith. Sometimes we do it to ourselves.

Every now and again, I will realize that what I thought was prayer was just an empty ritual. I realize that I was just saying words, but not really believing that the words had power. Other times, right in the middle of presiding at Mass, I realize that my mind has wandered. I am sure that you have been in the pews and experienced something very similar.

Some say they still have faith, but they just don't go to church anymore. Seems to me that if we have faith then going to church is part of living that faith.

What do you think?

Fourth Sunday of Easter (A)

But whoever enters through the gate is the shepherd of the sheep.
The gatekeeper opens it for him, and the sheep hear his voice,
as the shepherd calls his own sheep by name and leads them out.
When he has driven out all his own,
he walks ahead of them, and the sheep follow him.
because they recognize his voice.
Jn 10: 1 – 10

There are voices, and then there are those voices. Words are always important, but the speaker is more important than the words. The speaker gives life to the words. We know what a friendly voice is, and we know what a hostile one is as well.

Voices are as distinctive as fingerprints. I am always surprised when someone recognizes my voice when I am on the phone. This happened long before technology let people know who is calling.

There are conflicting voices calling for our attention all the time. There is the voice of Jesus, and there is the voice of the dominant culture. Often enough they call us in different directions. Jesus calls us to forgiveness; our culture invites us to seek revenge. Culture tells us to put ourselves first; Jesus invites us to put others first. Jesus asks us to lose our lives for his sake; culture encourages us to be selfish. Jesus asks us to take up our cross and follow him; culture suggests that we embrace the easiest solution.

What prevents us from hearing the voice of Jesus more clearly?

Fourth Sunday of Easter (B)

> Jesus said, "I am the good shepherd;
> the good shepherd lays down his life for the sheep.
> The hired hand, who is no shepherd nor owner of the sheep,
> catches sight of the wolf coming and runs away,
> leaving the sheep to be snatched and scattered by the wolf.
> That is because he works for pay;
> He has no concern for the sheep."
> Jn 10: 11 – 18

Unfortunately, in recent years we have experienced traumatic events such as the 9/11 attack on our country, or the many shootings in both schools and public gatherings. In the aftermath of these tragedies, we are reminded of the sacrifices made by our first responders. We are told, "They run toward danger as others are running away from it." That is what John is talking about in today's gospel. Jesus is a first responder. He embraced danger for us in order to save us.

There was a recent news story that reminded me of this gospel. A man in Florida was out walking his puppy when an alligator came out of a pond and snatched the puppy. Someone caught what happened next on a video that went viral. The owner of the puppy jumped into the pond, grabbed the alligator, and freed his puppy. The man's hands took a beating in the process, but the cigar he had in his mouth survived the ordeal. If you have never owned a puppy it would be hard to understand his behavior, but Jesus certainly knew what that man knew.

Jesus laid down his life for us. Just be still, and let that sink in.

Fourth Sunday of Easter (C)

> Jesus said:
> "My sheep hear my voice.
> I know them,
> and they follow me.
> I give them eternal life,
> and they shall never perish.
> Jn 10: 27 – 30

Oh, the sound of familiar voices. We can hear certain voices in a crowded and noisy room. I don't know much about sheep or shepherds, but I do know something about being attuned to certain sounds. The house where I live makes certain sounds. I have lived with those sounds, they are just part of where I live. Every now and again my house makes an unfamiliar sound. Only I can hear it; only I know that something is wrong.

I am always amazed at how well mothers can hear their children. Children are a lot like houses. They make certain sounds; the sounds are just part of who they are. Sometimes children make unfamiliar sounds; mothers always hear them first. Mothers know when their children are in trouble, and need assistance, and it makes no difference how old those children are. Even on the phone, our mothers can hear that something is wrong. They don't have to see our face; they just have to hear our voice.

That is the relationship that Jesus has with us. He calls us by name, by the name given to us at Baptism. He calls us each and every day. The problem is never about God not calling us. The problem is about our ability, or willingness, to hear God's voice. When we are preoccupied,

God's voice can get drowned out. When we are selfish, God's voice gets ignored. When we are angry, we shout over his voice. We need to attune our ears to hear better the gentle sound of God's loving call.

How have we muted the voice of God in our lives?

Monday of the Fourth Week of Easter

> I am the good shepherd,
> and I know mine and mine know me,
> just as the Father knows me and I know the Father;
> and I will lay down my life for the sheep.
> I have other sheep that do not belong to this fold.
> These also I must lead, and they will hear my voice,
> and there will be one flock, one shepherd.
> Jn 10: 11 – 18

Jesus did lay down his life for the sheep, but, thus far, that has not been enough to motivate Christians to overcome the scandalous barriers that separate us. Jesus envisioned one flock because he was the shepherd. We get lost because we focus on the sheep rather than the shepherd. When we focus on the sheep, we concentrate on our differences. This will never get the job done.

The following story is, I'm sure, apocryphal but, nevertheless, telling. A very well-known man died in his modest-sized town. The man's pastor, because of a previous commitment, was not able to be at the man's funeral, which was presided over by the assistant pastor. When the pastor returned to the rectory that evening he went right to the assistant pastor's room to hear all about the funeral. The assistant pastor told him that the church was full, and that the music was wonderful. He went on to say who had attended; it was a "who's who" of the town. He then told the pastor that the mayor, who was a Methodist, was at the funeral, and came up to receive communion. The pastor, filled with curiosity and anxiety blurted out, "What did you do?" The assistant pastor said, "I did what Jesus would have done." The pastor said, "Oh, no!"

How would Jesus solve the problem of division within our churches, and communities?

Tuesday of the Fourth Week of Easter

> So the Jews gathered around him and said to him,
> "How long are you going to keep us in suspense?
> If you are the Christ, tell us plainly."
> Jesus answered them, "I told you and you do not believe.
> The works I do in my Father's name testify to me.
> But you do not believe, because you are not among my sheep."
> Jn 10: 22 – 30

What a great question to ask God: "How long are you going to keep us in suspense?" The correct answer is, I think, a lifetime. God always keep us in suspense because his love, like all true love, makes him do unexpected things.

Jesus is the God of surprises, and his biggest surprise is that he loves us. Not only does he love us, but he loves us as we are.

Jesus could do so much better with his love. He could love others who are more deserving of his love. He does love others, but he loves us as well.

It all boils down to this: love is a gift not a reward. Jesus' love is not provisional like ours too often is.

Jesus doesn't love us if we say our prayers, or give to charity. He doesn't love us if we control our temper, or our language. We don't earn Jesus' love by our good deeds. We cannot earn God's love. God's love, expressed in Jesus, is a gift freely given. We need to stop trying to earn Jesus' love, and just learn to enjoy it. To accept Jesus' love as a gift is to surrender control of our lives to God. Easier said than done!

Where have I tried to earn Jesus' love?

Wednesday of the Fourth Week of Easter

I came into the world as light,
so that everyone who believes in me might not remain in darkness.
Jn 12: 44 – 50

Jesus is the light of the world. Yet too often we cling to the darkness. Jesus invites us to walk in the light of his love. Too often we stumble in our own darkness. Jesus is light, and he wants us to be light as well. As St. Matthew tells us in his gospel, "You are the light of the world. A city set on a mountain cannot be hidden. Nor do men light a lamp and put it under a bushel basket; it is set on a lampstand, where it gives light to all in the house. Just so, your light must shine before others, that they may see your good deeds and glorify your heavenly Father." (Mt 5: 14 – 16) So Jesus is light, and we are to live in that light, and, very importantly, we are to magnify that light by the way we live, and the choices we make. Our light is to help others glorify God. The light of our good deeds has the power to cast out the darkness that is so prevalent in our world. What is the darkness of our world? Greed, bigotry, injustice, violence, all forms of abuse, war, racism… That is just the beginning of the list.

Do we bring more light or darkness into the world?

Thursday of the Fourth Week of Easter

From now on I am telling you before it happens,
so that when it happens you may believe that I AM.
Amen, amen, I say to you, whoever receives the one I send
receives me, and whoever receives me receives the one who sent me.
Jn 13: 16 – 20

Talk about a powerful chain reaction! Jesus sends us to be his messengers. Whoever receives us, receives Jesus, and whoever receives Jesus receives God, the Father! Let that sink in a bit.
Talk about being lifted out of insignificance, and given a place of

honor. Only God can do that. Whenever we give witness to our faith in small or great ways, we bring God to people.

Think of the people who have been Jesus to us. Our parents who taught us what unconditional love was. The sisters and brothers who fashioned our first community of love. The spouses and lifelong friends who made enduring love come to life. The list seems endless – teachers, coaches, priests, religious sisters and brothers, neighbors, co-workers, and artists. Each in their own unique way became the face of Jesus, and led us to God.

Here is the humbling side of this reality. Each in her or his unique way, has been Jesus for others. We have led them to God. We can say with Mary in our Magnificat, "Our being proclaims the greatness of God."

Where have we failed in our challenge to proclaim the greatness of God?

Friday of the Fourth Week of Easter

> In my Father's house there are many dwelling places.
> If there were not,
> would I have told you that I am going to prepare a place for you?
> And if I go and prepare a place for you,
> I will come back again and take you to myself,
> so that where I am you also may be.
> Jn 14: 1 – 6

Because this gospel is frequently proclaimed at funerals too often we think it only applies to our transition from this life to the afterlife. I certainly does apply there, but it has present life meaning as well.

"In my Father's house there are many dwelling places." On a primal level, that means everyone is welcomed in God's house. Too often organized religion gets seduced into thinking that one size fits all. Too often it is the believers who have to contort so that we fit into the churches' categories. Some of that needs to happen, but where, and when, does the church have to meet the needs of her members?

All are welcomed is proclaimed, but too often not lived in our churches. You are welcomed if the Bible is your only guide. You are welcomed if you believe there are seven sacraments. You are welcomed only if you have no doubts, only if you tithe, only if you join a committee, only if you are married only once, are straight or willing to proclaim Jesus as your Lord and Savior.

Where do we need to work harder to remove the obstacles our churches create?

Saturday of the Fourth Week of Easter

> Amen, amen, I say to you,
> Whoever believes in me will do the works that I do,
> and will do greater ones than these,
> because I am going to the Father.
> Jn 14: 7 – 14

Clearly Jesus is using hyperbole here. He doesn't really believe that we will do greater works than the works he has done. Does he? I think maybe he does.

Think of this for a minute, who taught Einstein mathematics? Who taught Tom Brady to play quarterback? Who taught Shakespeare how to write?

How many people do you think Jesus met in his entire life? The story of the multiplication of the loaves says there were five thousand men, not counting women and children. Seems like a lot of people in one place for that time. I don't know what the number was, but it was relatively small. Jesus was the Messiah, he was the miracle worker, he gave sight to the blind, raised the dead, and set the captives free. Jesus knew he was starting a movement. He got the ball rolling, but he knew that his followers would bring his message farther than he could. He never painted a picture or wrote a hymn, but his followers certainly have.

It is not that we are better than Jesus, none of us are. Nevertheless, inspired by him, and motivated by the gift of the Spirit, we continue his work, and the results are greater than what he left us. We are blessed to be part of something bigger than ourselves.

What part do we play in the great experience that is Church?

Fifth Sunday of Easter (A)

> Philip said to him,
> "Master, show us the Father, and that will be enough for us."
> Jesus said to him,
> "Have I been with you for so long a time
> and you still don't know me, Philip?
> Whoever has seen me has seen the Father."
> Jn 14: 1 – 12

When it comes to our faith, what would be enough for us? Philip wanted to see the Father; Thomas wanted to touch the nail marks. What is it that we want?

One thing is certain, the answer is different for each of us, and most of us have more than one thing that we want see.

People frequently say to me, "God does not answer my prayers." They usually wince when I say, "God always answers our prayers. Sometimes the answer is not what we want to hear." Sometimes God, loving parent that he is, says, "No" to our prayers.

The perfect prayer, as far as I am concerned, is found in Mark's gospel. A father brings his son, who is possessed by mute spirit, to be healed. The father wants him cured; Jesus is exasperated. The father says to Jesus, "But if you can do anything, have compassion on us and help us." Jesus says, "'If you can!' Everything is possible to one who has faith." Then the boy's father cried out, "I do believe, help my unbelief." (Mk 9: 22 – 24) We need to ask God to help us know his will and embrace it more fully than we presently do.

How can we better embrace God's will for us?

Fifth Sunday of Easter (B)

> No more than a branch can bear fruit of itself apart from the vine,
> can you bear fruit apart from me.
> I am the vine, you are the branches.
> He who lives in me and I in him,
> will produce abundantly,
> for apart from me you can do nothing.
> Jn 15: 1 – 8

Together we can always do more than we can do alone. As the sport adage goes, "There is no I in team." Jesus gathered with his Apostles. Together they could do more than Jesus could do alone. That may sound like a heresy, but it is not. The twelve could go to more places, and connect with more people than Jesus could ever do alone.

This is why Christian community is so important. We gather together to celebrate Eucharist. We gather together to teach religious education classes. We gather together for social justice and for social activities.

Nothing is more destructive to community than individualism. Once the question changes from, "What is it I have to offer?" to "What's in it for me?" the community is in trouble. President Kennedy made that point in his inaugural address when he famously said, "Ask not what your country can do for you – ask what you can do for your country." Too often when it comes to our faith communities we get too hung up on what the community is supposed to do for us, and we forget that what really matters is what we can do for our faith community. Over the years, I have heard a lot of complaints about what the believing community was not doing, but seldom, if ever, have I heard people complain about what they were not doing for their faith community.

Where do we need to be sharing our gifts more generously?

Fifth Sunday of Easter (C)

> "My children, I am not to be with you much longer.
> I give you a new commandment:

> Love one another.
> Such as my love has been for you,
> so must your love be for each other.
> This is how all will know you for my disciples:
> your love for one another."
> Jn 13: 31 – 35

"I am not going to be with you much longer." These are words that none of us ever want to hear. In Jesus' case the words are even more poignant because he has already died, but he came back. The first time he left his disciples, his last words were, "Father, forgive them. They do not know what they are doing." Now he is preparing to leave his disciples for the second, and final time. In his first leaving, he was not in charge, so his message was forgiveness. This time he will be in charge, and this time his message will be to love one another.

If we love one another, if our love for each other reflects his love for us, then he will always be with us, and he will always be in charge. If we love those who would be our enemies, we make him present in our world. If we see dignity in those who have lost sight of their dignity, then our loving eyes make him present in our world. When we lovingly share from our plenty with those who are needed, we do as he would have done.

Where can we be more loving especially to those on the margins of life?

Monday of the Fifth Week of Easter

> "I have told you this while I am with you.
> The Advocate, the Holy Spirit
> whom the Father will send in my name,
> he will teach you everything
> and remind you of all that I told you.
> Jn 14: 21 – 26

We need to be lifetime learners with our faith. We have been taught well by our parents, our teachers, nuns, brothers, and priests. We have read about our faith, and we have prayerfully read the scriptures. But it takes a lifetime to learn what we need to know.

The Apostles in today's gospel have been taught by the greatest teacher and storyteller of all time, but the learning process is not complete. The Advocate, the Holy Spirit, will come and teach the Apostles everything, and remind them of what Jesus has already taught them.

The saddest of all people is the know-it-all. When a person thinks he has no need to learn anything new, life is not worth living. There is always something new to be learned.

Sometimes we have to be reminded of something we have forgotten. Not too long ago I was talking with a pastor of a parish where I had once given a parish mission. He told me, "I quote you all the time." I asked what quote, and he said, "You said that good is the enemy of better, and better is the enemy of best." I had completely forgotten ever saying it, but was glad to be reminded. It is a familiar quote of mine once again.

What truth of our faith needs to be refreshed in our lives?

Tuesday of the Fifth Week of Easter

> Jesus said to his disciples:
> "Peace I leave with you; my peace I give to you.
> Not as the world gives do I give it to you.
> Do not let your hearts be troubled or afraid."
> Jn 14: 27 – 31A

The peace that Jesus gives is pure gift. We don't earn it; we don't deserve it. Jesus gives his peace to us because he loves us, and he wants us to know that he will never abandon us.

One of the best feelings in the world is the contentment that comes from knowing someone we trust has our back. One of the worst feelings is that of being abandoned. Jesus has our back; he will never abandon us!

Jesus lived his life in peace. He discovered who he was, and he knew who the Father wanted him to be. Once he was rooted, he was at peace. Things did not always go as he planned. People did not always accept his teachings or his actions. Nevertheless, he was at peace.

He never took an opinion poll, and he certainly did not tell people what they wanted to hear. He told them the truth. He gave us beatitudes not commandments. And the beatitudes were, and still are, very countercultural. Who wants to be meek, who wants to hunger and thirst for justice, who wants to mourn? Disciples do that's who.

What has the peace of Christ allowed us to accomplish?

Wednesday of the Fifth Week of Easter

> I am the vine, you are the branches.
> Whoever remains in me and I in him will bear much fruit,
> because without me you can do nothing.
> Jn 15: 1 – 8

We need to remember at all times that we are part of something greater than ourselves. We are the church, the people of God, and the community of faith. Together we are more powerful than we can ever be alone.

Coaches, since time immemorial, have reminded their athletes that, "There is no 'I' in team." "We" has more power than "I". When the new English translation of the liturgy was introduced a number of years ago, there were many unfortunate, and, in my mind, unnecessary, changes. One was the beginning of the Creed. Because the Creed in Latin begins "credo" the translators went from having the congregation say, "we believe" back to "I believe." I know why they did it, but I wish they had left well enough alone. When we pray the Creed at Mass, we pray it as a community. A community is more than the sum total of the individuals present. A community has togetherness. A community is more powerful than the individuals present. When the community gathers, we are the branches and Christ is the vine. Together we bear the fruit of our faith.

Where do we need to focus more on community and less on ourselves?

Thursday of the Fifth Week of Easter

> Jesus said to his disciples:
> "As the Father has loved me,
> so I have loved you.
> Live on in my love.
> You will live in my love
> if you keep my commandments,
> even as I have kept my Father's commandments,
> and live in his love.
> All this I tell you
> that my joy may be yours
> and your joy may be complete."
> Jn 15: 9 – 11

What beautiful simplicity. Jesus gives his recipe for joy. It is a recipe that he has tested over and over again. A recipe he has perfected.

My grandmother used to make the best ginger cookies. After she died my aunt would make them. She would bring a big plate of them to every holiday celebration. She would wait patiently for our verdict. She desperately wanted to hear that she had perfected the recipe, but she never did. My aunt made her ginger cookies a few times a year. Grandma Barnes made them every week and the recipe was in her head. One of my prize possessions, which I got after my aunt died, is my grandmother's mixing bowl. I love it because she wore a spot on one side of the bowl with a wooden spoon. Every time I use that bowl, I am reminded what a labor of love is all about.

Jesus wore a hole in his life by being true to his Father's commandments. Jesus lived in his Father's love, and he passes that love on to us so that his joy might enrich us, and so that we might experience true joy. That is a labor of love!

Why are we not more joyful?

Friday of the Fifth Week of Easter

> I have called you friends,
> because I have told you everything I have heard from my Father.
> It was not you who chose me, but I who chose you
> and appointed you to go and bear fruit that will remain,
> so that whatever you ask the Father in my name he may give you.
> This I command you: love one another."
> Jn 15: 12 – 17

Friendship is mysterious. When I consider my friends, I enter into something mysterious. For example, when did an acquaintance become a friend? Why do some people remain acquaintances while others become friends? I don't know.

I just know that it happens.

I don't think I have ever chosen a friend. There have been people I wish were friends, but never were. The whole experience baffles me. Some people I thought were friends, but time has painfully taught me they were not.

So in today's gospel when Jesus calls his followers "friends" that is powerful. He chooses us, he chooses us as we are – warts, pimples and all. He chooses us, and sends us to continue his work of salvation. Like any true friend, he sees qualities and talents in us that we cannot see. He trusts us even though we have trouble trusting ourselves. When we were growing up our parents used to tell us, "Tell me who your friends are and I will tell you who you are." With Jesus as our friend we are indeed in good company.

How can we tell God, "Thank you for your friendship."?

Saturday of the Fifth Week of Easter

> Jesus said to his disciples:
> "If the world hates you, realize that it hated me first.
> If you belong to the world, the world would love its own;
> but because you do not belong to the world,

> and I have chosen you out of the world,
> the world hates you.
> Jn 15: 18 – 21

Unfortunately, too often it appears that we belong more to the world than to Jesus. We have let our Christian values and principles be pasteurized; we have become homogenized. We want to belong, to fit in, and to be accepted. Sometimes it costs us our identity.

There are some cultural values that are not compatible with our Christian values. Jesus taught us to put the needs of others before our own needs. Our culture balks at this. We are conditioned to take care of others after we take care of our own needs. We are taught to "take care of number one." We can't have it both ways. We resort to charity; the scriptures tell us to practice justice.

Then there is the whole forgiveness thing. Jesus tells us to forgive always. Our culture suggests that we keep count, and that there should be a limit to our forgiving. Once again we can't have it both ways.

Probably no part of scripture is more countercultural than the Beatitudes. Our culture is not inclined to think of being "poor in spirit" as a good thing. As for "mourning", we should avoid it if at all possible. Forget about being "meek." The list just won't end, "merciful", "clean of heart" or "hungering and thirsting for righteousness" just are not values that our culture is willing to embrace.

The world does not have to hate us, but the world should know that in some things we are different.

Where have we soft peddled our values in order to fit in?

Sixth Sunday of Easter (A)

> I will not leave you orphans; I will come to you.
> In a little while the world will no longer see me,
> but you will see me, because I live and you will live.
> On that day you will realize that I am in my Father
> and you are in me and I in you."
> Jn 14: 15 – 21

I remember when my father died. He died after my mother. When my mother died, I felt like I was adrift. I had been cut loose from my anchor. When my father died I remember thinking, "I'm an orphan now." It was not a good feeling.

Because of that feeling, today's gospel speaks to me in a profound way. Jesus will never abandon us. We will never be orphaned. Nothing can separate us from the love of God.

St. Paul speaks brilliantly of this love, "What will separate us from the love of Christ? Will anguish, or distress, or persecution, or famine, or nakedness, or peril, or the sword?... No, in all these things we conquer overwhelmingly through him who loved us. For I am convinced that neither death, nor life, nor angels, nor principalities, nor present things, nor future things, nor powers, nor height, nor depth, nor any other creature will be able to separate us from the love of God in Christ Jesus our Lord." (Rom 8: 35 – 39) Jesus assured his disciples, "I will be with you until the end of time."

Why do we sometimes think that Jesus has abandoned us?

Sixth Sunday of Easter (B)

> Jesus said to his disciples:
> "As the Father has loved me, so I have loved you.
> Live on in my love.
> You will live in my love if you keep my commandments,
> even as I have kept my Father's commandments,
> and live in his love.
> All this I tell you that my joy may be yours
> and your joy may be complete.
> This is my commandment
> love one another as I have loved you."
> Jn 15: 9 – 17

Why does Jesus command us to love one another? Short answer, because love is not the same thing as like. We like some people, and we dislike some people. Love is different. Love is a choice; love is a decision.

Let's go back to the beginning. God loves everyone unconditionally. God loves us when we listen to his word, and he loves us when we ignore his word. He loves us when we forgive our enemies, and he loves us even as our enemy list grows longer and longer. God's love is not conditional; it is not provisional. In today's gospel, Jesus invites us to love as his Father loves him, and as he loves his Father.

Why should we do this? Jesus gives us the answer when he says, "All this I tell you that my joy may be yours and your joy may be complete." Once again, just as love is different than like, so joy is different than happiness. Happiness comes and goes; it waxes and wanes. No one can be happy all the time; it is impossible. But anyone can be joyful all the time. When love guides all our life choices, the joy that Jesus knew will be ours, and not only will our joy be complete but our lives as well.

Nothing can fill us with joy like being embraced by the love of God.

Sixth Sunday of Easter (C)

> "This much have I told you while I was still with you;
> the Paraclete, the Holy Spirit,
> whom the Father will send in my name,
> will instruct you in everything,
> and remind you of all that I told you.
> 'Peace' is my farewell to you,
> my peace is my gift to you;
> I do not give it to you as the world gives peace.
> Do not be distressed or fearful."
> Jn 14: 23 – 29

Just how does the world give peace? Worldly peace is never given; it is always negotiated. Peace is too often described as the absence of violence. Peace in the world is what happens after violence. Peace means that one party has been victorious, or that both parties realize the benefits of ending the violence.

That is not the peace that Jesus gives to us. He does not negotiate peace; he gives it. That is why his peace is his gift to us. We cannot earn such a gift; we can only accept it. His peace is not the absence of violence; his peace is his being with us in a special way. We are never alone. Jesus is always with us. Because we are never alone, we never need to be fearful. We never need to be anxious.

Every time we gather to celebrate the Eucharist, we share the sign of peace. Before we can receive Jesus into our hearts and into our lives, we have to be at peace with one another. In the early church the sign of peace was called the kiss of peace. Unfortunately, that powerful image has been lost over the passage of time. Just remember Jesus' peace is not a handshake, it is a warm embrace that says, "Relax, together we can face whatever the world throws at us." And that is precisely what we need to say to each other before we receive communion.

Is there anyone in our lives from whom we have withheld the gift of peace?

Monday of the Sixth Week of Easter

> Jesus said to his disciples:
> "When the Advocate comes whom I will send you from the Father,
> the Spirit of truth who proceeds from the Father,
> he will testify to me.
> And you also testify,
> because you have been with me from the beginning."
> Jn 15: 26 – 16: 4A

The Advocate – one who defends a cause – will testify to Jesus. Jesus is keeping one eye on the future and one eye on the past. His disciples are going to need help in spreading the Good News. They have been indoctrinated in the truth of Jesus. They have traveled with him; they have learned at the feet of the Master. They have been present when he worked his miracles. You would think that would be enough, but Jesus knew better. It is one thing to be a learner and quite another to be a teacher.

Think of your first day of work on your career path. We had finished our education, at least the initial stage of our education, and we graduated. Now came the fun part, we had to do it. I remember the first time I presided at a liturgy. I was a nervous wreck. I remember my first homily; I remember clinging to the pulpit like it was a life raft. I knew I needed an advocate; I needed a mentor. I needed someone to walk with me until my confidence grew. Jesus knew what that was like so he promised his disciples a mentor until their confidence grew.

Where have we experienced the help of the Holy Spirit in our lives of faith?

Tuesday of the Sixth Week of Easter

> Jesus said to his disciples:
> "Now I am going to the one who sent me,
> and not one of you asks me, 'Where are you going?'
> But because I told you this, grief has filled your hearts."
> Jn 16: 5 – 11

Saying good-bye is hard to do. That is why we avoid saying it. Fr. Randy Chew, with whom I shared ministry when he was the Director of the Catholic Center at the University of Rhode Island and I was pastor of the university parish, Christ the King, used to give a wonderful homily at the last Mass of the academic year. He would exhort the graduates to make sure they said good-bye to one another. As I type this I can hear him saying, "Don't say, 'See you around.' You probably won't. Don't say, 'See you later.' You probably won't. Look your classmate in the eye and say, 'Good-bye' because your friendship, if it continues, will be different."

I'm not sure the graduates appreciated his homily as much as I did, but I'm sure that as time went on they grew to appreciate the wisdom he was sharing with them. When it is time to move on, move on. When we get married, we have to say good-bye to our family of origin so that we can begin our new family. When we move, we need to say good-bye to our neighbors. We will stay in touch for a while, maybe a long while, but it will be different.

Words of wisdom, "You have to close one door before you can open another."

We need to say good-bye to the security of our childish faith if we are to become mature disciples.

Wednesday of the Sixth Week of Easter

Jesus said to his disciples:
"I have much more to tell you but you cannot bear it now
but when he comes, the Spirit of Truth,
he will guide you to all truth."
Jn 16: 12 – 15

Sometimes we are just not ready to hear certain things. When we are mourners at a mother, brother, father, sister's wake we are not ready to hear, "She's in a better place," any more than in a few weeks' time will we be ready to hear, "You'll be OK." Then there are the times that a friend says, "Do you mind if I make a suggestion?" Seldom are we ready to hear what comes after that opening salvo.

What we are not ready or open to hear when we are fifteen we can grow to appreciate at twenty-five. This readiness to hear, understand, and appreciate things is painfully apparent when I think back to the reading lists that we were assigned in high school. Almost universally, I could not for the life of me understand why I was forced to read something so unimportant. A few years ago, I reread some of the books that were on my dreaded high school reading list. To my surprise when I did, I actually liked what I was reading. The problem was not with the reading list, but with me.

That's why Jesus had to send his Spirit to the disciples and to us. Even a teacher as great as Jesus had to wait until his students' minds were open. Come, O Holy Spirit come!

What new reality of our faith will the Holy Spirit teach us this year?

Thursday of the Sixth Week of Easter

Jesus said to his disciples:
"A little while and you will no longer see me,

> and again a little while later and you will see me."
> So some of his disciples said to one another,
> "What does this mean that he is saying to us,
> 'A little while and you will not see me,
> and again a little while and you will see me,'
> and 'Because I am going to the Father'?"
> Jn 16: 16 – 20

Sometimes we idealize the early church. We think that Mary and Joseph, the Apostles and disciples, even Jesus himself had a script. They knew what was going to happen. That they understood what was going to happen, and that they had no need for faith. Nothing could be further from the truth.

When the angel Gabriel appeared to Mary, her first response was, "How can this happen?" Joseph's first reaction to Mary's pregnancy was, "I will divorce her quietly." Peter told Jesus that he would not let him suffer. The Apostles deserted him in his hour of need. When the women first told the disciples of Jesus' resurrection they thought it was foolish. Does that sound like people who had the script to the story they were living?

Do not rob today's scripture of its questioning. The disciples were confused. They did not understand what Jesus was saying. They had to live with their doubts. They had to trust Jesus while they grew to discover what he was telling them. So do we!

Do we dare to live with our faith questions? Do we believe we will grow into the answers?

Ascension Thursday
(Some dioceses move the Ascension to Sunday)

> Then Jesus approached and said to them,
> "All power in heaven and earth has been given to me.
> Go, therefore, and make disciples of all nations,
> baptizing them in the name of the Father,
> and of the Son, and of the Holy Spirit.

> Teaching them to observe all I have commanded you.
> And behold, I am with you always, until the end of the age."
> Mt 28: 16 – 20

Jesus' growth plan was not terribly well thought out. The Apostles were not a bunch of Type A overachievers. They were very ordinary people. They were mainly fishermen, with a tax collector thrown in for good measure. Jesus was confident that the Holy Spirit would work through them, and he was correct.

Jesus wants them to make disciples of "all nations"; nevertheless, it took them a while and quite a bit of cajoling by Paul for them to bring the message to the Gentiles. It is hard to believe that eleven very ordinary individuals set in motion a church that now has 1.2 billion members.

Jesus chose very ordinary people at the beginning, and he chooses very ordinary people today to evangelize the world. Somehow it works. Each believer is unique and has a unique set of gifts. The challenge is to use our gifts to continue to spread the Good News. It will continue to work if we remember that God is working through us, and we don't become Pelagians. (Look it up if you have to.)

Where do we act as if we don't need God to work through us?

Friday of the Sixth Week of Easter

> But I will see you again, and your hearts will rejoice,
> and no one will take your joy away from you.
> On that day you will not question me about anything.
> Amen, amen, I say to you,
> whatever you ask the Father in my name he will give you.
> Jn 16: 20 -23

Whenever I fly somewhere I like to linger in the arrivals lounge. I like to watch the people who have gathered to greet someone. I stand off to the side and watch their faces. The longer they have to wait the more anxious they become. Then comes the moment of recognition. Anxiety melts from their faces, their eyes begin to sparkle, and smiles dominate their faces. They experience joy. If I am in a particularly reflective mood, and I don't have another flight to catch, I try to guess what kind of reunion I am witnessing. Friends reconnecting, families gathering for a celebration, boyfriend and girlfriend, a wedding or perhaps a class reunion, whatever it is joy is a byproduct.

That is what Jesus is talking about in today's gospel. He is going away and his disciples will be sad, but he will come back again. They will see him again, and when they do they will experience a joy that no one can take away from them.

Think back to a time when you thought God had abandoned you, and remember what it was like when you experienced his return.

Saturday of the Six Week of Easter

> The Father already loves you,
> because you have loved me
> and have believed that I came from God.
> I came into the world.
> Now I am leaving the world and going back to the Father.
> Jn 16: 23 – 28

Mission accomplished. Jesus came into the world to redeem the world. He came to heal the wound caused by the sin of Adam and Eve. He suffered, died, and he was buried. He was raised from the dead. Now what?

Mission accomplished. He will return to the Father. Sometimes people forget to move on to whatever is next in their lives. It is sad, very sad, when an athlete does not know it is time hang it up. The same is true with politicians. They don't seem to know when to give up the power or the prestige.

Jesus knew when to move on. He took his time; he prepared the disciples and Apostles. Now is the time to go. The disciples want to cling to him; the apostles want one last lesson. If he does not go, they will not grow. It is time for them to discover how to be his messengers to a waiting world.

How can we make Jesus' presence more vibrant in our world?

Seventh Sunday of Easter (A)

> Now this is eternal life,
> that they should know you, the only true God,
> and the one whom you sent, Jesus Christ.
> I glorified you on earth
> by accomplishing the work that you gave me to do.
> Jn 17: 1 – 11A

Jesus glorified God by accomplishing the work the Father had given him to do. We are called to do the same. The challenge is to believe that God has given each and every one of us a "work to accomplish." We know he gave Jesus a mission, and we know he fulfilled it totally because, "…he humbled himself, becoming obedient to death, even death on a cross." (Ph 2: 8)

Believing God gave Jesus a mission to accomplish is easy; believing that he has given us a mission as well is more difficult. I suspect most of us think that God has better things to do than to have a plan for each and every one of us. We might think that, but, as we know so well, God does not act according to our thoughts and plans. Recently sainted Cardinal John Henry Newman put it this way, "God has created me to do Him some definite service. He has committed some work to me which He has not committed to another. I have my mission. I may never know it in this life, but I shall be told it in the next. I am a link in a chain, a bond of connection between persons. He has not created me for naught. I shall do my good; I shall do His work." I have been haunted by that quote from the first time I read it. It should haunt us all. God has created us uniquely different, and has blessed us with unique talents so that we can complete our mission.

What is the portrait that God wants us to paint with the gifts he has given us?

Seventh Sunday of Easter (B)

> I do not ask that you take them out of the world
> but that you guard them from the evil one.
> They are not of the world,
> any more than I am of the world.
> Consecrate them by means of the truth –
> 'Your word is truth.'
> As you have sent me into the world,
> so I have sent them into the world;
> I consecrate myself for their sakes now,
> that they may be consecrated in the truth.
> Jn 17: 11 – 19

The trick is to be in the world, but not of the world. The world in which we Christians live is no longer a Judeo/Christian world. It is not an Islamic/Hindu world, or any other combination of religious identity we can think of. We are living in a post-religious world. That was an unthinkable reality not that long ago, but nonetheless that is where we are. More and more people consider themselves to be areligious or nonreligious.

How others identify themselves is not really our concern. What is important is how we identify ourselves. To be religious in a nonreligious world is our challenge. Jesus sends us into the world of our time just as he entered into the world of his time. Jesus had to speak the truth to his people; we have to speak the truth to our people.

The world in which we live tells us to put ourselves first; the gospel tells us to put others first. The world in which we live tells not to get mad, but to get even. The gospel tells us to forgive, and keep forgiving. The world tells us that the most important thing is to win. Our faith reminds us that our God wants us to fulfill our potential, not to be successful at all costs.

Like Jesus in his time, we have to show our age faith and love's transformative power. If it were easy, anyone could do it. There are many voices calling for our attention. The only voice that matters is the voice of God.

How can we hear his voice in the cacophony of our lives?

Seventh Sunday of Easter (C)

> Jesus looked up to heaven and said:
> "I do not pray for my disciples alone.
> I pray also for those who believe in me through their word,
> that all may be one as you, Father, are in me,
> and I in you;
> I pray that they may be [one] in us,
> that the world may believe that you sent me."
> Jn 17: 20 – 26

Passing on our faith is a process, a rich, diverse, and sometimes mysterious process. We are blessed to be part of that process. My college philosophy professor was fond of saying, "Religion is not taught, it is caught." Oh, there is a lot of teaching of religion going on, but the primary mover of religion is the lives we live, and the choices we make.

I am the believer I am today because of my parents. We were not what would be called an overly religious family. We did not say grace before meals very often. We would say the rosary as a family only when one of us brought home the statue of Mary from school on one of the days during May or October. We did however always say our evening prayers, we always went to Mass. We went to confession regularly, and my father insisted that we were dedicated to the First Friday devotions.

There is one childhood memory that reminds me that religion came first. Every Sunday on our way home from church we would stop at Dunkin' Donuts and buy a dozen doughnuts. We were not allowed to touch those doughnuts until we got home and had had a glass of water. Can you imagine four young boys actually honoring that custom? The smell of doughnuts would fill the car, but we had to wait. If our faith comes first, everything else will fit into place.

What childhood practice of faith has most fashioned the believer you are today?

Monday of the Seventh Week of Easter

> Jesus answered them, "Do you believe now?
> Behold, the hour is coming and has arrived
> when each of you will be scattered to his own home
> and you will leave me.
> I have told you this so that you might have peace in me.
> In the world you will have trouble
> but take courage, I have conquered the world."
> Jn 16: 29 – 33

The disciples of Jesus and we have something in common – we tend to overstate our faith. We profess our faith with our words, and with our public and private prayers. The only place we don't overstate our faith is with our deeds. Our deeds too often belie our faith.

Missouri is the "Show Me" state. Don't talk about it; show me. Don't tell me what you are going to do; do it. We know this spoof of the axiom, "When all is said and done, more is said than is ever done." Nothing describes our faith better than that.

I wonder if God ever gets tired of our hollow words? Will we ever exhaust God's patience? No, because God's patience, like his love, is endless.

In today's gospel, Jesus reminds the disciples that they need to remain united. He tells them, "when each of you will be scattered to his own home and you will leave me." This is Jesus' message, "If you try to grow without me, you will fail. If you think you don't need me, you are wrong." Jesus waits for us to be a believing community following him. That is the only way that leads to a faith that is strong in both words and deeds.

Where do we need to live up to our words of faith?

Tuesday of the Seventh Week of Easter

> I pray for them.
> I do not pray for the world but for the ones you have given me,

> because they are yours, and everything of mine is yours
> and everything of yours is mine,
> and I have been glorified in them.
> And now I will no longer be in the world,
> but they are in the world, while I am coming to you.
> Jn 17: 1 – 11A

Too often "the world" is seen as the enemy of religion, or a foil to our faith. The world and the flesh are presented as opponents. Our faith is worthless if it is not incarnated. Our faith has to take on flesh, and be lived in the world.

Jesus took on flesh, and in the words of scripture: "He pitched his tent among us." The world does not have to be in opposition to our faith. The world is our canvas; faith is our paint. We need to paint the world with our faith.

Jesus, in the end, had to leave this world. He, like us, was here for only a limited amount of time. Our time will come to leave this world. When that happens, God will say to us, "Show me what you have painted. Show me what you have created."

If we do the best we can during our lifetime, we need not fear that last day because God, our loving parent, will take what we have painted and, as our parents have done before him, give it a place of honor on his refrigerator.

Are we doing the best we can to make a masterpiece with our choices?

Wednesday of the Seventh Week of Easter

> Consecrate them in the truth.
> Your word is truth.
> As you sent me into the world,
> so I send them into the world.
> And I consecrate myself for them,
> so that they may be consecrated in truth.
> Jn 17: 11B – 19

We are all searching for the "Truth." We have all gotten lost, from time to time, on that journey. Most of what we call "truth" is "conditional truth." There comes a time when we have to move on from what we thought was true.

We live in a culture that tells us that things will make us happy. We are constantly told that we need to have the newest, biggest, best whatever, and, whatever that shiny bangle is, it will make us happy. Most of us have discovered that is not true, but not all of us. Some of us are still chasing around on the wheel of material things, grasping at empty promises.

We have to go through the phase of believing that people will make us happy. It is not our job to make someone happy. People can't make us happy any more than things can make us happy, but we have to learn that the hard way.

This is the truth: God loves us, and when we embrace that ultimate truth, our life we be lived in joyful response to that love. Our life will become our thank you note to God.

How have we thanked God for his love this day?

Thursday of the Seventh Week of Easter

> Lifting his eyes to heaven, Jesus prayed saying:
> "I pray not only for these,
> but also for those who will believe in me through their word,
> so that all may be one,
> as you, Father, are in me and I in you,
> that they also may be in us,
> that the world may believe that you sent me."
> Jn 17: 20 – 26

Too often we lose sight of the continuity of our faith. Faith is passed from one generation to the next. The process is dynamic not static. Nothing can be passed on without it being transformed. Too often we think of our faith as unchanging, hermetically sealed in tradition. We wrongly think our faith is to be preserved not lived. What a shame.

I have my faith heroes; you have yours. We would not be the believers we are today, without our parents. And our parents would not have been believers without their parents, and so it goes. But it is not just parents. Many people are responsible for our faith. Maybe it was the nun who taught us in the fifth grade. It could be that English professor in college who let her faith shine through what she was teaching. Perhaps it was a college chaplain or the priest who led youth ministry in our parish. We have our faith mentors, and we need to thank God for them.

But there is more than that. Not only do we have mentors; we are called to be mentors. There are people who need for us to live our faith fully so that it continues to be passed on through others. May we not break the continuity of faith!

Where is someone waiting for us to be the conduit of faith for them?

Friday of the Seventh Week of Easter

> He said to him a third time,
> "Simon, son of John, do you love me?"
> Peter was distressed that he had said to him a third time,
> "Do you love me?" and he said to him,
> "Lord, you know everything; you know that I love you."
> Jesus said to him, "Feed my sheep."
> Jn 21: 15 – 19

We don't often think of Jesus as being playful; nor do we think of Jesus has having a sense of humor. In today's gospel Jesus is having a little fun at Peter's expense.

Jesus keeps asking Simon Peter if he loves him. He asked him three times, "Simon, do you love me?" I wonder how long it took Simon Peter to figure out what was really happening. Jesus was reminding Peter that he had denied knowing him three times.

Jesus is being playful. Peter had denied him three times so, to even the score, he had to profess his love three times. I personally take great solace in the fact that Jesus has a playful side.

How many times has Jesus had to ask us, "Do you love me?" I know that in my life I have given Jesus cause to ask me that question more than three times. If we add one word to the question we end up with the worst question we can ever be asked. The new question is, "Do you still love me?" Fortunately, Jesus is too kind to add the word "still" to the question, but perhaps we should.

In what ways have we denied Jesus in our lives?

Saturday of the Seventh Week of Easter

> It is this disciple who testifies to these things
> and has written them, and we know that his testimony is true.
> There are also many other things that Jesus did,
> but if these were to be described individually,
> I do not think the whole world would contain the books
> that would be written.
> Jn 21: 20 – 25

Scripture exists to help us believe in God. The Bible exists to teach us about salvation history. Some people need more information; some need less. There are parts of scripture that don't speak to me; there are other parts that speak volumes. Rather than think of the Bible as one book, we should think of it as a library.

When it comes to the different books, we have different tastes. Some people like history, some like prose, and others like poetry. For some it is murder mysteries while for others it is romance novels. Fortunately, the Bible has all of these literary fronts covered.

We need to be open to the whole Bible of course, but realistically we need to accept that certain books of the Bible will speak to us more fully than other books. We need to revel in the books that speak to our soul; we need to respect the books that speak to our minds. In the end, all that matters is that the Bible helps us to believe that Jesus came to save us from sin and death. We need to listen with our ears, our hearts, and our souls so that the authors of the Bible can help us discover and profess our faith in Jesus as our Lord and savior. Remember Bible stands for **B**asic **I**nstructions **B**efore **L**eaving **E**arth.

Which book of the Bible speaks to us most clearly?

Pentecost Sunday (A, B, C)

The Sequence for Pentecost

Come, Holy Spirit, come!
And from your celestial home
Shed a ray of light divine!
Come, Father of the poor!
Come, source of all our store!
Come, within our bosoms shine.
You, of comforters the best;
You, the soul's most welcome guest;
Sweet refreshment here below;
In our labor, rest most sweet;
Grateful coolness in the heat;
Solace in the midst of woe.
O most blessed Light divine,
Shine within these hearts of yours.
And our inmost beings fill!
Where you are not, we have naught,
Nothing good in deed or thought,
Nothing free from taint of ill.
Heal our wounds, our strength renew;
On our dryness pour your dew;
Wash the stain of guilt away:
Bend the stubborn heart and will;
Melt the frozen, warm the chill;
Guide the steps that go astray.
On the faithful, who adore
And confess you, evermore

> In your sevenfold gift descend;
> Give them virtue's sure reward;
> Give them your salvation, Lord;
> Give them joys that never end. Amen.
> Alleluia!

> Jesus said to them again, "Peace be with you.
> As the Father has sent me, so I send you."
> And when he said this, he breathed on them and said to them,
> "Receive the Holy Spirit.
> Whose sins you forgive are forgiven them,
> and whose sins you retain are retained."
> Jn 20: 19 – 23

We had a longer version of this gospel on the Second Sunday of Easter. Back then we reflected on Thomas and his conditions for belief. Today's gospel stops just before the Thomas story.

"He breathed on them…" Does that have a familiar ring to it? It should because back in Genesis, the very first book of the Bible, in the second account of creation we are told that, "The Lord, God, formed man out of the clay of the ground and blew into his nostrils the breath of life, and so man became a living being." (Gn 2: 7)

Pentecost is the new creation; it is the beginning of the Church. Jesus breathes life into his disciples, just as the Father breathed life into Adam and Eve. There is no life without God's life-giving breath. On Pentecost, we are given both life and the ministry of continuing the healing forgiveness that Jesus began with the offering up of his life. From death comes life and a world transformed.

Where does the Spirit need to breathe new life into our hesitant faith?

Starting tomorrow the weekday readings revert back to Ordinary Time.

Holy Trinity – Corpus Christi

The Solemnity of the Most Holy Trinity (A)

For God did not send his Son into the world to condemn the world,
but that the world might be saved through him.
Whoever believes in him will not be condemned,
but whoever does not believe has already been condemned,
because he has not believed in the name of the only Son of God.
Jn 3: 16 – 18

God is mystery. Our journey of faith should not be an attempt to solve the mystery, but should be an invitation to get lost in it. The mystery should define us; we should not define the mystery.

The Trinity is important for many reasons not the least of which is that we are created in the image and likeness of God. The most important reality that the Trinity teaches us is that God exists in relationship. God the Creator is in union with God the Redeemer, and God the Sanctifier. God exists in relationship; we exist in relationships. It is as simple as that.

When we are born, we are born into a family, and family is a series of evolving, sometimes conflicting, but always affirming relationships. Secure in the multi-layered relationships that is family (mother, father, siblings, aunts, uncles, and cousins) we are empowered to welcome friends into our lives.

We do not learn alone, work alone, or celebrate alone. Schools are wonderful relationships, so ideally is work, and so are civic and faith celebrations. We know how relationships were missing or severely limited during when Covid 19 gripped our world. And we were diminished by our limited interactions. Relationships require work, and when they are bruised or broken they should be healed quickly so that we can be reflections of God's love.

Where do we need to work harder at building loving and healthy relationships?

The Solemnity of the Most Holy Trinity (B)

> Jesus came forward and addressed them in these words:
> "Full authority has been given to me
> both in heaven and on earth;
> go therefore, and make disciples of all the nations.
> Baptize them in the name
> 'of the Father
> and of the Son,
> and of the Holy Spirit.'
> Teach them to carry out everything I have commanded you.
> And know that I am with you always, until
> the end of the world!"
> Mt 28: 16 – 20

We began our lives of faith when we were baptized in the name of the Father, the Son, and the Holy Spirit! At the very beginning, we were welcomed into the most loving of all relationships. The Trinity is three persons, one nature. We say that like we understand it, but we do not, and we never will. The Trinity is the relationship of pure love. There are differences without distinction, and togetherness without unmistakable individuality.

What the Trinity really means is that we will never be alone on life's journey. In Baptism we become the daughters and sons of God. We become brothers and sisters in one family made up of millions and millions of people. Most we will never meet, but we have the same ministry – to make God more visible in our world. Like our God we are together, but uniquely different. All believers have a unique set of skills and talents, which they are called to fuse together. We are not in competition; we are in cooperation. We are a community of believers. This is what Jesus had in mind when he prayed to his Father that we might be one just as he and the Father are one. Alone we could never accomplish this, but with Jesus all things are possible.

How can we be more together as believers?

The Solemnity of the Most Holy Trinity (C)

> Jesus said to his disciples:
> "I have much more to tell you,
> but you cannot bear it now.
> When he comes, however,
> being the spirit of truth
> he will guide you to all truth.
> He will not speak on his own,
> But will speak only what he hears,
> and will announce to you the things to come.
> Jn 16: 12 – 15

I remember once hearing a very good preacher say, "Anyone can give a twenty minute sermon. Only a preacher can give a ten minute sermon." Not every sermon needs to contain all the truths of our faith. A sermon should make a point not to cast away all doubt.

Jesus, always the teacher, gave his disciples what they needed. He did not burden them with all that he had to say. He realized that if he did his part, and the Holy Spirit did her part then eventually we would hear what we needed to hear.

Today we celebrate the Trinity of our God. No one aspect of the triune God is sufficient; but together they are sufficient. We need to be created in order to be redeemed, and once redeemed we have to be inspired to live holy lives. Each aspect of God has its role to fulfill. The Trinity reminds us that God is a relationship of persons with the same nature. The divine relationship, like all relationships, must always be growing. Each event, each experience enlarges who we are so we are never finished. Just as God is both an active relationship and a mystery, so all of our relationships are mysterious. We need to enjoy our relationships not dissect them; just as we need to enjoy God not dissect him.

Where has God become more a puzzle to be solved than a relationship to be enjoyed?

Solemnity of the Body and Blood of Christ (A)

Jesus said to the Jewish crowds:
"I am the living bread that came down from heaven;
whoever eats this bread will live forever;
and the bread that I give
is my flesh for the life of the world."
Jn 6: 51 – 58

What does it mean to be "life giving?" Anything that lifts up, enhances, enriches, or gives meaning is "life giving." In today's reading Jesus says he is "the living bread." Bread is often called the staff of life. Every culture, it seems, has its own bread, similar but different.

When we gather to share a meal, we frequently say, "We will break bread together." The word "companion" comes from two Latin words "cum" and "panis" which means to share bread with someone.

So when Jesus wanted to find a way to be present to his followers after he had returned to the Father, he chose the setting of a meal. Not just any meal, but the Passover meal. The annual meal where the Jewish people tell the story of their being set free from slavery in Egypt. Set free by the blood of the lamb.

Jesus became our lamb; his blood, shed on the cross, sets us free from slavery to sin. His death gives life; he is life-giving bread. He has given us his body to eat and his blood to drink to nourish us for our journey home to him.

We need to deepen our appreciation of the Eucharist. What will be our first step?

Solemnity of the Body and Blood of Christ (B)

During the meal he took bread,
blessed and broke it, and gave it to them.

> "Take this," he said, "This is my body."
> He likewise took a cup, gave thanks and passed it to them
> and they all drank from it.
> He said to them,
> "This is my blood, the blood of the new covenant,
> to be poured out on behalf of many."
> Mk 14: 12 – 16, 22 – 26

Jesus gathered with his disciples, his apostles, his mother, and we assume other people as well. In spite of Michelangelo's magnificent fresco, we know there were more than thirteen people at the Last Supper. We also know from scripture that they reclined at table, they did not all sit on one side of the table as depicted in the fresco.

We do know that Jesus, true to his Jewish heritage, gathered to celebrate the Passover meal with a group of his fellow Jews. We know that Jesus took the unleavened bread and the final cup of blessing of the Passover, and gave them new meaning.

I doubt seriously that Jesus envisioned what we now call Holy Mass; I doubt that he envisioned something called daily Mass. Remember the Passover was celebrated once a year. What we do know was that Jesus wanted to make sure that his followers remembered him. That is why he said, "Do this to remember me." He chose the setting of a meal, a religious meal, and he took the basic elements of that meal, bread and wine, and he made them different so that we can be different. In the history of the Eucharist, something was lost when the focus was changed from why Jesus is present in the Eucharist to how he is present in the Eucharist. We need to refocus our attention on why Jesus chose to be present to us in the breaking of the bread and the sharing of the cup.

Where have we forgotten Jesus in our lives?

The Solemnity of the Body and Blood of Christ (C)

> Jesus spoke to the crowds of the reign of God,
> and he healed all who were in need of healing.
> As sunset approached the Twelve came to him and said to him,

> "Dismiss the crowd so that they can go into the villages
> and farms in the neighborhood and find
> themselves lodging and food,
> for this is certainly an out-of-the-way place."
> He answered them,
> "Why do you not give them something to eat yourselves?"
> Lk 9: 11 – 17

There are two parts to problem solving. First we have to recognize that there is a problem; secondly we have to come up with a solution. The Twelve saw the problem, but did not want to be part of the solution. They wanted to send the crowd away. They wanted to move the problem rather than solve it. Jesus would not let them off the hook that easily.

Our church seems to excel at letting someone else fix what is wrong. The parishioners think the pastor should solve whatever is wrong. The pastor thinks the bishop should solve whatever is wrong, and the bishops think the pope ought to fix whatever is wrong. Then the process is reversed. The pope offers a solution, but the bishops don't think it is the right solution. Nevertheless they pass it on to the pastors, who wonder just how the pope and bishops keep coming up with the wrong solution. With little or no enthusiasm, the pastors try to implement what they were told to do, and the parishioners wonder what's wrong with the pastor. As long as problems go up the chain of command, and solutions come down, nothing will be solved. When the people see a problem, they should solve it, same is true for pastors and bishops. After a while the Pope will be able to do what popes are supposed to do – pray for the Church.

What problems in the church do we need to help solve?

Ordinary Time

Monday of the First Week in Ordinary Time

> As he passed by the Sea of Galilee,
> he saw Simon and his brother Andrew
> casting their nets into the sea; they were fishermen.
> Jesus said to them,
> "Come after me and I will make you fishers of men."
> They left their nets and followed him.
> Mk 1: 14 – 20

Whenever I read the scriptural accounts of people being called to serve God, I feel inadequate. What we read is so neat, clear, and unambiguous. My own call was, and is, so much more conflicted and messy.

I think it would be helpful if we can un- romanticize the call of Simon and Andrew in today's gospel. For the longest time I thought that Jesus just happened to be walking by their boat and called them and they answered on the spot. That can't be what happened. Simon and Andrew had to have met Jesus a number of times. They had the chance to hear him preach. Perhaps they had heard a parable or two. They certainly had met Jesus, and were fascinated by him. They had thought about becoming one of his followers. Today's gospel is the final stage of their vocational assessment.

Jesus did not call Simon and Andrew just once. He called them over and over again. Jesus calls us over and over again. No matter how many times he calls us the quality of our response can always be better.

Where are we ignoring Jesus' call in our lives?

Tuesday of the First Week in Ordinary Time

> The unclean spirit convulsed him
> and with a loud cry came out of him.
> All were amazed and asked one another,
> "What is this?
> A new teaching with authority.
> He commands even the unclean spirits and they obey him."
> His fame spread everywhere throughout the whole region of Galilee.
> Mk 1: 21 – 28

It is too bad that belief in unclean spirits is a thing of the past. We don't cast out unclean spirits anymore. We diagnose them, given the symptoms, and treat them. In short, we make believe that we are in charge.

Seems to me there are more than enough unclean spirits that need to be driven out in our present day and age. God will help us get rid of unclean spirits. All we have to do is ask.

Racism is an unclean spirit, as is materialism. How about greed? Violence is certainly an unclean spirit. Discrimination with regard to age, gender, religion, or sexual orientation is an unclean spirit. What St. John Paul II called "the culture of death" is an unclean spirit.

The list could go on and on but that is not the point. The point is that if we call upon God to help us remove the unclean spirits that pollute our generation, he will respond as powerfully as he did in the early church. God has not lost his power; we have lost faith in his power.

Where do we need to invite God to help us clean up our act?

Wednesday of the First Week in Ordinary Time

> Rising very early before dawn,
> he left and went off to a deserted place, where he prayed.
> Simon and those who were with him pursued him
> and on finding him said,
> "Everyone is looking for you."
> He told them, "Let us go on to the nearby villages

> that I may preach there also.
> For this purpose I have come."
> Mk 1: 29 – 39

Jesus knew his purpose. He knew what was important. He had his priorities in order. His life was not organized around activity; his life was rooted in prayer. He would not let himself get so busy that he did not have time for prayer. We need to learn from him.

We are super busy. We like to brag about how busy we are. We think we need an eight-day week with days that last 30 rather than 24 hours. Who has time for relaxation? Maybe next year we will be able to take a vacation. Retired people are too busy. People tell me all the time, "I don't know how I ever found time to work."

Two Americans go to Africa to explore the jungle. They hire guides and the guides hire porters to carry all their stuff. On the first day they set out very early in the morning and push themselves until late in the day. The second day is more of the same as is the third day. At the beginning of the fourth day, the two Americans are eager to be off once again but the guides tell them they have to wait. "Why?" they wanted to know. The guides just pointed at the porters quietly resting. The guides then said, "The men aren't going to move until their spirits catch up with their bodies."

Where do we need to rest so that our souls can catch up with our bodies?

Thursday of the First Week in Ordinary Time

> "Why has the Lord permitted us
> to be defeated today by the Philistines?
> Let us fetch the ark of the Lord from Shiloh
> that it may go into battle among us
> and save us from the grasp of our enemies."
> 1 Sm 4: 1 – 11

What is the difference between superstition and faith? In today's first reading the Israelites are defeated in battle. They don't regroup;

they don't change their strategy. They get the ark of God and that will save them. But it didn't. Why? Because they confused superstition and faith.

When I was still in active ministry, I used to love it when someone would come into the sacristy after Mass and ask me to bless a statue of St. Joseph. I would smile and ask them why they had such devotion to my patron saint. More often than not the statue had nothing to do with St. Joseph and everything to do with the superstition that if you buried a statue of St. Joseph upside down somewhere on your property you would be able to sell your house. I would bless their statue, wish them good luck, and most of the time I resisted telling them that if they lowered the price it would probably work better than St. Joseph. I hope that God just smiles when we confuse superstition and faith.

Where have we let magical thinking corrupt our faith?

Friday of the First Week in Ordinary Time

> They came bringing to him a paralytic carried by four men.
> Unable to get near Jesus because of the crowd,
> they opened up the roof above him.
> After they had broken through they let down the mat
> on which the paralytic was lying.
> When Jesus saw their faith, he said to him,
> "Child, your sins are forgiven.
> Mk 2: 1 – 12

Today's gospel is great inspiration for those who are inclined to give up too easily. We need to realize that one of the reasons for their perseverance was that there were five people involved not just one. If the paralytic was going to get somewhere, he had to depend on others. I suppose that one person could have carried him on his back but it was better when the help was shared. One person most likely would not have climbed up on the roof. Alone the roof might not even have occurred to the paralytic and one helper. Because this was a group effort persistence was assured.

Too often we go it alone. Too often we do not ask for help. We love to help others; we dislike asking for help. Henri Nouwen, in one of his many wonderful books, said, "If you can only give and not receive, then the only honest thing to do is question why you give." Since I first read that quote many years ago it has haunted me. I hope now it will haunt you.

Where do we need to let others support us and help us to grow?

Saturday of the First Week in Ordinary Time

> Some scribes who were Pharisees saw Jesus was eating
> with sinners and tax collectors and said to his disciples,
> "Why does he eat with tax collectors and sinners?"
> Jesus heard this and said to them,
> "Those who are well do not need a physician, but the sick do.
> I did not come to call the righteous but sinners."
> Mk 2: 13 – 17

Obviously Mary and Joseph never told Jesus "You'll be known by the company you keep." Or if they did, then, fortunately for us, Jesus grew to ignore their advice.

Several years ago a reporter asked Pope Francis to describe himself. He paused for a few moments and said, "I am a sinner." What a delightful, refreshing answer from a pope. Of course the pope is a sinner. So are we. There would have been no need for a Messiah except for the sin of Adam and Eve, which is passed on to each generation as original sin. But Francis was speaking of more than generic, original sin. He was saying that he is not perfect, that he has weaknesses, that he sometimes fails to completely live the faith given to him at Baptism.

We are all sinners. Sometimes we sin in small ways; other times in more serious ways. We need to own our sins. Own not brag about them. We need forgiveness; we need salvation. There is a great saying that should give us comfort, "The Church is not a gathering of saints but of sinners who have not yet given up."

What darkness in our hearts needs to be exposed to the light of God's loving forgiveness?

Second Sunday in Ordinary Time (A)

> I did not know him, but the one who sent me
> to baptize with water told me,
> 'On whomever you see the Spirit come down and remain,
> he is the one who will baptize with the Holy Spirit.'
> Now I have seen and testified that he is the Son of God.
> Jn 1: 29 – 34

Just imagine – it took John the Baptist a while to figure out what he was supposed to do with his life. It took Jesus a while as well. Guess it should not come as a surprise that we need time to figure out who God is calling us to be. The most challenging thing we get to do as human beings is answer the question, "Who am I?" The second most challenging question we have to answer is, "Is this what God wants me to do with my life?"

A wise person once said, "Life is like a jigsaw puzzle. Once you have the border in place all the other parts fall into place. If God is the border of our lives then all the pieces will fall into place. Perhaps "Whose am I" is as important as "Who am I?" Once we realize and accept that we belong to God, then we will know the path we need to follow. St. John reminds us, "Beloved, now we are children of God, and it has not appeared as yet what we shall be." (1 Jn 3: 2)

What would change in our lives if we truly believed that we are the daughters and sons of the God of love?

Second Sunday in Ordinary Time (B)

> John was in Bethany across the Jordan with two of his disciples.
> As he watched Jesus walk by he said,
> "Look! There is the Lamb of God."
> The two disciples heard what he said, and followed Jesus.

> When Jesus turned around and noticed them following him,
> he asked them,
> "What are you looking for?"
> They said to him,
> "Rabbi where do you stay?"
> "Come and see," he answered them.
> So they went to see where he was lodged,
> and stayed with him that day.
> Jn 1: 35 – 42

Something is obviously lost in the translation of today's gospel. "Rabbi where do you stay?" just seems lame. I think a better translation would be, "What makes you tick?" They had followed John the Baptist, now at John's invitation, they were being asked to become followers of Jesus. They had seen Jesus; they had probably heard him teach. Perhaps they had seen him cure someone. But they needed more.

They wanted to know what his values were. They wanted to know what kept him grounded. They had become used to John the Baptist; they had grown to respect his odd ways. They probably enjoyed his wild and blunt ways. Jesus was different. He was gentler. He did not hang out in the desert: he moved from village to village. They knew that people went out to meet John; they could see that Jesus went to the people.

To answer their questions they had to spend time with Jesus. The only way relationships grow and deepen is by spending time with the other. Every day, Jesus says to us, "Come and see." Come and spend time with me. We do that in quiet prayer, prayerful reading of the scriptures, and by just sitting attentively waiting for him to speak to us.

How can we help our relationship with Jesus grow deeper?

Second Sunday in Ordinary Time (C)

> There was a wedding at Cana in Galilee,
> and the mother of Jesus was there.
> Jesus and his disciples had likewise been invited to the celebration.

> At a certain point the wine ran out,
> and Jesus' mother told him,
> "They have no more wine."
> Jesus replied,
> "Woman how does this concern of yours involve me?
> My hour has not yet come."
> His mother instructs those waiting on table,
> "Do whatever he tells you."
> Jn 2: 1 – 12

As for Jesus changing the water into wine, I will leave the explanation to the poets and the theologians. "The conscious water saw its Master and blushed" is attributed to both Richard Crashaw and Alexander Pope. Whoever said it captured the moment.

What I find more interesting is that the conversion of water into wine is the dialogue between Mary and Jesus. Mary perceives the embarrassment that is about to fall upon the host family. To run out of wine would be the talk of the town. Imagine being forever known as the "family that ran out of wine at their son's wedding." Mary's concern is not shared by Jesus. He basically says to his mother, "That's not my problem." It is Mary's response that always moves me. She ignores him. She turns to the waiters and says, "Do whatever he tells you."

Mary, like so many mothers both before and after her, will not tolerate her child's lack of concern. She knows she and Joseph have brought Jesus up better than he is behaving. There is no debate, there is no discussion; she does not remind Jesus of his manners. She sets the scene, so that Jesus has to act; he has to do the right thing. At Cana Mary was the mother, and Jesus was the son, and sometimes that is just the way the world works.

Can we think of a time when our mothers helped us do the right thing?

Monday of the Second Week in Ordinary Time

> Likewise, no one pours new wine into old wineskins.
> Otherwise, the wine will burst the skins,

> and both the wine and the skins are ruined.
> Rather, new wine is poured into fresh wineskins.
> Mk 2: 18 – 22

The challenge for any institution, especially the church, is how do I preserve what is good yet continue to grow and adapt? Tradition is good. It keeps us rooted; it is our anchor. Tradition is not a room without windows; it is not a bunker. There are old truths and new errors, but there are also new truths and old errors. We need to sift through our life experiences so we can keep what is of value and discard what is no longer useful. Our lives can easily be cluttered with junk.

Sometimes we do things that once had a purpose, but no longer do. During World War II the British were having trouble firing their artillery shells fast enough. They called in an efficiency expert to see what was wrong. The expert watched the soldiers fire their cannons. He noticed that before they would fire the cannons two soldiers would run to the back of the cannon and salute. The expert asked why; no one knew. It turns out that during World War I the cannons were moved into place by horses. The two soldiers would run back to grab the horse by the bridle so that the cannon would not move from its target. By the time World War II came around jeeps were used to move the cannons. The two soldiers still ran back but there were no horses so they saluted. It is difficult to break old habits even if they no longer serve a purpose.

Where in our faith do we cling too tightly to traditions that no longer serve a useful purpose?

Tuesday of the Second Week in Ordinary Time

> The Sabbath was made for man; not man for the Sabbath.
> That is why the Son of Man is lord even of the Sabbath.
> Mk 2:23 – 24

Laws and rules are a good and necessary fact of human existence. Nevertheless, we must remember that laws and rules exist for a reason.

They exist to help all people live together in peace and harmony. The contemporary church, under the guidance and leadership of Pope Francis, is trying to find its way out of the dead end street that is too rigidly rule bound. Remember rules and laws are good, but they must be reviewed and re-evaluated from time to time.

Allow me to share an example of rules that got lost. There was a time when in order to receive Holy Communion you had to fast from all solid food from midnight. This rule was intended to increase reverence for the Eucharist and for a time maybe it did just that. As time went on, all the rule achieved was to make it difficult for believers to receive communion. It took a while but eventually the church changed the rule and more and more people began receiving Holy Communion.

Obviously there are more serious examples of church rules that need to be changed, but I will leave that to your imagination.

What rules do you think the Church should examine so that she can become a more vibrant and fulfilling community of faith?

Wednesday of the Second Week in Ordinary Time

> Jesus entered the synagogue.
> There was a man there who had a withered hand.
> They watched him closely to see if he would cure on the Sabbath
> so they might accuse him.
> Mk 3: 1 – 6

Today's gospel has the same message as yesterday so we will have to find a different angle of approach. The Pharisees were committed to catching Jesus breaking the Law. Once their sights were so narrowly focused, they were unable to discover Jesus doing anything correct.

It is not too much of a stretch to point out that what was true in Jesus' time is true in our time as well. The best example of that – cable news and the twenty-four hour news cycle. One channel has nothing good to say about the Democrats while another has nothing good to say about Republicans. Some try to find a middle ground but few succeed.

During the papacy of both St. John Paul II and Benedict XVI, some of my brother priests would accuse me of being a cafeteria catholic. Now that Francis is the Pope, I ask them how they like the food in the cafeteria.

Imagine how much more healthy our Church would be if we would do away with the labels that divide and separate us and focus on what binds us as one.

Thursday of the Second Week in Ordinary Time

> Jesus withdrew toward the sea with his disciples.
> A large number of people followed him from Galilee and from Judea.
> …He told his disciples to have a boat ready for him
> because of the crowd,
> so they would not crush him.
> Mk 3: 7 – 12

We all know that public support is a fickle reality. Today's hero is tomorrow's villain. My local newspaper has a feature that runs from time to time. It is called, "Where Are They Now?" I usually find it a fascinating feature. Someone who used to be someone has fallen off the radar.

There is a great story that Tom Brokaw would tell on himself. When he was at the height of his career with NBC Nightly News, he was shopping in one of New York City's famous department stores. A man approached him and said, "Are you Tom Brokaw and did you used to be on KMTV in Omaha, Nebraska?" Tom smiled and said, "Yes," but was not expecting what the man said next. The man looked right at him and said, "What are you doing now?" Public support is fickle indeed.

Jesus was not about currying public support; he was about being the Messiah. That is why two thousand years later he is better known than ever. Which proves the validity of this quote, "What we do for ourselves dies with us. What we do for others and the world remains and is immortal."

How would Jesus' example lead us to do more for others?

Friday of the Second Week in Ordinary Time

Jesus went up the mountain and summoned those whom he wanted
and they came to him.
He appointed twelve, whom he also named Apostles,
that they might be with him
and he might send them forth to preach
and have authority to drive out demons.
Mk 3: 13 – 19

No one doubts the importance of the twelve Apostles but only the most serious Christians could name them. Part of the problem is that several of them went by different names but the real problem is that what they did is more important than who they were. The same thing can be said of the signers of the Declaration of Independence. What they did is more important than who they were.

In a very real way, we are believers today because Jesus chose and sent the Twelve to preach and cast out demons. The preaching of the Twelve impacted the people who heard them. Each listener heard something similar but not identical. Those people then became apostles who continued to spread the Good News.

The Word of God is heard through the prism of our uniqueness. The English word "person" comes from two Latin words, "per" (through) and "sonare" (to sound); person means to sound through. God sounds through you and me differently. Apostles beget apostles from one generation to the next. The end result is a full orchestra proclaiming the Good News of Jesus Christ.

Where have our lives muted rather than amplified the Word of God?

Saturday of the Second Week in Ordinary Time

Jesus returned to the house with his disciples
and again the crowd assembled,

> making it impossible for them to get any food whatsoever.
> When his family heard of this
> they came to take charge of him saying,
> "He is out of his mind."
> Mk 3: 20 – 21

Today's gospel is a classic case of someone working too hard, which leads to a family intervention. Mary is worried about her son. He is not taking proper care of himself. He is not eating right, and he is probably not getting enough sleep. Parents always worry about such things. My parents did, and so did yours. The thing that is different here is that the one doing the worrying is Mary, and the one who is working too hard is Jesus. We don't think of Mary and Jesus having to deal with such issues. But if Jesus took on our human condition, then he has to deal with all the issues we have to deal with.

Family interventions are never easy. They are always filled with tension. Family interventions are held because someone needs to be confronted. Family interventions are always a last resort. They are held only when all other remedies have been exhausted. How many times did Mary express her concerns to her son?

How many times did Jesus roll his eyes and tell his mother that he was fine, and she should not be worrying about him?

What we do know is that somehow the issue did get resolved, and that both sides had to give a little ground.

Is there an issue of conflict in our family that could be resolved if we gave a little ground?

Third Sunday in Ordinary Time (A)

> From that time on, Jesus began to preach and say,
> "Repent, for the kingdom of God is at hand."
> As he was walking by the Sea of Galilee,
> He saw two brothers,
> Simon who is called Peter, and his brother Andrew,
> casting a net into the sea; they were fishermen.

> He said to them,
> "Come after me, and I will make you fishers of men."
> Mt 4: 12 – 23

The gospel stories of Jesus calling his Apostles always leave me feeling inadequate.

I compare my response with the response of Peter and company and I conclude that they were much better at responding than I am. I suspect that I am not alone in this regard.

We fail to realize or forget to account for the fact that the accounts in scripture are very subjective. When we read of Jesus calling Peter and Andrew and then James and John we assume that they had never met Jesus. That Jesus was just walking by and called them and they dropped everything and followed him. But that cannot be what happened. We don't know how many times Jesus taught them, walked with them, or even shared a meal with them. The call of God is not instantaneous. It evolves over time. We have to pray about it; we have to imagine what it will demand. Eventually comes the day when we say, "Yes! I will follow you." Even after that day comes, even after we are all in, we still have to renew our response each and every day. Answering God's call takes a lifetime!

How can we respond more fully to God's call this day?

Third Sunday in Ordinary Time (B)

> As he made his way along the Sea of Galilee
> he observed Simon and his brother Andrew casting their nets
> into the sea; they were fishermen.
> Jesus said to them,
> "Come after me; I will make you fishers of men."
> They immediately abandoned their nets
> and became his followers.
> Proceeding a little farther along,
> he caught sight of James, Zebedee's son, and his brother John.
> They too were in their boat putting their nets in order.

> He summoned them on the spot.
> They abandoned their father Zebedee,
> who was in the boat with the hired men,
> and went off in his company.
> Mk 1: 14 – 20

People will frequently ask me, "Why did you become a priest?" I really wish I had a dynamic story to tell them. Paul got knocked off his horse; that was his call. Andrew and Peter, James and John, they were working when Jesus called them. I have nothing to compare with these vocation stories. Since I don't have a great call story, people have to settle with hearing me tell them why I remain a priest.

Perhaps it is time to demystify the scriptural accounts of Jesus calling his disciples.

The stories always sound like Jesus met them for the first time, called them by name, and they dropped everything and followed him. Do you think that's what happened? I don't. First of all he knew their names; he knew what they did for a living. He knew where to find them. They had been in his company before this day. This day is important because it was decision day. Were they going to continue on as fishermen or were they going to become disciples? There is a great verb that described their answer – "they abandoned their nets." They did not leave them; they did not walk away from them. No, they abandoned them. There is finality about abandonment. They were open to becoming different people. Before this day they were curious about Jesus; now they were committed to him. There is a big difference, but they were entering into a process that would profoundly change how they looked at the world.

What do we need to abandon if we are to become better believers?

Third Sunday in Ordinary Time (C)

> He came to Nazareth where he had been reared,
> and entering the synagogue on the Sabbath
> as he was in the habit of doing,

> he stood up to do the reading.
> When the book of the prophet Isaiah was handed to him,
> He unrolled the scroll and found the passage where it was written:
> "The Spirit of the Lord is upon me,
> therefore he has anointed me.
> He has sent me to bring glad tidings to the poor,
> to proclaim liberty to captives,
> recovery of sight to the blind
> and release to prisoners,
> to announce a year of favor from the Lord."
> Rolling up the scroll he gave it back to the assistant
> and sat down.
> All in the synagogue had their eyes fixed on him.
> Then he began by saying to them,
> "Today this Scripture passage is fulfilled in your hearing."
> Lk 1: 1 – 4, 4: 14 – 21

I'm not sure we can fully appreciate the impact today's gospel had on Jesus and the people of Nazareth. Jesus has begun his public ministry. He is a wandering preacher, and he is working signs and wonders. His neighbors were beginning to hear things about the carpenter's son. Jesus comes back home. Goes to the synagogue, as was his custom. Why was he asked to do the reading? What did the assistant have in mind? What was Jesus thinking when they handed him the scroll for Isaiah? There are no answers for these questions; we just know what Luke tells us.

What we do know is that Jesus knew his scriptures. He knew the words of Isaiah very well. He went right to the passage about the coming Messiah. He reads it clearly but then everything changes. He sits down and says the most outrageous and shocking thing that any Jewish man could ever think of saying. He says, "Today this Scripture passage is fulfilled in your hearing." It is one thing to know the prophecy, but it is something completely different to be the prophecy. Jesus tells his neighbors that he is the "anointed one of God." They knew him as neighbor, classmate, apprentice carpenter, and cousin. They did not know him as Messiah. The silence in that synagogue must have been deafening.

Where is the most surprising place we have ever encountered God?

Monday of the Third Week in Ordinary Time

> Amen, I say to you, all sins and all blasphemies that people utter
> will be forgiven them.
> But whoever blasphemes against the Holy Spirit
> will never have forgiveness, but is guilty of an everlasting sin.
> Mk 3: 22 – 30

What could possibly be an everlasting sin? What happened to the loving father of the prodigal son? Where is the father who runs out to greet his wayward son when he is still a long way off? How do we blaspheme against the Holy Spirit?

When we despair, or when we lose hope we sin against the Holy Spirit.

God never gives up on us. No matter how low we sink, no matter how depraved we let ourselves become, God never gives up on us. God always sees the goodness that in our dark times we hide so well.

The problem is that God has given us the gift of free will. We can choose to go against God and he will not fight us. He will keep loving us, but he will not force his love on us. We have the power to render the all-powerful God powerless.

That being said, in my heart of hearts, I think God will always find a way to overcome our obdurate behavior. There is no everlasting sin because the light of God's love is always greater than the darkness of our despair!

Where is God calling us to be our better selves again?

Tuesday of the Third Week in Ordinary Time

> But Jesus said in reply, "Who are my mother and my brothers?"
> And looking around at those seated in the circle he said,
> "Here are my mother and my brothers.

> for whoever does the will of God
> Is my brother, sister and mother."
> Mk 3: 31 – 35

Is Jesus downgrading his mother and siblings? No! He is upgrading his believers. We all know that when Mom comes calling we are supposed to drop everything and give her our full attention. The same is true for our siblings albeit at a slightly less intense level. Family comes first. We all know that; we all practice that.

I remember many years ago, I was transferred from one parish to another. The parish I was leaving was trying to get a date from me so they could schedule a little going away party. I was doing my best to frustrate their planning. Since they were getting nowhere with me they called my mother. My mother called me and said, "I brought you up better than that. You will be at your former parish this coming Friday night, you will be gracious, and you will say 'Thank You' when the night is over." Guess where I was on Friday night.

The respect and honor we give to our parents is the same respect that Jesus gives to us when we prayerfully discover his will and faithfully act on it.

Jesus welcomes us to his inner circle; our lives need to thank him for holding us so dear.

Wednesday of the Third Week in Ordinary Time

> Hear this! A sower went out to sow,
> and as he sowed, some seed fell on the path,
> and the birds came and ate it up.
> Other seed fell on rocky ground where it had little soil.
> Mk 4: 1 – 20

The seed of faith is sown generously at Baptism. On that day, God plants the gift of faith in our hearts. Unlike today's parable the results are not instantaneous. God is patient; he waits years for us to produce fruit. Sometimes we are the good soil, and we live lives of faithful service.

Sometimes we slip into bad habits, and become selfish and self-serving. When we get it right, Jesus is affirming; when we regress, he is forgiving.

A number of years ago there was a craze called WWJD? (What would Jesus do?) I was never a big fan of that movement. We really don't know what Jesus would do in certain situations. The real question is what should we do because we are followers of Jesus? We always know the answer to that question. We may not always live the answer but we always know what it is.

The more we do what is right, the more we bear good fruit; the more we bear good fruit, the more Jesus blesses our efforts.

How can we be more faithful in doing Jesus' will?

Thursday of the Third Week in Ordinary Time

> Jesus said to his disciples,
> "Is a lamp brought in to be placed under a bushel basket
> or under a bed, and not be placed on a lampstand?
> For there is nothing hidden except to be made visible;
> Nothing secret except to come to light."
> Mk 4: 21 – 25

Light always helps us to see better. If we can't find our glasses during the day, all we have to do is walk over to a window and use natural light to see better. When we eat in a fancy restaurant where soft lighting enriches the atmosphere all we have to do is take out our cell phone and switch on the flashlight function. Light helps us to see better.

When we were baptized, the priest gave our parents and godparents a candle while he said, "Receive the light of Christ." We need to understand what that ritual means. We don't have to generate light. Christ gives us his light, and all we have to do is pass it on. Perhaps the whole prayer that is said at Baptism will help us understand who we are and how we are to live: "Child of God, receive the light of Christ. Christ entrusts this light to us and we pass it on to you. May this light always be kept burning brightly, for you are now a child of that light.

May the flame of faith be ever alive in your heart and when the Lord comes may you go out to meet him with all the saints in the heavenly kingdom."

Pick a situation where we need to let God's light cast out the darkness of our sins.

Friday of the Third Week in Ordinary Time

> He said, "To what shall we compare the Kingdom of God.
> or what parable can we use for it?
> It is like a mustard seed that, when it is sown in the ground,
> is the smallest of all the seeds on the earth.
> But once it is sown, it springs up and becomes the largest of plants
> and puts forth large branches,
> So that the birds of the sky can dwell in its shade."
> Mk 4:26 – 34

I used to have a sign on my refrigerator that said, "God give me patience. NOW!" Things take time, but we don't like to wait. We want it, and we want it now! God on the other hand takes the long view. God is the patient farmer. He plows the field, he plants the seed, and he waits for the harvest. He waits for us to reach our harvest time, to fulfill our potential.

Faith, like all of life's blessings, is a work in progress. Hopefully we are better believers this year than we were last year. And if all goes according to God's plan, we will be better believers next year than we are this year.

We live in a world that is ruled by instant gratification. We crave speed. We hate to wait. Instant-on appliances, and instant results are all that matter. How can a culture that is fed on fast food ever embrace God's timeline? One thing most of us have learned is that fast food is seldom good food. God wants us to produce good food so we need to learn to take our time. There are no instant prayers, rituals, or sacraments. 2 Peter 3: 8 – 9 says it best, "But do not forget this one thing, dear friends: With the Lord a day is like a thousand years, and a thousand years are like a day. The Lord is not slow in keeping his promise, as some understand slowness. He is patient with you, not wanting anyone to perish, but everyone to come to repentance."

Where is God waiting for us to turn back to the path that leads to him?

Saturday of the Third Week in Ordinary Time

> The wind ceased and there was great calm.
> Then he asked them, "Why are you terrified?
> Do you not have faith?"
> They were filled with great awe and said to one another,
> "Who then is this whom even wind and sea obey?"
> Mk 4: 35 – 41

"I believe; help my unbelief!" (Mk 9: 24) That scripture should be the only prayer we ever pray. At some level, we all believe. Nevertheless, the level of our belief can always be better. We have experienced God's love, his providential care for us on the journey called life. We know that God is with us, but we doubt. Is he really with us; does he really care. When doubts enter, it can cause us to wonder if we really believe.

We frequently petition God to enter our lives and change things. At Mass we have the general intercessions. We ask God to send his Spirit on those who govern in both the church and in society that they might rule wisely. We pray for those who are unemployed, sick, suffering from addiction. We pray that hearts might be healed. The same is true in our private prayers. There is a thing called A.C.T.S., the four forms of prayer, Adoration, Confession, Thanksgiving, and Supplication. We need to be more balanced when it comes to our praying. Most of us spend too much prayer time asking for things, and nowhere near enough time adoring, confessing and giving thanks.

How can we create a more balanced prayer life?

Fourth Sunday in Ordinary Time (A)

> When Jesus saw the crowds,
> He went up on the mountainside.
> After he had sat down his disciples gathered around him,
> and he began to teach them:
> "How blessed are the poor in spirit;
> the reign of God is theirs."
> Mt 5: 1 – 12

I think that some gospel passages become so familiar that they lose the power to inspire us. The Beatitudes is one such passage.

Jesus, the teacher, is challenging his students. By calling Jesus' disciples "his students" we give this gospel a new meaning. The disciples did not have all the answers; they did not fully understand everything Jesus said. They had to ask clarifying questions; they had to be reminded of lessons that they had forgotten. They were like students everywhere.

All of us have had good teachers; all of us have a favorite teacher. That one teacher who made a connection. The teacher whose love for her specialty was both palpable and infectious. Favorite teachers stay with us throughout our lives. We quote them, and they continue to inspire us long after they are no longer a daily part of our lives. There is a strong bond between a student and a favorite teacher.

Sometimes I think it is hard to imagine having a relationship with Jesus. He is just too distant, too special, or too perfect. Frequently, I fear, we think we don't deserve to be in a relationship with Jesus. Try thinking of Jesus as our teacher, our favorite teacher, and think of ourselves as his students. See if that works.

What is the best lesson Jesus has taught us?

Fourth Sunday in Ordinary Time (B)

> There appeared in the synagogue a man
> with an unclean spirit that shrieked:

> "What do you want of us, Jesus of Nazareth?
> Have you come to destroy us?
> I know who you are – the Holy one of God!"
> Jesus rebuked him sharply:
> "Be quiet! Come out of the man!"
> At that the unclean spirit convulsed the man violently
> and with a loud shriek came out of him.
> All who looked on were amazed.
> Mk 1: 12 – 28

Why is it that unclean spirits shriek? Why don't they just whisper seductively? There seems to have been more evil, more unclean spirits in Jesus' time. I'm not sure that there are many people around now who believe in unclean spirits. Dr. Karl Menninger in his book *What Ever Happened to Sin?* offers an explanation. He describes a process where the police and judges took over for priests, ministers, and rabbis, and then the doctors and the pyschologists took over for the police and the judges. What used to be a sin became a crime, and what used to be a crime is now an illness that just needs to be treated. There is a lot of truth in what he says, but we will never be able to explain sin away. Sin is part of the human condition.

What we have lost is our taking responsibility for our sins. Many of us act like Flip Wilson and say, "The Devil made me do it." The devil cannot sin for us. Sin is personal; it is an abuse of the gift of freedom. With God's help we can drive out whatever it is that leads us to wander from the right path.

Where have we failed to take responsibility for our evil deeds?

Fourth Sunday in Ordinary Time (C)

> At these words the whole audience in the synagogue
> was filled with indignation.
> They rose up and expelled him from the town,
> leading him to the brow of the hill on which it was built

> and intending to hurl him over the edge.
> But he went straight through their midst and walked away.
> Lk 4: 21 – 30

So much for the local boy makes good fairytale ending. I guess there will be no hometown hero's welcome for Jesus. Jesus had invited his neighbors to open their minds to experience God in new and better ways, and they recoiled in fear. They rejected the one who was inviting them to change.

Many years ago, I took a course called Small Group Dynamics. It was a strange course, and, truth be told, I remember very little about it. One thing that I do remember is this, "If you crawl out on a limb, someone will start sawing." I remember it because I have experienced its truth over and over again. If someone invites people to change, people will turn on him. How many times in life have you heard, "That's not how we do things here!" As a parish priest one of the most traumatic things you can ever attempt is changing the Mass schedule for weekends.

Jesus faced resistance to his ministry right up until his death on the cross. The scribes, the Pharisees, the elders, all the religious and political leaders rejected him, and just as at Nazareth, he walked through their midst. He kept climbing out on that limb, and they kept sawing away.

As my father was fond of telling my brothers and me, "You may be on the wrong side of a lot of 10 to 1 votes, but that doesn't automatically mean you are wrong!"

Where have we let others deter us from doing what is right?

Monday of the Fourth Week in Ordinary Time

> As they approached Jesus, they caught sight of the man
> who had been possessed by Legion,
> sitting there clothed and in his right mind.
> And they were seized with fear.
> Those who witnessed the incident explained to them

> what had happened
> to the possessed man and the swine.
> They began to beg him to leave their district.
> Mk 5: 1 – 20

When Jesus enters our life, things are supposed to happen. Unfortunately, we have allowed history and culture to defang our Christian faith. As one Catholic observer once said, "We used to be Catholics trying to be American, now we are Americans trying to be Catholic." When our faith takes a back seat to our culture our faith is always impoverished.

Our faith teaches the dignity of all people; our culture insists that some are more important than others. We cannot have it both ways. Our faith tells us that our environment is a gift from God; capitalism says it is permissible to use the earth as a disposable commodity. Our faith teaches that all human life is precious; our culture says that abortion is legal. Our faith is dedicated to the common good; our culture is dedicated to profits that create inequality.

We need to rediscover the power of Jesus to cast out the demons we have unwittingly embraced. When we invite Jesus to make us whole once again, there will be disruption and confusion.

Will we cling to our comfortable ways and values or return to our gospel values?

Tuesday of the Fourth Week in Ordinary Time

> One of the synagogue officials, named Jairus, came forward.
> Seeing him he fell at his feet and pleaded earnestly with him saying.
> "My daughter is at the point of death.
> Please, come lay your hand on her
> that she may get well and live."
> Mk 5: 21 – 43

Before Jesus can make his way to the sick girl, he is told that she had died. Nevertheless, Jesus keeps on going, insisting that the girl is sleeping not dead. When he gets to her home, he takes the mother and father and Peter, James, and John into the girl's room. Jesus says, "Little girl, I say to you, arise!" and she does.

Jesus saw life where others saw death. Jesus saw goodness where others saw sinfulness. Jesus looked on Peter and saw a leader not a denier. Jesus did not see the woman at the well with five husbands as a blight on society, but a disciple. The town folk thought Nicodemus was a tax collector and a cheat; Jesus saw a follower. Jesus always sees the more to come in people; too often we see only their past. We need to look on the world with the eyes of faith.

When I find myself being critical of others, I say to myself, "Time to have a ten minute past two mentality." I have to catch people doing good and not focus on their misdeeds.

With whom do we need to develop a ten-minute past two attitude?

Wednesday of the Fourth Week in Ordinary Time

> When the Sabbath came he began to teach in the synagogue,
> and many who heard him were astonished.
> They said, "Where did he get all of this?
> What kind of wisdom has been given him?
> What mighty deeds are wrought by his hands!
> Is he not the carpenter, the son of Mary…"
> And they took offense at him.
> Mk 6: 1 – 6

Familiarity breeds contempt. Jesus went to school with their children; they played together. They knew Mary, and probably remembered Joseph, her deceased husband. He was the village carpenter; he had fixed the broken leg on their table. He was Jesus, the kid next door.

He had left town; they heard he was preaching. It was normal for him to go to synagogue. What was different was that now he was the teacher not the student. And they took offense at him.

We don't like it when people change. We like to think we know the people in our lives. We know how to deal with them; there should be no surprises. Jesus would not stay in the box they had built for him!

St. John Cardinal Henry Newman was fond of saying, "To live is to change, and to be perfect is to have changed often." The problem with aphorisms is that they are easier to say than to live. Jesus did not start out as the Messiah; he ended up as the Messiah. To be the one his father was calling him to be required that he was never satisfied with who he was until he had fully embraced the will of his father.

Where is God calling us to grow out of who we are to become the people he is calling us to be?

Thursday of the Fourth Week in Ordinary Time

Jesus summoned the Twelve and began to send them out two by two
and gave them authority over unclean spirits.
He instructed them to take nothing for the journey
but a walking stick –
no food, no sack, no money in their belts…
Mk 6: 7 – 13

The simplicity of Jesus' sending the Twelve always impresses me. He trusted them. They were not well educated, they had not been with him that long. They had attended no classes. They had walked with him; they had listened to him tell his stories. They had encountered his spirit. They had a relationship with him.

Pope Francis, in his writings and his daily homilies, frequently says what is too often missing in our lives of faith is a genuine relationship with Jesus.

Too often we look to people with advanced degrees, theologians, and teachers. They have the knowledge but is that enough? Education is essential but it will never replace a real relationship.

A few years ago there was a popular saying in church circles, "Going to church will not make you a Christian any more than standing in a garage will make you an automobile." We have to encounter Jesus in the Word, in the Eucharist, in the community, and in the lives of others.

There is a great story about an evangelical woman who went to a very staid church one Sunday. When the preacher made a good point she stood and said, "Amen!" She did this several times until one of the ushers came over and told her to stop. She said that when she encounters Jesus she has to say, "Amen!" The usher said "Ma'am, we don't encounter Jesus in this church." How true and how sad!

Have we ever really personally encountered Jesus as our Lord and Savior?

Friday of the Fourth Week in Ordinary Time

> Herod was the one who had ordered John arrested,
> Chained, and imprisoned on account of Herodias,
> the wife of his brother Philip, whom he had married.
> That is because John had told Herod,
> "It is not right for you to live with your brother's wife."
> Herodias harbored a grudge against him for this
> and wanted to kill him but was unable to do so.
> Mk 6: 14 – 29

When we harbor grudges nothing good ever happens. Nevertheless, harbor them we do. Most of us are familiar with the quote, "I don't get mad; I get even." The truth of the matter is we get both mad and even.

On October 2, 2006, Charles Roberts IV entered the one-room Amish schoolhouse in Nickel Mines, PA and opened fire killing five young girls and wounding three others before he took his own life. The killings shocked the nation, but the attitude of the Amish people also shocked the nation. They went to the Roberts family, and offered them comfort and forgiveness. They did not resort to revenge; they offered forgiveness. Why? Because that is what their faith taught them to do.

Their extraordinary act of forgiveness resulted in a book, Amish Grace: How Forgiveness Transcended Tragedy. In that book there is a quote from Fred Lufkin, who is the head of the Stanford University Forgiveness Project (I am always amazed that Stanford University has a Forgiveness Project and Catholic University does not.) "Forgiveness determines whether we will be the hero or the victim in the story we tell." That is why Jesus said, "Father, forgive them. They do not know what they are doing," and invites us to do the same.

To whom do we need to extend forgiveness?

Saturday of the Fourth Week in Ordinary Time

> The Apostles gathered together with Jesus and reported all
> they had done and taught.
> He said to them,
> "Come away by yourselves to a deserted place and rest awhile."
> Mk 6: 30 – 34

We need to live balanced lives – more balanced lives. We are a people who have made a god out of being busy. We brag about how many hours we work, and how long it has been since we took a vacation. We get caught up in the rush of life and get lost in the process.

All of us need a "quiet place." We need to go to our "quiet place" in order to keep our priorities straight. We need a place where we can unplug from social media and the constant bombardment of information. We need to shut off the television, put away our cell phones, and talk to the people with whom we live and work.

Whenever I go out to dinner, I see people sitting at nearby tables paying more attention to their cell phones than to each other. How have we let that happen? How did such rude behavior become acceptable? It happened because we failed to find the time to reflect on our business. It happened because we wrongly concluded that it is more important to be connected to a thing than to another person.

What should be more important people or things?

Fifth Sunday in Ordinary Time (A)

> Jesus said to his disciples: "You are the light of the world.
> A city set on a mountain cannot be hidden.

> Nor do they light a lamp and then put it under a bushel basket;
> it is set on a lampstand
> where it gives light to all in the house.
> Just so, your light must shine before others,
> that they may see your good deeds
> and glorify your heavenly Father."
> Mt 5: 13 – 16

Many of us are familiar with the song, "This little light of mine, I'm going to let it shine." We sang it as children; we need to live it as adults. Our light may be little but it is magnified when it is shared. One of my college philosophy professors was fond of saying, "Religion is caught not taught." How right he was.

I am a believer today because my parents were believers. They lovingly taught me my prayers; they were genuinely thrilled when I made the sign of the cross correctly for the first time. Your parents did the same and now, hopefully, you are doing the same for your children.

Shortly after my ordination, I taught high school religion for five years. Early on I discovered the importance of parents night, which was usually scheduled to take place about a month after school began. After my first parent night, I lobbied the principal to schedule parent night the first week of the school year. He asked, "Why?" and I responded, "Once I meet the parents, I know who my troubled students will be."

Of all the values our parents handed on to us, which serve us best?

Fifth Sunday in Ordinary Time (B)

> Rising early the next morning,
> he went off to a lonely place in the desert;
> there he was absorbed in prayer.
> Simon and his companions tracked him down;
> and when they found him, they told him,
> "Everyone is looking for you!"
> He said to them,

> "Let us move on to the neighboring villages
> so that I can proclaim the good news there also.
> That is what I have come to do."
> Mk 1: 29 – 39

Jesus is teaching in their synagogues, he is healing the sick, and casting out unclean spirits. It had to be exhilarating, but it had to be draining as well. Jesus seems to remain above the fray. Peter and his companions not so much. The gospel says, "they tracked him down"; they had to find him because "everyone is looking for you."

Jesus knew something that the others had yet to learn. There will always be more work to be done. There will always be someone who needs assistance. Nevertheless, it is important not to get lost in the "doing part of life." Jesus knew he needed quiet time so that he could stay focused. Without prayer, without time spent talking with his father, he would get lost. Jesus came to announce the Good News of salvation. He did not come to heal people. The healing was just a way to announce that the Kingdom of God was at hand.

We all lead busy lives. Too often it feels like we need a few twenty-eight hour days to get done all that needs to get done. Perhaps what we need is not more time, but better priorities. If we spend time in prayer, then our time will be put to better use. It worked for Jesus, and it will work for us.

Do we find time for prayer every day?

Fifth Sunday in Ordinary Time (C)

> Upon doing this they caught such a great number of fish
> that their nets were at the breaking point.
> They signaled to their mates in the other boat
> to come and help them.
> They came, and together they filled the two boats
> until they nearly sank.
> At the sight of this, Simon Peter fell at the knees of Jesus saying,
> "Leave me, Lord. I am a sinful man."

> For indeed, amazement at the catch they had made seized him
> and all his shipmates, as well as James and John, Zebedee's sons,
> who were partners with Simon.
> Jesus said to Simon,
> "Do not be afraid. From now on you will be catching men."
> With that they brought their boats to land,
> left everything, and became his followers.
> Lk 5: 1 11

When we realize that we are in the presence of God, we automatically act like Simon Peter, "Leave me, Lord. I am a sinner." This just reminds us that we see our sins more clearly than God sees them. God knows we are sinners; he just doesn't care. He chooses not to focus on our sins; he leaves that to us. Jesus does not dwell on our past but on our future.

He promises Peter and Andrew, James and John that in the future they will be catching people not fish. By saying this, Jesus is telling them that he will take all the qualities that made them good fishermen and use those qualities in a new and better way. To be a fisherman requires patience; to be an Apostle will require patience. To be a good partner requires cooperation; the same is true of Apostles.

There will be days of great success and days of scarcity. As Apostles they will have days when people will cling to their every word, and there will be days when no one will listen to anything they say.

All the Apostles had to do was leave everything especially their sins. We are called to do the same. Every time we celebrate the sacrament of reconciliation the priest ends the process by saying, "Peace. Go and sin no more."

What sins do we need to leave behind?

Monday of the Fifth Week in Ordinary Time

> As they were leaving the boat,
> people immediately recognized him.
> They scurried about the surrounding country

> and began to bring the sick on mats
> to wherever they heard he was.
> Mk 6: 53 – 56

It is too easy to get distracted from what should be the task at hand. Jesus' task was to be the Messiah; he was not in the business of curing people. He was not put on this earth so that the blind could see, the deaf hear, the lame walk, and the poor have the Good News preached to them. It is hard to let the important thing be the important thing.

There was a college professor who came to class one day with a big glass jar and three bags. He opened the first bag and took out some large rocks, which he put in the jar. He then asked the students if the jar was full, and they answered in the affirmative. Next, he reached into the second bag and took out some pebbles, which he put into the jar. He shook the jar to make sure it took as many pebbles as possible. Again, he asked the students if the jar was full, and again they answered in the affirmative. Finally, he reached into the third bag, which was filled with sand, which he put into the jar. Finally the jar was full. The professor then told them that the jar was their life. The rocks were the important things in life – your spouse, your family, and your home. The pebbles were the next level of importance – your job, your friends, and your community involvement. The sand represents everything else in life. If we put the important things first there will always be room for the other stuff. However, if we put the sand first there will be no room for what is really important.

Does the way we organize our life allow the important things to come first?

Tuesday of the Fifth Week in Ordinary Time

> Well did Isaiah prophesy about you hypocrite, as it is written:
> *This people honors me with their lips*
> *but their hearts are far from me;*
> *In vain do they worship me,*
> *Teaching as doctrines human precepts.*
> Mk 7:1 – 13

Lip service is when we say all the right things but don't believe them or live them. How many people go to communion and say, "Amen" without intending to live what they receive? How many people say, "I love you" because it is expected but never owned? How often has someone said, "If you need anything, you can count on me" but are never available when they are needed? How often do we say more than we are ready to live?

There is a story about a man from Milwaukee who was visiting Poland. A member of the Communist Party was showing him around. After several days together they began to ask and answer more personal questions. The Polish communist asked the man from Milwaukee, "Are you a Christian?" The answer was "Yes, believing not practicing." The man from Milwaukee asked, "Are you a communist?" to which he was told, "Practicing not believing."

In one of Flip Wilson's comedy routines, he would say, "I'm a Jehovah bystander. They wanted me to be a witness but I did not want to get involved." I fear that far too many of us are Catholic bystanders rather than witnesses!

If we are asked, "Are you a Catholic?" what would be the most honest answer?

Wednesday of the Fifth Week in Ordinary Time

> But what comes out of the man, that is what defiles him.
> From within the man, from his heart,
> come evil thoughts, unchastity, theft, murder,
> adultery, greed, malice, deceit,
> licentiousness, envy, blasphemy, arrogance, folly.
> All these evils come from within and they defile.
> Mk 7: 14 – 23

If God is all good, then where does evil come from? Did God create the evil that is in the world? These questions rank up there with, "Can God make a boulder so big that he can't lift it?"

God did not create evil; he created us, and we created evil. God gave us free will. We can either use it or abuse it. When we choose to do what is right and just we use our precious gift of freedom. When we choose to do what is bad and unjust we abuse our freedom. It doesn't get simpler than that. As Albert Pike said, "What we do for ourselves dies with us. What we do for others and the world remains and is immortal."

The challenge for all of us is to leave this world a better place than the one we entered. We determine what comes out of us; we are in charge of the influence we have on others. God has blessed us with many gifts. We need to open those gifts, develop them, and share them lovingly in justice with others. That is all the return God wants.

Where can we make better choices so that the darkness of evil can be changed into light?

Thursday of the Fifth Week in Ordinary Time

> The woman was a Greek, a Syrophoenician by birth,
> and she begged him to drive the demon out of her daughter.
> He said to her, "Let the children be fed first.
> For it is not right to take the food of the children
> and throw it to the dogs."
> She replied and said to him,
> "Lord, even the dogs under the table
> eat the children's scraps."
> Mk 7: 24 – 30

Jesus was fully human and fully divine. Because he was human, he was born in time and was influenced by the culture of his time. In today's gospel passage, Jesus speaks the prejudice of his time. As a practicing Jew, he believed his people were the chosen people and that all other people were inferior. The mother in today's gospel is a Greek, a foreigner, considered unclean, known as the "goyim."

Jesus had to outgrow the prejudices of his time and culture. All of us have to do the same.

That there was a time when women in America were not allowed to vote is embarrassing, but it is a fact. That people of color were forced to sit in the back of the bus is embarrassing, but it happened during my lifetime. That slaves were once bought and sold in America boggles my mind, but it is part of our history. We or our ancestors had to outgrow the prejudices of our time. So did Jesus. And in today's gospel passage that is precisely what Jesus did. He listened not to a Greek or a foreigner but a mother. He heard a mother's concern and healed her daughter. Prejudice always wilts when we listen with an open mind.

What prejudices do we need to outgrow?

Friday of the Fifth Week in Ordinary Time

> He put his fingers into the man's ears and, spitting,
> touched his tongue;
> then he looked up to heaven and groaned,
> and said to him, "Ephphatha!" (that is, "Be opened!")
> And immediately the man's ears were opened.
> Mk 7: 31 – 37

Jesus did not heal from afar. Healing for him was up close and personal. In today's story, Jesus touched and opened the ears of the deaf man. A number of years ago at a day of reflection, I invited the group to reflect on what it would be like to lose one of our six senses. They were invited to judge which would be the easiest sense to lose, and which would be the hardest. It was not my most memorable day of reflection.

Most of us are familiar with convenient deafness. We make believe we don't hear someone. We turn a deaf ear. We don't want our schedule interrupted. Sometimes the person we do not listen to is God. God calls out to us in the needy; we turn away. He speaks to us in the person who is being treated unjustly; we do not act. The next-door neighbor needs a ride to the doctor, the child down the street needs someone to tutor him in math, the parish asks for help with the food pantry, and we don't hear God calling to us in the needs of those around us.

Where is God calling us to be more involved in easing the burdens of others?

Saturday of the Fifth Week in Ordinary Time

> Then, taking the seven loaves, he gave thanks, broke them,
> and gave them to his disciples to distribute,
> and they distributed them to the crowd.
> They also had a few fish.
> He said the blessing over them and ordered them distributed also.
> They ate and were satisfied.
> They picked up the fragments left over – seven baskets.
> Mk 8: 1 – 10

Sharing multiplies what we have so we always have more than we think. There probably is a psychological name for this phenomenon but I don't know what it is. Actually, I am not sure sharing multiplies what we have or changes our expectations. Either way, sharing is the way to go.

Jesus and the disciples had a problem – too many mouths to feed. Jesus asks the tough question, "What do we have?" He does not ask, "What do we need?" The second question begets doubt; the first question invites creativity.

My parents, mainly my father, passed on to my brothers and me an attitude of "Make do!" As a result, the four of us learned early on to focus on what was possible rather than get lost in what could not be done. It has served us well, but has caused a certain level of frustration for others.

A minister was at a prayer breakfast where the leader of the group introduced a new program that was going to cost $10,000. When the leader finished his explanation he called on the minister to pray that the money would be quickly raised. The minister stood and said, "The people in this room have the wherewithal to fund this project so there is no need to trouble God with our request." The minister focused on what the group had; the members focused on what they needed. It is not part of the story, but I am fairly sure the group went looking for a new minister.

Where can we make better use of the gifts and talents we have?

Sixth Sunday in Ordinary Time (A)

> But I say to you, do not swear at all;
> not by heaven, for it is God's throne;
> nor by earth, for it is his footstool;
> nor by Jerusalem, for it is the city of the great King.
> Do not swear by your head,
> for you cannot make a single hair white or black.
> Let your 'Yes' mean 'Yes' and your 'No' mean 'No.'
> Anything more is from the evil one.
> Mt 5: 17 – 37

There is a movie scene that is burned into my memory. The scene is from the *The Godfather*. Don Corleone is godfather at a baptism. The priest is asking the threefold profession of faith to the parents and godparents, "Do you believe in God the Father almighty…" Don Corleone says yes as his henchmen are violently killing his perceived enemies. "Do you believe in Jesus Christ…?" More violence. "Do you believe in the Holy Spirit…" The final act of violence. The juxtaposition of dishonest words of belief and senseless acts of violence was jarring.

Too often, we say words because we think others want to hear them. Too often, we give partial or misleading answers because it seems easier at the time. When some people say you can count on their support, you know it is true. When others say the same thing we know we can count on them unless they get a better offer. It is just the way of the world.

There was a time not too long ago when a handshake and a look in the eye were the only contract that honest people needed. It would be nice to get back there once again!

Where do we need to be more honest with the words we speak?

Sixth Sunday in Ordinary Time (B)

> A leper approached Jesus with a request,
> kneeling down as he addressed him,

> "If you will to do so, you can cure me."
> Moved with pity, Jesus stretched out his hand,
> touched him and said,
> "I do will it. Be cured."
> The leprosy left him then and there, and he was cured.
> Mk 1: 40 – 45

Lepers were known as the "untouchables" because their disease was considered highly infectious. Jesus knew this, but touched him nonetheless. What must that moment have been? Having gone years without the healing balm of human touch, having seen people recoil from his presence for who knows how long, to finally have someone stand their ground and without fear reach out and touch him. It was then that he was cured; it was then that he was part of the community once again. Why did it happen? Because Jesus felt his pain; because Jesus had empathy.

Empathy seems to be in short supply in our world. We won't let ourselves feel the pain of others. If someone is begging at an intersection we do our best not to make eye contact. We look straight ahead. We avoid conversation. We pray more for the light to change than we do for the person who has been reduced to begging. We are content to write out a check or make an online donation, but we don't want to go to a soup kitchen and help out.

Instead of seeing the dirty clothing, or the bloodshot eyes, we need to see a fellow human being who is hurting. Like Jesus, we need to will to make them whole once again.

Where have we shut down so as not to feel the pain of those in need?

Sixth Sunday in Ordinary Time (C)

> When Jesus came down the mountain,
> He stopped at a level stretch where there were many of his disciples;
> a large crowd of people was with them from all Judea and Jerusalem
> and the coast of Tyre and Sidon.
> Then, raising his eyes to his disciples, he said:

> "Blest are you poor; the reign of God is yours
> Blest are you who hunger; filled you shall be.
> Blest are you who are weeping; you shall laugh.
> Blest shall you be when men hate you,
> when they ostracize you and insult you
> and proscribe your name as evil because of the Son of Man.
> On the day they do so,
> Rejoice and exult for your reward shall be great in heaven."
> Lk 6: 17 – 26

In Matthew's gospel, Jesus goes up on a mountain, sits down, and gives the beatitudes. In Luke's gospel, Jesus comes down the mountain and gives the beatitudes. Matthew gives us eight beatitudes; Luke gives us only four. But the number is not what counts. What counts is we realize that being a believer is not going to be a walk in the park. Being a believer must cost us.

Jesus is not exulting the poor, the hungry, and the sorrowful; he is telling those who live in misfortune that God is with them. God is greater than our poverty, however that poverty gets expressed. God will fill us with good things. Our hunger, whether physical, spiritual, or psychological, will not last forever. God feeds us with his love.

Finally, just as Jesus was hated, ostracized, and insulted, so shall we be. We need to exult and rejoice when our beliefs make others feel guilty. We will be rewarded in heaven, but we will be rewarded here on earth as well. We will be rewarded with little victories, small conversions, and mini successes. If we can persevere, if we can live as Jesus lived, then the Kingdom of God will slowly come to fruition.

Where have we watered down our faith in order to embrace the values of this world?

Monday of the Sixth Week in Ordinary Time

> The Pharisees came forward and began to argue with Jesus,
> seeking from him a sign from heaven to test him.
> He sighed from the depth of his spirit and said,

> "Why does this generation seek a sign?"
> Mk 8: 11 – 13

God is love. God is mercy. God is forgiveness. God is many things but mostly God is patient. He is patient with us. He keeps waiting for us to get it; we keep disappointing him.

God, if you want me to do this, just send me a sign. We always want more reassurance from God. There is a great line in the gospel story of Lazarus and the rich man. In the story, the rich man dies and is in torment because he ignored the plight of Lazarus who used to beg at his gate. The rich man wants Lazarus to dip his finger in water and touch his lips. Abraham says no. The rich man then asks Abraham to send Lazarus back to earth to warn his brothers of their fate unless they change their ways. Abraham says "They have Moses, and the prophets, let them listen to them." He said, "Oh no, father Abraham, but if someone from the dead goes to them, they will repent." Then Abraham said, "If they will not listen to Moses and the prophets, neither will they be persuaded if someone should rise from the dead.'"

Well someone did rise from the dead and we still are not persuaded. Not only is our God patient; he is prescient.

How can we pay more attention to the signs God has already shared with us?

Tuesday of the Sixth Week in Ordinary Time

> Do you not understand or comprehend?
> Are your hearts hardened?
> Do you have eyes and not see, ears and not hear?
> Mk 8: 14 – 21

What does it mean to have a hardened heart? What does it mean to have a closed mind? They mean pretty much the same thing as far as I can tell. In our partisan world and church there are plenty of hardened hearts, and closed minds, and the condition is not of recent vintage.

"For John the Baptist came neither eating food or drinking wine, and you said, 'He is possessed by a demon.' The Son of Man came eating and drinking and you said, 'Look, he is a glutton and a drunkard, a friend of tax collectors and sinners.'" For some the bishop can speak no truth; for others he can speak no falsehood. Still others love to quote St. John Paul II or Benedict XVI because their truth lines up with their truth but can find nothing truthful in the words of Pope Francis.

My father was a man of few words, but many sayings. One of his favorite sayings was, "When a man's [sic] mind is made up never confuse him with the facts." I reflect on these words of wisdom frequently in our unfortunately divided church.

What group have I learned to ignore, and how can I reverse that decision?

Wednesday of the Sixth Week in Ordinary Time

> When Jesus and his disciples arrived at Bethsaida,
> people brought to him a blind man and begged Jesus to touch him.
> He took the blind man by the hand and led him outside the village.
> Putting spittle on his eyes he laid his hands on the man and asked,
> "Do you see anything?"
> Looking up the man replied,
> "I see people looking like trees and walking."
> Then he laid hands on the man's eyes a second time
> and he saw clearly.
> Mk 8: 22 – 26

Since the blind man knew what trees look like, and what people look like, it is safe to assume that there was a time when he could see, and then he went blind. He had the ability, and he lost it.

Sometimes we fail to appreciate things until we no longer have them! The older we get the more our lives shrink. Recently, I read this on social media, "I don't know if 70 is the new 50 but I know that 9 pm is the new midnight." Boy is that true.

There was a time when we had more patience. There was a time when we had more energy. And there certainly was a time when we were more self-assured. We would like to get back some of our energy and time, but not our sense of self-assurance. People can be hurt by our self-assurance. We need to lose whatever makes us insensitive to the needs of others.

Where have we allowed ourselves to ignore the plight of others?

Thursday of the Sixth Week in Ordinary Time

> Jesus and his disciples set out for the villages of Caesarea Philippi.
> Along the way he asked his disciples,
> "Who do people say that I am?"
> Mk 8: 27 – 33

Jesus went from "Who do people say that I am?" to "Who do you say I am?" He went from a general question to a particular question. The human part of Jesus was wrestling with the most important question of our lives, "Who am I?" Everything depends on the answer to that question.

We believe that God has a plan for us. That plan has been described in myriad ways but I think St. John Cardinal Henry Newman said it best, "God has created me to do Him some definite service. He has committed some work to me which he has not committed to another. I have my mission. I may never know it in this life, but I shall be told it in the next. I am a link in a chain, a bond of connection between persons."

Let that sink in a bit. There is a task that is mine, a task that is yours. The coming of God's Kingdom depends on our figuring out to the best of our ability what God wants us to do with our lives and then doing it to the best of our ability.

What does God want us to do with our gifts and talents?

Friday of the Sixth Week in Ordinary Time

> Jesus summoned the crowd with his disciples and said to them,
> "Whoever wishes to come after me must deny himself,
> take up his cross and follow me.

> For whoever wishes to save his life will lose it,
> but whoever loses his life for my sake
> and that of the Gospel will save it."
> Mk 8: 34 – 9: 1

Being a disciple of Jesus is not for the faint of heart. Jesus does not sugar coat the cost of being his disciple. It is all about sacrifice and discipline. Think of Jesus as a coach. Most everyone can make the roster but only the supper dedicated make the starting team.

Right after ordination I taught in a Catholic boys high school that had great success in both academics and sports. My second year at the high school, I was having lunch with the basketball coach and asked him what kind of a team he was going to have. He shocked me when he said, "There will be a better team walking the corridors, but we should be OK." What he was saying was that some students, even though they were talented, did not have the desire to work hard enough to be part of the team. That is true in so many different aspects of life.

In a similar vein, I used to tell all my students, "Anyone can get a B or a C; if you want an A or a D, you have to ask for it." If they wanted to excel they had to work hard; there are no short cuts. If we want to be a disciple, we have to make sacrifices. There are no short cuts in Christianity!

Where do we need to work harder at living out the promises we made at Baptism?

Saturday of the Sixth Week in Ordinary Time

> Jesus took Peter, James, and John off by themselves with him
> and led them up a high mountain.
> He was transfigured before their eyes
> and his clothes became dazzlingly white –
> whiter than the work of any bleacher could make them.
> Elijah appeared to them along with Moses;
> the two were in conversation with Jesus.
> Mk 9: 2 – 13

The thing that always amazes me about this gospel is how low key the description of the transfiguration is. It is almost ho hum. We went up a mountain, saw a vision that had Elijah and Moses having a chat with Jesus. Then Peter had something interesting to say, and we left the mountain. What's for lunch?

They had a religious experience on that mountain. Jesus' divinity broke through his humanity ever so briefly. Elijah, speaking for all the prophets, put his seal of approval on Jesus; then Moses, representing the Law, put his seal on Jesus.

Religious experiences are few and far between, and usually they don't make a lot of sense. Can you imagine Peter, James, and John trying to explain to the others what happened? Can you imagine the look of bewilderment that would be on the faces of the other apostles?

One thing is certain. The vision did not last. It had a profound effect on them, but they had to treasure it in their memory. It became their religious touchstone. When things got bad or confusing, they had to go back and remember what they saw. All of us need a religious touchstone.

What is your religious touchstone?

Seventh Sunday in Ordinary Time (A)

"You have heard that it was said,
'You shall love your neighbor and hate your enemy.'
But I say to you, love your enemies
and pray for those who persecute you,
that you may be children of your heavenly Father
for he makes his sun rise on the bad and the good.
and causes rain to fall on the just and the unjust."
Mt 5: 38 – 48

There is a story about W.C. Fields, a notorious atheist, who was in the hospital and very sick. A friend went to visit him and was surprised to find Mr. Fields sitting in bed reading the Bible. His friend said, "What are you doing?" and Fields replied, "Looking for a few loopholes." When it comes to gospel imperatives like today's, I think many of us go looking for loopholes.

Mark Twain once said, "It is not the parts of the Bible that I don't understand that bother me; it is the parts that I do understand," I think the truth of that statement is found in today's challenge, "Love your enemies."

Having enemies requires a lot of work; it can dominate our lives. I think it is very important to remember that Jesus challenges us to "love our enemies" he does not ask us to "like our enemies." That is an important distinction. Love is a choice. We have almost no control over whom we like or dislike; liking just sort of happens. Love on the other hand is a choice; we decide whom we love. And we need to follow the example of Jesus who loved everyone, but was not terribly fond of the Scribes and Pharisees.

Pick one enemy to forgive and then do it. Repeat the process tomorrow.

Seventh Sunday in Ordinary Time (B)

> While he was delivering God's word to them,
> some people arrived bringing a paralyzed man to him.
> The four who carried him were unable to bring him to Jesus
> because of the crowd, so they began to open up
> the roof over the spot where Jesus was.
> Mk 2: 1 – 12

There is always so much we don't know about the people in the gospels. Take the paralyzed man in today's story. How long had he been paralyzed? Was he in an accident, or had he been sick? We don't know. How long had his friends been carrying him around? Whose idea was it to bring him to Jesus? Who owned the house where Jesus was preaching? Did anyone remember to fix the hole in the roof? These and other details would help the story come alive, but what we have will have to do.

The reason why Jesus forgives his sins is because it was believed that any deformity was because of sin. Remember the question in the story of the blind man in John's gospel, "Who sinned, this man or his parents that he was born blind?" Sin does not cause physical deformity; it causes spiritual deformity. The deformity of sin cannot be seen. Only the sinner knows it is there. Every sinner carries around in his mind and heart the scars of past sins. Everyone reading this has at least one spiritual scar that needs to be healed. We need to go to Jesus and ask for healing. There will be obstacles that get in the way of asking for healing. There will be embarrassment perhaps or doubt that we can really be healed. Just say a prayer to the four friends in today's gospel asking them not to let you give up on getting to Jesus.

Where are we letting our sins dictate who we are?

Seventh Sunday in Ordinary Time (C)

> "Do to others what you would have them do to you.
> If you love those who love you, what credit is that to you?
> Even sinners love those who love them.
> If you do good to those who do good to you,
> how can you claim any credit?
> Sinners do as much.
> If you lend to those from whom you expect repayment,
> What merit is there in it for you?
> Even sinners lend to sinners, expecting to be repaid in full."
> Lk 6: 27 -38

The Golden rule: "Do to others what you would have them do to you." So easy to say, but so difficult to live. We need to treat everyone with dignity and respect. EVERYONE! Unfortunately, we treat people differently.

We used to be a people who could believe different things, and still live together peacefully. That seems like a long time ago. So long ago, that we may be in danger of forgetting how to live peacefully with one another. Divisions abound in politics, in work, in church, and in neighborhoods. We take sides too easily. Those who disagree with us become the enemy, and we attack their position. Divisions are dangerous anywhere, but especially in our church.

In one of my first assignments after ordination, I was assigned to a parish with a pastor who was clearly a pre-Vatican II pastor, and I was clearly a post-Vatican II assistant. That pastor had a priest friend who was an ultra-conservative pastor. One day, I returned to the rectory to find that priest sitting in my room, reading my copy of the progressive magazine, Critic. I said to him, "Are you coming over to the dark side?" He smiled and said, "No", but I want to know what you and your ilk are up to." There was no acrimony, no bitterness, no name calling, just two adults who held different theological opinions on what our religion should look like. There was civility, and we need to relearn how to act that way once again in the church that we all love.

Where have we allowed divisions to fester in our Church?

Monday of the Seventh Week in Ordinary Time

Jesus said to him,
"'If you can!' Everything is possible to the one who has faith."
Then the boy's father cried out, "I do believe, help my unbelief!"
Mk 9: 14 – 29

Ambivalence is part of the human condition, but we wish it were not. Part of us loves; part of us hates. We want all of us to love and none of us to us hate, but that is not the way it works. We want to live in a world of certainty without any doubt, but that can't happen. Without doubt there can be no certainty. Same thing is true of faith. Unless we wrestle with unbelief there can be no real belief!

Rainer Maria Rilke, the poet-philosopher, expresses it thus, "Be patient toward all that is unsolved in your heart and try to love the questions themselves, like locked rooms and like books that are now written in a very foreign tongue. Do not seek the answers, which cannot be given because you would not be able to live them. And the point is, to live everything. Live the questions now. Perhaps then, someday far in the future, you will gradually, without even noticing it, live your way into the answer."

Where in our lives do we need to be more patient with our questions?

Tuesday of the Seventh Week in Ordinary time

> Then he sat down, called the Twelve, and said to them,
> "If anyone wishes to be first,
> he shall be the last of all and the servant of all."
> Taking a child, he placed it in their midst,
> and putting his arms around it, he said to them,
> "Whoever receives a child such as this in my name, receives me;
> and whoever receives me, receives not me but the One who sent me."
> Mk 9: 30 – 33

Jesus' values were at odds with the culture of his day and certainly are at odds with our contemporary culture. Earlier in today's gospel passage, we are told that the disciples were discussing who among them was the greatest. Did you ever wonder how that discussion got started? I don't think I have ever been in a discussion about who is the greatest. We discuss who is the greatest shortstop, the greatest playmaker, the best actress, or the best song. But the greatest person, never.

I know if people think about who is the greatest, that conversation is usually a mental monologue that seldom rises to the level of dialogue. We tend to measure greatness by fame and fortune. Jesus uses other criteria. If we want to be great, we have to put others first. We have to defer to others; we have to serve others.

God comes to us in the needy; we need to recognize that, and serve the needy. Then, and only then, will we be great in the Kingdom of God

Where in our lives have we let a warped notion of greatness cloud our vision?

Wednesday of the Seventh Week in Ordinary Time

> Jesus said in reply:
> "Do not try to stop him.

> No one can perform a miracle in my name
> and at the same time speak ill of me.
> Anyone who is not against us is with us."
> Mk 9: 38 – 40

Jesus makes a very subtle change to a phrase we often use, and it makes a tremendous difference. Common wisdom says, "If you are not with me, you are against me." Jesus' wisdom says, "If you are not against me, you are with me." What a difference.

Jesus' way of thinking includes more people than our way of thinking. Our way of thinking is limiting; Jesus' way of thinking is more inclusive. Exclusivity is important to us. The more limited an event is the more important we deem it to be. We seek out gated communities, exclusive clubs, posh zip codes, and tickets to sold out events. We call it human nature.

Jesus invites us to a different way of thinking and behaving. Jesus wants us to live life with our arms and our hearts wide open. Jesus did not come to save some of us, but rather all of us. That is his nature, and he invites us to share his more inclusive love.

Where do we need to be more open with our love?

Thursday of the Seventh Week in Ordinary Time

> Jesus said to his disciples:
> "Any man who gives you a drink of water
> because you belong to Christ will not,
> I assure you, go without his reward.
> But it would be better if anyone
> who leads astray one of these simple believers
> were to be plunged into the sea
> with a great millstone fastened around his neck."
> Mk 9: 41 – 50

I wonder what Jesus meant by "leads astray one of these simple believers…" Given the harsh punishment Jesus attaches to anyone who leads astray a believer we would be well advised to avoid such behavior.

I don't think I have ever met anyone who deliberately tried to destroy someone's faith. I know people whose faith has been destroyed, but usually the person whose behavior diminished someone's faith has no idea they did anything wrong.

There are many different reasons why believers go astray. We need to hope that we have never done anything to cause someone to abandon their faith. We need to live our faith to its full expression. We need to meet the needs of those in trouble; we need to work on being kind to people.

There has to be more to our lives of faith than being rewarded for good deeds, and punished for bad behavior. Faith is about love not rewards and punishments. We need to live our faith out of love, and trust that God will judge us mercifully

Where have we allowed fear of punishment to motivate our lives of faith?

Friday of the Seventh Week in Ordinary Time

> Once more crowds gathered around him
> and he began to teach them.
> Then some Pharisees came up
> and as a test began to ask Jesus
> whether it was permissible for a husband
> to divorce his wife.
> Mk 10: 1 – 12

That question has been asked over and over again ever since. I wonder if there will ever be an acceptable answer. In Jesus' time, only men had the right to divorce. Women had no rights. Whatever solution worked in Jesus' time could not work in our time. Too much has changed.

One thing is certain – divorce will be with us forever, and we need to discover a better way as a church to deal with the issue of divorce and remarried believers. Our present way of dealing with the issue is just lacking. Cutting people off from the sacraments is harmful for those who are trying to live their lives to the best of their ability. We need to find a way to uphold the ideal of marriage as lasting until death do us part without condemning those who fail to achieve the ideal. Can we expand the notion of death to include emotional death or psychological death? We need to keep searching for a solution. As a church, we need to relearn that our ministry is to serve people where they are not where we want them to be.

How can we help our church be less judgmental and more welcoming?

Saturday of the Seventh Week in Ordinary Time

> "It is to just such as these
> that the kingdom of God belongs.
> I assure you that whoever does not accept
> the kingdom of God like a little child
> shall not enter into it."
> Then he embraced them and
> blessed them, placing his hands on them.
> Mk 10: 13 – 16

Children have wonderful and creative imaginations. Children don't overthink things. As we grow older our inner child is too often sacrificed on the altar of maturity.

This delightful story can teach us how we need to be more like a little child. An ocean liner was going through a patch of bad weather. Everyone was confined to quarters to wait out the storm. One passenger grew tired of his cabin, and decided to go exploring. All of the corridors were outfitted with ropes so people could pull themselves along. The passenger had gone but a short distance when he came upon a child kneeling on the deck playing jacks. He watched for a while, and then said to the child, "Aren't you afraid?" The child replied, "No." The passenger asked, "Why not?" and the child said, "My daddy is the captain!" That's the attitude that will get us into heaven.

Where do we need to be more trusting of God?

Eighth Sunday in Ordinary Time (A)

> Your heavenly Father knows all that you need.
> Seek first his kingship over you, his way of holiness,
> and all these things will be given you besides.
> Enough, then, of worrying about tomorrow.
> Let tomorrow take care of itself.
> Today has troubles enough of its own.
> Mt 6: 24 – 34

Worrying is by in large a waste of time. Nothing has ever been solved by worrying. Actually, worrying usually just makes things worse. Nevertheless, most of us are dedicated worriers.

When it came to worrying my parents were exact opposites. My mom was a gold medal worrier. Truth be told I think worrying may have shortened her life. My father's philosophy was, "If you can do something about an issue do it. If you can't then let it go." I suspect his approach added years to his life.

I remember one time when I was having dinner with them at home, and they were having a discussion about a problem. I have no recollection of what the problem was; I just remember the dynamics of the discussion. My mother in exasperation finally said to my father, "Why aren't you more worried about this?" My father calmly said, "You are doing enough worrying for both of us." Thank God they loved each other because otherwise his comment would have caused more trouble than it did.

Where do we need to let go and let God?

Eighth Sunday in Ordinary Time (B)

> The day will come, however,
> when the groom will be taken away from them;
> on that day they will fast.
> No one sews a patch of unshrunken cloth on an old cloak.
> If he should do so, the very thing

> he has used to cover the hole would
> pull away – the new from the old – and the tear would get worse.
> Similarly, no man pours new wine into old wineskins.
> If he does so, the wine will burst the skins
> and both wine and skins will be lost.
> No, new wine is poured into new skins.
> Mk 2: 18 – 22

I love it when Jesus gets folksy. Today is a perfect example. The Pharisees are trying to pick a fight with him, but he will not get sucked into their trap. Instead he uses the example of how to mend a cloak, and of how to store new wine to make his point.

Basically, he is reminding his listeners that there is always a correct and an incorrect way of doing things. Sometimes the solution to a challenge is a tried and true method from the past; sometimes the solution is entirely new and different. Sometimes we try to fix something and we make matters worse; sometimes we succeed at fixing the problem. The challenge is knowing when to employ a traditional solution and when to be creative. Some problems need creative thinking; some don't. The Pharisees want everything to fit into their neat categories. Life just doesn't work that way.

Where are we letting stubbornness frustrate our problem solving?

Eighth Sunday in Ordinary Time (C)

> "Why look at the speck in your brother's eye
> when you miss the plank in your own?
> How can you say to your brother,
> 'Brother, let me remove the speck from your eye.'
> yet fail to see the plank lodged in your own?
> Hypocrite, remove the plank from your own eye first;
> then you will see clearly enough to remove
> the speck from your brother's eye."
> Lk 6: 39 – 45

The most obvious result of original sin is that we can see the faults of others clearly, and yet be so blind to our own. The devil must take great delight in this most human foible.

We never seem to run out of advice for others. We are blessed (or is it cursed) with knowing just how to tell our friends how they can live better lives.

Many years ago, a couple in the parish asked me if I would help them celebrate their 50th wedding anniversary by renewing their vows. Their anniversary fell on a weekday, so they came to daily Mass, and after the Mass they renewed their vows. The couple had several priest friends whom they invited to their mundane celebration. After they renewed their vows their small group of friends congratulated them. One of their priest friends followed me into the sacristy, and proceeded to tell me how he would have renewed their vows. It felt like he was criticizing how I had renewed their vows. Finally, I had to remind him that they had invited me not him to do the renewal. Undaunted he continued to tell me how I could have done it better.

Where do we need to cut others some slack?

Monday of the Eighth Week in Ordinary Time

> He replied, "Teacher, I have kept all these since my childhood."
> Then Jesus looked at him with love and told him,
> "There is one more thing you must do.
> Go and sell what you have and give to the poor;
> you will then have treasure in heaven.
> After that come and follow me."
> At these words the man's face fell.
> He went away sad, for he had many possessions.
> Mk 10:17 – 27

The rich man in today's gospel must have never heard the aphorism, "Don't ask a question unless you are ready to accept the answer." He thought he wanted eternal life so he asked Jesus what he had to do to gain it. At first, Jesus gives him a sort of checklist; he reminds him of the commandments. The rich young man boasts that he is faithful to the commandments all his life. At which point he must have been feeling pretty good about himself.

That is when Jesus tests him to see if he was really interested in sharing everlasting life. Jesus tells him his possessions are the problem. He needs to get rid of his possessions, and then come back. Notice once the man gets rid of his possessions his salvation is not achieved; he has to get rid of his possessions so that he can begin to follow Jesus.

Every believer I know has something that prevents them from following Jesus more fully. For some it is possessions, for others it is success, or fame, or recognition, or pleasure. For some of us it is more than one thing. We need to identify our stumbling blocks to salvation and deal with them.

What is it that keeps us from being better believers?

Tuesday of the Eighth Week in Ordinary Time

> Peter was moved to say to Jesus:
> "We have put aside everything to follow you!"
> Jesus answered: "I give you my word,
> there is no one who has given up home,
> brothers or sisters, mother or father,
> children or property, for me and for the gospel
> who will not receive in this present age
> a hundred times as many homes,
> brothers and sisters, mothers, children
> and property – and persecution besides –
> and in the age to come, everlasting life.
> Mk 10: 28 – 31

Jesus realizes that the Apostles had to leave behind their former way of life. They had given up fishing or tax collection to follow him. He had entered their lives, and they would never be the same.

He assures them that their new lives will be better than their former lives. They had to trust what he was saying, and they had to pay very close attention. Not only would their new lives be better, there would also be hardship. There would be persecution as well. Jesus kind of slips the persecution detail in the midst of the good things they will receive for being his followers.

Once we decide to be followers of Jesus we have our goal. Once we have our goal we know that some things will help us achieve that goal, while other things will be obstacles. Jesus knows that following his way of love will fulfill our lives. We need to embrace those values that will help us experience the transforming power of his love in our lives.

What are our obstacles to being better believers?

Wednesday of the Eighth Week in Ordinary Time

> The other ten, on hearing this,
> became indignant at James and John.
> Jesus called them together and said to them:
> "You know how among the Gentiles those who
> seem to exercise authority lord it over them;
> their great ones make their importance felt.
> It cannot be like that with you.
> Anyone among you who aspires to greatness
> must serve the rest;
> whoever wants to rank first among you must
> serve the needs of all.
> The Son of Man has not come to be served but to serve –
> to give his life in ransom for the many."
> Mk 10: 32 – 45

What does it mean to "aspire to greatness?" Greatness is not fame; greatness is being comfortable in our own skin. Greatness is a byproduct of doing God's will. Jesus not only aspired to greatness; he achieved it.

We need to follow Jesus' example if we are to achieve greatness. We need to put others before ourselves. That is not easy to do. We are all for helping out the poor and the needy, but only after we take care of our needs first. That is not what Jesus demands. Jesus wants us to diminish our needs so we can take care of others. This is never easy. Remember that in the garden on the night before he was to die, Jesus asked his Father to "let this cup pass me by." In the end he achieved greatness because he said, "Not my will but your will be done."

We need to adjust our needs so that others can be served. Gandhi highlighted what Jesus was teaching in today's gospel when he said, "There will always be enough for our need, but never enough for our greed."

How can we adjust our needs so as to serve others more generously?

Thursday of the Eighth Week in Ordinary Time

> Then Jesus stopped and said,
> "Call him over."
> So they called the blind man over,
> telling him as they did so,
> "You have nothing whatever to fear from him!
> Get up! He is calling you!"
> He threw his cloak aside, jumped up and came to Jesus.
> Jesus asked him,
> "What do you want me to do for you?"
> "Rabboni," the blind man said,
> "I want to see."
> Mk 10: 46 – 52

There are so many themes in this rather short gospel. There is the theme of the blind man Bartimaeus' persistence. He cries out for help, the crowd tries to silence him, but he cries out louder. He was not going to be discouraged.

Next, there is Jesus telling the crowd to call him over. I have always found it strange that Jesus did not go to Bartimaeus; he waited for Bartimaeus to come to him. It was more difficult for Bartimaeus to go to Jesus, but that is what happened. Was Jesus testing Bartimaeus? We don't know. The way this gospel story is written reads like Jesus calling the Apostles. Jesus is saying to the blind man, "Follow me." Perhaps this gospel is more of a calling than a cure.

The reason I think this is more of calling than a cure is that Bartimaeus jumps up, and throws away his cloak. Just like Peter and Andrew, and James and John abandoned their nets, so Bartimaeus abandons his cloak, which was used to beg for coins from the crowd. Bartimaeus gives up his livelihood to follow Jesus.

Next comes a very strange twist in the story. Jesus asks Bartimaeus, "What do you want me to do for you?" Jesus does not presume that the blind man wants to see. Once Bartimaeus says he wants to see, Jesus gives him his sight, and "immediately he received his sight and started to follow him up the road."

Where do we need to be more persistent in asking for Jesus' help?

Friday of the Eighth Week in Ordinary Time

> In reply Jesus said to them,
> "Put your trust in God.
> I solemnly assure you,
> Whoever says to this mountain,
> 'Be lifted up and thrown into the sea'
> and has no inner doubts but believes what he says will happen,
> shall have it done for him.
> I give you my word, if you are ready to believe
> that you will receive whatever you ask for in prayer,
> it shall be done for you.
> When you stand to pray, forgive anyone
> against whom you have a grievance
> so that your heavenly Father may in turn
> forgive you your faults."
> Mk 11: 11 – 26

When our prayers are not answered, we blame God, but today's gospel suggests that the blame falls elsewhere. The fault is that we don't believe enough; we suffer from inner doubts.

We ask God to heal a sick husband. We ask, but our inner voice tells us we are wasting our time. The healing never happens. We pray that God will heal our daughter's addiction, but she has relapsed so often we are afraid our prayers are futile. The addiction remains. We want to get a job, or a promotion, or a raise, but we suspect that God has better things to do than answer our prayers. We don't get what we want, and we wonder why God doesn't answer our prayers.

God will answer our heartfelt prayers if we believe those prayers. Too often we see our prayers as requests or suggestions, but not as prayers. Has the time come for us to accept that too often there is insufficient faith behind the words we offer in prayer?

How can we put more faith into our prayers?

Saturday of the Eighth Week in Ordinary Time

> As he was walking in the temple precincts
> the chief priests, the scribes, and the elders
> approached him and said to him,
> "On what authority are you doing these things?
> Who has given you the power to do them?"
> Mk 11: 27 – 33

When it came to the Jewish religion who had the power and the authority?

The very same people who were challenging Jesus had the power and the authority – the chief priests, the scribes, and the elders of the people.

What these people were really saying is we have not given you permission to be doing the things you are doing.

They were losing control; their power and authority were slipping away from them. Jesus was giving sight to the blind, he was helping the lame to walk, the mute to speak and the deaf to hear. In other words, Jesus was performing all the things that the Messiah would do, but the chief priests, the scribes, and the elders of the people could not see those signs. They could not see the Messiah. All they could see is that they were being diminished.

Too often we are like the chief priests, scribes, and the elders of the people; we question the process rather than embrace the result.

Where does our faith need to be better focused?

Ninth Sunday in Ordinary Time (A)

> "Anyone who hears my words and puts them into practice
> is like the wise man who built his house on rock.
> When the rainy season set in, torrents came
> and the winds blew and buffeted his house.
> It did not collapse;
> it had been solidly set on rock."
> Mt 7: 21 – 27

There are two parts to our faith – believing and doing. Too often we give lip service to our faith. We say our prayers, and we go to church. We neglect to live what we say we believe. We pray, but we hold grudges and withhold forgiveness. We go to church, but we neglect the needs of the marginalized. Or it can be the other way around. We are very forgiving, but we never pray. We are very active in peace and justice issues, but are too busy to worship on Sunday.

A union carpenter from Chicago was part of an exchange program with carpenters in Poland. While on a visit to Poland he was assigned a guide for the program. After a few days they got into a rather personal conversation. The man from Chicago asked his guide if he was a communist. The man thought for a few moments and then said, "Yes. Practicing but not believing." The American had another question for him, "Are you a Catholic?" There was another pause and then the guide said, "Yes. Believing but not practicing." Turns out the guide was neither a good communist nor a good Catholic. Neither his soul nor his life was built on rock!

Is our faith one dimensional or two dimensional?

Ninth Sunday in Ordinary Time (B)

> They kept an eye on Jesus to see whether
> he would heal him on the Sabbath,
> hoping to be able to bring an accusation against him.
> He addressed the man with the shriveled hand:
> "Stand up here in front."
> Then he said to them:
> "Is it permitted to do a good deed on the Sabbath –
> or an evil one?
> To preserve a life – or to destroy it?"
> At this they remained silent.
> He looked around at them angrily,
> for he was deeply grieved that they had closed
> their minds against him.
> Then he said to the man, "Stretch out your hand."
> The man did and his hand was perfectly restored.
> When the Pharisees went outside,
> they immediately began to plot with the
> Herodians on how they might destroy him.
> Mk 2: 23 – 3: 6

Rules are meant to be broken. There is no rule that does not have an exception. There may be disagreement on what the exception is, but there is always at least one if not more.

Was keeping the Sabbath holy important? Of course it was. Jesus, the Pharisees, and the Herodians would agree on that. Where they disagreed was whether healing was a holy or an unholy activity. Jesus believed healing was holy, and, therefore, did not violate the Sabbath. The Pharisees and Herodians believed that healing should be confined to the other six days of the week. As Jesus says elsewhere in Scripture, "The Sabbath was made for man; man was not made for the Sabbath." Priorities are important.

Whenever a penitent confesses that they missed Mass on Sunday, I always ask if there was a reason. I am always stunned when they say, "I was in the hospital." How can anyone think that is a sin? Yes there is an obligation to attend Mass on all Sundays and holydays but that obligation is not absolute. All rules need to be filtered through common sense.

Where are we too black and white when it comes to rules?

Ninth Sunday in Ordinary Time (C)

> A centurion had a servant he held in high regard,
> who was at that moment sick to the point of death.
> When he heard about Jesus he sent some Jewish elders to him,
> asking him to come and save the life of his servant.
> Upon approaching Jesus they petitioned him earnestly,
> "He deserves this favor from you," they said,
> "because he loves our people, and even built our synagogue for us."
> Jesus set out with them.
> Lk 7: 1 – 10

The last part of today's gospel passage is the inspiration for the prayer we say just before receiving communion, "I am not worthy for you to enter under my roof, say but the word and my soul will be healed." I have already written a reflection on those powerful words.

Today I want to reflect on the centurion. He was certainly an outstanding person. He goes out of his way to take care of his servant. He was a man of empathy. His servant was not a possession; he was someone for whom he cared a great deal.

He was part of the occupying Roman army, but even there he was different. Remember what the elders said of him, "He loves our people." Occupying armies don't love the people they rule. He did more than love them, he built a house of prayer for them. He was obviously an outstanding person.

There is a saying that applies to the centurion, "Always do the best you can, and then some." He was not one to rest on his laurels. We need to follow his example.

Where do we need to live our faith better? What is the "then some" we need to be about?

Monday of the Ninth Week in Ordinary Time

> Jesus began to speak to the chief priests, the scribes,
> and the elders in parables.
> "A man planted a vineyard, put a hedge around it, dug a wine press,
> and built a tower.
> Then he leased it to tenant farmers and left on a journey.
> At the proper time he sent a servant to the tenants to obtain
> from them some of the produce of the vineyard."
> Mk 12: 1 – 12

Too often we think of parables as nice little stories, and sometimes they are. But not always. One theologian summed up the power of parables this way, "Jesus told parables and they put him to death." Today's gospel parable would be a reason why that is true.

Today's parable is the story of the chosen people. God put his people in charge of his vineyard. He was the owner; they were not. The owed him his share of the produce, but they did not want to pay. Then God out of desperation sent his son to collect what was owed to him. They dragged the son outside of the vineyard, and they killed him. Sound familiar?

The chief priests, scribes, and elders knew the parable was about them, and how they would reject Jesus as the messiah, and kill him. It would be convenient for us if the parable were meant only for the scribes, chief priests, and elders, but that is not the case. God has entrusted his vineyard (the world) to us. We are stewards of his creation, and we are not always good stewards. We are in the process of ravaging our environment, and we think we can because it is our world. It is not. As Pope Francis reminds us in *Laudati Si*, we need to take better care of what has been entrusted to us.

What change can we make in our daily routine that will enrich rather than deplete our world?

Tuesday of the Ninth Week in Ordinary Time

> They came and said to him,
> "Teacher, we know that you are a truthful man
> and that you are not concerned with anyone's opinion.
> You do not regard a person's status
> but teach the way of God in accordance with the truth.
> Is it lawful to pay the census tax to Caesar or not?"
> Mk 12: 13 – 17

Jesus should have said to the Pharisees and Herodians, "Psalm 12, verse 2 and 3" and walked away. I will save you the trouble of running for your Bible. Here is what that reference says, "Help, Lord, for no one loyal remains; the faithful have vanished from the children of men. They tell lies to one another, speak with deceiving lips and a double heart."

Jesus knew to be suspect of their flattery. They were just setting him up, but Jesus flipped the scene on them. It was idolatry for them to have a coin with Caesar's image on it, but they had one anyway. Jesus, having flushed them out, then gives the simplest response, "Repay to Caesar what belongs to Caesar and to God what belongs to God." Unfortunately, the issue of the separation of Church and State is still a lively issue in our day and age, and will continue to be for the foreseeable future. A simpler answer would have been, "Figure out what belongs to God first and everything else will fall into place." If we put God first, then our lives will be rightly ordered.

Where are we giving God what is left over in our lives?

Wednesday of the Ninth Week in Ordinary Time

> "As for the dead being raised,
> Have you not read in the book of Moses,
> in the passage about the bush, how God told him,
> *'I am the God of Abraham, the God of Isaac, and the God of Jacob?'*

> He is not God of the dead but of the living.
> You are greatly misled."
> Mk 12: 18 – 27

Our God is the God of the living. Our faith should be life-giving; our church should be the same. Change is the only true sign of life. Too often our faith and our church are known for rigidity, and not for change. Too often we look to the past rather than to the future. Give me that old time religion is more than a song.

Jesus, throughout his life, taught, "The Sabbath was made for man, not man for the Sabbath." The Pharisees of his time, like the Pharisees of today, were more interested in controlling people than teaching and leading them.

Under the leadership of Pope Francis we are rediscovering what a living faith means. He expressed the best and most concrete expression of the change that needs to happen in our church when he said he wanted priests to be, "shepherds living with the smell of the sheep."

Francis has brought the touch of "the common man" to the highest office in our church. He eschews the lavish trappings of his office. He is the Bishop of Rome living with and inspiring his people, both in Rome and throughout the world, to discover and share the God of the living.

Where in our lives of faith do we need to imitate the living faith of Pope Francis?

Thursday of the Ninth Week in Ordinary Time

> One of the scribes came to Jesus and asked him,
> "Which is the first of all the commandments?"
> Jesus replied, 'The first is this:
> *Hear, O Israel!*
> *The Lord our God is Lord alone!*
> *You shall love the Lord your God with all your heart,*
> *With all your soul, with all your mind,*
> *And with all your strength.*

> The second is this:
> *You shall love your neighbor as yourself.'"*
> Mk 12: 28 – 34

The scribe is trying to trip up Jesus, but Jesus is just too nimble to be lured into the trap. First of all Jesus quotes directly from Deuteronomy, chapter 6, verse 2. It is hard to argue with a direct quote from the Hebrew Scriptures. Every member of the Jewish faith knew this quote by heart. This quote is called the Schema of Israel. Jesus states the obvious. God loves us and we need to love God back with all we've got, all of our heart, mind, soul, and strength. God is the lover; all we have to do is love him back with all we've got.

But is that enough? Jesus says, "No!" What does it mean if we love God with our whole being, but don't love our neighbor or ourselves? Love of God that is not translated into our everyday interactions makes no sense. If we love God and God loves us, then we need to trust his love. Sometimes I think it is harder to love ourselves than it is to love our neighbor. Many of us are too hard on ourselves. We focus too intently on what is wrong with us rather than focus on the fact that God loves us. He does not love us provisionally or conditionally. No! He loves us as we are. It is not that he does not see our faults; he chooses not to dwell on then. If God does that for us, we need to do that for one another.

How can we love ourselves better?
(I know you want to focus on how we can love God and neighbor better, but I think that is the wrong starting point.)

Friday of the Ninth Week in Ordinary Time

> As Jesus was teaching in the temple area he said,
> "How do the scribes claim that Christ is the son of David?
> David himself, inspired by the Holy Spirit, said:
> 'The Lord said to my lord,
> "Sit at my right hand
> until I place your enemies under your feet."

> David himself calls him 'Lord';
> so how is he his son?"
> The great crowd heard this with delight."
> Mk 12: 35 – 37

Usually it is the scribes and the Pharisees who are asking the trick questions. Today it's Jesus' turn.

Most ordinary people were afraid of the scribes and the Pharisees. They held positions of both honor and power. But over time they had grown aloof; they lost the ability to see that they were called to serve the people. Remember when Jesus said to the scribes and Pharisees, "Woe to you Pharisees! You love the seats of honor in synagogues and greetings in marketplaces"…Then one of the scholars of the law said to him in reply, "Teacher, by saying this you are insulting us too." And he said, "Woe also to you scholars of the law! You impose on people burdens hard to carry, but you yourselves do not lift one finger to help them." (Lk 11: 43 – 47) In today's gospel, Jesus is much less strident, but is nevertheless calling them to repentance.

Jesus gives us, as always, a new teaching. "Sit at my right hand until I place your enemies under your feet." What a great image. Triumph over our enemies. We can crush them. Jesus and the scribes and Pharisees were enemies, but Jesus did not want to crush then. He wanted the scribes and Pharisees to repent, and he lovingly calls them to that repentance.

Where do we need to love those people who have become our enemies?

Saturday of the Ninth Week in Ordinary Time

> He sat down opposite the treasury
> and observed how the crowd put money into the treasury.
> Many rich people put in large sums.
> A poor widow also came
> and put in two small coins worth a few cents.
> Calling his disciples to himself, he said to them,
> "Amen, I say to you, this poor widow put in more

> than all the other contributors to the treasury.
> For they have all contributed from their surplus wealth,
> But she, from her poverty, has contributed all she had,
> her whole livelihood."
> Mk 12: 38 – 44

Generosity is a funny thing. Some people just seem to be more generous than others. And how much people have is seldom an accurate indicator of how generous they will be. Being a pastor has validated this observation over and over again.

A parish was having a capital campaign to renovate the parish church. One very affluent member of the parish had not given a gift so the pastor paid him a visit to ask for his gift. The parishioner greeted the pastor, and after a bit of chit chat the pastor made his request for a large donation. After a brief pause the man said to him, "Father are you aware that my mother is very ill and needs care twenty-four hours a day? Are you aware that my sister's husband recently died of cancer without benefit of life insurance and is constantly asking me to help her and her four children? Or that my blind brother is constantly asking for my financial help?" The room was silent, and the pastor struggled to say something.

Before he could the man said, "And if I don't give them any help, why do you think I will be giving to our parish campaign?"

People who don't have a lot usually are more generous than those who are more fortunate, but not always.

How can we more generously share our time, talent, and treasure?

Sunday of the Tenth Week in Ordinary Time (A)

> As Jesus passed on from there, he saw
> a man named Matthew sitting at the customs post.
> He said to him, "follow me."
> And he got up and followed him.
> While he was at table in his house,
> many tax collectors and sinners came and sat

> with Jesus and his disciples.
> The Pharisees saw this and said to his disciples,
> "Why does your teacher eat with tax collectors and sinners?"
> He heard this and said, "Those who are well
> do not need a physician, but the sick do."
> Mt 9: 9 – 13

Matthew has a conversion experience. He is called, and like Peter and Andrew, James and John before him, he abandons his livelihood and chooses a new direction for his life. The Pharisees would do well to imitate Matthew's behavior. Would that they had abandoned their judgmental ways and had learned to look at people in new ways. All they can see is "tax collectors and sinners." Jesus looks at Matthew and sees his future not his past; the Pharisees are so locked in to his past they cannot imagine that he even has a future.

There is a great story about Michelangelo and his magnificent statue of David. The block of marble from which it was chiseled had been ignored for years because of a flaw. Only a genius like Michelangelo could see the bend in David's leg. He turned a flaw into a work of art. Jesus had that same genius that helped him see goodness where others could only see flaws! He does it over and over in the New Testament, and he does it every day in our lives. He refuses to fixate on our flaws; he only has time for our success. It is not just beauty that is in the eye of the beholder; goodness finds a home there as well. We need to look at our lives and the lives of those around us as Jesus does.

How can we better see the goodness that others try to hide?

Sunday of the Tenth Week in Ordinary Time (B)

> Summoning them,
> he began to speak to them in parables,
> "How can Satan drive out Satan?
> If a kingdom is divided against itself,
> that kingdom cannot stand.
> And if a house is divided against itself,

> that house will not be able to stand.
> And if Satan has risen up against himself and is divided
> he cannot stand; that is the end of him."
> Mk 3: 20 – 35

Division is always a scandal. Be it a family, a business, a church, a political party, or a neighborhood that is fractured, it is always a scandal. Right now our church is scandalously fractured. We have Pope Francis who is patiently trying to steer the church in a new direction. There are some who will not rest until they block his every move. Presently, he is trying to introduce synodality into our church structures. He has the courage to believe that all believers should be given a chance to share their vision of how the church needs to change in order to continue to guide people on their journeys of faith. Too many of those who presently wield power in the church see this as a foolish idea. Like Francis, they know the influence of the church is waning, but they have convinced themselves that a smaller church will be a more faithful church even though there is no evidence or hard data to back up this belief. Francis believes a church that is open to the needs of the baptized and reaches out to them with compassion and understanding is the church of the future. Francis wants to walk with the People of God; too many others want to tell the People of God where to walk. The schism that is growing in our church is indeed a scandal.

What can we do to re-establish the unity that Jesus wants for his Church?

Sunday of the Tenth Week of Ordinary Time (C)

> Soon afterward he journeyed to a city called Naim,
> and his disciples and a large crowd accompanied him.
> As he drew near to the gate of the city,
> a man who had died was being carried out,
> the only son of his mother, and she was a widow.
> A large crowd from the city was with her.
> Lk 7: 11 – 17

I am not sure when it dawned on me that the Widow of Naim and the Widow of Nazareth faced the same hardship. Mary would one day be called upon to bury her only son as a widow. The only difference is that there would be no one to intervene to lighten her load. Well that is not entirely true, is it? Jesus would intervene. In John's gospel we are told that from the cross, "When Jesus saw his mother and the disciple there whom he loved, he said to his mother, 'Woman, behold your son.' Then he said to the disciple, 'Behold, your mother.' And from that hour the disciple took her into his home" (Jn 19: 26 – 27). This was Jesus' way of living out, "Where there's a will, there's a way."

Just like Jesus we need to be ever vigilant in searching for creative ways to live out our faith. When confronted with a difficult situation, we try to come up with a solution but often we give up too easily. What we need to do when our faith is challenged by a difficult problem is ask Jesus and his mother to inspire us to be more creative.

Where have we avoided creative thinking when it comes to living out our faith?

Monday of the Tenth Week in Ordinary Time

> Blessed are they who are persecuted for the sake of righteousness,
> for theirs is the Kingdom of heaven.
> Blessed are you when they insult you and persecute you
> and utter every kind of evil against you falsely because of me.
> Rejoice and be glad,
> for your reward will be great in heaven.
> Mt 5: 1 – 12

I've been insulted more than once, people have spoken ill of me and my views, but I've never been persecuted. And I must say I am still working at rejoicing when the insults and ill speech come my way. I suspect that I am not alone.

My reward in heaven is guaranteed as is yours. Nevertheless, the whole reality of heaven as a reward does not work for me. Heaven is a gift not a reward. We don't earn a place in heaven; Jesus gives it to us as a gift. I remember having a long and serious conversation about heaven with a friend. He was more invested in heaven than I was or am. I remember the look on his face when I said, "I when I breathe my last if all I hear is someone laughing, that would be fine with me."

No one should do what is right because she expects a reward. We should do right because it is the right thing to do. When we think we "earn" our place in heaven, we are going down the wrong path. God loves us, died for us, was raised for us, and he opened the gates of heaven for us. We can't earn a place there; we can only lose our place there.

How can we thank God for heaven, and stop trying to earn our way there?

Tuesday of the Tenth Week in Ordinary Time

> "Just so, your light must shine before others,
> That they may see your good deeds
> and glorify your heavenly Father."
> Mt 5: 13 – 16

We represent God wherever we go. Where we walk, God is either more or less present. Whenever we speak, we either bring the light of God's love or the darkness of Satan's hate.

When my brothers and I were growing up our parents made it very clear to us that we should never disgrace our family name. It was, and still is, sage advice. We have another name that we should never disgrace. That name is Christian. We are Christians, Catholic Christians, and our lives should give dynamic witness to how God's love is transforming our lives.

When we are confronted with the opportunity to forgive or seek revenge, we need to act in a way that glorifies God. When we can be selfish or selfless, we know which to choose. Whose needs come first, ours or our neighbors? Micah the prophet said it best, "You have been told, O mortal, what is good, and what the Lord requires of you: only to do justice, to love goodness, and to walk humbly with your God." (Micah 6: 8) We have been told how to live so that God is glorified by our deeds. All we have to do is do it.

Where in our lives can we give more witness to God being at work in us?

Wednesday of the Tenth Week in Ordinary Time

Jesus said to his disciples:
"Do not think that I have come to abolish the law or the prophets.
I have come not to abolish but to fulfill.
Amen, I say to you, until heaven and earth pass away,
Not the smallest letter or the smallest part of a letter
will pass from the law,
until all things have taken place."
Mt 5: 17 – 19

Legalists love today's reading because they can twist it to serve their agenda. Fortunately, Jesus was not endorsing their very limited agenda. In fact, Jesus was taking the long view. He knew that the law and the prophets existed for a reason. The law was to guide the chosen people; the prophets were to call the wayward back to the ways of God.

The law and the prophets were not God; they were to lead people to God. The chosen people should have known that things had gotten out of hand when they needed a special group of people to interpret the law. They should have known something was wrong, when instead of listening to the prophets, they killed them.

When Jesus told his disciples, "I am the way, the truth, and the life" he was telling his followers that he was the fulfillment of both the law and the prophets, and that from then forward he was the way that led to God. His law was "love one another." His prophetic message was, "Repent for the Kingdom of God is at hand." And like the prophets who preceded him, they tried to silence him by killing him. That just made his voice louder.

Have we truly let Jesus be our way, truth, and life?

Thursday of the Tenth Week in Ordinary Time

> Therefore, if you bring your gift to the altar,
> and there recall that your brother
> has anything against you,
> leave your gift there at the altar,
> go first and be reconciled with your brother,
> and then come and offer your gift.
> Mt 5: 20 – 26

Surely Jesus must have been misquoted. I am sure what he meant to say was, "If you bring your gift to the altar and there recall that you have something against your sister or brother…" go and straighten it out, and then offer your gift. That is what you and I would say and do, but Jesus, as always, goes a step farther. He wants us to engage in "normal" forgiveness, but he also wants us to practice "extraordinary" forgiveness as well.

What Jesus is teaching us is what he has shared with us – unconditional forgiveness! He does not want us to get bogged down in casuistry. He does not want us to evaluate the veracity of what a brother or sister has against us. He just wants us to ask for forgiveness. Why? Because Jesus knows that the better we get at asking for forgiveness, the better we will be at extending forgiveness. Forgiveness is the original "pay it forward" virtue.

Do we have a broken relationship that is crying out for healing?

Friday of the Tenth Week in Ordinary Times

> If your right eye causes you to sin,
> tear it out and throw it away.
> It is better to lose one of your members
> than to have your whole body thrown into Gehenna.
> If your right hand causes you to sin,
> cut it off and throw it away.
> Mt 5: 27 – 32

I'm not sure how you sin with one eye and not the other, or, for that matter, with one hand and not the other. Jesus is not teaching biology; he is teaching salvation.

We are all experts with the obstacles to salvation. Sin is highly personal. What is a temptation for one person can be an invitation for virtue for another. Every now and again there will be a story in the news of a person who finds a wallet full of money, and returns it to its rightful owner. When that happens, we can be sure that the finder had to wrestle a bit with her conscience. Should she keep it, or turn it in? For others there is no wrestling at all. For them it is, "Finders keepers; losers weepers." The first group have their eyes clearly fixed on the Kingdom to come. The second group are interested in the here and now. The long view is always the better view.

A disciplined approach to food is, "A minute in my mouth, an hour in my stomach, but a lifetime on my hips." Same is true for sin, "A minute of pleasure, an hour of gratification, but a lifetime in hell."

Which will it be for us?

Saturday of the Tenth Week in Ordinary Time

> "Do not swear by your head,
> for you cannot make a single hair white or black.
> Let your, 'Yes' mean 'Yes,' and your 'No' mean 'No.'
> Anything more is from the evil one."
> Mt 5: 33 – 37

Giving your word used to mean something. That seems to be fading. We couch our words; we dull them. It used to be easier to separate fact from fiction, or truth from lies. Now we call lies misinformation, and believe that distinction means something. It doesn't.

If we don't like something we are told, we can dismiss it as fake news. But something is fake because it is made up, not because we don't agree with it. Athletes sign letters of intent, but then change their minds. Coaches have three or five year contracts, but nevertheless they walk out on the contract if they get a better offer. We all know at least one person who freely gives us his word, and we know that word is worthless.

Jesus offers us a simple solution to the confusion we create with words. Mean what you say, and say what you mean. Nothing is more simple, or straightforward, than that.

Where in our lives do we need to live up to the faith words we so too easily speak?

Eleventh Sunday in Ordinary Time (A)

> At the sight of the crowds, the heart of Jesus
> was moved with pity.
> They were lying prostrate from exhaustion,
> like sheep without a shepherd.
> He said to his disciples:
> "The harvest is good but laborers are scarce.
> Beg the harvest master to send out laborers to gather his harvest."
> Mt 9: 36 – 10: 8

Whenever there is a Mass to pray for vocations this gospel or one of its synoptic cousins is always read. Unfortunately, that just demonstrates that the church has historically narrowed the definition of a Christian vocation. We have been conditioned to think of a religious vocation as a call to serve as a priest, or a religious sister or brother.

Fact of the matter is that every baptized person has a religious vocation. To be a wife or a husband is a religious vocation. To be a teacher or a nurse is a religious vocation. Plumbers, electricians, mechanics, first responders, and landscapers are all living out their call from God. Once we rediscover this wider notion of vocation our church will be both more vibrant and more engaged. Clericalism will diminish; involvement will increase.

We don't need more laborers to do God's work; we need to empower the laborers God had already sent to gather his harvest.

How can we live our vocation more fully?

Eleventh Sunday in Ordinary Time (B)

> He went on to say:
> "What comparison shall we use for the reign of God?
> What image will help to present it?
> It is like a mustard seed which,
> when planted in the soil, is the smallest of all the earth's seeds,
> yet once it is sown, springs up to become the largest of shrubs,
> whose branches are big enough for the birds of the sky
> to build nests in its shade."
> Mk 4: 26 – 34

The seed of faith is planted in our hearts at Baptism, and slowly it begins to grow. Our parents lovingly and patiently taught us how to make the sign of the cross. It took a while, but finally we got it right. Then came the Hail Mary followed by the Our Father. In due time came First Communion, and we entered into a lifetime of letting Jesus enrich and nourish us. Because our sacramental life is always evolving our faith must evolve as well. We are enriched by the gifts of the Holy Spirit in Confirmation; we are forgiven our sins in Reconciliation. For many life's journey is anchored in either Holy Orders or Marriage.

Remember our faith grows only if we live it fully. Each day we are invited to get lost in the mystery of God's love. We are part of something much greater than our efforts. The Church in every age receives the gift of faith, a living faith. Unfortunately, there is the temptation to safeguard that faith, to protect it from growing. Sometimes the institutional church tries too hard to safeguard "the deposit of faith" and clings too much to the past. Sometimes we settle for the God we know and are afraid to experience God in new and better ways. Too often we lose the joy and excitement of our faith. Too often we exchange the adventures of faith for the security of religion. That is not how growth happens.

How can we be better risk takers with our faith?

Eleventh Sunday in Ordinary Time (C)

> He said to her then,
> "Your sins are forgiven,"
> at which his fellow guests began to ask among themselves,
> "Who is this that he even forgives sins?"
> Meanwhile he said to the woman,
> "Your faith has been your salvation. Go now in peace."
> Lk 7: 36 – 8: 3

At the beginning of today's gospel passage, Jesus is invited to dine at the home of a Pharisee. While he reclined at table, "A woman known in town to be a sinner," enters the scene. Imagine, being known around town as "a sinner." It is one thing to be aware of our sins, but something altogether different to be aware of another person's sins.

Hearing confessions is a very humbling reality. At the beginning of every confession I say, "May the Lord strengthen your faith that with courage you may confess your sins, and with loving kindness you may receive his forgiveness." Then I listen to the penitent's confession, offer a bit of guidance, assign a penance, and give absolution. The last thing I say is, "Go now in peace."

The woman in today's gospel left the Pharisee's house not as a sinner, but as a new saint with a bright future. It would take both her and all the people of the town awhile to figure her new life out, but at least she was off to a good start. We don't need to drag our past sins around with us. God will lighten our burden.

What sins do we need to bring to God in confession?

Monday of the Eleventh Week in Ordinary Time

> Jesus said to his disciples:
> "You have heard it said,
> *An eye for an eye and a tooth for a tooth.*
> But I say to you, offer no resistance to one who is evil.

> When someone strikes you on your right cheek,
> turn the other cheek to him as well."
> Mt 5: 38 – 42

"An eye for an eye, and a tooth for a tooth" when it is quoted today is usually an excuse for why it is all right to seek revenge. Nothing could be further from that saying's original meaning. This quote, known as the Law of the Talon (lex talionis), was contained in early Babylonian law, and was later incorporated into biblical and Roman law as well. It was created to make sure that those who sought punishment or revenge did not go overboard. The punishment should match the offense.

Jesus wants us to use the Law of the Talon as a starting point not an end point. Jesus is saying don't seek revenge. Offer forgiveness. When today's quote is put in that context then the "turn the other cheek" admonition becomes the end, and not the starting point.

Jesus has already arrived at the point of unconditional forgiveness. Dying on the cross, he asks his Father to "forgive them for they do not know what they are doing." Most of us are not there yet; many of us will never get there. What is important is that we do not give up believing that, like our Savior, we can grow strong enough to offer forgiveness rather than to seek revenge.

Where are we presently withholding forgiveness in our lives?

Tuesday of the Eleventh Week in Ordinary Time

> Jesus said to his disciples:
> "You have heard that it was said,
> *You shall love your neighbor and hate your enemy.*
> But I say to you, love your enemies
> and pray for those who persecute you,
> that you may be children of your heavenly Father,
> for he makes his sun rise on the bad and the good,
> and causes rain to fall on the just and the unjust."
> Mt 5: 43 – 48

Jesus never wants us to stop at the usual places. Society has set up certain rules or customs that are meant to guide people to live good lives. But Jesus does not want us to just live good lives, he wants us to imitate him. He wants us to be "perfect as our heavenly Father is perfect."

Jesus will not be satisfied until we are the best people we can be. How do we become the best? We never give up; we don't let ourselves be satisfied. There is always more we can do.

Too often we learn to settle. We have our dreams and our goals, but we are not fanatical about them. We file them under "It would be nice if, but…" Jesus does not just want us to love our enemies; he doesn't want us to have enemies at all. He does not want us to lash out at those who persecute us; he wants us to pray for them.

Jesus knows that love conquers all, and he will not let up on us until we live in and by the power of his love. We could never live up to Jesus' standards without his presence in our lives. He is with us as we strive for perfection.

Where have we prevented the light of God's love from shining on those who hurt us?

Wednesday of the Eleventh Week in Ordinary Time

Jesus said to his disciples:
"Take care not to perform righteous deeds
in order that people may see them;
otherwise you will have no recompense from your heavenly Father.
Mt 6: 1 – 6, 16 – 18

The best sermons are the ones that don't require words. There is a quote, falsely attributed to St. Francis of Assisi, that says as much, "Preach the Gospel at all times and if necessary use words."

It all comes down to words and deeds. Words that don't lead to action are hollow. Deeds not rooted in principle are likewise hollow. What Jesus is exhorting us to do in today's Gospel is to translate our faith into action. To do what we do because it is the right thing to do not to reap some future reward.

When we are getting our picture taken, someone always says, "smile." But since a commanded smile always looks phony, we are told to say, "cheese" which produces a sincere smile. What happens if someone says to us, "look religious." After a brief hesitation, we would fold our hands, cast our eyes toward heaven, and tilt our head to the side. And that would look phony, indeed. We can't look religious; we can only be religious. We can't look like we believe in God; we can only act like we believe in God. Let's not worry what "being religious" looks like. Let's just trust that God knows what is in our hearts.

Where can we be more sincere in living our faith?

Thursday of the Eleventh Week in Ordinary Time

> Jesus said to his disciples:
> "In praying, do not babble like the pagans,
> who think that they will be heard because of their many words.
> Do not be like them.
> Your Father knows what you need before you ask him."
> Mt 6: 7 – 15

"Babel" is a great word. We get it from the Genesis story of the Tower of Babel, (Gn 11: 1 – 9) a story that explains why language too often separates rather than unites us. It is also a great word because it sounds like what it means, which linguists call an onomatopoeic word.

When we pray too often we babel, which happens because, I think, we feel that our prayers are inadequate. The prayers of others are fine, but ours always seem to fall short. Almost everyone I know has a favorite prayer, and it is always someone else's prayer. We just do not trust our words when it comes to God.

This happens because we focus on ourselves rather than on God. God is our loving creator. He knows us inside and out. He has the habit of filling in the gaps in our lives. He focuses on what we get right not on what we get wrong. So when it comes to praying we need to give up trying to fashion the perfect prayer, and learn how to trust that God will listen with loving patience, and hear what we are trying to say. When it comes to prayer, we should let God do all the heavy lifting.

How would our prayer life change if we would just trust that God listens better than we speak?

Friday of the Eleventh Week in Ordinary Time

> Jesus said to his disciples:
> "Do not lay up for yourselves an earthly treasure.
> Moths and rust corrode; thieves break in and steal.
> Make it your practice instead to store up heavenly treasure,
> which neither moths nor rust corrode nor
> thieves break in and steal.
> Remember where your treasure is,
> There your heart is also."
> Mt 6: 19 – 23

What do we really treasure? What captures our attention?

Every now and again I will pull into a store parking lot and there I will see a brand new car parked diagonally across two parking spaces. The owner of that car is clearly saying, "I treasure my car more than your convenience." Very few people would be so crass as to say that out loud, but, then again, actions speak louder than words.

Relationships should be treasured more than possessions. Nevertheless, we have all seen families torn apart when someone dies and there is a squabble over a desk or a chair. Really a desk or a chair, should that be enough for people to stop speaking?

A good friend of mine had to go into a rehabilitation facility after she fell at home. Several weeks after she was home she discovered that some of her jewelry had been stolen. One of the rings had been her mother's, another had been her grandmother's. She did not know what the rings were worth. She never had them appraised. What broke her heart was the loss of memories that the rings gave to her. Her loss was personal not financial. Her heart was in the right place.

Where are our hearts rooted?

Saturday of the Eleventh Week in Ordinary Time

> Jesus said to his disciples,
> "No man can serve two masters.
> He will either hate one and love the other
> Or be attentive to one and despise the other.
> You cannot give yourself to God and money.
> I warn you, then:
> do not worry about your livelihood,
> what you are to eat or drink or use for clothing.
> Is not life more than food?
> Is not the body more valuable than clothes?"
> Mt 6: 23 – 34

Oh to be able to live in a black and white world! We don't live in a love or hate world; we live in a like and like world. In that world, we can like God, and like money. We live in a gray world. Unfortunately, a gray world is not the real world.

Even in our gray world, decisions ultimately have to be made. What happens when the money we like is in conflict with the God we like? In the end, we are going to like one more than the other, and the one we like more will rule our decisions.

Two ministers were vacationing in Europe. Every day they visited another magnificent church. After one such visit, one minister said to his fellow minister, "How come we don't build churches like this anymore?" His friend paused for a few thoughtful moments, and then replied, "You don't build churches like this on opinions." When our faith becomes an opinion rather than a conviction everyone loses. When convenience replaces conviction, we, and the world in which we live, are impoverished. Indeed, we cannot serve two masters because one master will always outrank the other.

Where have we let our faith be an opinion rather than a conviction?

Twelfth Sunday in Ordinary Time (A)

> Jesus said to the Twelve:
> "Fear no one.
> Nothing is concealed that will not be revealed,
> nor secret that will not be known.
> What I say to you in the darkness, speak in the light;
> what you hear whispered, proclaim on the housetops."
> Mt 10: 26 – 33

Eventually everything comes to light. People go to great lengths to hide things from other people. Eventually all is revealed. People lie on their resumes; the truth always prevails. Why do people think they will get away with making stuff up?

We keep secrets; we convince ourselves that others are better off not knowing our secrets. Maybe they are, but who are we to decide. God blesses us every day with the light of his love; too often we prefer to linger in the shadows of prejudice. We whisper our nasty comments, and get embarrassed when we realize that someone has heard our pettiness.

In our relationship with God, we are free to be ourselves. We don't have to hide anything; God knows everything about us. He knows the good we do, and the bad we do. But he still loves us. I remember saying in a homily once that there was nothing I could ever do that would cause my parents to stop loving me. Oh, I could hurt them, disappoint them, cause them to shake their heads, but they would always love me. Real friends are like that as well. It is wonderful to have people who just accept us as we are. We don't have to be someone; we just have to be ourselves.

We cannot earn what is freely given. Why do we still think we have to earn God's love?

Twelfth Sunday in Ordinary Time (B)

> It happened that a squall blew up.
> The waves were over the boat and it began to ship water badly.

> Jesus was in the stern through it all,
> Sound asleep on a cushion.
> They finally woke him and said to him,
> "Teacher, doesn't it matter to you that we are going to drown?"
> He awoke and rebuked the wind and said to the sea:
> "Quiet! Be still!"
> The wind fell off and everything grew calm.
> Mk 4: 35 – 41

We have almost no idea how much time Jesus spent on boats with his disciples, but we know that Peter and Andrew, James and John were seasoned fishermen. They knew their way around boats, and they knew about sudden squalls. I assume that initially they were glad that Jesus was asleep. If he were awake he would probably get seasick or, at the very least, get very nervous. Leave well enough alone; let him stay asleep. But then things changed. This was more than a sudden squall. There was a real chance that their boat was going to sink.

Then they do what you and I do all the time. We blame God when things go wrong. "Don't you care that we are going to drown?" they ask. He was asleep; he did not know they were going to sink. When all else fails, ask God for help. We tell ourselves that God knows everything; he knows we need help. We should not have to ask for help; God should just intervene.

God will not always rescue us. We need to ask for his help, but more than asking for help, we need to ask God to make us strong enough to accept his will.

Why do we wait so long to ask for God's help?

Twelfth Sunday in Ordinary Time (C)

> One day when Jesus was praying in seclusion
> and his disciples were with him,
> he put the question to them,
> "Who do the crowds say that I am?"
> Lk 9: 18 – 24

The gospel says Jesus was praying in seclusion and his disciples were with him. I thought I knew what seclusion was but apparently I was wrong. Jesus needed to find the time to pray so he found a semblance of seclusion. What is really important is that Jesus found the time to pray even in a situation that was not ideal. Prayer, not his schedule, dictated his prayer time.

In our hectic schedules prayer is often the first thing that gets eliminated. We need to learn from Jesus. We have to find a way to pray in our busyness. Maybe we just have time to say to ourselves, "Jesus have pity on me." Or perhaps we can just say a quick "thank you for this day." We could always shut off the radio when we are in our automobile, and our prayer could just be enjoying the silence.

We always seem to be able to find the time to be online. Why not give up five minutes of being electronically connected with others to be spiritually united with our God? The more time we find to pray to God, the more our lives will be grounded in what really matters.

How can we be better at finding time to pray?

Monday of the Twelfth Week in Ordinary Time.

> Why do you notice the splinter in your brother's eye
> but do not perceive the wooden beam in your own eye?
> How can you say to your brother,
> 'Let me remove that splinter from your eye.'
> while the wooden beam is in your eye?
> You hypocrite, remove the wooden beam from your eye first;
> then you will see clearly
> to remove the splinter from your brother's eye."
> Mt 7: 1 – 5

Whenever I go out to eat, I wonder about my fellow diners. I wonder if the mother with the three kids is a single mother or is her husband still at work. When I see a couple, I wonder are they celebrating an anniversary, a birthday, are they married or just friends, or is it just date night. Then I focus on behaviors that annoy me. Grown men who wear baseball hats indoors, people on cell phones, folks who don't remember to use their quiet voice, or those who are not respectful of the waitstaff.

I do all of this while engaging in conversation with my dinner companions. The only problem is if I did less wondering about the other people in the restaurant, I would pay better attention to my companions. I am bothered by the rudeness of others, but fail to see my own rudeness.

This reflection is in the first person because each one of us has our own beam. I cannot point out your splinter; you cannot point out mine. All of us are too critical of others, and too kind to ourselves.

Where do we need to be a little more focused on our bad behaviors?

Tuesday of the Twelfth Week in Ordinary Time

> "Enter through the narrow gate;
> for the gate is wide and the road broad that leads to destruction,
> and those who enter through it are many.
> How narrow the gate and constricted the road that leads to life.
> And those who find it are few.
> Mt 7: 6, 12- 14

C.K. Chesterton was fond of saying, "Christianity has not been tried and found wanting. Christianity has been found difficult and left untried." More often than not we know the correct thing to do; more often than not we don't do what is correct. In the seminary we used to joke about "the primrose path to perdition." More often than not we are better off not following the crowd because the crowd is lost.

We have allowed ourselves to believe there is a pill for every pain, that you can lose weight without diet or exercise, that we can learn without effort, etc. P.T. Barnum was correct, "There is a sucker born every minute." I always thought the quote ended with, "and two to take advantage of him." That's the way I always heard it but I can find no justification for that ending. I guess someone took advantage of me.

The surest way to succeed is to work hard. Be good to other people.

Mean what you say, and say what you mean. Most people don't plan to fail; they fail to plan. The road that leads to life may be narrow, but God, our faith, and our fellow believers will always guide us there.

Where have we left good undone because it was too difficult to do?

Wednesday of the Twelfth Week in Ordinary Time

> Jesus said to his disciples:
> "Be on guard against false prophets,
> who come to you in sheep's clothing
> but underneath are wolves on the prowl.
> You will know them by their deeds."
> Mt 7: 15 – 20

Somewhere in our brain is an alarm that should go off when things don't make sense. Actually the alarm does go off, but sometimes we ignore it. As the old saying goes, "When something is too good to be true, it is." Sometimes we want something to be true so badly that we ignore the warning signs.

Just look at how many people fall for Ponzi schemes. Why do they fall? Greed, pure and simple. The promise of incredibly high rates or returns blinds them from what can be logically sustained.

Sometimes our faith can be viewed as a Ponzi scheme. Sometimes we follow the preacher who says what we want to hear rather than the one who says what we need to hear. There is the gospel of prosperity, and the gospel of Jesus Christ. We know which one to be true but that is not always the one we follow. Dom Helder Camara, the Brazilian archbishop of Olinda and Recife who died in 1999, and whose cause for sainthood is underway, was fond of saying, "When I give food to the poor, they call me a saint. When I ask why the poor have no food, they call me a communist."

A prophet is not false because he says something I disagree with; he is a prophet when he forces me to listen to what has to change in my life. The job of a prophet, indeed the job of all believers, is "to comfort the disturbed, and to disturb the comfortable."

What true prophets have we tuned out of our lives?

Thursday of the Twelfth Week in Ordinary Time

> Everyone who listens to these words of mine and acts on them
> will be like a wise man who built his house on rock.
> The rain fell, the floods came,
> and the winds blew and buffeted the house.
> But, it did not collapse; it had been set solidly on rock.
> Mt 7: 21 – 29

Always it is about the foundation. If the foundation is sturdy, the building will be secure. That is true of buildings and it is true of people – the better the foundation the better the life. That is what parenting is all about. Giving children the foundation, the values, the principles, and the courage do always do what is right. Fortunately, parents don't have to go it alone. There are grandparents, aunts and uncles, brothers and sisters, cousins, teachers, coaches, scout leaders and other mentors who work hard to give us the tools we need to live well.

My father had a thing about our family name. He did not talk about it a lot, but he frequently sent his message by the choices he made and encouraged my brothers and me to make. Your signature is important. You don't get to sign everything you do but never forget that your name, your good name, goes on everything you do!

Never do anything to bring discredit to your family name. Too many people, through many generations, have added honor to that name. It is entrusted to you; it is precious. Make it more so.

What are we doing to make the name Christian more honored and precious?

Friday of the Twelfth Week in Ordinary Time

> When Jesus came down from the mountain,
> great crowds followed him.
> And then a leper approached, did him homage, and said,
> "Lord, if you wish, you can make me clean."

> He stretched out his hand, touched him, and said,
> "I will do it. Be made clean."
> Mt 8: 1 – 4

The most important thing that Jesus did in today's gospel is that he touched the leper. That was against the order of the day. Lepers were unclean; they lived in exile. The leper in today's gospel is a man of great courage. Against all customs of the time, he approached Jesus. He was tired of being unclean; he was tired of being an outcast. He wanted back into mainstream life. He was tired of living on the periphery of life. There is so much we don't know about him. Was the leper married, did the leper have children, what was his job before he was inflicted? We don't know.

What we do know is that Jesus felt his pain and knew his shame. He got involved. He healed the leper and sent the leper to reclaim his place in the community.

We need to learn from Jesus. We need to feel the shame and the pain of those who are forced to live on the fringes of society because of poverty, sickness, or prejudice. We have to reach out and touch those who are hurting.

Where are we afraid to get involved in easing the pain of others?

Saturday of the Twelfth Week in Ordinary Time

> When Jesus entered Capernaum,
> a centurion approached him and appealed to him, saying,
> "Lord, my servant is lying at home paralyzed, suffering dreadfully."
> He said to him, "I will come and cure him."
> The centurion said in reply,
> "Lord, I am not worthy to have you enter under my roof;
> only say the word and my servant will be healed."
> Mt. 8: 5-17

The centurion's recognition of the power that Jesus had to heal is powerful. He has power as a centurion, and he knows how to use it.

He gives orders and his soldiers carry them out. He wants Jesus to do the same thing. He encourages Jesus to command that his servant be healed, and that is what happened.

The centurion's request for healing has found its way into our celebration of the Eucharist. Just before communion we say, "Lord, I am not worthy for you to enter under my roof, say but the word and my soul will be healed." The amazing thing is that we have forgotten the context of the prayer and as a result we have made the words a prayer of humility rather than a proclamation of the transforming power of God's love.

None of us are worthy to receive communion, but all of us need God's love to heal and make us whole. We don't receive communion as a reward for being good. No, we receive communion because Jesus invites us to receive communion. Jesus does not ask that we be worthy. He asks that we be willing to let him help heal what is broken in our lives. We need Jesus if we are going to get better.

Where do we need the love of Jesus to heal what is broken in our lives?

Thirteenth Sunday in Ordinary Time (A)

Jesus said to his apostles:
"Whoever loves father or mother more than me is not worthy of me,
and whoever loves a son or daughter more than me
is not worthy of me;
and whoever does not take up his cross
and follow after me is not worthy of me.
Whoever finds his life will lose it,
and whoever loses his life for my sake will find it."
Mt 10: 37 – 42

Jesus is not in a competition for our love. He wants us to love him fully. So he uses examples that are meant to shock us. What is stronger than our love for our parents, or parents' love for their children? Nothing!

Love cannot be doled out in portions that are more or less. Love is just totally given. True love is not provisional or conditional. When it comes to love, we are blessed to be able to return what we have been given. Parents and God don't love because they expect something back. They love because that is a gift they are able to give.

Jesus' love led him to the cross where he seemed to lose his life. But instead of losing his life he found it. He found his glory; he fulfilled his mission. Parents sacrifice so much for their children. When we are infants our parents lose sleep. When we are adolescents, they lose sleep as they wait for us to come home. They work extra hours so we can have a better life. Parenting is not an investment; parenting is a choice. Both God and our parents show us how to put others first.

Where is God calling us to surrender our security in order to grow?

Thirteenth Sunday in Ordinary Time (B)

> Jesus took the child's father and mother and his own companions
> and entered the room where the child lay.
> Taking her hand he said to her,
> "Talitha, koum," which means, "Little girl, get up."
> The girl, a child of twelve, stood up immediately
> and began to walk around.
> At this the family's astonishment was complete.
> He enjoined them strictly not to let anyone know about it,
> and told them to give her something to eat.
> Mk 5: 21 – 43

It always amazes me how Jesus can be so out of it one minute and so down to earth the next. In today's gospel, Jesus heals a young girl who is very sick or he raises her from the dead. Either way, it was a big deal. There was no way people were not going to talk about it. Nevertheless, Jesus says, "Don't let anyone know about it." That is a great example of Jesus being out of it.

The very next minute, Jesus tells the parents to give the girl something to eat. That is an example of Jesus being down to earth. In all the commotion going on, with the pure delight of the parents seeing their daughter walking around perfectly healthy, they could have forgotten to feed her. But Jesus, the bachelor, tells them to give her something to eat. It just proves that Jesus was calm when everyone else was ecstatic. Jesus was doing what his Father sent him to do. He was demonstrating that he was the Messiah. He also knew that his signs and miracles could become the main focus and distract from his being the Messiah. He had to keep things in proper perspective. We need him to teach us how to keep things in proper perspective in our lives.

What is presently out of whack in our lives?

Thirteenth Sunday in Ordinary Time (C)

> To another Jesus said,
> "Come after me."
> The man said to him,
> "Let me bury my father first."
> Jesus said to him,
> "Let the dead bury the dead;
> come away and proclaim the kingdom of God."
> Yet another said to him,
> "I will be your follower, Lord, but first let
> me take leave of my people at home."
> Jesus answered him,
> "Whoever puts his hand to the plow
> but keeps looking back
> is unfit for the reign of God."
> Lk 9: 51 – 62

At first glance it sounds like Jesus is being harsh. But the fact is that all excuses are hollow. Why would anyone whose father just died be out listening to Jesus or anyone else for that matter? Why was he not at home with his family taking care of his father's burial? Remember in the Jewish tradition the deceased should be buried before sunset on the day of death. Asking for time to bury his father was an excuse pure and simple.

The same is true with asking for time to say goodbye to a family.

Jesus was not signing up disciples for a cloistered monastery; he was not asking them to go on a long journey. He was asking people to be followers. They would be home most nights with their family. So what we have is just another excuse.

Jesus wants his followers to focus on what is to come not what has already happened. He does not want excuses; he wants action. Jesus wants us to keep our eyes on the prize. He wants us to say "yes" to his call, but, too often, all we can muster is "maybe" or "I'll think about it."

What excuses do we use not to be better followers?

Monday of the Thirteenth Week in Ordinary Time

> A scribe approached him and said,
> "Teacher, wherever you go I will come after you."
> Jesus said to him,
> "The foxes have lairs, the birds in the sky have nests,
> but the Son of Man has nowhere to lay his head."
> Another, a disciple, said to him,
> "Lord, let me go and bury my father first."
> But Jesus said to him,
> "Follow me, and let the dead bury the dead."
> Mt 8: 18 – 22

Mary Poppins created the phrase "pie crust promises. Easily made. Easily broken." I have never thought that pie crusts are easily made, but I know they are easily broken.

Too often we say what is convenient rather than what we are prepared to live. In today's gospel, Jesus is testing the depth of both the scribe and the disciple. It is easy to say, "Wherever you go I will follow." It is much more difficult to live it than to say it. I know Jesus sounds insensitive when he says, "Let the dead bury the dead," but that is not the case. He is just pointing out that there will always be something that we will allow to distract or dissuade us from putting our faith into action.

"I promise, it will never happen again." It doesn't really matter what "it" is; it is a pie crust promise. We have all made them. When we want God to grant us our wish, we make all kinds of promises. Once we get what we want, we often renege.

Every time we pray the Act of Contrition we end by saying, "I firmly resolve with the help of Thy grace to sin no more and to avoid the near occasion of sin. Amen"

How are we doing with that promise?

Tuesday of the Thirteenth Week in Ordinary Times

> He said to them, "Why are you terrified, O you of little faith?"
> Then he got up, rebuked the winds and the sea,
> and there was great calm.
> The men were amazed and said, "What sort of man is this,
> whom even the winds and the sea obey?"
> Mt 8: 23 – 27

I wonder how often Jesus refers to us as, "O you of little faith." I suspect more often than we would like. Faith is a gift, but, like any gift, it has to be opened. Too often our gift of faith is left unopened. Faith becomes our last resort rather than our first choice.

Lou Holtz, the great Notre Dame football coach, describes most people's faith with this story. There is a man who is going to an important meeting but can't find a parking spot. On his third trip around the block, the man begins to panic and says this prayer, "God, if you can find me a parking spot, I will never miss Sunday Mass again and I will tithe on my income." Just as the man was finishing up his prayer a parking spot came open right in front of him. So the man says, "Never mind God. I found a spot on my own."

Remember, it is not God who suffers when we live our faith as if it were a game.

Where do we make a game out of our faith?

Wednesday of the Thirteenth Week in Ordinary Time

> The demons pleaded with him,
> "If you drive us out, send us into the herd of swine."
> And he said to them, "Go then."
> They came out and entered the swine,
> And the whole herd rushed down the steep bank into the sea where they drowned.
> The swineherds ran away,
> And when they came to the town they reported everything,
> including what had happened to the demoniacs.
> Thereupon the whole town came out to meet Jesus,
> And when they saw him they begged him to leave their district.
> Mt 8: 28 – 34

The demoniacs (imagine living in a culture that has a specific name for people thought to be possessed by the devil?) were Gentiles. So once again, as with the child of the Centurion, we have a cross faith healing. Knowing that they were Gentiles explains why there was a herd of pigs in that place. Jews don't eat pork; they consider pigs to be unclean.

So the demons recognize Jesus as the Son of God before any of the people do. The demons request a place with the unclean animals. Their request is granted, but even the swine reject the demons by drowning. All this seems pretty far removed from our lives. Nevertheless, what can we learn?

First of all, we have no need to fear demons, evil spirits, or the devil. Jesus commands and they obey. Evil is powerless in the presence of Jesus. This should not lead us to be foolish, but it should help us be confident in our ability to trust that Jesus will keep us from evil, if that is what we want.

The other lesson is a painful one. The people of the town meet Jesus and ask him to leave. Why? Because their possessions, the swine, were more important to them than the demoniacs. The demoniacs were healed; they were made whole but the people would not focus on that. When Jesus enters our lives our priorities have to change. We cannot be a believer and put things ahead of people.

Where have we put things ahead of people in our priorities?

Thursday of the Thirteenth Week in Ordinary Time

> Jesus knew what they were thinking, and said,
> "Why do you harbor evil thoughts?
> Which is easier to say, 'Your sins are forgiven'
> or to say, 'Rise and walk'?
> But that you may know that the Son of Man
> has authority on earth to forgive sins" –
> he then said to the paralytic,
> "Rise, pick up your stretcher, and go home."
> Mt 9: 1 – 8

In Jesus' time it was accepted belief that people who lived with a handicap – deafness, blindness, being mute, crippled, or possession by an evil spirit – were inflicted because of sin. Therefore, when Jesus sees the man being carried on a stretcher, it makes all the sense in the world for Jesus to say, "Courage, child, your sins are forgiven."

The problem is that only God can forgive sins. So the Scribes accuse Jesus of blasphemy. Jesus rejects their accusation and then proves that he has the power to forgive sins because he orders the man to walk and he does.

One thing is certain, forgiveness of sin was an issue in Jesus' time and it is an issue in our time as well. But there is one massive difference. In our time, we have trouble letting ourselves be forgiven. We know God forgives us, but we cling on to our sins. We drag them around in our memory. We sometimes define ourselves by our sins.

Jesus forgives us. He orders us to walk once again on the path of goodness. Too often we are afraid to trust his forgiveness.

To what past sins are we clinging?

Friday of the Thirteenth Week in Ordinary Time

Now it happened that, while Jesus was at table in Matthew's home,
> many tax collectors and those known as sinners
>> came to join Jesus and his disciples at dinner.
>
> The Pharisees saw this and complained to his disciples,
>> "What reason can the Teacher have for eating with
>>> tax collectors and those who disregard the law?"
>
> Overhearing the remark, he said,
> "People who are in good health do not need a doctor;
>> sick people do.
>
> Go and learn the meaning of the words,
>> 'It is mercy I desire and not sacrifice.'
>
> I have come to call not the self-righteous, but sinners."
>> Mt 9: 9 – 13

Seems like in every age it is the self-righteous who forget the meaning of mercy. God is the God of mercy, love, and forgiveness, and we need to be more like our God.

It is just too easy to divide the world into two camps. The good guys, and the bad guys. Once we have divided up the world in this fashion all that remains is to reward the good folks and punish the bad folks. Would that the world was that easy to manage.

A young mother was doing her food shopping with her two young children. One of the children, her son, was running a bit wild through the store. Mom was clearly frustrated and at the end of her rope. Just at that moment an older woman turned into her aisle and quickly assessed the scene. She pushed her cart up to the frustrated mother and quietly said, "I had one like that. Today he is the CEO of a very successful company. Hang in there; don't lose hope." The tension was broken and a frustrated mother had been given a glimmer of hope.

God, like the older woman, knew how to look toward the future. To see in advance that a certain wildness can be tamed and put to good use. Jesus does that with us. We need to do it more often with one another.

Where do we need to see possibilities rather than opportunities for punishment?

Saturday of the Thirteenth Week in Ordinary Time

No one patches an old cloak with a piece of unshrunken cloth,
for its fullness pulls away from the cloak and the tear gets worse.
People do not put new wine in old wineskins.
Otherwise the skins will burst, the wine spills out,
and the skins are ruined.
Rather, they pour new wine into fresh wineskins,
and both are preserved."
Mt 9: 14 – 17

I just love it when Jesus goes folksy. I can almost see people's heads snap when he does it. He does it quite a bit. Most often it is his way of saying, "I'll give your question the answer it deserves." That is certainly the case here. Jesus is not going to get drawn into a discussion about his disciples not fasting while the disciples of John do fast. He's got better things to do.

However, in his heart Jesus is a teacher and a storyteller, so he cannot resist a chance to teach. There are new ways and there are old ways. Not all the old ways are perfect and not all the new ways imperfect. We have to be flexible. Our faith needs to be anchored in tradition but not imprisoned by it. Tradition is the foundation, but what good is a foundation if nothing is built on it?

Many years ago a friend shared this quote from the conductor Kurt Herbert Adler, "Tradition is what you resort to when you don't have the time or the money to do it right." I don't fully agree with the quote. I would put "energy" where he put "money," but that is quibbling. I know the quote is a good conversation starter, and that is always a good thing.

What do we need to let go of if our faith is to grow?

Fourteenth Sunday in Ordinary Time (A)

> "Come to me, all you who labor and are burdened,
> and I will give you rest.
> Take my yoke upon you and learn from me,
> for I am meek and humble of heart;
> and you will find rest yourselves.
> For my yoke is easy, and my burden light."
> Mt 11:25 – 30

We need to learn from everything Jesus did. He took on our human condition to show us how to live. He is our role model; he is our mentor. Jesus knows what it is to be frustrated. He got aggravated with the disciples. The Scribes and Pharisees got on his nerves. He had good days and bad days, but he never let those people or those days distract him from who he was or what his mission was. When we are out of sorts, we need to go to Jesus. We need to let Jesus dictate our choices not people or events. Jesus was proactive not reactive, and we need to learn that from him. Too often we give to people we neither like nor respect the ability to make decisions in our lives. When we react to others, they are controlling our lives.

Lou Holtz, the legendary Notre Dame football coach, provided us with an example of what I mean. He and his wife were in Miami for a bowl game. The night before the game they went out to eat. When the waiter came over, he said, "You're Lou Holtz, aren't you?' Coach Holtz said, "Yes" as he was reaching for pen to give the waiter an autograph. The waiter said, "What's the difference between Notre Dame and Cheerios?" The coach said, "I have no idea." The waiter said, "Cheerios belong in a bowl." That set Holtz off. He was fuming. His wife said to him, "Why are you letting that waiter dictate your mood?" Holtz cooled off, but before they paid the bill, he called the waiter over and said, "What's the difference between Lou Holtz and your golf pro?" The waiter said, "I have no idea." Coach Holtz said, "Golf pros give tips."

Who or what do we give too much power in our lives?

Fourteenth Sunday in Ordinary Time (B)

> They found him too much for them.
> Jesus' response to all this was:
> "No prophet is without honor except in his native place,
> among his own kindred, and in his own house."
> He could work no miracle there,
> apart from curing a few who were sick
> by laying hands on them,
> so much did their lack of faith distress him.
> He made the rounds of the neighboring villages instead,
> And spent his time teaching.
> Mk 6: 1 – 6

Jesus goes home; everyone knows him. He went to school with their children. They knew his aunts and uncles and all his cousins. He was one of them. He was the carpenter's son. Mary was his mother.

That's how it used to be before Jesus went off and began to collect disciples and teach people about the will of God. The town folks thought he was being uppity. All Jesus had to do was be who he used to be, and everything would be all right. But that was not to be.

There is something in human nature that makes us want to keep people from changing. We want to live stable lives in a stable world, and that cannot happen if people keep changing. We don't want others to change, and we are not very keen on changing ourselves.

Every now and again, we will read about someone who just walks away from his job, walks away from a good life, and goes in a different direction. The account always has that person saying something like, "I just wasn't happy." "I knew there had to be more to life." We read about it, wish we could do the same, but instead we return to what does not fulfill us and never will fulfill us. Change is hard.

What part of our lives really needs to change?

Fourteenth Sunday in Ordinary Time (C)

> The Lord appointed a further seventy-two
> and sent them in pairs before him
> to every town and place he intended to visit.
> He said to them,
> "The harvest is rich but the workers are few;
> therefore ask the harvest-master to send workers
> to his harvest.
> Be on your way, and remember;
> I am sending you as lambs in the midst of wolves."
> Lk 10: 1 – 12, 17 – 20

Jesus always needs more disciples. At every baptism, the Church makes more disciples. On the surface there should be enough disciples to get the job done, but that is obviously not the case.

What is wrong? Not enough people take their baptism seriously. In baptism we receive a call from God. We are given a mission and a ministry from God not from the church. We know this because if an adult Baptist, Methodist, Episcopalian, or Lutheran wants to join the Catholic Church, we do not re-Baptize them. They are already baptized; they have already been given a mission and a ministry from God. We need to know that it is not the church that calls us; it is God.

I suspect that we act as if it is the church that calls us because it is easier to ignore a call from the church. A call from God, however, is much more difficult to ignore.

When I was still in parish ministry, I would occasionally tell the staff I was not taking any calls until I got a given project done, and they would hold all calls. Now if the bishop or the governor called, they would put that call through. As I said, some calls are more difficult to ignore than others.

How is God calling us to live out our Baptism more fully?

Monday of the Fourteenth Week in Ordinary Time

> When Jesus arrived at the official's house
> and saw the flute players and the crowd
> who were making a commotion,
> he said, "Go away! The girl is not dead but sleeping."
> And they ridiculed him.
> When the crowd was put out, he came and took her by the hand,
> And the little girl arose.
> Mt 9: 18 – 26

No one likes to be ridiculed. It is demeaning. Not only that, we let the fear of being ridiculed have too much power in our decision making. We want approval; we want to be accepted. When we go against the crowd, we risk being ostracized.

Jesus did not let the crowd in today's gospel dictate his choices or limit his power.

He got rid of them mentally so he was able to remove them physically.

My father was a man of few words, but when he spoke we listened. He would tell my brothers and me, "In life you maybe on the wrong side of a lot of 10 to 1 votes; that does not mean you are wrong." That wisdom has served me well. Another of his aphorisms was, "Make up your mind slowly, and change it even more slowly." One final saying, "If you think you are right, do not back down or buckle under pressure to change your mind." I can think of at least two bishops who wish I had a different father. We need to go where the truth leads us not where the wind blows us.

Where have we let public opinion cramp our thinking?

Tuesday of the Fourteenth Week in Ordinary Time

> At the sight of the crowds, his heart was moved with pity for them
> because they were troubled and abandoned,
> like sheep without a shepherd.
> Then he said to his disciples,

> "The harvest is abundant but the laborers few;
> so ask the master of the harvest
> to send out laborers for his harvest."
> Mt 9: 32 – 38

Apathy and empathy seem to be in combat to be the guiding principle in our lives. That was never the case with Jesus. He was always empathetic. When he was confronted with the woman caught in adultery, he let empathy guide his actions. Empathy led him to be gentle with the woman at the well with five husbands, with Zacchaeus the tax cheat, with the good thief, and with so many other folks in his life.

We need to learn from Jesus. Too often we get tired of the hurt and need that seems to surround us. The 24/7 news cycle is awash with bad news about bad people. It overwhelms us, and we shut down, and we shut off. We give in to apathy. Fear leads to apathy; love leads of empathy. The choice is ours.

C. K. Chesterton gives us this gem, "There is no safe investment. To love at all is to be vulnerable. Love anything, and your heart will certainly be wrung and possibly broken. If you want to make sure of keeping it intact, you must give your heart to no one, not even to an animal. Wrap it carefully round with hobbies and little luxuries; avoid all entanglements; lock it up safe in the casket or coffin of your selfishness. But in the casket – safe, dark, motionless, airless – it will change. It will not be broken; it will become unbreakable, impenetrable, irredeemable." Maybe apathy is not the answer.

Where have we been afraid to love and get involved?

Wednesday of the Fourteenth Week in Ordinary Times

> Jesus sent out these Twelve after instructing them thus,
> "Do not go into pagan territory or enter a Samaritan town.
> Go rather to the lost sheep of the house of Israel.
> As you go, make this proclamation:
> 'The Kingdom of heaven is at hand.'"
> Mt 10: 1 – 7

When it comes to our religion (our religion, not our faith) we are frequently confronted with the "fact" that we cannot change. This is in spite of the fact that change is everywhere in our institutional history, as it should be.

Today's gospel is a prime example. Were Jesus' instructions to the Twelve an end point or a starting point? Was Jesus saying, "Never go into pagan territory or a Samaritan town" or was he saying, "Start out with the lost sheep of the house of Israel and then enlarge your audience."

It took a while but the Twelve ultimately saw the need to take the message to the pagans. There was a confrontation between Paul and Peter. It took a vision on the roof of Cornelius' house, but Peter finally was able to understand that Christ's message was for the whole world not just the chosen people.

Our church will die unless it learns better how to expand her mission. The church will continue to be wounded if she continues to focus on maintenance of what we have rather than the ministries and mission we are called to embrace. We need to find the courage to live out the ancient aphorism, "Ecclesia semper reformanda" (the church always being reformed). We lost that wisdom for a few hundred years, but it is not too late to embrace that saying's wisdom.

Where do we need to speak out on the changes our church needs to make?

Thursday of the Fourteenth Week in Ordinary Time

> As you enter a house, wish it peace;
> If the house is worthy,
> let your peace come upon it;
> if not, let your peace return to you.
> Mt 10: 7 – 15

Many years ago, I read about a missionary who was impressed by one tribe's custom. Whenever the Elder called a meeting there was the custom known as "the passing of the grass." The Elder would begin the passing. If the grass did not return to him that meant that there was an active wounded relationship among the tribe. The meeting could not begin until everyone was at peace.

When the tribe was converted they adapted the "passing of the grass." When the priest visited, the tribe would gather for the passing of the grass. The Eucharist could not begin until the grass was returned to the Elder.

Imagine if we instituted a similar custom in our parishes. What would happen if we were to move the sign of peace to the very beginning of our Eucharistic celebrations. The presider would offer the sign of peace to the deacon who would then offer peace to the lector. And so it would go until the peace was returned to the presider. Too often we gather and we ignore the divisions that exist within our community. No Eucharist if there are any active wounded relationships. I suspect that most Eucharistic celebrations would not begin on time.

Where do we need to offer peace to heal a wounded relationship?

Friday of the Fourteenth Week in Ordinary Time

> When they hand you over,
> do not worry about what how you are to speak
> or what you are to say.
> You will be given at that moment what you are to say.
> For it will not be you who speak
> but the Spirit of your Father speaking through you.
> Mt 10: 16 – 23

Jesus is warning his followers that they will be persecuted because they believe in him and in the power of his name. Over time those persecutions have diminished; indeed in many places they have disappeared altogether. In some ways that is too bad. Faith should cost us something.

When I was in high school, the whole school went on retreat. The priest giving the retreat was a young Paulist priest; he gave a great retreat. One point that he made is still with me all these years later. He said, "If Catholics were persecuted in America would there be enough evidence for you to be found guilty?" It was a great question then, and it is a great question now. What he was asking us to consider is do our lives show that we are followers of Jesus.

In the early church the people said about Jesus' followers, "See how they love one another." They don't say that anymore, and for good reason. In the early church they took care of those in need. We still do but we could certainly do more. Our neighbors and our coworkers should not have to wonder if we are believers. They should know it by the way we live and the choices we make.

Do they?

Saturday of the Fourteenth Week in Ordinary Time

> "Therefore do not be afraid of them.
> Nothing is concealed that will not be revealed,
> nor secret that will not be known.
> What I say to you in the darkness, speak in the light;
> what you hear whispered, proclaim on the housetops."
> Mt 10: 24 – 33

Fear and secrecy go hand in hand. Everyone has secrets. Everyone. There are parts of our past that we want to keep to ourselves. We are afraid of what people would think if they knew everything about us.

I am always amazed when someone is caught doctoring their resume. Why do people make up degrees? Why do they say they graduated from a "better" college or university than the one they actually attended? Once we make something up, we live in fear that the truth we come out. Why not just go with the truth the first time?

We whisper things because we do not want our real thoughts to be known. What a waste of time. We hide in the shadows so our flaws won't be clearly seen. Another waste of time. God knows all about us, and he still loves us. We need to learn how to walk in the light and to always speak the truth.

What darkness do we need to abandon?

Fifteenth Sunday in Ordinary Time (A)

> And he spoke to them in parables, saying:
> "A sower went out to sow.
> And as he sowed, some seed fell on the path,
> and the birds came and ate it up.
> Some fell on rocky ground, where it had little soil.
> It sprang up at once because the soil was not deep,
> and when the sun rose it was scorched,
> and withered for lack of roots.
> Mt 13: 1 – 23

The sower is God, the seed is faith, and we are the soil. There was a time when I used to think of the different kinds of soil and different kinds of people. Some people were the path, others the rocky ground, some were surrounded by thorns, and a few people were the rich soil.

Now, I realize that, at different times, we are different kinds of soil. There are times when we are the rich soil. The seed of faith planted in us has grown and thrives. We hear the challenge of the gospel and respond, with God's help, to the challenge. There are other times when our faith is choked off by the thorns in our life. We get too busy with material things. We act out of selfishness. Then there are the times when we reduce our faith to going through the motions. A prayer here, a kindness there, but our faith is sporadic at best. That is when we are the soil that is beaten down to become a path. Lastly, we are the rocky ground. We start off with the best of intentions, but as soon as there is any resistance we fold like a house of cards. We are going to set aside time to read the Bible, but we don't. We are going to pray more, but we don't. We are going to be more faithful to Sunday Mass, but when the time comes we are just too tired.

We need to work harder at being rich soil so God's message will grow in our lives and in our world.

How can we better cultivate the seed of faith planted in our lives at Baptism?

Fifteenth Sunday in Ordinary Time (B)

> He instructed them to take nothing on the journey
> but a walking stick – no food, no traveling bag
> not a coin in the purses in their belts.
> They were, however, to wear sandals.
> "Do not bring a second tunic,"
> he said and added:
> "Whatever house you find yourself in,
> stay there until you leave the locality.
> If any place will not receive you or hear you,
> Shake its dust from your feet in testimony
> against them as you leave."
> With that they went off, preaching the need of repentance.
> They expelled many demons, anointed the sick with oil,
> and worked many cures.
> Mk 6: 7 – 13

And so our church began. Ordinary people, inspired by Jesus, calling others to repent. What could be simpler? We are all familiar with the axiom, "The longest journey begins with a single step."

Do you know who Rev. Chad Varah is? In 1953 in London, he issued a call for volunteers to work a new helpline he established for people contemplating suicide. That was the first step. Today the Samaritans is an organization with 20,000 volunteers worldwide. Do you know who Peter Benenson is? In 1961, he founded Amnesty International, which today is an organization with more than seven million members. It all began with a single step. One more, do you know who Dru Joyce II is? He was LeBron James' high school basketball coach at St. Vincent-St. Mary High School. When he convinced LeBron's mother to let him be his coach, he took a single step that helped produce one of the greatest basketball players of all time.

Most likely we will not be part of anything so wonderful as these stories, but all of us are called to make a difference in our world. When parents bring a child into the world, it is a first step. When they present that child for Baptism, it is a first step. When a young woman offers to be a lector at her parish, or a young man decides to become a Eucharistic minister, those are first steps.

We are all part of something bigger than ourselves, and the more we realize that the more we will be willing to share our talents to make our world a better place.

Where have we realized that we are part of something greater than ourselves?

Fifteenth Sunday in Ordinary Time (C)

> On one occasion a lawyer stood to pose this problem to Jesus.
> "Teacher, what must I do to inherit everlasting life?"
> Jesus answered him:
> "What is written in the law? How do you read it?"
> He replied:
> "You shall love the Lord your God
>   with all your heart,
>   with all your soul,
>   with all your strength,
>   and with all your mind;
>   and your neighbor as yourself."
> Jesus said, "You have answered correctly.
> Do this and you shall live."
> But because he wished to justify himself he said to Jesus,
>   "And who is my neighbor?"
> Lk 10 :25 – 37

We know what comes next. The parable of the good Samaritan. We know the story by heart; we don't need to read it. A man was beaten and robbed – a priest did not stop to help him, nor did the Levite, but a foreigner, a Samaritan, took care of the victim. He did not just take care of him; he went above and beyond. He paid for the victim's care.

The lawyer asks the question, "Who is my neighbor?" Jesus tells a story and then asks the lawyer, "Which of these three, in your opinion, was neighbor to the man who fell in with the robbers?" Jesus switches the focus. The lawyer wants to limit the meaning of neighbor; Jesus wants to expand it. The issue is not who is our neighbor, but rather, to whom am I called to be a neighbor. The answer is everyone. Remember the golden rule? "Do unto others what you want them to do unto you."

We are called to treat everyone with respect, not just people we know. We are called to see the good in everyone, not just in the people we like. If we do this then we will hasten the coming of the Kingdom of God.

How have we narrowed the list of people we need to care for?

Monday of the Fifteenth Week in Ordinary Time

> "Whoever loves father or mother more than me is not worthy of me,
> and whoever loves son or daughter more than me is not worthy of me;
> and whoever does not take up his cross
> and follow after me is not worthy of me.
> Whoever finds his life will lose it,
> and whoever loses his life for my sake will find it.
> Mt 10: 34 – 11:1

Sometimes I wonder why Jesus has any followers at all. Today's gospel would provide one of those times. At the beginning, Jesus is using a bit of hyperbole to make a point. Jesus does not want to be second in our lives. He knows the special bond between a son and his mother and father. He lived it. His mother was with him through the good and the bad in his life. She was there at the end, watching her son die unjustly. But she was there because of her love for Jesus.

That is what Jesus wants from us. He wants us to believe in him when it is convenient but especially when it is inconvenient. He wants us to believe when it hurts, when we want to give up, or when it costs us to believe. Jesus knows that our faith will provide us plenty of opportunities to take up our cross and follow him. When Sunday rolls around and you can either sleep in or go to Mass. We need to take up our cross. When the choice is eat out or give to the needy, do we take up the cross? When someone betrays us, do we seek revenge or offer forgiveness? We don't have to go looking for crosses to take up. All we have to do is live our faith each and every day and there will be more crosses than we could ever want to carry.

It may feel like we are losing too much of our life, but when love and faith guide our choices, we grow to learn what living to the fullest means.

Where have we cut corners so we don't have to take up our cross and follow Jesus?

Tuesday of the Fifteenth Week in Ordinary Time

> Jesus began to reproach the towns
> where most of his mighty deeds had been done,
> since they had not repented.
> "Woe to you, Chorazin! Woe to you Bethsaida!
> For if the mighty deeds done in your midst
> had been done in Tyre and Sidon,
> they would long ago have repented in sackcloth and ashes."
> Mt 11: 20 – 24

Jesus' constant call is repentance. "Repent, the Kingdom of God is at hand." We wander; we get lost. Jesus wants us to turn our lives around. He wants on the right path.

He does not dwell on the past. He leaves that us to us. We cling to the past; we define ourselves by the past. We forget our past good deeds, but not our bad deeds. Those we cling to. We let our past mistakes define our present choices, and in so doing allow our future to be polluted over and over again.

Go back in your memory to the story of the woman caught in adultery. The Pharisees and Scribes want her defined by her sin. Jesus takes a different approach. He clears the air by inviting those accusing her to focus on their sins rather than her sin. When they do that, they quickly see the foolishness of their supposed superiority.

When Jesus is left alone with the woman, he asks her, "Woman, where are they? Has no one condemned you?" When she says they have gone away, Jesus tells her, "Neither do I condemn you. Go and from now on do not sin any more."

Repentance is Jesus' invitation to learn from our sins rather than be defined by them!

What past sin(s) do we need to let go of so that we can grow?

Wednesday of the Fifteenth Week in Ordinary Time

> At that time Jesus exclaimed:
> "I give praise to you, Father, Lord of heaven and earth, for although
> you have hidden these things
> from the wise and the learned
> you have revealed them to the childlike.
> Yes, Father, such has been your gracious will."
> Mt 11: 25 – 27

Children are inquisitive; they are trusting. Children have wonderful imaginations, and dare to hope. In short, children have all the attributes necessary to be believers. Unfortunately, somewhere on the journey from childhood to adulthood, we lose most of those attributes. The first thing to be suppressed is our imagination, next is curiosity, then trust, and lastly is hope. We end up plodding through life. We want to survive and we lose the zest to live.

In today's gospel, Jesus is not encouraging us to be childish, but rather to be childlike. There is a big difference. To be childlike is to live a simple life. The childlike know that people are more important than things. Children have not yet been taught to filter their emotions. When they are sad, they cry; when they are happy their exuberance is unrestrained.

A reporter once asked Karl Barth, the famous theologian, what his greatest theological insight was. Professor Barth paused briefly and then said, "Jesus loves me this I know, because the Bible tells me so." What could be more simple or childlike than that?

Where do we need to be less sophisticated with our faith and our prayers?

Thursday of the Fifteenth Week in Ordinary Time

Jesus said:
"Come to me, all you who labor and are burdened,
and I will give you rest.
Take my yoke upon you and learn from me,
For I am meek and humble of heart;
and you will find rest for yourselves.
For my yoke is easy, and my burden light."
Mt 11: 28 – 30

Jesus does not promise to lighten our burdens or put us on permanent vacation. What he does offer is a place of rest. Sometimes that is all we need. With our crazy schedules, we forget to rest or we rest at the wrong times.

The third commandment invites us to, "Keep Holy the Sabbath." When God created the world, he worked for six days, and then he took a day off. If a day off was good for God, it should be good for us. Unfortunately, we have forgotten how to rest. Bits of solitude need to be found in the midst of our activity.

Every year I go on retreat during the first week of Advent. Anyone who knows me knows that's what I do. I am amazed by how many people say to me, "I would love to get away. You are so lucky." Luck has nothing to do with it. My celibate life makes it easier for me to get away, but it still requires discipline. When I was still in active ministry, I had to clear five days in my calendar. I did it because I knew I needed it. Now that I am retired from active ministry, I still go on retreat. Why?, because I need it. I need time away to focus on what my priorities should be.

Sometimes I think we are afraid to rest because we will discover that much of what we do is not really all that essential. At least once a week we need to take a walk with Jesus and let him guide our reflection on what needs to be important in our lives.

Where have used our business as an excuse not to be reflective?

Friday of the Fifteenth Week in Ordinary Time

> Jesus was going through a field of grain on the Sabbath.
> His disciples were hungry
> and began to pick the heads of grain and eat them.
> When the Pharisees saw this, they said to him,
> "See, your disciples are doing what is unlawful to do on the Sabbath."
> Mt 12: 1 – 8

We have all had encounters with Pharisees. Maybe it was at work, in the neighborhood, at church, or, God forbid, at home. Pharisees don't know how to enjoy life so they spend a lot of energy making sure no one else enjoys life. They are constantly on watch to make sure that everyone follows the rules. Their only joy is when they catch someone else doing something not allowed. Their life blood is to be critical.

In John's gospel, Jesus says, "… I came so that they might have life and have it more abundantly." The Pharisees must have cringed when he said that. Life is not about abundance; life is about the rules. Rules are important, but they are not the be all or end all of life. There are situations where the rules just don't make sense. When that happens we need to ignore the rules, and just do what makes sense.

Yes there will always be Pharisees around to point out the error of our ways when that happens, but it is best to ignore them, and pray for them. Perhaps they will learn how to enjoy life.

Where do we need to be less law bound in our lives?

Saturday of the Fifteenth Week in Ordinary Time

> This was to fulfill what had been spoken through Isaiah the prophet:
> *Behold, my servant whom I have chosen*
> *my beloved in whom I delight;*
> *I shall place my Spirit upon him,*
> *and he will proclaim justice to the Gentiles.*
> *He will not contend or cry out,*
> *Nor will anyone hear his voice in the streets.*

> *A bruised reed he will not break,*
> *a smoldering wick he will not quench,*
> *until he brings justice to victory;*
> *And in his name the Gentiles will hope.*
> *Mt 12: 14 – 21*

I have always loved the part that says, "A bruised reed he will not break, a smoldering wick he will not quench." Jesus will not give up on us. If we are bruised by our sins, he forgives us. If the flame of our faith is reduced to a smoldering wick, he will gently blow on our wick until it is aflame once again.

For me that image gives great hope.

Our God looks at us with loving kindness. He always sees the more to come in us. He does not fixate on what we do wrong, but sees what we are capable of achieving in our lives. So much good happens when we know there is someone who believes in us. The teacher who convinces us we can do better and is willing to spend time with us to coax that goodness out of us. There is the coach who affirms rather than criticizes us. There is the friend who won't abandon us.

All of us have been blessed with people who believe in us. We need to be thankful for those people, but thankfulness is not enough. We have to pay it forward. We have to believe in others so that they can fulfill their potential.

Who do we know who could use someone to believe in them?

Sixteenth Sunday in Ordinary Time (A)

> He proposed another parable to them.
> "The kingdom of heaven is like a mustard seek
> that a person took and sowed in a field.
> It is the smallest of all the seeds,
> yet when it is full-grown it is the largest of plants.
> It becomes a large bush,
> and the 'birds of the sky come and dwell in its branches.'"
> Mt 13: 24 – 43

When the parish where I served for many years decided to publish a monthly newsletter, we had a competition to see who could come up with the best name for the newsletter. The winner was, "The Mustard Seed." That was more than thirty years ago and the newsletter is bigger and better than ever. It has lived up to its name.

"The longest journey starts with the smallest step" applies to so many things in our lives. Our parents patiently taught us how to make the sign of the cross many years ago. It took us a while to get it right, but look where that first prayer has brought us. It is always a joy to join in a Golden Anniversary celebration. We know there were good times and bad times, but we also know that the couples' loves has grown deeper and stronger. Whenever I do a wedding, I tell the couple, "Remember, the love that brings you here today will never keep you married. It must grow richer, deeper, and stronger with the passage of time. May God be with you on your journey of love." Faith and love are like the mustard seed. They start off small, but their growth borders on the miraculous.

Pause for a few moments, and call to mind those people who have helped our faith and love grow.

Sixteenth Sunday in Ordinary Time (B)

> The apostles returned to Jesus and reported to him
> all that they had done and what they had taught.
> He said to them,
> "Come by yourselves to an out-of-the-way place
> and rest a while."
> People were coming and going in great numbers
> making it impossible for them to so much as eat.
> So Jesus and the apostles went off in the boat
> by themselves to a deserted place.
> Mk 6: 30 – 34

Jesus, ever the great teacher, teaches his apostles a very important life lesson. In order to be successful at any task, you have to get some rest. Too often we forget the wisdom of this teaching. I'm sure the apostles, fresh off their successful first mission, were eager to go back at it again. But Jesus had a different idea. He wanted them to get some rest, to enjoy their success and learn how to do even better the next time.

How do we hear this message in our culture, which has been described by Patricia Datchuck Sanchez, in Celebration Preaching Resources, in this fashion, "A life that is too busy, a life whose priorities are askew or whose values are not clearly defined will become dissipated and distracted…In a society that seems to revel in 60 – 70 hour work weeks and wears the title 'workaholic' like a badge of honor, today's Gospel presents a challenge of balance, i.e., balancing work with play as well as prayer with service."

As a good friend of mine likes to say, "No one on their death bed has ever said, 'I wish I had spent more time at work.'"

Where have we forgotten how to enjoy quiet time?

Sixteenth Sunday in Ordinary Time (C)

> Jesus entered a village where a woman named Martha
> welcomed him to her home.
> She had a sister named Mary,
> who seated herself at the Lord's feet and listened to his words.
> Martha, who was busy with all the details of hospitality,
> came to him and said,
> "Lord, are you not concerned that my sister
> has left me all alone to do the household tasks?
> Tell her to help me."
> Lk 10: 38- 42

There is a name for what is going on in this gospel – triangulation. Martha should have gone to Mary and said, "I need your help." But instead she goes to Jesus and tries to drag him into the problem.

This happens all the time. At work, we have a problem with a co-worker, but instead of trying to work things out with the co-worker, we go to the boss, and complain. That always makes things worse. There may come a time when we need to go to a supervisor, but that should be the last step not the first.

There are many things I miss about parish ministry, but dealing with personal conflicts is not one of them. People would come to me all the time to complain about this or that member of the parish. When I recognized what was happening I always said, "Have you talked to them about the problem?" Invariably they would say, "No." I would encourage them to try the direct method, but very often that was the end of the issue. The problem would go unaddressed, and fester until it became a much bigger issue.

Going behind someone's back has never resolved an issue. Nevertheless, we do it all the time. Nothing is more divisive for a community.

Where have we tried to get someone else to solve problems for us?

Monday of the Sixteenth Week in Ordinary Time

> Some of the scribes and Pharisees said to Jesus,
> "Teacher, we wish to see a sign from you."
> He said to them in reply,
> "An evil and unfaithful generation seeks a sign,
> but no sign will be given it
> except the sign of Jonah the prophet."
> Mt 12: 38 – 42

God would give us more signs if we were willing to read the signs he already gives us. The problem is not signs from God, but our ability to read those signs. More signs would just be a waste of God's time.

There is a story about a railroad company that needed someone to send out Morse code messages for them. They took out an advertisement in the local paper announcing that interviews would be held the following Saturday at 9 o'clock in the morning. On Saturday more than thirty people showed up for an interview. One man arrived around 9:15, took a look around at the waiting room, then walked over to the door and knocked on it. The door opened and the man went inside. Before the interviewer closed the door he told all the others they could go home. They all complained, but the interviewer told them that the whole time they had been sitting there the loudspeaker had been announcing in Morse code that the first person who listened to the message, and knocked on the door would be hired.

God talks to us all the time through signs, but often we are too preoccupied to see or hear them.

What sign from God are we presently missing?

Tuesday of the Sixteenth Week in Ordinary Time

> Someone told him,
> "Your mother and your brother are standing outside,
> asking to speak with you."
> But he said in reply to the one who told him,
> "Who is my mother? Who are my brothers?"
> Mt 12: 46 – 50

We know that Mary was without sin, but I'll bet she was perturbed when she heard her son's answer. Jesus is not dissing his mother, nor is he making light of his relatives. He is merely making a point. I'm sure Mary, his mother, told him to make the point a different way next time.

For Jesus, doing the will of his Father was the measure of his life. Toward the end of his life, in what we know as the Agony in the Garden, Jesus hesitated but finally said to his Father, "Not my will, but your will be done." Throughout his life, Jesus found time for prayer. In his prayer time, he sought to discover his Father's will for him. In all things, he was true to what his Father wanted him to do.

We know part of that experience. We know, sometimes better than others, what God wants us to do. That we have in common with Jesus. Unlike Jesus too often we follow our own will rather than the will of the Father. Every day we need to ask Jesus to give us the strength to do our Father's will.

Where are we stubbornly clinging to what we want to do rather than what God wants us to do?

Wednesday of the Sixteenth Week in Ordinary Time

> On that day, Jesus went out of the house
> and sat down by the sea
> Such large crowds gathered around him
> that he got into a boat and sat down,
> and the whole crowd stood along the shore.
> And he spoke to them at length in parables.
> Mt 13: 1 – 9

Jesus was a storyteller; he was a great storyteller. We, as a people, are storytellers. It is what we do. When we gather as families, we tell our stories. We pass on the oral history of our families. That is how one generation teaches the next generation.

William Bausch, parish priest and prolific author, speaking of today's gospel has this to say in A World of Stories, "Jesus told the crowds all these things in parables, without a parable he told them nothing. Why? Because parables, or stories, are wisdom bearers. Individuals, families, and indeed nations, for better or worse are defined and sustained by their stories. This fact causes some to worry because, as George Gebner of the Annenberg Center for Media Studies at the University of Pennsylvania observes, for the first time in history the major stories our children learn are not from their parents, teachers, families or their religious tradition, but from global media corporations interested in making a profit." We need to make sure we tell our children our religious parables and our family faith stories. That is the only way that our faith gets passed on to the next generation.

Where do we need to be better storytellers of our faith?

Thursday of the Sixteenth Week in Ordinary Time

> This is why I speak to them in parables, because
> they look but do not see and hear but do not listen or understand.
> Isaiah's prophecy is fulfilled in them, which says:
> "You shall indeed hear but not understand;
> you shall indeed look but never see.
> Gross is the heart of this people,
> they will hardly hear with their ears,
> they have closed their eyes,
> lest they see with their eyes
> and hear with their ears
> and understand with their hearts and be converted
> and I will heal them."
> Mt 13: 10 – 17

God is in constant communication with us. He surrounds us with signs of his presence, and he speaks to us through the beauty of nature and the people around us. God communicates, but too often we fail to connect.

As Isaiah says, we "hear but we do not listen or understand." I love to travel and I love to people watch. I especially love to watch Americans when they try to communicate with people from other countries. Most Americans assume that everyone speaks English. So they just blurt out their question in English. When the person does not respond, what do Americans do? They assume that the person is hard of hearing so they ask the question louder. When that does not work they think that the person must be learning disabled, so they repeat the question louder and more slowly. What never dawns on them is that the person "hears" what they are saying, but does not "understand." I think that is how God must feel when he tries to communicate with us. We need to be more attuned to God's words and signs of his presence. Presently we miss too much of what God is trying to say to us.

How can we hear better God's language of love and forgiveness?

Friday of the Sixteenth Week in Ordinary Time

> But the seed sown on rich soil
> is the one who hears the word and understands it,
> who indeed bears fruit and yields a hundred or sixty or thirtyfold.
> Mt 13: 18 – 23

The part of today's gospel that always fascinates me is why the rich soil does not always produce a hundredfold. Why can the yield sometimes be as low as sixtyfold or even thirtyfold?

I'm not much of a gardener. I plant a few flowers on my deck along with some herbs that I use for cooking. One thing I have noticed is that I can use the same potting soil for all my plantings, but some do better than others. Some plants and some herbs like lots of sun while others like a mixture of sun and shade. Plants do better when they are in the proper environment.

The same is true with us when it comes to the seed of faith that God has planted in our lives. When everything is in order with our lives our faith will produce a hundredfold. But things are not always in order. We get sick, we get depressed, or we just get overwhelmed. When that happens our faith production is going to suffer. God has already told us that he understands that sometimes our production is going to be off, and that he is fine with that. We need to be as understanding of our yield as God is. God is willing to cut us some slack. Are we?

Sometimes "good enough" has to be "good enough." Where are we more demanding of ourselves than God is?

Saturday of the Sixteenth Week in Ordinary Time

> The slaves of the householder came to him and said,
> 'Master, did you not sow good seed in your field?
> Where have the weeds come from?'
> He answered, 'An enemy has done this.'
> His slaves said to him, 'Do you want us to go and pull them up?'

> He replied, 'No, if you pull up the weeds you might
> uproot the wheat along with them.'
> Mt 13: 24 – 30

As I mentioned yesterday, I am not much of a gardener. I remember when I was a little boy, and my grandfather was trying to teach me about gardening. I asked him, "What's the difference between a plant and a weed." I have never forgotten his answer. He looked at me with all seriousness and said, "Pull it up. If it grows back it's a weed." His answer was true but not very helpful.

One thing that a good gardener needs is patience. That is probably why I am not that good a gardener. But God is because he is patient. He waits patiently for our faith to bloom. He tills our soil, he waters us with his grace, and he lets the sunshine of his love envelop us. He gives us everything we need to grow our faith, but when our sinfulness becomes the weeds in our life, he chooses to focus on our potential not our subpar performance.

The harvest time will come. We will be held accountable for how well we cultivated the gift of faith. God lets us remove the sinful weeds from our lives by forgiving them. He keeps on shining his love on our lives, and waits patiently for us to be who he wants us to be.

What sinful weed do we need to ask God to remove from our lives?

Seventeenth Sunday in Ordinary Time (A)

> Jesus said to his disciples:
> "The kingdom of heaven is like a treasure buried in a field,
> which a person finds and hides again,
> and out of joy goes and sells all that he has and buys that field.
> Again, the kingdom is like a merchant
> searching for fine pearls.
> When he finds a pearl of great price,
> He goes and sells all that he has and buys it."
> Mt 13: 44 – 52

In poker there is a phrase "all in." That is the point at which a player pushes all his chips to the center of the table. The player is going for it all. He either wins and stays in the competition or he goes home. There is both a risk and a reward, and the reward is big enough to absorb the risk.

In that regard poker is like our faith. We need to be all in when it comes to our faith. Faith should not be a Sunday thing, nor should it be reality only when we say our morning or evening prayers. I do not remember where I read this, but it is apropos of this gospel. "For too many people, God is like a reference book in the library called life. When we need something, we take God off the shelf to get what we want. Then we put him back on the shelf until we need him again." That is the God of convenience; what we need is the God of conviction.

If faith is going to be our guide then we need to rid our lives of hatred, bigotry, pride, laziness, and a host of other vices. God should be our first consideration not an afterthought at the end of our day.

How can we make God and our faith more central in our lives?

Seventeenth Sunday in Ordinary Time (B)

> When they had had enough, he told his disciples,
> "Gather up the crusts that are left over
> so that nothing will go to waste."
> At this, they gathered twelve baskets full of pieces left over
> by those who had been fed with the five barley loaves.
> Jn 6: 1 – 15

Sometimes when we have plenty we get wasteful. Jesus wanted to prevent this from happening when he multiplied the five barley loaves. I am not sure what you do with twelve baskets full of bread crusts, but at least they did not go to waste.

It seems like the more we have, the more we throw away. When I studied theology in Belgium more than fifty years ago, I was amazed at how respectful the Belgians were of water. How efficient they were with heating, and how small their refrigerators were. They even had reusable bags for when they did their shopping, a practice that did not become popular here until many years later. If memory serves me correctly they were already into the early phase of recycling. They seemed to get the waste not, want not philosophy. We on the other hand still have a lot to learn.

I am writing this during the time of the Covid 19 pandemic. We have lost so much of our personal freedom. We have to wear masks everywhere. We have had to give up family gatherings at Easter, Thanksgiving, and Christmas. Millions of people are out of work, and millions of children are being taught virtually. Church attendance is being dictated by the state. Our life is out of whack.

By the time you are reading this hopefully life will be back to some semblance of what we used to call normal. And hopefully we will be more thankful for what we had temporarily lost. However, I fear that once our freedom of assembly, and our freedom to move about without restriction, as well as the ability to hug the people we love return, we will become prodigal once again. Hopefully that will not happen.

Where do we need to be more grateful for what we have?

Seventeenth Sunday in Ordinary Time (C)

> "For whoever asks, receives;
> whoever seeks, finds;
> whoever knocks, is admitted.
> What father among you will give his son a snake
> if he asks for a fish; or hand him a scorpion if he asks for an egg?
> If you with all your sins,
> know how to give your children good things,
> how much more will the heavenly Father
> give the Holy Spirit to those who ask him."
> Lk 11: 1 – 13

There is a difference between asking and asking for the right thing. Growing up we asked our parents for all sorts of things. Sometimes they said yes, and sometimes they said no. Most of the time, we graciously accepted their decision. Sometimes we threw a hissy fit, and then accepted their decision. Ultimately, we knew we were not in charge.

God is just like our parents. If we ask for a forgiving heart, he will give it to us. If we ask to win the lottery, he ignores us. If we ask that he give us the Holy Spirit, he will give it to us. If we ask God to make life difficult for those who oppose us, he will wait for us to grow up.

Too often we complain that God does not answer our prayers. What we need to realize is that God frequently answers our prayers in ways we don't like. Just as we had to learn as children that our parents were in charge, so as adults we need to learn that God is in charge. We need to ask him to help us hear and accept his answers, and we need to be more sensible in what we request.

How can our prayers of petition be less selfish and more faith-filled?

Monday of the Seventeenth Week in Ordinary Time

He spoke to them another parable.
"The Kingdom of heaven is like yeast
that a woman took and mixed with three measures of wheat flour
until the whole batch was leavened."
All these things Jesus spoke to the crowds in parables.
He spoke to them only in parables,
to fulfill what had been said through the prophet:
I will open my mouth in parables,
I will announce what has lain hidden from
the foundation of the world.
Mt 13: 31 – 35

I have made bread only a few times in my life. There is something very healing about making bread. The whole process is very therapeutic. Most of all it takes time; it cannot be rushed. The yeast has to do its thing twice for bread to be born.

The dough has to rise up only to be beaten down so that it can rise up again.

When the dough goes in the oven, all the patience and all the hands-on work begins to pay its dividends. The smell of bread fills the whole house. Nothing is untouched. Bread is better when it is shared.

That is why Jesus compares the Kingdom to yeast. For the Kingdom to come we need patience. There will be times when we rise to the occasion, and there will be times when we get beaten down. There will be times when our progress will be hard to see. We will certainly have to take some heat for the Kingdom to be born. Finally, the Kingdom will come only when we learn to share better.

Bread is the staff of life, so is our faith. How can we share our faith better?

Tuesday of the Seventeenth Week in Ordinary Time

"The harvest is the end of the age, and the harvesters are angels.
Just as weeds are collected and burned up with fire,
so will it be at the end of the age.
The Son of Man will send his angels,
and they will collect out of his Kingdom
all who cause others to sin and all evildoers.
They will throw them into the fiery furnace,
where there will be wailing and grinding of teeth.
Then the righteous will shine like the sun
in the Kingdom of their Father.
Whoever has ears ought to hear."
Mt 13: 36 – 43

Precisely who are those "who cause others to sin" as opposed to those who are evildoers? Evildoers are easy to spot. All we have to do is look in a mirror. We are all sinners; we are all evildoers. There are Hall of Fame sinners and there are minor league sinners. Fortunately, most of us are in the latter category.

How do we "cause others to sin"? I'm not sure I know the answer to that question. I don't think I have ever caused someone to sin. At least I hope I have not. Did the Pharisees cause others to sin when they laid heavy burdens on others and did nothing to help carry the burden?

Is that what Jesus had in mind? Maybe. When we are insensitive to others, and they lash out, have we caused them to sin? Maybe. If we get on someone's nerves by riding them unmercifully, and they finally erupt in vulgar language is that what Jesus had in mind? Could be.

Perhaps we need to focus on what will make us righteous so that we can shine like the sun. We need to treat everyone with dignity and respect. If we do that we certainly will not "cause others to sin."

Who in our lives do we need to treat better?

Wednesday of the Seventeenth Week in Ordinary Time

> Jesus said to the crowds,
> "The reign of God is like a buried treasure
> which a man found in a field. He hid it again,
> and rejoicing at his find
> went and sold all he had and bought that field.
> Or again, the kingdom of heaven is like a merchant's search
> for fine pears.
> When he found one really valuable pearl,
> He went and put up for sale all that he had
> and bought it."
> Mt 13: 44 – 46

This parable is not about whether or not the person who finds the treasure has an obligation to tell the owner of the field what he has found. So don't go there. This parable is about how we decide what is important in our lives.

There is a wonderful little story about an elderly gentleman out for a mid-day walk. As he goes his way, he hears a little, squeaky voice say, "Hello." He looks around but does not see anyone so he continues on his way; again he hears a little voice say, "Hello." This time he looks down, and sees a frog. He picks up the frog, and the frog says, "I am a beautiful princess. If you kiss me I will be set free, and will be yours for the rest of your life." The gentleman pauses a bit and then puts the frog in his pocket. The frog cries out, "What are you doing? Didn't you hear me?" The gentleman says, "I heard you, but frankly at this time in my life I would rather have a talking frog." It is all about priorities.

God wants to be first in our lives. He wants us to get rid of anything that prevents us from putting him first in our lives. Too often we put other things first. Thankfully our God is patient, and will love us into doing what is right.

What is preventing us from putting God first in our lives?

Thursday of the Seventeenth Week in Ordinary Time

>Jesus said to his disciples:
>"The Kingdom of heaven is like a net thrown into the sea,
>which collects fish of every kind.
>When it is full they haul it ashore
>and sit down to put what is good into buckets.
>What is bad they throw away.
>Thus it will be at the end of the age."
>Mt. 13: 47 – 53

We can avoid what Jesus is saying for only so long. Eventually, we have to face the reality that there will be a day of accountability. The age will end, and he will be our judge. We want to be saved; we don't want to be thrown away. We want to end up with the good folks.

My father was a man of simple faith. Early in his life someone taught him that his purpose in life was "to save his immortal soul." And that is how he lived his life. He said his prayers every night. He made the nine First Fridays, and he completed the First Saturday devotion. He prayed the rosary, went to Mass every Sunday and on the days of obligation, he was faithful to the Ten Commandments and the six precepts of the church. He treated others as he wanted them to treat him. He lived a good life.

The only thing that bothers me is how much he worried about saving his soul. He let his life be turned into a spiritual obstacle course. He thought it was hard to be saved. I wish that he, and a lot of other people, would realize that salvation is a gift freely offered not a victory earned.

Where do we let fear enter into our salvation history?

Friday of the Seventeenth Week in Ordinary Time

> Jesus came to his native place and taught in their synagogue.
> They were astonished and said,
> "Where did this man get such wisdom and mighty deeds:
> Is he not the carpenter's son?
> Is not his mother named Mary
> and his brothers James, Joseph, Simon, and Judas?
> Are not his sisters all with us?
> Where did he get all of this?"
> Mt 13: 54 – 58

Mary is called by name. Jesus' brothers all get names. His sisters don't get names, even his father does not get called by name. He becomes "the carpenter." Even though Jesus returned home, they know full well his given name and yet he is called "this man." It is because of situations like this that we have the saying, "Familiarity breeds contempt". People don't like people to change. Once he have a label for someone we want that label to be permanent.

Jesus had certainly at one time been an assistant to his father, and when Joseph died, Jesus probably took over his carpentry business. Then he heard the call. Then he became a wandering preacher, and sometime worker of wonders. He was getting a name for himself. What does the gospel say? "Where did he get all of this?" Short answer, he got it from God.

We are surrounded by people with wonderful talents, and we have great talents. We need to create an environment that calls forth and affirms the talents of others. We need to encourage people to grow. They in turn recognize and affirm our talents. That is how the Kingdom of God grows.

Who do we know who needs a little encouragement to develop their talents?

Saturday of the Seventeenth Week in Ordinary Time

> But at a birthday celebration for Herod,
> the daughter of Herodias performed a dance before the guests
> and delighted Herod so much
> that he swore to give her whatever she might ask for.
> Prompted by her mother, she said,
> "Give me here on a platter the head of John the Baptist."
> Mt 14: 1 – 12

Revenge never works, but that does not discourage us from trying. There are a lot of not nice people in today's gospel. Herodias was the wife of Herod's brother, Philip, but was living with Herod. That makes them both questionable people. Then there is Salome, the daughter of Herodias, who did the dance.

She went to her mother for advice, and did not hesitate to have someone killed to help her mother seek revenge. As I said, there are some not so nice folks in today's gospel.

Rather that focus on the people who made bad or questionable choices, we need to focus on John the Baptist. When he had the opportunity to confront Herod, he did just that. John spoke the truth to power, and paid the ultimate price. John had the courage of his convictions. He lived his life out of conviction rather than convenience. We need more people like John the Baptist. Too many of us see things that are wrong, but remain silent. We need to embrace the wisdom of Sir Edmund Burke, "The only thing necessary for evil to triumph is for good men [sic] to do nothing."

Where have we bowed to temerity, and let evil go unchecked?

Eighteenth Sunday in Ordinary Time (A)

> When it was evening, the disciples approached him and said,
> "This is a deserted place and it is already late;
> dismiss the crowds so that they can go to the villages
> and buy food for themselves."

> Jesus said to them, "There is no need for them to go away;
> give them some food yourselves."
> Mt 14: 13 – 21

The disciples were aware enough to recognize a problem but did not want it to be their problem. They wanted to send the people away and send the problem with them. Jesus wanted to teach them a better way.

If the disciples had proceeded with their solution, their lives would not have been changed. By following Jesus' advice their lives were changed. Jesus taught them to share what they had.

Because of the sharing everyone got something. Maybe everyone did not get enough, but everyone got something. Food was not the only, or even real, issue. Lifestyle was the issue. The disciples wanted to solve a problem; Jesus wanted them to go further; he wanted them to examine how their choices were part of the problem. The wisdom of Jesus, and the generosity of a little boy who was willing to share his "five loaves and two fish," lead to not just a new and better way of thinking, but a new and better way of living.

What lifestyle changes do we need to make so that no one goes hungry in our world?

Eighteenth Sunday in Ordinary Time (B)

> When they found him on the other side of the lake,
> they said to him,
> "Rabbi, when did you come here?"
> Jesus answered them:
> "I assure you, you are not looking for me
> because you have seen signs but because you
> have eaten your fill of the loaves.
> You should not be working for perishable food
> but for food that remains unto life eternal,
> food which the Son of Man will give you;
> it is on him that God has set his seal."
> Jn 6: 24 – 35

Toward the end of John's gospel he writes, "Now Jesus did many other signs in the presence of his disciples that are not written in this book. But these are written that you may come to believe that Jesus is the Messiah, the Son of God, and that through this believe you may have life in his name." (Jn 20: 30) John's gospel is frequently called the gospel of signs because John's purpose in writing the fourth gospel is to lead more and more people to believe in Jesus as the Messiah.

The problem happens when the signs are not transparent. People are supposed to pass through the signs to experience Jesus as the Messiah. Today's gospel passage shows us what happens when signs are misunderstood.

The people have been fed in a miraculous way. They flock after Jesus not because he is the Messiah, but because he fed them. Now they want to be taken care of like their ancestors were fed with manna in the desert.

I was watching football this past Sunday. One of the defensive players was able to sack the quarterback. As the camera zoomed in on him, he knelt and made the sign of the cross. It was not the first time I had seen a player do that, but it was the first time that I questioned why he was doing it. I have never seen a quarterback throw an interception, and then make the sign of the cross. I have never seen a player make a mistake, and then make the sign of the cross. I don't want to ruin your football watching forever, but it seems to me that making the sign of the cross only when you are successful might not be respectful to the sign of the cross or the one who died on it. Just saying!

How have we misused the signs of our faith?

Eighteenth Sunday in Ordinary Time (C)

Someone in the crowd said to Jesus,
"Teacher, tell my brother to give me my share of our inheritance."
He replied, "Friend, who has set me up as your judge or arbiter?"
Then he said to the crowd,
"Avoid greed in all its forms.

> A man may be wealthy,
> but his possessions do not guarantee him life."
> Lk 12: 13 – 21

"Avoid greed in all its forms." We tend to limit greed to money and possessions, but greed can, and does, affect so much more than money and possessions.

We can be greedy with our words. We can withhold words of praise and encouragement. We can be greedy with our forgiveness. We can hang on to grudges long after their expiration date. We can be greedy with our attention as well as our understanding.

Turns out that greed has myriad faces and disguises. All of us have a form of greed that needs to be avoided. First we need to figure out where we have been greedy unknowingly. Not just where are we tight fisted, but where have we closed our minds, our eyes, and our hearts?

The spirituality of stewardship inspires us to share our time, talent, and treasure, and is a four-step process. We receive gratefully, develop responsibly, share justly, and make a return with increase to our God, who is after all the giver of all our gifts.

How have we allowed greed to prevent us from being better stewards of God's gifts?

Monday of the Eighteenth Week in Ordinary Time

> Jesus made the disciples get into a boat
> and proceed him to the other side of the sea,
> while he dismissed the crowd.
> After doing so, he went up on the mountain by himself to pray.
> When it was evening he was there alone.
> Mt 14: 22 – 36

If you read the entire gospel story for today, you will discover that it deals with Jesus walking on the water to save the disciples from rough seas. Why then have I chosen to focus on Jesus finding time to pray rather than his calming the waters? Because, if Jesus had not regularly found time to pray, he would not have been able to calm the waters.

We live busy lives. There is so much that needs to be done, so much that cries out for our attention. In our busyness the first thing to suffer is our prayer life. We cannot live our lives, as God wants us to, if we do not find the time to be with God. Go back for a moment to the gospel passage that I chose for this reflection. Jesus and the disciples had been busy. The crowd was big, and they had found a way to feed them. Now it is time to move on. Jesus becomes proactive, not reactive. He dismisses the disciples, and then he dismisses the crowd. By doing so he found time to be alone; he found time to pray. There will always be time for prayer if we are more clever about the way we steward the gift of time.

How can we find a time and a place for prayer in our lives?

Tuesday of the Eighteenth Week in Ordinary time

> Then his disciples approached and said to him,
> "Do you know that the Pharisees took offense
> when they heard what you said?"
> He said in reply, "Every plant that my heavenly Father
> has not planted will be uprooted.
> Let them alone; they are blind guides of the blind.
> If a blind man leads a blind man
> Both will fall into a pit."
> Mt 15: 1 – 2, 10 – 14

Jesus was not worried about people taking offense at what he was saying; Jesus was worried about speaking the truth. More of us should imitate Jesus in this regard. Please note that Jesus did not set out to offend anyone. He just spoke the truth, and let others worry about whether they should listen or take offense.

I saw a post on Facebook the other day that reminded me of today's gospel. The post said, "I won't be remembered as a woman who kept her mouth shut. I'm okay with that." Jesus is not remembered as a teacher who was politically correct, and he is okay with that.

Do you know what Irish diplomacy is? It is being able to tell someone to go to hell in a way that he looks forward to the journey. We need to learn how to tell the truth in a way that encourages others to listen. What good is the truth if it is spoken in a way that turns people off rather than opens them up?

Where have we been less than truthful in communicating with others?

Wednesday of the Eighteenth Week in Ordinary Time

> His disciples came and asked him,
> "Send her away, for she keeps calling out after us."
> He said in reply,
> "I was sent only to the lost sheep of the house of Israel."
> But the woman came and did him homage, saying,
> "Lord, help me."
> He said in reply,
> "It is not right to take the food of the children
> and throw it to the dogs."
> She said, "Please, Lord, for even the dogs eat the scraps
> That fall from the table of their masters."
> Then Jesus said to her in reply,
> "O woman, great is your faith!
> Let it be done for you as you wish."
> And her daughter was healed from that hour.
> Mt 15: 21 – 28

There is an old-time song called, "Something's Gotta Give." It was sung by all the old-time crooners, Ella Fitzgerald, Frank Sinatra, Bing Crosby, Sammy Davis Jr., and Johnny Mercer. The powerful words in that song were these, "When an irresistible force such as you, meets an old immovable object like me. You can bet just as sure as you live, something's gotta give. Something's gotta give." That's what today's gospel passage is all about.

We believe that Jesus took on our human condition. Today's gospel proves that he truly did. In this gospel passage, Jesus shows the prejudice, or if you can bear it, the bigotry that his age and his faith passed on to him. The Jews are the chosen people, all others are "goyim," which means that they are inferior.

In today's gospel, Jesus and his culture are the "immovable object." The Canaanite woman, whose daughter is possessed by a demon, is the irresistible force. She is first and foremost a mother, a mother with a sick child, a mother who will do whatever is necessary to take care of her daughter. She matches Jesus step for step. She counters every objection he has to getting involved. Finally, a mother's love wins out. Jesus leaves his comfort zone, and heals the daughter. Love triumphs over prejudice.

What historical prejudices does love need to banish from our lives?

Thursday of the Eighteenth Week in Ordinary Time

> From then on Jesus started to indicate to his disciples
> that he must go to Jerusalem to suffer greatly there
> at the hands of the elders, the chief priests, and the Scribes,
> and to be put to death, and raised up on the third day.
> At this Peter took him aside and began to remonstrate with him.
> "May you be spared, Master!
> God forbid that such a thing happen to you!"
> Jesus turned on Peter and said,
> "Get out of my sight, you satan!
> You are trying to make me trip and fall.
> You are not judging by God's standards but by man's."
> Mt 16: 13 – 23

Parents try to prevent their children from suffering; friends do the same. We want others to have it easier than we had it. That is always a mistake. We are who we are because of what we have suffered.

We have learned more from our failures than our successes. That is just the way life works. I'm not saying we should set out to fail. That would be crazy. I am just saying that not everything we try is going to succeed. When our efforts fail, we find out who we truly are.

It is not important that Jesus fell three times on his way to crucifixion. It is important that he got up three times. He did not give up; he fought to do his Father's will.

In sports there are two kinds of people when the big moment comes. Some rise to the challenge; others shrink from it. Some say, "Give me the ball" while others try to blend into the crowd. The person who wants the ball is not always successful, but gives it his best. The one who blends into the crowd is always successful but never succeeds.

Are we willing to suffer a little so that our faith can grow?

Friday of the Eighteenth Week in Ordinary Time

Jesus said to his disciples,
"Whoever wishes to come after me must deny himself,
take up his cross, and follow me.
For whoever wishes to save his life will lose it,
But whoever loses his life for my sake will find it.
What profit would there be for one to gain the whole world
and forfeit his life?
Or what can one give in exchange for his life?"
Mt 16: 24 – 28

We must constantly examine our values and our priorities to make sure that we are on the right path. It is too easy to get lost if we don't pay attention.

Leo Tolstoy wrote a short story titled, "How Much Land Does A Man Need." Pahom is the lead character in the story. He spends his life working hard and acquiring more and more land. However he is never satisfied. Finally, he comes across the Bakhkirs who are a simple-minded people with a lot of land, and a deal is struck. Pahom will pay one thousand rubles, and then he will buy as much land as he can walk around from sunrise to sunset. If he does not make it back to his starting point by sunset, he loses his thousand rubles and gets no land. Pahom is delighted with the deal. He sets out at sunrise and makes good progress. Toward the end of the day with sunset approaching he has to run furiously to make it to his starting point. He makes it before sunset, but exhausted from his running he drops dead and is buried where he died. He lost his life because of his greed for more and more land. Sometimes we make the same foolish mistake.

Where has seeking more and more ruined the quality of our lives?

Saturday of the Eighteenth Week in Ordinary Time

> Jesus rebuked him and the demon came out of him,
> and from that hour the boy was cured.
> Then the disciples approached Jesus in private and said,
> "Why could we not drive it out?"
> He said to them, "Because of your little faith.
> Amen, I say to you, if you have faith the size of a mustard seed,
> You will say to this mountain,
> 'Move from here to there,' and it will move.
> Nothing will be impossible for you."
> Mt 17: 14 – 20

Faith is tricky business. We believe in God; we believe in the power of prayer. But do we really believe? Sometimes we do, but too often we just go through the motions.

The was a severe drought in the Midwest. The people in one small town decided that what they needed to do was have an ecumenical prayer service asking God to send rain. On the appointed Sunday after all the morning services, the whole town gathered at the town square and for an hour they sang and prayed that God would send rain, but nothing happened. Dejected the people headed home. It was the minister who figured out what went wrong. Everyone gathered to plead for rain, but only one small boy showed up with an umbrella. Only he believed that their prayers would work.

There is a big difference between saying prayers, and believing in the power of prayer. When we doubt God's power, we prevent his working miracles.

Where have our prayers lacked conviction?

Nineteenth Sunday in Ordinary (A)

> Peter said to him in reply,
> "Lord, if it is you, command me to come to you on the water."
> He said, "Come."
> Peter got out of the boat and began to walk on the water toward Jesus.
> But when he saw how strong the wind was he became frightened;
> and, beginning to sink, he cried out, "Lord, save me!"
> Immediately Jesus stretched out his hand and caught him,
> and said to him, "O you of little faith, why did you doubt?"
> After they got into the boat, the wind died down.
> Those who were in the boat did him homage, saying,
> "Truly, you are the Son of God."
> Mt 14:22 – 33

Many years ago, I was on a study fellowship for psychiatry and religion at the Menninger Clinic then in Topeka, Kansas. During orientation, the director of our program said, "All of you are good amateur counselors or you would not be here. We are going to make you professional counselors." My hand went up immediately, and I asked, "What's the difference between an amateur and a professional counselor?" The director said, "An amateur is never sure he can repeat his successes."

In today's gospel, Jesus is the professional and Peter is the amateur. Peter lacked the confidence that he could, with Jesus' help, actually walk on water. Even though he was walking on water. He let himself be distracted by the wind and the waves. Doubt entered in, and he began to sink.

My father was fond of saying to my brothers and me, "If you don't think you can do it, you can't." There is a pre-set button in our brains that knows what we have, and what we can do. We need another button – one that looks to the future and sees what we can achieve if we do not limit ourselves to what we have already done. If we cannot overcome the pre-set button that limits us to the past, we will never grow into the future.

Where are fear, doubt, and a lack of confidence holding us back?

Nineteenth Sunday in Ordinary Time (B)

> This is the bread come down from heaven,
> for a man to eat and never die.
> I myself am the living bread come down from heaven.
> If anyone eats this bread
> he shall live forever;
> the bread I will give
> is my flesh for the life of the world.
> Jn 6: 41 – 51

Bread is a basic building block of every culture. Seems like every culture has its signature bread. Knowing this Jesus decided to leave his followers their signature bread – The Eucharist. This new bread was built on the unleavened bread of the Seder meal of the Passover. The Seder where the Jewish people call to mind their captivity in Egypt, their following Moses through the Red Sea to wander for forty years to enter the Promised Land. This matzo already had a rich history, and Jesus was going to add on to it. Jesus was the New Lamb whose blood shed on the cross would set his people free from sin. This is the living bread Jesus gave to his followers.

This bread would be life giving; this bread would nourish his people on their faith journey. We need to understand what Jesus means when he says, "If anyone eats this bread, he will live forever…" What he says cannot be taken literally because we all know people who fed on the Eucharist their whole life, but died nonetheless. He did not say we would live forever in this world. What he is promising is that the bread that sustains us here on earth will reserve for us a place at the eternal banquet in heaven. Why? Because if we are faithful to the Eucharist, and we receive it frequently, we will never forget Jesus and how he died for us. This remembering will keep us on the path that leads to heaven.

How could we be more faithful to the Eucharist?

Nineteenth Sunday in Ordinary Time (C)

> "Let your belts be fastened around our waists
> and your lamps be burning ready.
> Be like men awaiting their master's return from a wedding,
> so that when he arrives and knocks,
> you will open for him without delay.
> It will go well with those servants
> when the master finds them wide-awake on his return."
> Lk 12: 32 – 48

In my dreams I am going to live a long life, and then experience a brief illness and die. In my dreams, I will be prepared to meet my master. My brother, Mike, died after a two-year battle with cancer. He was prepared to meet his maker. My brother, Bill, went very early in the morning to swim as he did most mornings, and dropped dead of a heart attack. Because of who he was and how structured and organized he was about his life, I know he was prepared, as well as surprised, when his Master came.

Life is a gift. None of us knows how long we are going to live. Nevertheless most of us think we are going to live longer than we actually will. That is one of the foibles of the human condition. This quote from The Tablet magazine helps to keep me focused. I hope it will do the same for you. "It is the fact that each day counts us down that makes each one such a gift. There are only two days with fewer than twenty-four hours in each lifetime sitting like bookends astride our lives. One is celebrated every year but it is the other one that makes us see living as precious."

If we live each day as our last day, we will always be prepared to meet our Master.

Where have we lost sight of life as precious?

Monday of the Nineteenth Week in Ordinary Time

> When they entered Capernaum,
> the collectors of the temple tax approached Peter and said,
> "Does your master not pay the temple tax?"
> "Of course he does," Peter replied.
> Then Jesus on entering the house asked,
> Without giving him time to speak,
> "What is your opinion, Simon?
> Do the kings of the world take tax or toll from their sons,
> or from foreigners?"
> Mt 17: 22 – 27

Obviously Simon said, "From foreigners." But notice something else. The temple tax collectors approached Peter; Jesus questions him as Simon. Peter still has a lot to learn. His transformation from Simon to Peter is not yet complete. It never will be complete. Becoming who God wants us to be takes a lifetime.

We are all on a journey. Hopefully, we are becoming better believers with each passing day. Part of us wants to cling to the status quo, while part of us wants to move on. Some of us want to live while others are content to survive.

Jesus does not want us to survive when it comes to our faith. He wants us to live our faith. He sends us opportunities each and every day so that we can become more faithful. That's where ambivalence comes into our lives.

We can cling to our former ways. We can keep saying our old prayers and addressing them to the God of our past. Or we can keep some old prayers, but dare to speak to God using our own words as well. We can pray our rosary, and say our novenas and be done with it. Or we can pray the rosary some of the time, and dare some of the time to just sit and be quiet and let God speak to us.

Remember our faith is not an either or proposition. It is both. The past and our traditions are the foundation. But what good is a foundation if we never build on it?

Where have we let our faith stagnate?

Tuesday of the Nineteenth Week in Ordinary Time

"What is your opinion?
If a man has a hundred sheep and one of them goes astray,
will he not leave the ninety-nine in the hills
and go in search of the stray?
And if he finds it, amen, I say to you, he rejoices more over it
than over the ninety-nine that did not stray.
In just the same way, it is not the will of your heavenly Father
that one of these little ones be lost."
Mt 18: 1 – 5, 10, 12 – 14

It seems like with each passing year more and more believers go astray. I don't think I know a Catholic family, with children who are teenagers and older, that does not include at least someone who no longer is an active member of our faith. Young parents have difficulty finding Godparents who qualify to be Godparents. More and more Catholics are choosing to marry in non-religious ceremonies. The reasons for this waning of interest are many. For too many people going to church was a habit that has morphed into the habit of not going to church.

We, as a church, need to be more creative in finding ways to invite those who have gone astray to return to the fold.

One very effective way to re-evangelize lapsed Catholics is to be welcoming to people who go to church for weddings and funerals. Likewise, we need to be attentive to those Catholics whose practice of the faith has shrunk to Christmas, Ash Wednesday, Palm Sunday, and Easter, or some portion of that cluster. When I was still in active parish ministry, I was amazed by how many people would say to me, "We came to Christmas Mass, and we were reminded of what was missing in our lives. Thank you for making us feel welcomed." Sometimes all people need is an invitation, and a little encouragement.

Who can we invite back to Church? (Remember it might take more than one invitation. Be gentle.)

Wednesday of the Nineteenth Week in Ordinary Time

> Jesus said to his disciples:
> "If your brother sins against you,
> go and tell him his fault between you and him alone.
> If he listens to you, you have won over your brother.
> If he does not listen,
> Take one or two others along with you,
> so that every fact may be established
> on the testimony of two or three witnesses.
> If he refuses to listen to them, tell the Church."
> Mt 18: 15 – 20

The process that is mentioned in today's gospel is known as fraternal correction, and almost no one follows it. When there is a problem between two people, seldom if ever does the person who is offended say so. Instead, the offended person goes to a third person and complains. The third person then spreads the "news" with several others, and so it goes. People used to come to me to complain about someone else's behaviors. I would listen as best I could, but eventually I would say, "Have you spoken about this with him?" No one ever says yes. They wanted me to speak to the person. I remind them that I should be the last person involved in the process not the first one.

This is how things get blown out of proportion. When there is an issue, the two people involved should talk it through. In most cases, that will heal whatever rift there is. Once a third, or fourth person is added to the mix the chances of healing diminish. The sooner the third or fourth person removes himself from the equation the better the chance of resolution becomes.

Is there someone with whom we need to have a heart to heart conversation?

Thursday of the Nineteenth Week in Ordinary Time

> Peter approached Jesus and asked him,
> "Lord, if my brother sins against me,

> how often must I forgive him?
> As many as seven times?"
> Jesus answered,
> "I say to you, not seven times but seventy-seven times."
> Mt. 18: 21 – 19: 1

Peter is trying to measure out forgiveness; Jesus gently corrects him. In God's mind, and therefore in Jesus' mind, forgiveness is endless. To put it another way, we cannot exhaust God's mercy or forgiveness.

Imagine if Jesus had said to Peter, "Pick a number of times that you think I should forgive you." What would be a generous number? For Jesus and Peter the number seven and seventy-seven are filled with significance. Just think of the seven days of creation, and think of the Sabbath, which is the seventh day. There are seven laws of Noah and seven Patriarchs. The menorah in the temple has seven branches, the first verse of the Torah consists of seven words, and the walls of Jericho fell after the Israelites encircled it seven times. So there is special significance in Peter saying seven times, and in Jesus saying seventy-seven times.

One thing we know is that God will forgive us as often as we ask for forgiveness. He does not keep score; neither should we. Since God is prodigal in his forgiveness of us, we need to be prodigal in our forgiveness of others.

With whom do we need to offer forgiveness more generously?

Friday of the Nineteenth Week in Ordinary Time

> Some Pharisees approached Jesus, and tested him, saying,
> "Is it lawful for a man to divorce his wife for any cause whatever?"
> He said in reply, "Have you not read that from the beginning
> the Creator *made them male and female and said,*
> *For this reason a man shall leave his father and mother*
> *and be joined to his wife, and the two shall become one flesh?*
> So they are no longer two, but one flesh.
> Therefore, what God has joined together, man must not separate."
> Mt 19: 3 – 12

Few passages in scripture have caused as much confusion as today's passage. The Jewish people wrestled with the issue of divorce in Jesus' time; Catholics are still wrestling with the issue.

Today's gospel gives us food for thought. Jesus goes back to the beginning. The Pharisees cast their lot with Moses, "Then why did Moses command that the man give the woman a bill of divorce and dismiss her?" Back and forth they go.

There are several things to notice. First of all, there had been a change with regard to divorce. Second, it was a partial change. A man could divorce a woman, but, back then, women had no rights so they could not divorce a husband.

Jesus is calling the people of his time back to full observance of the meaning of marriage.

Nevertheless, the last line of today's gospel passage is very important, "Whoever can accept this ought to accept it." Lifelong marriage is the ideal. Not everyone will be able to fully embrace the ideal. We, as a church, need to find a better way to minister to those who divorce and remarry.

How can we help the church we love minister to those who have failed to achieve the marriage ideal?

Saturday of the Nineteenth Week in Ordinary Time

> Children were brought to Jesus
> so that he could place his hands on them in prayer.
> The disciples began to scold them,
> but Jesus said,
> "Let the children come to me.
> Do not hinder them.
> The kingdom of God belongs to such as these."
> Mt 19; 13 – 15

Sometimes in our rush to grow up we abandon our inner child. Children cry to get their way. We plot in more devious ways to get what we want. Children just experience their emotions; we manage them.

When we get a big promotion at work, we don't jump up and down and clap our hands. No, we tell the boss, "Thanks for putting your confidence in me. I will do my best not to disappoint you." Then we go and find a place where we can jump up and down and clap our hands.

Children are open to trying new things. We get set in our ways. If a child needs a hug, she will just crawl up in our lap and wait to be hugged. Children love to be complimented; we pretend that it is not necessary, but secretly crave to be complimented. Children readily ask for help; we think asking for help makes us look weak. Children are filled with gratitude, thanks, and praise. We grow hardened, satisfied, and focused on ourselves. Children have vivid imaginations; we forget how to dream.

To approach our God we need to rediscover our inner child.

How can we be more child like when we approach God?

Twentieth Sunday in Ordinary Time (A)

At that time, Jesus withdrew to the region of Tyre and Sidon. And behold, a Canaanite woman of that district came and called out,
"Have pity on me, Lord, Son of David!
My daughter is tormented by a demon."
But Jesus did not say a word in answer to her.
Mt 15: 21 – 28

The secret to powerful prayer is persistence. The woman in today's gospel is persistent. I think she is persistent because she is a mother, and mothers will not be deterred from getting help for their children.

Jesus ignores her; she persists. Finally, Jesus gives in and answers her prayer.

The question I have been asked most frequently in my years of ministry is, "Why doesn't God answer my prayers?" God always answers our prayers. Sometimes he says "yes" sometimes he says "no." The problem is we think God hears our prayers only when he grants what we want.

There is a Russian proverb that says, "Most prayer is that two plus two will equal five." We spend too much time asking God to change his mind. We get things backwards. We want God to do our will. That is not how it works. We are called to do his will.

Jesus has given us the perfect prayer and it is not the Our Father. Rather it is his prayer in the garden. He tells his Father what he wants, "Let this cup pass me by." But then he ends the way all prayers should end, "Not my will but yours be done."

Are we willing to surrender to the will of God?

Twentieth Sunday in Ordinary Time (B)

> The man who feeds on my flesh
> and drinks my blood
> remains in me, and I in him.
> Just as the Father who has life sent me
> and I have life because of the Father,
> so the man who feeds on me
> will have life because of me.
> Jn 6: 51 – 58

The English word "companion" helps to explain today's gospel. Our English word, as I mentioned previously, comes from two Latin words, "cum" which means with, and "panis" which means bread. A companion is someone with whom we break bread. Sharing a meal, sitting at table with others, breaking bread have lost some meaning in our fast-paced world. Families seldom find the time to gather at table. For a while this deficiency was ameliorated by Sunday dinner, but unfortunately that ritual of extended family gathering at table is now just a relic.

We Catholics have lost a sense of breaking bread together. Attendance at Mass is at an all time low. Because of the pandemic we could only gather in limited numbers. After being vaccinated, will our people come back? Our only hope is that since we have been unable to break bread together, we will once again realize how important it is to break bread together. Like the two disciples on the road to Emmaus hopefully we will recognize Jesus in the breaking of the bread, and learn how to be brothers and sisters once again.

How does the Eucharist give us life?

Twentieth Sunday in Ordinary Time (C)

> "Do you think I have come to establish peace on the earth?
> I assure you, the contrary is true;
> I have come for division.
> From now on, a household of five will be divided
> three against two, two against three;
> father will be split against son and son against father,
> mother against daughter and daughter against mother,
> mother-in-law against daughter-in-law,
> daughter-in-law against mother-in-law."
> Lk 12: 49 – 53

Whatever is Jesus talking about in this gospel? Of course he wants peace and togetherness. In another gospel Jesus says, "I pray that they might be one, just as you and I are one." Jesus can't have it both ways.

In today's gospel Jesus is using hyperbole. He does not really want people in the same family to be at each other's throats. Nevertheless, he wants his followers to be all in. If our faith puts us at odds with anyone, we will be tempted to water down our faith to preserve our friendships. Jesus is warning us not to water down our faith.

Too often this gospel is used as an either or argument. Either you agree with me or I'm done with you. Jesus' entire life mitigates against such a rigid stance. In spite of this some of us and some of our church leaders allow ourselves to get trapped in such dichotomies. This is especially true when we mix religion and politics. Without delving into particulars, let me just point out that when it comes to immigration, abortion, and capital punishment the church would be better off if she chose dialogue over condemnation.

Where have we allowed condemnation to interfere with dialogue?

Monday of the Twentieth Week in Ordinary Time

> The young man said to him,
> "All of these I have observed. What do I still lack?"
> Jesus said to him, "If you wish to be perfect, go,
> sell what you have and give to the poor,
> and you will have treasure in heaven.
> Then come, follow me."
> When the young man heard this statement, he went away sad,
> for he had many possessions.
> Mt 19: 16 – 22

The young man asks Jesus what he has to do to gain eternal life. Jesus tells him to keep the commandments. The young man says he is keeping the commandments. He then asks the question that is his downfall. "What more do I need to do?" That is when Jesus drops the hammer. "Sell all your possessions."

For the young man in today's gospel the thing that prevented him from giving his life to God was his possessions. For some of us possessions aren't the problem; for some of us pleasure is the problem. For some it is not possessions or pleasure; for some of us it is power. And so it goes.

There is always something that gets in the way of being a better believer. We need to recognize what that is, we need to name it, and then we need to take away its power.

Here is a wonderful story that reminds us that the best is yet to come. An elderly parishioner who is very sick asks for her pastor to pay her a visit. The priest comes, visits, anoints her and is about to leave when the woman says to him, "When I die, I want you to bury me with a fork in my right hand." The priest says he will, but he does not understand the request. The woman says to him, "You know at church suppers when they clear away the plates just before desserts are served, someone always says. 'Save your fork. The best is yet to come.' I want to remember that when I'm buried."

What have we allowed to get in the way of our being better believers?

Tuesday of the Twentieth Week in Ordinary Time

Jesus said to the disciples:
"Amen, I say to you, it will be hard for one who is rich
to enter the Kingdom of heaven.
Again I say to you,
it is easier for a camel to pass through the eye of a needle
than for one who is rich to enter the Kingdom of God."
Mt 19: 23 – 30

There is an unverified story that there was a small gate in the wall around the city of Jerusalem that was called, "The eye of the needle." Camels were used to carry heavy loads. A camel could get through the "eye of the needle" but only if the load was removed.

Let me try to explain. What is the difference between a pane of glass and a mirror? A mirror is a pane of glass which has one side coated with silver. Once the silver is applied you can only see yourself. The pane of glass is transparent and lets us see the beauty around us; the mirror only permits us to see ourselves. Our possessions are like the silver; our possessions make it difficult to see others.

The comedian George Carlin had a wonderful routine about "stuff." Life is all about stuff. Buying stuff, moving stuff, protecting stuff, insuring stuff, and getting more stuff. We never will have enough stuff; we are always on the lookout for more stuff. My mother was a good shopper; she never met a sale she did not love.

I remember once when I was quite young, and my mother was showing my father something she had bought on sale. My father, who was not a good shopper, and whose favorite saying was, "make do" was pretending to look at whatever my mother had bought. My mother was saying how much money she had saved. My father finally said, "You know, Kit, if you keep saving us money this way, we will go broke."

How does my stuff prevent me from seeing the needs of others?

Wednesday of the Twentieth Week in Ordinary Time

> "He said to one in reply,
> 'My friend, I am not cheating you.
> Did you not agree with me for the usual daily wage?
> Take what is yours and go.
> What if I wish to give this last one the same as you?
> Or am I not free to do as I wish with my own money?
> Are you envious because I am generous?'
> Thus, the last will be first, and the first will be last."
> Mt 20: 1 – 16

The landowner created this problem when he told his foreman to pay those who were hired at the end of the day first. By doing this he raised the expectations of those who had toiled the whole day. When they saw that those who worked the least got a full day's pay, they assumed that they would get more than the agreed amount. If he had paid the workers in the order they were hired, then those who had labored the whole day would have gotten their pay, and been on their way none the wiser.

Why did the landowner do what he did? He wanted to teach the workers about the dangers of comparisons. Comparisons create competition, and competition creates winners and losers. Once we start keeping score rifts are inevitable.

If we have siblings, we have had the discussion about who is mom's favorite. If we ask mom she will always say she has no favorite. Parents love each child fully, but differently. That's the way it should be. God does the same. We know that it would be a waste of time to discuss whom God loved the most, and that is the way it should be!

Where have we allowed comparisons to create divisions in our relationships?

Thursday of the Twentieth Week in Ordinary Time

> Jesus again in reply to the chief priests
> and elders of the people spoke in parables saying,
> "The Kingdom of heaven may be likened to a king

> who gave a wedding feast for his son.
> He dispatched his servants to summon the invited guests to the feast,
> but they refused to come.
> A second time he sent other servants, saying,
> 'Tell those invited: Behold, I have prepared my banquet,
> my calves and fattened cattle are killed,
> and everything is ready, come to the feast.'"
> Mt 22: 1 – 14

Every Sunday, Jesus invites us to the Eucharistic feast. As time goes on fewer and fewer of us go to the feast. We come up with our excuses. We are tired, Sunday is our one day to sleep in, or there are races to be run, and games to be played. I wonder how that makes God feel.

When I was in active ministry, we would have an appreciation celebration every year to thank all the members of the parish who had shared their time and talent to keep our parish a vibrant community of faith. The first time we had the celebration we had to give the caterer the number of people who would attend. We counted up the RSVPs we had received, and that was our number. Or so we thought.

We learned the hard way that there are hard RSVPs and soft RSVPs. Turns out that some people were going to come unless they got a better offer. They were going to come, but when the day arrived they just didn't feel like attending. We learned the hard way that an invitation to a free celebration is easier to ignore than when we buy a ticket. Maybe Jesus should have found a way to sell the Eucharist rather than give it away.

How can we be more faithful to Jesus' invitation to remember him?

Friday of the Twentieth Week in Ordinary Time

> When the Pharisees heard that Jesus had silenced the Sadducees,
> they gathered together, and one of them,
> a scholar of the law, tested him by asking,
> "Teacher, which commandment in the law is the greatest."
> Mt 22: 34 – 40

There are only two kinds of questions, sincere or insincere. The question in today's gospel is insincere. The scholar of the law who asked the question knew the answer. He was not interested in an answer. He was interested in putting Jesus in an uncomfortable position.

Jesus knew what was going on, and refused to be limited in his answer. He ignored the question, and gave a teaching about loving God with our whole being and loving our neighbor as ourself.

Anyone who has ever taught a class or given a lecture knows that not all questions are created equal. Some questions are sincere while others are insincere. I used to love when someone would ask me, "Is it a sin if I…?" In almost every case the person knew the answer, but they were looking for an out.

Too often our search for the truth is short circuited by I search to find someone who will tell us what we want to hear.

How can we be more sincere on our search for the truth?

Saturday of the Twentieth Week in Ordinary Time

> "As for you, do not be called, 'Rabbi.'
> You have but one teacher, and you are all brothers.
> Call no one on earth your father;
> you have but one Father in heaven.
> Do not be called 'Master';
> you have but one master, the Christ.
> The greatest among you must be your servant.
> Whoever exalts himself will be humbled;
> But whoever humbles himself will be exalted."
> Mt 23: 1 – 12

Most of us enjoy seeing someone get knocked down a peg or two. Especially if the one getting knocked down has an inflated opinion of her or himself. We know such folks exist. If we get to do the take down that is just the cherry on the sundae.

President George H. W. Bush liked to tell this story. He was at his home in Texas, and he was having a video made for his re-election campaign. He went to a nearby nursing home. He was being filmed walking down the main corridor. There was a man in a wheelchair outside his room. The president stopped, bent down, and said to the man, "Do you know who I am?" The man looked at him, smiled, and said, "No but this is your lucky day. Nurse Ellen is on duty. She is down at the nurses' station. She knows everyone's name. She'll be able to tell you who you are." Needless to say, that clip did not make the final cut. The fact that President H. W. Bush took great delight in telling the story is proof that he did not have an inflated opinion of himself.

Sometimes we get overly impressed with rank and/or titles. We should never forget that rank or title does not make the person, the person makes the rank or the title.

It is easy to think of others who have an inflated opinion of themselves, but can we see it in ourselves?

Twenty-first Sunday in Ordinary Time (A)

> Jesus went into the region of Caesarea Philippi and
> he asked his disciples,
> "Who do people say that the Son of Man is?"
> They replied, "Some say John the Baptist, others Elijah,
> still others Jeremiah or one of the prophets."
> He said to them, "But who do you say that I am?"
> Simon Peter said in reply,
> "You are the Christ, the Son of the living God."
> Mt 16: 13 – 20

Jesus, having taken on our human condition, was subject to all of the challenges that we face. We have to discover who we are, who God wants us to be, and communicate to others who we are. That is what the journey called life is all about.

Many years ago the staff and I went on a retreat. We had taken the Myers-Briggs personality test. The facilitator who was guiding us on the retreat went through all of the possible arrangements of the letter assigned to the four principle psychological functions – sensation, intuition, feeling and thinking. Then she gave each of us our four initials. One staff member was highly offended by her initials. The rest of the staff thought she had been correctly identified. Finally, the facilitator let her pick the initials she wanted and we continued on with the day. She either did not know or could not accept who she was.

Jesus knew who he was. He figured it out by prayer and feedback from others. In today's gospel he is measuring how well he was communicating who he was. It is always a two-part process – discovery and communicating.

I was once stationed with a pastor who would frequently tell me, "I am the most available priest in the diocese." One day, when things were not going well for me, he made the declaration one time too often. I, imprudently and impertinently, said, "It is too bad you are so unapproachable." My next assignment was much better. That is just who I am, but I am still working at improving.

Is our sense of self evolving or static?

Twenty-first Sunday in Ordinary Time (B)

> From this time on, many of his disciples broke away
> and would not remain in his company any longer.
> Jesus then said to the Twelve,
> "Do you want to leave me too?"
> Simon Peter answered him,
> "Lord, to whom shall we go?
> You have the words of eternal life.
> We have come to believe; we are convinced
> that you are God's holy one."
> Jn 6: 60 – 69

Our faith is filled with many difficult teachings. When one of those teachings conflicts with the life we are living, we have two choices. We can follow the teaching, or we can walk away. There are lots of ways to walk away, and we have perfected most of them.

The most popular way of walking away is to convince ourselves that we can act against our faith, but still be a believer. There is a certain truth in this method. We are still a believer, but we are diminished believers. In our secular lives, we have friends and diminished friends. We want true friends; God wants true believers.

Another way of walking away is to cut a few corners. We tell ourselves that we will just dissent this one time. Seldom, if ever, does this work because one time leads to a second time, and the third time is not far behind.

We need to be able to separate the teachings of God that are difficult, and the teachings of the Church that are difficult.

There was a cartoon many years ago that showed a woman arriving at the Gate of Heaven being greeted by St. Peter. Peter asks for the woman's name, and the woman says, "My name won't be in that book, I was excommunicated." Peter, taking off his glasses looks up and says, "exco… what?"

All God wants is for us to love him with all we've got and to love each other. How are we doing?

Twenty-first Sunday in Ordinary Time (C)

> Jesus went through cities and towns teaching – all the while
> making his way toward Jerusalem.
> Someone asked him,
> "Lord, are they few in number who are to be saved.?"
> He replied,
> "Try to come in through the narrow door.
> Many I tell you, will try to enter and be unable."
> Lk 13:22 – 30

We have been taught that our major task in life is to save our immortal souls. We have likewise been taught that saving our souls is hard work, and that many of us will fail. There was a time when most believers just hoped to make it to purgatory, and then hope that family and friends would pray them home to heaven.

I have no idea where this attitude came from, but I know it did not come from scripture. God, our Father, went to a lot of trouble to send his son, Jesus, into the world. Jesus knew his vocation was to be our redeemer. He even died on the cross so that we might be saved.

Jesus has given us salvation as a gift. We don't have to earn our salvation. Actually, we cannot earn our salvation. Salvation comes from God, and is pure gift. The only way not to be saved is to be committed to rejection of God's most precious gift. I have never met a believer who did not want to spend eternity with God in heaven. Admission to heaven is in God's hands; we need to trust God's love for us more fully.

God has given us the gift of salvation. Why are we still trying to earn it?

Monday of the Twenty-first Week in Ordinary Time

A man came up to Jesus and said,
"Teacher, what good must I do to possess everlasting life?"
…The young man said to him,
"I have kept all these; what do I need to do further?"
Jesus told him,
"If you seek perfection, go, sell your possessions,
and give to the poor.
You will then have treasure in heaven.
After that, come back and follow me."
Hearing these words, the young man went away sad,
for his possessions were many.
Mt 19: 16 – 22

The amazing thing about this gospel is that getting rid of his possessions was just the first step for the young man in becoming a follower of Jesus. As the dialogue reveals, the young man was already keeping all the commandments; he thinks he is ready for more, but Jesus sees his weakness – his possessions. He was not ready to give up his things. All of us have something that prevents us from being better believers.

We need to discover what our Achilles' heel is, and it will be different for all of us. For some it will be possessions; for others it will be status. For some it will be appearances; for others it will be notoriety.

C. S. Lewis, in Screwtape Letters, which is a wonderful little book about the devil training an apprentice devil on how to lead people astray, expresses it this way, "It does not matter how small the sins are provided that their cumulative effect is to edge the man away from the Light and out into the Nothing. Murder is no better than cards if cards can do the trick." There is something that keeps each one of us from being a better believer.

What is it that keeps us from being a better believer?

Tuesday of the Twenty-first Week in Ordinary Time

Jesus said:
"Woe to you, scribes and Pharisees, you hypocrites.
You pay tithes of mint and dill and cumin,
And have neglected the weightier things of the law;
judgment and mercy and fidelity.
But these you should have done, without neglecting the others.
Blind guides, who strain out the gnat and swallow the camel!"
Mt 23: 23 – 26

From time to time, we all need to evaluate our priorities. The scribes and Pharisees did not start off in the wrong; they slowly drifted there. It happens all the time.

Whenever a politician gets arrested it is the same thing. They start off with all the best intentions, but then because of some combination of power, greed, and arrogance, they drift off the straight and narrow. The same can happen in every occupation and profession. Police, doctors, nurses, lawyers, mechanics, priests, electricians, contractors, or cooks all start off with the best and purest of intentions. Unfortunately, not everyone stays on the right path.

One of my favorite cartoons in the newspaper is Shoe. In one cartoon the senator, Batson D. Belfry, is seated at the bar and he says to Roz Specklehen, the bartender, "My life has come full circle." She sarcastically responds, "You cut enough corners and that is bound to happen."

Chesterton, as I have already stated in a previous reflection, once said, "Christianity has not been tried and found wanting. It has been found difficult and left untried." The creators of Shoe, Gary Brookins and Susie MacNally, Chesterton, and Jesus are all saying the same thing. Pick which iteration works best for you.

Where are we guilty of cutting corners? What actions of ours would cause Jesus to say, "Woe to you"?

Wednesday of the Twenty-first Week in Ordinary Time

> Jesus said,
> "Woe to you, scribes and Pharisees, you hypocrites.
> You are like whitewashed tombs,
> which appear beautiful on the outside.
> but inside are full of dead men's bones and every kind of filth.
> Even so, on the outside you appear righteous,
> but inside you are filled with hypocrisy and evildoing."
> Mt 23: 27 – 32

I wonder if Jesus would ever have said, "You put lipstick on a pig. It is still a pig." We will never know, but we do know that Jesus knew how to use colorful language to make a point. Where did he ever come up with "whitewashed tombs"? It needs no explanation, and once you hear it you cannot erase it from memory. Even though it needed no explanation, Jesus went right ahead and gave them a full explanation.

We know all about hypocrisy. We have been hypocrites on one level or another. When we are nervous and we project confidence. We are hypocrites. When we see a police car and get a cramp in our right leg. We are hypocrites. Sometimes we are hypocrites in church.

We know who we are, and God knows who we are. We need to learn how to be more straightforward in our dealings with others. If there is something not right in our lives we need to confront it, and change it not try to hide it.

Where have we learned to accept cosmetic rather than real change in our lives?

Thursday of the Twenty-first Week in Ordinary Time

> Jesus said to his disciples:
> "Stay awake!
> For you do not know on which day your Lord will come.
> Be sure if this:
> if the master of the house
> had known the hour of night when the thief was coming,
> he would have stayed awake
> and not let his house be broken into.
> So too, you also must be prepared,
> for at an hour you do not expect, the Son of Man will come."
> Mt 24: 42 – 51

When our time comes, we will not be ready. That is a given. No one can stay in prepared mode perpetually. So rather than be prepared, what we need is to just do what is right all the time, and then we will automatically be prepared.

We had a bishop when I was ordained who used to love to throw out Latin quotes. One of his favorite quotes was, "Age quod agis!" which means, "Do what you are doing!"

If you are praying, pray. If you are working, work. If you are playing, play. "Do what you are doing!" Easier said than done. We tend to blur the lines between our prayer, work, and leisure. We are all too familiar with distractions in prayer.

There is a story about a poor man who told his King that he admired his horse. The King said to the man, "If you can say the Our Father all the way through without a distraction, I will give you my horse." The man agreed. He closed his eyes and began the Our Father. When he got to "give us this day our daily bread" he opened his eyes and said, "Does the saddle come with it?"

How many people check in on work while on vacation? How many of us are unwilling to leave our cell phones in the car while we play a round of golf?

How can we learn to focus better so that we can do what we are doing?

Friday of the Twenty-first Week in Ordinary Time

> Five of them were foolish and five were wise.
> The foolish ones, when taking their lamps,
> brought no oil with them,
> but the wise brought flasks of oil with their lamps.
> Mt 25: 1 – 13

This is a very strange parable because it sounds like Jesus is telling his disciples not to help people in need. But we know that is not the case. We are always to put the needs of others ahead of our needs.

What Jesus is saying is be wise rather than foolish. We need to think about our faith. We need to anticipate challenges to our faith, and be prepared to overcome them.

We know that prayer is important; we know that time is precious. We need to find time for prayer. We can go about that in two different ways. The wise thing to do is to understand ourselves. Are we morning people? Then we need to find time to pray in the morning when we are at our best. If we are evening people we do the same. The one thing we don't want to do is plan to pray when we find the time because that never happens. We have to schedule prayer time. Important things we plan for, we put them in our calendar and we work our day around those important events. God is important; prayer is important. We need to schedule both God time and prayer time into every day. Be prepared to be amazed at how much better life is when we find time for God.

How can we be more disciplined about our prayer time?

Saturday of the Twenty-First Week in Ordinary Time

> It will be as when a man who was going on a journey
> he called in his servants and entrusted his possessions to them.
> To one he gave five talents; to another, two;
> to a third, one –
> to each according to his ability.
> Then he went away.
> Mt 25: 14 – 30

We in our uniqueness have different God-given talents. The challenge of life is to take the talents that God has given us, and develop them to the best of our ability, and then to share our talents with others.

Developing talent is hard work. Some do it better than others. We need to do the best we can with what has been given to us. That is all God asks.

Unfortunately, too often, rather than be satisfied with what we have, we wish we had something more or something different. In today's gospel, we can be sure that the person who got one talent wanted to have five talents. The same is true of the person who got two talents. We might think that the person who got the five talents was satisfied, but we know he wasn't. He was probably wondering why he did not get all eight talents.

We will never be grateful. We will never develop the attitude of gratitude until we learn to be satisfied with what we have. We live in a world that keeps telling us we need more. There is always something we don't have that is going to make us happier. That is a lie. Things don't make us happier. We make ourselves happier by thanking God for what we have and by making the most of all he has given us.

What talents have I let go fallow in my life?

Twenty-second Sunday in Ordinary Time (A)

> Jesus began to show his disciples
> that he must go to Jerusalem and suffer greatly
> from the elders, the chief priests, and the scribes,
> and be killed and on the third day raised.
> Then Peter took Jesus aside and began to rebuke him.
> "God forbid, Lord! No such thing shall ever happen to you."
> He turned and said to Peter,
> "Get behind me Satan! You are an obstacle to me.
> You are thinking not as God does, but as human beings do."
> Mt 16: 21 – 27

There is nothing worse than a well-intended friend who wants to protect us from all danger. There is an old saying, "I have learned more from my failures than my successes," and it is true.

There is no such thing as a life without suffering or pain. Hurt and disappointment are part of life. We don't have to like them, but we do need to learn to befriend them. We live in a culture that believes there must be a pill for everything that makes us uncomfortable. Nothing could be further from the truth.

We grow stronger when we wrestle with the challenges of life. No one has ever learned to ride a bicycle without falling. The bumps and bruises are part of the process. We fall, we get up, and we try again. Eventually, we learn how to balance ourselves so we don't have to fall anymore.

As adults my brothers and I quote our father quite a bit. Looking back, it seems like he had a saying for every situation. When we were young we would roll our eyes at his sayings, but as adults we cherished them. One of his favorites was, "Many a young man has been deprived of working hard at precisely those things that made a man of his father." That is what Jesus is teaching Peter in today's gospel.

Where have we let failure or fear of failure keep us from growing?

Twenty-second Sunday in Ordinary Time (B)

He said to them:
"How accurately Isaiah prophesied about you
hypocrites when he wrote,
'This people pays me with lip service
but their hearts are far from me.
Empty is the reverence they do me
because they teach as dogma mere human precepts.'
You disregard God's commandments,
and cling to what is mere human traditions."
Mk 7: 17 – 18, 21 – 22, 27

There is a bit of hypocrisy in the best of us. We condemn others for the very things that hide in the shadows of our conscience. Or we line up behind the boss not because he is right but because he is the boss. Unfortunately, we can be a little bit hypocritical when it comes to our faith as well. We know how to look holy when the situation calls for the "holy look." We can go into church, genuflect, slide into our pew, lower the kneeler, close our eyes, tent our hands, and then pretend to be praying.

In recent years we have had to confront that some of our bishops were more interested in the institutional church than they were of abused minors. I am sure God will forgive their hypocrisy but he will also understand if it takes the rest of us awhile to forgive them. They paraded around in all their glory, speaking out boldly about the moral evils in our culture, but were mute concerning the moral evil in their culture.

Everyone knows right from wrong. We know it in our heart of hearts. Too often for reasons that are torturous at best, we do not do what we know is right. This problem has been around for a long time because St. Paul tells us, "What I do, I do not understand. For I do not do what I want, but I do what I hate." (Rom 7: 15) The correction has to begin within each one of us. Once our house is in order, we can move on to help others.

What is the most hypocritical thing about us?

Twenty-second Sunday in Ordinary Time (C)

> "What you should do when you have been invited
> is go and sit in the lowest place,
> so when your host approaches you he will say,
> 'My friend, come up higher.'
> This will win you the esteem of your fellow guests.
> For everyone who exults himself shall be humbled
> and he who humbles himself shall be exulted."
> Lk 14: 1, 7 – 14

This gospel represents a middle step not a final step. The final step would be to not care where you are seated. If there is going to be a high table, there have to be low tables. The whole notion is sort of foolish. Just go, and be seated. Jockeying for position is a waste of time. Go, sit down, enjoy the meal, and don't overstay your welcome.

Deliberately exalting ourselves is as foolish as false humility. I think God is equally offended when we have a puffed up opinion of ourselves as when we have too low an opinion of ourselves. In my life, I have met far more people who have too low an opinion of themselves. God wants us to have an honest opinion of ourselves. God has blessed each and every one of us with a unique set of gifts. We need to discover our gifts, develop them, and share them with others. Too often, we have been taught to hide our gifts, or even worse deny that we have gifts. When we cooperate in sharing our gifts, our world is improved. When we compete with our gifts, our world is diminished.

What gifts have we hidden from others?

Monday of the Twenty-second Week in Ordinary Time

> Jesus came to Nazareth, where he had grown up,
> and went according to his custom
> into the synagogue on the Sabbath day.
> He stood up to read and was handed a scroll of the prophet Isaiah.
> He unrolled the scroll and found the passage where it was written:
> *The Spirit of the Lord is upon me*
> *to bring glad tidings to the poor.*
> *He has sent me to proclaim liberty to captives*
> *and recovery of sight to the blind,*
> *to let the oppressed go free,*
> *and to proclaim a year acceptable to the Lord.*
> Lk 4: 16 – 30

This gospel is important because Jesus proclaims to his hometown people that he is the Messiah. In my opinion, it is more important because of this detail, "and went according to his custom into the synagogue on the Sabbath day." To be more specific, it is important because of "according to his custom."

This small detail has enormous consequences. Would he have ever discovered himself to be the Messiah if he was not accustomed to going to the synagogue? Was it just his custom? No! He was introduced to the Sabbath by Mary and Joseph just as their parents had introduced them. The practice of our faith is a learned experience.

One of my favorite college professors was fond of saying, "Religion is caught not taught." The contemporary church needs to find better ways to pass on the faith. We need to support and encourage parents as they pass on the faith to their children. It seems that with each passing generation the gift of faith grows weaker and weaker whereas it should be growing stronger and stronger.

How can we do a better job in making sure the next generation of believers are churchgoers?

Tuesday of the Twenty-second Week in Ordinary Time

> In the synagogue there was a man
> with the spirit of an unclean demon,
> He cried out in a loud voice,
> "What have you to do with us, Jesus of Nazareth?
> Have you come to destroy us?
> I know who you are – the Holy One of God!"
> Jesus rebuked him and said, "Be quiet! Come out of him!"
> Then the demon threw the man down in front of them
> and came out of him without doing him any harm.
> Lk 4: 31 – 37

The demons recognized Jesus as the "Holy One of God" long before the chosen people did. The people following Jesus around were still trying to figure out who he was, not the demons. The demons knew Jesus was different. As scripture tells us, "He spoke with authority not like the scribes and the Pharisees."

When some people say, "I give you my word," we know that they are speaking the truth. When others say it, they are just empty words.

Some people just command attention. It is difficult to say why or how, but we just know it is true. Jesus commanded attention. He did not tell people to pay attention; he spoke in a way that commanded attention. Was it his voice? Was it the look in his eye? Was it the words he used? Probably a combination of all of the above, and a few more that we don't know about.

He commanded demons and they obeyed; he invites us to "follow him" and we demure.

How can we hear the call of Jesus better and follow him more surely?

Wednesday of the Twenty-second Week in Ordinary Time

> After Jesus left the synagogue, he entered the house of Simon.
> Simon's mother-in-law was afflicted with a severe fever,
> and they interceded with him about her.
> He stood over her, rebuked the fever, and it left her.
> She got up immediately and waited on them.
> Lk 4: 38 – 44

So Peter had a mother-in-law. As far as I know there is only one way to get a mother-in-law. So Peter was married, but maybe not. Maybe Peter's wife was dead. The gospel does say that the mother-in-law got up and waited on them. If Peter's wife was there you would think that she would have let her mother take a bit of a rest. This has nothing to do with my reflection for today. It is just an example of how my mind sometimes works.

So what is today's message? Healing is part of everyday life, and healing is not reserved to Jesus. We need to continue Jesus' healing ways. We are probably not going to be faith healers, but that's all right because there are many ways to heal.

When we visit someone who is homebound, we help to heal their isolation. When we find the time to listen to someone whose life is weighing him down, we lighten his burden. When we smile with someone who is suffering, we lessen her pain. When we bring food to the parish food pantry, we ease the food insecurity of who knows how many people. Chances are we are not going to heal illness or raise the dead, but we certainly can heal feelings and give hope to the suffering.

How can we see more clearly the wounds that need healing in our world?

Thursday of the Twenty-second Week in Ordinary Time

> Then he sat down and taught the crowds from the boat.
> After he had finished speaking, he said to Simon,
> "Put out into deep water and lower your nets for a catch."
> Simon said in reply,
> "Master, we have worked hard all night and have caught nothing,
> but at your command I will lower the nets."
> When they had done this, they caught a great number of fish
> and their nets were tearing.
> Lk 5: 1 – 11

"Put out into deep water" was a favorite saying of St. John Paul II. He would say it in Latin, "Duc in altum!" None of us like to be told what to do. Fishermen certainly don't like being told how to fish by a traveling preacher. Fishermen know their trade; they have their spots. They trust their knowledge.

The Latin phrase quoted above uses the imperative tense. It is not a request; it is a command. Peter hears his tone of voice, and responds. That is how all growth happens. Someone draws us out of our comfort zone, and we try something new.

We are by nature not risk takers. We get set in our ways. On one level, we know we can be more and do more, but we learn to settle. Our God invites us to live – too often we choose to survive.

Thank God for good parents, who keep encouraging their children to grow. Thank God for friends who see our potential and encourage us to go for it. Thank God for those wonderful teachers who motivate us to keep growing in mind and spirit. Thank God for coaches who push us to get better and better.

Thank you, God, for always inviting us to become better believers and more complete people.

Who are the people who have kept us growing?

Friday of the Twenty-second Week in Ordinary Time

> And he also told them a parable,
> "No one tears a piece from a new cloak to patch an old one.
> Otherwise, he will tear the new
> and the piece from it will not match the old cloak.
> Likewise, no one pours new wine into old wineskins.
> Otherwise, the new wine will burst the skins,
> and it will be spilled, and the skins will be ruined.
> Rather, new wine must be poured into fresh wineskins.
> And no one who has been drinking old wine desires new,
> For he says, 'The old is good.'"
> Lk 5: 33 -39

Today's gospel sounds more like something from the Old Farmer's Almanac than scripture. Every now and again, Jesus gets folksy and talks about lighting candles, searching for lost coins, or how to mend clothing and store wine. Jesus was a great teacher because he could connect with people on their level, and then gently lead them to the next level.

What Jesus is saying in today's reading is that things do not stand still. Clothes wear out, wine needs to mature. We need to approach things with a positive attitude. We need to learn how to make better choices.

If we get to pick between a new coat or an old coat, we will pick the new coat. If we can drink a nice mature, full-bodied wine or a yet undeveloped wine, we will choose the mature wine. Sometimes new is better; sometimes old is better. It depends on other factors.

When it comes to the institutional church, too often what is old is seen as the only good thing. This attitude is what too often is holding back the growth of our church. There is a saying, which I have already used several times in these reflections, but it bears repeating: Ecclesia semper reformanda, (the church always reforming) in our Catholic tradition that too often is ignored.

We need to constantly sift through new ideas and old customs. The trick is finding the correct balance. This is what the Second Vatican

Council tried to do. This is what Pope Francis is trying to do. The traditionalists are trying to defeat the winds of change that need to blow through our church.

Where do we need to be more open-minded when it comes to passing on our faith?

Saturday of the Twenty-second Week in Ordinary Time

> While Jesus was going through a field of grain on a sabbath,
> his disciples were picking the heads of grain,
> rubbing them in their hands, and eating them.
> Some Pharisees said,
> "Why are you doing what is unlawful on the sabbath?"
> Lk 6: 1 – 5

Jesus and the Pharisees had a running battle over sabbath rules. It seems like Jesus is always healing someone on the sabbath, and the Pharisees were always complaining about it. Jesus was trying to help them see that the Sabbath and its accompanying laws, rules, and regulations were there to help people serve God. The Pharisees thought the law, rules, and regulations were there to be served.

From time to time, I have had a similar issue with an occasional bishop. I would get called in to the bishop's office, and was told, "You can't do such and such." I would always respond, "Obviously I can do such and such because I have done it. You can disagree and disapprove of what I have done, which you are. Now we can have a discussion." Most bishops were not interested in a discussion, much like the Pharisees in today's gospel.

When disagreements are approached as accusations resolution seldom happens. When disagreements are discussed, and sides are clarified, resolution frequently happens. Since this is so, why do we waste so much time making accusations, and so little time having discussions?

Where in our lives have we confused understanding with agreement?

Twenty-third Sunday in Ordinary time (A)

> "Again, amen, I say to you,
> if two of you agree on earth
> about anything for which you pray,
> it shall be granted to them by my heavenly Father.
> For where two or three are gathered in my name,
> there am I in the midst of them."
> Mt 18: 15 – 20

I have experienced today's gospel; I hope you have as well. Sometimes when we gather with other believers, we feel the presence of Jesus among us. I wish it happened more often. Perhaps it can if we remember that Jesus can be present in a variety of ways.

Whenever a family invites me to pray with them when someone is dying it almost always happens. The prayers for the anointing of the sick are very powerful, and they can be very specific. When someone is dying of old age the prayer talks about having grown weak under the burden of years. When death is because of an illness the prayer talks about the person having shared the sufferings of Jesus. A family united in suffering and praying for one of their own can be a very powerful experience.

When we gather to celebrate a wedding, the uniting of two people and two families, the prayers offered by the church give added meaning to the celebration. When the gathering is to offer our final prayers for a deceased family member or a friend and together we pray, "Lord, for your faithful people life is changed, not ended. When the body of our earthly dwelling lies in death, we gain an everlasting dwelling place in heaven," frequently we can feel Jesus guiding us through our grief.

When we gather in community, we become part of something bigger than our individuality. We belong together, and together we are stronger because Jesus wraps us in his loving embrace.

When and how have we felt the presence of Jesus in community?

Twenty-third Sunday in Ordinary Time (B)

> Some people brought to him a deaf man with a speech impediment
> and begged him to lay his hand on him.
> Jesus took him off by himself away from the crowd.
> He put his fingers into the man's ears
> and, spitting, touched his tongue;
> then he looked up to heaven and emitted a groan.
> He said to him, "Ephphatha!" (That is "Be opened!")
> At once the man's ears were opened;
> He was freed from his impediment, and began to speak plainly.
> Mk 7: 31 – 37

There is much to like in this gospel passage. The first thing that hits me is that Jesus took the man off by himself; he took him away from the crowd. By so doing, he gave the man both privacy and dignity. That was his first gift to the man.

The second gift is that Jesus did more than lay a hand on him. He touched him intimately and personally. He stuck his fingers in the man's ears, and then, the part that I like best, he spit into his hands. Just pause and get a picture of that in your mind. Jesus spitting. Indeed he really did take on our human condition.

Finally, he looked up to heaven, the source of his healing strength, and he groaned. This was not easy. Jesus had to give something of himself for the man to be healed. This intimacy, this personal touching, was Jesus' second gift.

Then came the "Ephphatha!" moment. He opened his ears and loosened his tongue. He made him whole once again. This is the final gift.

How many times in our life has Jesus touched us, and opened us up to new experiences? How many times has he helped us see the hidden dignity in others?

How many times has he helped us hear truth from an unlikely source? How many times has he helped us see the bigotry we were unaware of?

Where do we still need Jesus to open us up to the more to come in our lives?

Twenty-third Sunday in Ordinary Time (C)

> On one occasion when a great crowd was with Jesus,
> he turned to them and said,
> "If anyone comes to me without turning his back
> on his father and mother, his wife and his children,
> indeed his very self, he cannot be my follower.
> Anyone who does not take up his cross and follow me
> cannot be my disciple."
> Lk 14: 25 – 33

Jesus is not looking for part-time followers; Jesus wants only full-time followers. In reality, there is no way we can be part-time Christians any more than we can be a part-time human being.

To follow Jesus is a decision, and one that should not be made lightly. Officially, we become Christians when our parents present us for Baptism. Unofficially, we become Christians when as adults we decide to own our Baptism. In reality, there are far fewer Christians than there are people who have gone through a ceremony and had some water poured on their heads.

Important decisions in our lives require a process. Where we are going to go to college, what work are we going to do, where will we live, will we marry, who will we marry? None of these decisions are snap decisions. We deliberately go through a process, and evaluate the pros and the cons. Then we act. We don't always make the best decision, but we try.

Have we ever made a decision to be a believer?

Monday of the Twenty-third Week in Ordinary time

> Then Jesus said to them,
> "I ask you, is it lawful to do good on the sabbath
> rather than to do evil,

> to save life rather than to destroy it?"
> Looking around at them all, he said to him,
> "Stretch out your hand."
> He did so and his hand was restored.
> But they became enraged
> and discussed together what they might do to Jesus.
> Lk 6: 6 – 11

Rather than discuss what they were going to do about Jesus they should have been discussing how can we get more people healed. Life gave them a gift, and they turned it into a problem.

All of us should be dedicated to making life better for as many people as possible. That is what Jesus did; we should be following his example. Jesus was not worried about what the Pharisees were going to do or say. He wasn't even worried about it being the Sabbath. He saw a man who was hurting, and he did something about it.

The simple fact is that ultimately Jesus was put to death because he cared more about people than he did about rules and regulations, and the Pharisees cared more about the rules and regulations than they did about people.

Would that the mentality of the Pharisees died with them, but it did not. The church has lots of laws, rules, and regulations none of which should come before people, but they do. Pope Francis is trying to follow the example of Jesus when it comes to the divorced and remarried, the issue of gender and sexual attraction, the undocumented, and a whole host of other sensitive issues. Unfortunately, the old guard has decided to emulate the Pharisees rather than Jesus. Will the church, will we, ever learn?

Where are we guilty of putting rules and regulations ahead of people?

Tuesday of the Twenty-third Week in Ordinary Time

> Jesus went out to the mountain to pray,
> Spending the night in communion with God.
> At daybreak, he called his disciples

> and selected twelve of them to be his apostles:
> Simon, to whom he gave the name Peter,
> and Andrew his brother,
> James and John, Philip and Bartholomew,
> Matthew and Thomas, James son of Alphaeus,
> and Simon called the Zealot,
> Judas son of James, and Judas Iscariot,
> who turned traitor.
> Lk 6: 12 – 19

No one will challenge that the twelve apostles are important, and yet most believers cannot name all twelve. Who they are is less important that what they did. They were sent to be Jesus' messengers.

Nevertheless, the thing I want to emphasize is what Jesus did just before he chose his apostles. He spent the night in prayer. He sought his Father's guidance, and he followed it. Imagine how our lives would change if we spent more time in prayer. Unfortunately, prayer is the first thing to go in our busy lives. We know prayer is important, and we say we want to pray more often, but when it comes to allocating our time prayer is the first thing to go. It should not be that way.

I am amazed at how many very busy people find time to pray. Usually, they find the time by getting up one hour earlier, and dedicating that "new found" time to prayer.

One advantage of praying early is that the rest of the day is built on a strong foundation. Some people are not morning people so this solution probably won't work for them. What is important is to find time (perhaps an hour is too much at the beginning but it should be a goal), and use that time for prayer. Everyone's day is different but we all find time to eat, sleep, watch TV, exercise, and be electronically connected. Adding prayer to the list of things we do every day will make us better people.

What is our best time to pray?

Wednesday of the Twenty-third Week in Ordinary Time

> Blessed are you when people hate you,
> and when they exclude and insult you,
> and denounce your name as evil
> on account of the Son of Man.
> Rejoice and leap for joy on that day!
> Behold, your reward will be great in heaven.
> For their ancestors treated the prophets
> in the same way.
> Lk 6: 20 – 26

Unfortunately, we have learned to live our faith in a way that offends no one. As a friend of mine likes to say, "We have defanged Christianity." If we were to live our faith full throttle, we would stand apart from most other people.

I remember presiding at Mass for a community of religious brothers. In my homily I asked if anyone had ever said, "I think you are crazy." I then went on to give examples of how we are to put the needs of others before our own needs, how we are to forgive others even if they aren't sorry for what they have done, how we are to minister to those on the fringes of society, or how we need to turn the other cheek when we are attacked. At the sign of peace just before communion, one of the brothers who had spent almost all of his religious life in the missions responded to my "Peace be with you" by saying, "I think you are crazy." He caught me completely off guard. I never had the courage to ask him if I was crazy because of what I said in my homily, or because of the way I live my life. I hope it was the latter.

Where have we "defanged" our faith commitment?

Thursday of the Twenty-third Week in Ordinary Time

> "Stop judging and you will not be judged.
> Stop condemning and you will not be condemned.
> Forgive and you will be forgiven.

> Give and gifts will be given to you;
> a good measure, packed together, shaken down, and overflowing,
> will be poured into your lap.
> For the measure with which you measure
> will in return be measured out to you."
> Lk 6: 27 – 38

We spend too much time judging other people. At least I do, and I don't think I am alone. Not only do we spend too much time judging others, we encourage others to do the same. Stories are the best way to teach. A minister went into a restaurant and sat at the counter. Seated next to him was a truck driver. The behind the counter staff person walked by the two of them several times. Finally, the minister in exasperation said, "Maybe we are invisible." The truck driver said, "Maybe they are understaffed." After a few minutes the minister mumbled out loud, "Why can't we place our order." The truck driver said, "I'm sure they will get to us as soon as they can." A little while later the minister said, "Maybe when hell freezes over, they will get to us." The truck driver responded, "They are doing the best they can." Finally, the behind the counter person came over and said, "Thanks for being patient, we had a water pipe burst and things are a bit crazy right now." The embarrassed minister thought to himself, "The truck driver lives what I preach. I need to learn from him."

Where do we need to be more understanding in our dealings with others?

Friday of the Twenty-third Week in Ordinary Time

> Why do you notice the splinter in your brother's eye,
> but do not perceive the wooden beam in your own?
> How can you say to your brother,
> 'Brother, let me remove that splinter in your eye'
> when you do not even notice the wooden beam in your own eye?
> You hypocrite! Remove the wooden beam in your eye first;
> then you will see clearly
> to remove the splinter in your brother's eye."
> Lk 6: 39 – 42

Have you ever seen someone do an imitation of you? If you have chances are you did not recognize yourself. We see ourselves from the inside out; others see us from the outside in. We and they see very different realities.

Many years ago I was on a study fellowship in psychology and religion. One of the courses was in pastoral counseling. As part of the program, I had to get one of the couples that I was counseling to come into the institute, and agree to have one of our sessions monitored. When my session was over, I gathered with my fellow students, and our supervisor critiqued my session. He asked, "Why do you favor the wife's opinions more than the husband's?" I said I did not; he showed me the video. He was correct; I was unaware that I was doing it. A lot of that goes on in life. We are more attuned to the faults of others than to our own!

Another story might help. On a Saturday afternoon a husband and wife were having lunch. Their new next-door neighbor was hanging out her wash to dry. The wife said to her husband, "Why would anyone hang out dirty clothes to dry?" The husband tried to ignore the question; the wife repeated it. Without saying a word the husband got up, took a paper towel, went outside and wiped the dirt off of the kitchen window. Turns out the clothes were clean; their window was dirty.

Where have we become blind to our faults?

Saturday of the Twenty-third Week in Ordinary Time

> Jesus said to his disciples:
> "A good tree does not bear rotten fruit,
>   nor does a rotten tree bear good fruit.
> For people do not pick figs from thornbushes,
>   nor do they gather grapes from brambles.
> A good person out of the store of goodness in his heart produces good,
>   but an evil person out of a store of evil produces evil;
>   from the fullness of the heart the mouth speaks."
> Lk 6: 43 – 49

At first glance, today's gospel passage seems pretty cut and dry. There are good people, and they do good things; there are bad people, and they do bad things. Next.

Not quite so fast. Jesus' entire life says something different. Yes, there are good people and there are bad people. The challenge is to affirm the good people, and to invite the others to change. Jesus was the master of this behavior; we need to learn from the master.

Jesus looked at the world this way – every saint has a past and every sinner has a future. Sometimes we are saints; sometimes we are sinners. Jesus affirms our good behaviors, and invites us to repent and change our sinful behaviors. As the old saying would have it, "There is a little bit of good in the worst of us, and a little bit of bad in the best of us. So it ill behooves any of us to speak ill of the rest of us."

Here is another old saying: "The church is not a gathering of saints, but a gathering of sinners who have not yet given up." God has not given up on us, neither should we!

Where do we need the light of God's love to shine on whatever is dark in our lives?

Twenty-fourth Sunday in Ordinary Time (A)

"His master summoned him and said to him, 'You wicked servant!
I forgave you your entire debt because you begged me to.
Should you not have had pity on your fellow servant,
as I had pity on you?'
Then in anger his master handed him over to the torturers
until he should pay back the whole debt.
So will my heavenly father do to you,
Unless each of you forgives your brother from your heart."
Mt 18: 21 – 35

I never cease to be amazed at how prodigal God is when it comes to forgiving us our transgressions. His forgiveness is both voluntary and total. God's mercy knows no limits, and that is the problem. We become too comfortable with God's mercy. We forget what a tremendous blessing and gift God's forgiveness is!

What we receive as a gift we are supposed to give as a gift. Unfortunately, too often our mercy and forgiveness do not live up to God's standards. We are provisional when it comes to forgiving others. We keep score; we don't want to be seen as being too forgiving. Our forgiveness has a string tied to it so that we can withdraw it at any time. God never withdraws his forgiveness.

Too often our forgiveness is tentative; too often it is provisional. God's forgiveness is wholehearted and unconditional. We are too often like the man in today's gospel who forgets what he has been forgiven, but remembers what he is owed.

If we can just stop, remember God's loving mercy and forgiveness, and appreciate it more fully, we will grow to become more forgiving of those who offend or betray us from time to time. We have all received the gift of God's forgiveness; now is the time to pay it forward.

Where do we need to be more lavish with our forgiveness?

Twenty-fourth Sunday in Ordinary Time (B)

> He began to teach them that the Son of Man had to suffer much,
> be rejected by the elders, the chief priests, and the scribes,
> be put to death, and rise three days later.
> He said this quite openly.
> Peter took him aside and began to remonstrate with him.
> At this he turned around, and eyeing the disciple,
> reprimanded Peter in turn:
> "Get out of my sight, you satan!
> You are not judging by God's standards but by man's!"
> Mk 8: 27 – 35

We have to love Peter. He is a lug. In the matter of several minutes he goes from being the hero because he said to Jesus, "You are the Messiah!" Then, a bit full of himself no doubt, he decided it is time to tell Jesus how to live his life. Now he is the goat. Now he gets called satan. In sporting terminology, "He turned the cheers into jeers."

As much as I love Peter, I love Jesus even more. He looked at Peter, and did not see a lug, but a leader. He did not see the Peter who would deny him, but rather the Peter who would die for him. This is normative behavior for Jesus.

For some reason Jesus chose us to be his disciples. To do this he had to see beyond our faults, failures, and sins. For some reason, he could see me as a priest. He could see you as a wife or husband, mother or father, daughter or son. He did not see any of us as perfect. He did not see Peter as the perfect leader of the early church. I will not speak for any of you, but I can assure you he did not see me as the perfect priest. He saw me as a good priest who could get the message to certain people. And he did not see all of you as perfect, but as a good individuals and able to reach certain people. Together with his continued help and encouragement we can make this world a better place.

Can we grow into the people that Jesus knows we can be?

Twenty-fourth Sunday in Ordinary Time (C)

> The tax collectors and sinners
> were all gathering around to hear Jesus,
> at which the Pharisees and the scribes murmured,
> "This man welcomes sinners and eats with them."
> Then he addressed a parable to them:
> "Who among you, if he has a hundred sheep and loses one of them,
> does not leave the ninety-nine in the wasteland
> and follows the lost one until he finds it?
> And when he finds it,
> he puts in on his shoulders in jubilation.
> Once arrived home, he invites friends and neighbors in
> and says to them,
> 'Rejoice with me because I have found my lost sheep.'
> I tell you, there will likewise be more joy in heaven
> over one repentant sinner than over ninety-nine
> righteous people who have no need to repent."
> Lk 15: 1 – 32

We love the underdog. When I taught high school religion many years ago, it was a delight to teach bright students, but the students that gave me the greatest joy were the ones who had to struggle, those who flirted with failure for different reasons. Some just were not interested, some were openly rebellious, while others were just academically challenged. When one of these students had a breakthrough, when they got it or applied themselves, I felt like I was being a good teacher.

The same thing is true in sports. Some players are just natural. It comes easy to them, they listen to their coaches and achieve wonderful results. Then there are the average players, and finally there were those who had great desire but limited talent. Working with this last group was always the most rewarding. Every now and again one of this group would make the winning play, and that was always more satisfying than when one of the stars did so.

That is what Jesus is getting at in today's gospel parable. When one of us goes astray on our faith journey, and who among us has never gone astray, Jesus always comes after us. He always finds us, and he always invites us back to the right path. How fortunate are we?

From what lost place has Jesus rescued us?

Monday of the Twenty-fourth Week in Ordinary Time

> When he was only a short distance from the house,
> the centurion sent friends to tell him,
> "Sir, do not trouble yourself,
> for I am not worthy to have you enter my house.
> That is why I did not presume to come to you myself.
> Just give the order and my servant will be cured."
> Lk 7: 1 – 10

We are very familiar with this gospel story because it is the foundation for a prayer we say every time we celebrate the Eucharist. Just before communion we say, "Lord, I am not worthy for you to enter under my roof, say but the word and my soul will be healed."

What is truly amazing is that many of us misunderstand why we say this prayer. Many of us think it is a prayer of humility. Indeed, in the old Mass we would say the prayer three times, and each time we would bow our head and touch our heart as we professed our unworthiness. In truth, we groveled! Fortunately, today's gospel provides us with the proper context for this prayer. It is not a prayer of humility; it is a prayer that proclaims our belief in God's power.

No one is worthy to receive communion, yet everyone is in need of its saving power. We go to communion not because we have been good, but because we need God's loving presence in our lives so that we can become better. We say this prayer not to announce our unworthiness, but to announce to one and all that we need communion to be better people.

How else can we demonstrate our need for God's power in our lives?

Tuesday of the Twenty-fourth Week in Ordinary Time

> Jesus went to a town called Naim,
> and his disciples and a large crowd accompanied him.
> As he approached the gate of the town
> a dead man was being carried out,
> the only son of a widowed mother…
> The Lord was moved with pity upon seeing her
> and said to said to her,
> "Do not cry."
> He then stepped forward and touched the litter;
> at this, the bearers halted.
> He said, "Young man, I bid you get up."
> The dead man sat up and began to speak.
> Then Jesus gave him back to his mother.
> Fear seized them all and they began to praise God.
> Lk 7: 11 – 17

On one level this gospel is just a story about Jesus being compassionate. The widow of Naim, as we call her, was on the brink of nothingness. Her husband was dead, and now her only son was dead. In the culture of her time, she was about to become nothing. Jesus rescued her.

On another level, Jesus is announcing that he is the Messiah. He is checking off the deeds that will announce the Messiah's arrival. Scripture tells us that "the lame will walk, the mute will speak, the blind will see, the dead will rise, and the poor will have the good news proclaimed to them."

That is why fear seized the people. When God enters he brings fear with him. That is why the phrase, "Do not be afraid" is so popular in scripture. Scriptural fear is not fear as we know it. These people were not terrified, they weren't shaking in their sandals, they were awestruck. They knew they were in the presence of greatness, in the presence of great goodness. They knew, but they did not understand. They wanted to draw near, but were unsure what would happen to them. They wanted to be able to wrap their minds around what they had just experienced, but it was too soon for that. All they could do was enter the mystery and trust in God.

When have we been most aware of God's loving, mysterious presence in our lives?

Wednesday of the Twenty-fourth Week in Ordinary Time

Jesus said:
"What comparison can I use for the men of today?
What are they like?
They are like children squatting in the city square
and calling to their playmates
'We piped for you a tune but you did not dance.
We sang you a dirge but you did not wail.'
I mean that John the Baptist came
neither eating bread nor drinking wine
And you say, 'He is mad!'
The Son of Man came and he both ate and drank,
And you say,

> 'He is a glutton and a drunkard, a friend of tax collectors and sinners!'
> God's wisdom is vindicated by all who accept it."
> Lk 7: 31 – 35

Over the years, I have heard just about every excuse there is for not going to church. The pastor does not know who I am, or the music is bad. The homilies are too intellectual or not intellectual enough. The people are not friendly. Mass is too long; Mass is too short. These are but a few of the excuses that I have heard. Do you know what they all have in common? They are excuses; they are made up. They are not the real reason why people don't go to church.

The real reasons are more mundane. For many people it boils down to the fact that they just got out of the habit of going. For many people who go to Mass the reason is they are just in the habit of going.

Faith needs to be more than a habit. Jesus at the Last Supper told us why we should gather for the breaking of the bread. He said, "Do this to remember me."

Do this to remember that I love you. Gather to give thanks that I was willing to die for you. Do this so that I can be more actively present in your lives.

When we gather to remember all that Jesus has done for us, we are automatically filled with gratitude. That gratitude leads to giving thanks to God, which is best done in the Eucharist.

What can we do to make the practice of our faith more than a habit?

Thursday of the Twenty-fourth Week in Ordinary Time

> A certain Pharisee invited Jesus to dine with him,
> And he entered the Pharisee's house and reclined at table.
> Now there was a sinful woman in the city
> who learned that he was at table in the house of the Pharisee.
> Bringing an alabaster flask of ointment,
> she stood behind him at his feet weeping
> and began to bathe his feet with her tears.

> Then she wiped them with her hair,
> kissed and anointed them with the ointment.
> Lk 7: 36 – 50

I cannot imagine allowing anyone to cry on my feet, and then dry my feet with her hair. You can be sure that no one is going to kiss my feet or anoint them with fragrant ointment. Jesus allows all of this to happen. Why? I imagine her machinations made Jesus very uncomfortable, but he knew the moment was not about him but about her. She needed these rituals to cleanse her soul.

Obviously she was tired of being known as "the sinful woman of the city." She was making a public display of her desire to change her ways. Jesus let her be. He let her proclaim her change of heart.

People have different customs, and we need to learn how to respect those customs. I can remember when I was ordained that some people, when they knelt to receive my first priestly blessing, wanted to kiss my hands after I blessed them. I was shocked when the first person did it, and I know I tried to remove my hands. But when the next person wanted to kiss my hands, I did not resist. I did not enjoy it, but I realized it was not about me. It was about their love for the priesthood. We need to learn how to let others express themselves even if it sometimes makes us uncomfortable.

Where have we stifled the free expressions of others?

Friday of the Twenty-fourth Week in Ordinary Time

> Jesus journeyed from one town and village to another,
> Preaching and proclaiming the good news of the Kingdom of God.
> Accompanying him were the Twelve
> and some women who had been cured of evil spirits and infirmities,
> Mary, called Magdalene, from whom seven devils had gone out,
> Joanna, the wife of Herod's steward, Chuza,
> Susanna, and many others who provided for them
> out of their resources.
> Lk 8: 1 – 3

Jesus and his entourage went about doing good. It does not get more bare boned than that. We have a charismatic leader and some followers. Look what they have wrought, a worldwide church with 1.2 billion members. Who could have predicted that?

What is necessary for growth to happen? First there needs to be a vision. The vision is formed by recognizing what is wrong with a situation, and then coming up with a solution, a way to improve what is going on. Once there is a vision there needs to be a leader, a person who can articulate the vision. But a leader, even a charismatic one, is not enough. The leader needs followers, people who embrace the vision, and are willing to give their blood, sweat, and tears to make that vision a reality.

Once there is a community of believers the challenges don't go away, they just take on different forms. There is a preacher's story about a lighthouse in a small village. People gave their time, people were rescued, and life was good. Over time the lighthouse became famous. People who were rescued gave money to build a better lighthouse and a gathering room. Over time the gathering room got new carpet, better chairs, and some nice decorations. After a while the people were more attached to the clubhouse than the lighthouse. They lost the vision of who they were supposed to be. Their mission got lost in the maintenance of their clubhouse.

That can happen with our church. Our church has a mission, but it also has the maintenance of the institution. When maintenance becomes more important than mission we are in serious trouble. It happens more than we think.

Where have our church institutions become more important than announcing the Kingdom of God?

Saturday of the Twenty-fourth Week in Ordinary Time

Then his disciples asked him
what the meaning of this parable might be.
He answered,
"Knowledge of the mysteries of the Kingdom of God

> has been granted to you;
> but to the rest, they are made known through parables
> *so that they may look but not see, and hear but not understand.*
> Lk 8: 4 – 15

Today's parable is the sower who sows his seed and some falls on the path, some on rocky ground, some amid the thorns, and some on good soil. We have heard this parable many times. (We had Matthew's version of it on the Fifteenth Sunday of Ordinary Time, Cycle A.) We know what it means. We hear and we understand. Would that it were that easy. With parables there is always a new and deeper level.

What can this familiar parable teach us today? Usually we focus on what kind of soil we are for the Word of God. Today let's shift our focus just a bit. Let's not focus on what kind of soil we are, but on what kind of sowers we are. We are followers of Jesus; he calls us to spread his message. We need to imitate him.

I am always amazed that the sower did not give up. Three quarters of what he sowed failed. Only one quarter bore fruit. That is not a good average. But Jesus did not give up. He chose to focus on the good, and not let the bad discourage him. We need to develop that attitude.

All the important people in our lives are the ones who have not given up on us. Our parents, teachers, coaches, scout leaders, friends, and co-workers have this attitude. Thank God. They chose to focus on what we do right, and build on that. We need to do the same thing if we are to sow God's love generously in the world.

Where have we given in to discouragement in our lives?

Twenty-fifth Sunday in Ordinary Time (A)

> "He said to them in reply,
> 'My friend, I am not cheating you.
> Did you not agree with me for the usual daily wage?
> Take what is yours and go.
> What if I wish to give this last one the same as you?

> Or am I not free to do as I wish with my own money?
> Are you envious because I am generous?'
> Thus, the last will be first, and the first will be last."
> Mt 20: 1 – 16

Too often we keep score as if life were a game. It is not! We need to stop keeping score and stop making comparisons. If we think that one of our siblings gets what she wants too often, we complain that we are not being treated fairly. If the coach seems to play someone else more than us, we grouse about it. If a co-worker makes more money than we do and does less work, we file a grievance.

Jesus is trying to teach us to appreciate what we have rather than complain about what we don't have. Someone will always have a better car, live in a nicer home, and have the latest fashion. So what?

We are bombarded every day with the message that we should not be satisfied with what we have; we need to focus on what we need rather than what we have. Our economy is based on the false notion that things, new and better things, will make us happy. We know that is not true, but we embrace the lie anyway.

Things do not make us happy, and people don't make us happy. What should make us happy is doing what we know is right, treating others with the dignity they deserve, and putting the needs of others ahead of our own needs.

If we want to be happy, we need to live in a way that will leave the world a better and more caring place.

Where have we put things before people in our lives?

Twenty-fifth Sunday in Ordinary Time (B)

> They returned to Capernaum and Jesus, once inside the house,
> began to ask them,
> "What were you discussing on the way home?"
> At this they fell silent, for on the way they had been arguing
> about who was the most important.
> So he sat down and called the Twelve around him and said,

> "If anyone wishes to rank first, he must remain the last one of all and the servant of all."
> Mk 9: 30 – 37

Who is the most important? Why do we care? We love to make lists. The ten best songs of the year, the all-star team, the MVP, the best Italian restaurant, and the lists go on and on.

I can only imagine how embarrassed the Twelve were when they had to admit that they were arguing about which one of them was the most important. Jesus has taught us that, "Wherever two or three are gathered together, I am there in their midst." He should have warned us, "That wherever two or three are gathered together competition will always be present." And wherever competition is present community is endangered.

Parish life can be wonderful; it can also be awful. Cooperation makes it wonderful; competition makes it awful. Allow me a banal example. Most parishes select people to bring up the gifts in the offertory procession. Every parish seems to have it unique selection process. Sometimes the presider asks a family, sometimes it is the head usher, sometimes it is the family that has asked for a deceased relative to be remembered at the Mass. Each method invites complaints because of fairness. Some get asked too much; some don't ever get asked.

My former parish (after I retired) came up with a great solution. A member of the parish made a wooden fish. That fish is placed on the gift table. Whoever wants to bring up the gifts just takes the wooden fish off the table, and returns it there when it is time for the offertory procession. To the best of my knowledge the self-selection process has worked flawlessly because it is built on cooperation.

Where can we be more cooperative in our faith communities?

Twenty-fifth Sunday in Ordinary Time (C)

> "No servant can serve two masters.
> Either he will hate one and love the other
> or be attentive to the one and despise the other.
> You cannot give yourself to God and money."
> Lk 16: 1 – 13

Fact is we can keep God and money in creative tension most of the time, but the time will come when we have to make a choice. My father, who was a man of few words but many quoted sayings, was fond of telling my brothers and me, "It is a shame that we have let money become the sign of success." Unfortunately, he was absolutely correct.

In our culture, we idolize professional athletes, pay them obscene amounts of money, and grant them status in society. We know in our heart of hearts that none of them deserve obscene salaries, and few deserve their high status, but that is the way capitalism works. Owners of franchises don't deserve the obscene amounts of money they make either, nor do those very creative people who conjure up things that people just cannot live without. No one needs a billion dollars; but no one who has a billion is going to give it away freely.

I do not know how to solve the problem of income inequality, but I know income inequality is bad. We need a society where the people who truly make a difference in the lives of others – the teachers, nurses, police, firefighters, all first responders, and ordinary good folks don't have to worry about how they are going to keep a roof over their heads. Poor Pope Francis gets beat up every time he talks like this, but we know he is on to something.

Where have we put profits before people, and comfort before justice?

Monday of the Twenty-fifth Week in Ordinary Time

> Jesus said to the crowds:
> "No one lights a lamp and puts it under a bushel basket
> or under a bed;
> he puts it on a lampstand so that whoever comes in can see it.
> Therefore nothing is hidden that will not be exposed,
> Nothing is concealed that will not be known and brought to light."
> Lk 8: 16 – 18

Everyone I know has something to hide. We have all done wrong. We would be embarrassed if those deeds were to come to light. We do our best to make sure they stay buried.

There are a few people who just don't seem to care. We had a local mayor who went to jail twice. He was referred to warmly as "our felon." His base loved him; in their eyes he could do no wrong.

My father used to tell my brothers and me, "Never do anything that you don't want to see on the front page of the newspaper." Pretty much we have followed his advice.

I do not watch a lot of television, but when I do I watch either sports or crime shows. The crime shows all have one thing in common, at some point out comes the powerful little flashlight. One sweep of the room and the missing piece of evidence appears that allows the good guys to prosecute the bad guys. If we are to walk in the light of God's love we need to stop trying to hide in the shadows.

Have we confessed all that we try to hide from others?

Tuesday of the Twenty-fifth Week in Ordinary Time

> The mother of Jesus and his brothers came to him,
> but were unable to join him because of the crowd.
> He was told, "Your mother and your brothers are standing outside
> and they wish to see you."
> He said to them in reply, "My mother and my brothers
> are those who hear the word of God and act on it."
> Lk 8: 19 – 21

Jesus is making a point, but we know it cost him. Mothers don't take lightly to being ignored even if it is done to make a point! Mary would not be happy coming in second to a crowd.

This probably sounds crazy. How could there be tension between Mary and Jesus? They were members of the Holy Family. They did not have the problems that you and I have. Right? Wrong! Mary's feelings were hurt by Jesus' cavalier attitude. Jesus was getting a bit too big for his britches. They had to work things out, and they did.

If we lose sight of the very fact that Jesus, Mary, and Joseph suffered through all the same growing pains as every family's, then we deprive them of serving as role models for us. Too often, we think that the Holy Family was the perfect family. They were not. There is no perfect family. Just as there is no perfect wife, or perfect husband, or perfect son, or perfect mother, or perfect father. We have problems, and we need to work through them. We need to grow, we need to learn how to cope, and we need to learn how to forgive. No one gets a free pass. Being a family is hard work, but is certainly worth the effort.

What part of being family needs a little work at this time?

Wednesday of the Twenty-fifth Week in Ordinary Time

> Jesus summoned the Twelve and gave them power and authority
> over all demons and to cure diseases,
> and he sent them to proclaim the Kingdom of God
> and to heal the sick…
> "Whatever house you enter, stay there and leave from there.
> And for those who do not welcome you,
> when you leave that town,
> shake the dust from your feet in testimony against them."
> Lk 9: 1 – 6

Yesterday we reflected on the problem of romanticizing the Holy Family. Today we need to reflect on how we romanticize the Twelve. We think Jesus sent them out, and they drove out demons and healed all who were sick. That their efforts were blessed with success, and that nothing ever went wrong. At some level, we know that is incorrect, but we cling to the fantasy anyway.

There is a line in today's gospel that shows that Jesus was more realistic than we are when it comes to how people would react to the disciples. He prepares them for the fact that not everyone is going to welcome them with open arms. He tells them how to react when rejected. They are not to ignore or deny that they are rejected. He merely tells them to, "shake their dust from your feet." Don't argue; don't respond angrily. Accept that it will happen from time to time, and get back to work.

The worst thing that could have happened to the Twelve was that they would get disappointed and quit. That was a problem at the beginning of the church; it is still a problem today. When we try something in our parishes, and it is not met with success and praise, we get discouraged and give up. What we should do is dust ourselves off and try something else.

Where have we let discouragement limit our faith?

Thursday of the Twenty-fifth Week in Ordinary Time

> But Herod said, "John I beheaded.
> Who then is this about whom I hear such things?"
> And he kept trying to see him.
> Lk 9: 7 – 9

Herod was a man easily fascinated. He was fascinated by John the Baptist, but had him beheaded nonetheless. Now he hears about Jesus, and the work that his disciples are doing. Ultimately, he would play a role in putting Jesus to death. Fascination gets us only so far. Fascination is a beginning move, but not a lasting one. Herod's problem was that he got stuck at fascination. His curiosity never led anywhere.

Sometimes we are like Herod especially when it comes to our faith. We are fascinated by Jesus, we are fascinated by the church, and we are fascinated by the liturgy. Fascination with Jesus should lead to a personal relationship with him. As Pope Francis said in *Evangelium Gaudium*, "I invite all Christians, everywhere, at this very moment, to a renewed personal encounter with Jesus Christ, or at least an openness to letting him encounter them. I ask all of you to do this unfailingly each day." (EG #3)

When it comes to the church fascination must lead to involvement. "Sitting in church won't make you a Christian any more than standing in a garage will make you an automobile." The same is true for liturgy. Unless we enter into the celebration and actively participate its transforming power, liturgy will never lead us to a deeper experience of faith.

Where do we need to enter more fully into our faith?

Friday of the Twenty-fifth Week in Ordinary Time

> Once when Jesus was praying in solitude,
> and his disciples were with him,
> he asked them, "Who do the crowds say that I am?"
> Lk 9: 18 – 22

There is a contradiction in today's gospel. It says, "Jesus was praying in solitude" and then it says, "and his disciples were with him." How can that be? My dictionary defines solitude, as "The state or quality of being alone or remote from others." Perhaps there is no contradiction after all. Jesus was with his disciples, but he was praying. He was paying no attention to his disciples, they just happened to be there. Solitude is easier when we are alone, but being alone is not essential to finding solitude.

Prayer needs solitude, and it needs disciplined focus. Too often we let ourselves get distracted. Too often we fail to quiet all the voices and all the sounds that clutter our lives. Too often we are unwilling to silence our electronic devices. Pope Francis gets up at 4:30 and prays for two hours at the beginning of his day. We need to find prayer time in our days. We need to have a place of prayer, and we need to have a time to pray. We know if we wait for prayer time to appear, it will never happen. When we find the time, and when we actually pray, it is very important that we listen as well as speak. If our prayer time consists of us talking to God all the time, when does God get to respond?

When is the best time of the day for us to pray?

Saturday of the Twenty-fifth Week in Ordinary Time

> While they were all amazed at his every deed,
> Jesus said to his disciples,
> "Pay attention to what I am telling you.
> The Son of Man is to be handed over to men."
> But they did not understand this saying;
> its meaning was hidden from them

> so that they could not understand it,
> and they were afraid to ask him about this saying.
> Lk 9: 43B – 45

The disciples did not understand the meaning of suffering; we do not understand the meaning of suffering. Yet suffering is part of life, an important part of life.

In the world of fitness there is a saying, "No pain no gain!" Progress never comes without sacrifice. We don't want to hear that, but it is true. Nothing good in life come without suffering.

One of life's greatest joys is watching a child take her first step. The first step is important, but the lead up to the first step is what can teach us. The instinct to walk is there before the ability to do so. No one just gets up and walks. Someone holds our hands, and encourages us. When the person lets go, we fall down. We fall down quite a bit before that actual first step. Even after the first step there is more falling than walking. Eventually, we learn to walk without falling down.

What would life be like if the first time we fell we just stayed down?

Walking takes time; if we are going to learn how to walk we have to endure learning from falling down. The same is true of everything we do. We did not just start talking in sentences one day, nor did we just pick up a musical instrument and play it. Suffering is an essential part of life. Our faith is part of our life. Therefore suffering has to be a part of our faith.

Where have we tried to live faith without it costing us anything?

Twenty-sixth Sunday in Ordinary Time (A)

> Jesus said to the chief priests and elders of the people:
> "What is your opinion?
> A man had two sons.
> He came to the first and said,
> 'Son, go out and work in the vineyard today.'
> He said in reply, 'I will not,'
> but afterwards changed his mind and went.

> The man came to the other son and gave the same order.
> He said in reply, 'Yes, sir, but did not go.
> Which of the two did his father's will?"
> Mt 21: 28 – 32

Jesus exposes a human foible in today's gospel. We humans are a very fickle bunch, especially when it comes to our words and our deeds. Too often, we promise more than we can deliver. Sometimes we go the extra mile, but that is the exception. The problem is we cannot predict, nor can others, when we will live up to what we have promised.

We all know people who over promise. They are the people who RSVP that they will attend, but their response is provisional at best. What they really mean is they will attend unless a better offer comes along. It is difficult to take such people at their word.

I once served with a priest who did not take constructive criticism very well. He would explode and storm off before the issue at hand could be resolved. Then he would do the most amazing thing. He would change his behavior to what had set him off just the day before. It was an amazing sort of transformation. I had to learn to ignore his initial response, and he worked at being more receptive to criticism.

Too often we glibly say, "I believe in God…" but then behave in a way that suggests we don't believe in God. Other times we try to reject God in our lives, but end up acting like a believer. It is all very confusing. Fortunately, Jesus took on our human condition, and he pays more attention to our deeds than our words.

Where do we need to have more transparency between our words and deeds?

Twenty-sixth Sunday in Ordinary Time (B)

> "If your hand is your difficulty, cut it off!
> Better for you to enter life maimed than to keep both hands
> and enter Gehenna,
> with its unquenchable fire.
> If your foot is your undoing, cut it off!
> Better for you to enter life crippled

> than to be thrown into Gehenna with both feet.
> If your eye is your downfall, tear it out.
> Better for you to enter the kingdom of God with one eye
> than to be thrown with both eyes into Gehenna,
> where 'the worm dies not and the fire is never extinguished'"
> Mk 9: 38 – 43, 45, 47 – 48

Jesus is obviously being hyperbolic. Nevertheless, I must confess this gospel has always given me great joy. As a preacher I have frequently wondered what the congregation would look like if it took this gospel literally. However that is foolish because if I took this gospel literally I would not be able to either see the congregation or preach to them.

So what is Jesus' message here? There will always be something that can get in the way of our being better believers. Temptation is very subjective, but nonetheless very real.

I remember giving a homily once on the reality of temptation. In that homily, I said, "I don't have a problem with will power, I have a problem with won't power." The following week, a member of the parish presented me with a rock that had "won't power" painted on it. That rock had a place of honor on my desk for many years. When I retired, the rock went missing, but its message is still with me.

I have my litany, which I will share with you now. I won't give in to anger. I won't speak hurtful words. I won't discriminate. I won't be silent in the face of injustice… These are only some of the issues I have to confront every day.

What would your litany look like?

Twenty-sixth Sunday in Ordinary Time (C)

> Jesus said to the Pharisees:
> "Once there was a rich man who dressed in purple
> and linen and feasted splendidly every day.
> At his gate lay a beggar named Lazarus, who was covered with sores.
> Lazarus longed to eat the scraps that fell from the rich man's table.

> The dogs even came and licked his sores.
> Eventually the beggar died.
> He was carried by the angels to the bosom of Abraham.
> The rich man likewise died and was buried.
>
> Lk 16: 19 – 31

This parable gets everything backwards, and it does so on purpose! First of all, when is the last time you heard a story where the rich man was anonymous, and a beggar had a name? That's just not how our world works. The rich and famous have names, and the spotlight shines brightly on them. The poor and the folks on the margins of life are too often nameless.

In this parable, the rich person is punished for not reaching out to Lazarus, while Lazarus rests in the bosom of Abraham. That's the stuff of fairy tales, not reality. As the parable develops we realize that the rich man even knows Lazarus' name. There was some sort of relationship between the two, but not enough of a relationship to lead the rich man to action. He was aware, but unmoved.

The part of the parable that I like the most is when the rich man knows his fate is fixed. When he knows there will be no end to his punishment, he asks Abraham to send Lazarus to warn his five brothers. Abraham says that his brothers have Moses and the prophets. The rich man does not think that is enough because he had Moses and the prophets and it did not save him. This is how the parable ends, "No, Father Abraham," the rich man replied, "but if someone would only go to them from the dead, then they would repent." Abraham said to him, "If they do not listen to Moses and the prophets, they will not be convinced even if one should rise from the dead."

We prove Abraham correct almost every day because Jesus did rise from the dead, and we still ignore those in need.

We need to improve both our charity and our justice.

Monday of the Twenty-sixth Week in Ordinary Time

> An argument arose among the disciples
> about which of them was the greatest.
> Jesus realized the intention of their hearts and took a child
> and placed it by his side and said to them,
> "Whoever receives this child in my name receives me,
> and whoever receives me receives the one who sent me.
> For the one who is least among all of you
> Is the one who is the greatest."
> Lk 9: 46 – 50

I have had and listened to many conversations about who was the greatest quarterback of all time, the greatest debater of all time, the greatest singer of all time, the greatest actor/actress of all time, but I have never been part of a group where we argued about who was the greatest. That discussion may go on in our head, but the words never come out of our mouth.

For this reason, I doubt that the disciples ever had such a discussion. Jesus made up the discussion to make a point. The point was we have to see God in everyone. That is why Jesus picks a child. When we welcome a child, we welcome Jesus, and when we welcome Jesus we welcome God who sent him. When we are caught up in this dynamic, we don't have to worry about greatness. Everyone is a vessel that carries God each in her own unique way.

In the history of our church there have been saints whom we call great. Gregory the Great comes to mind as does Leo the Great. History called them "great" – they never called themselves that. It would, I think, be impossible to call yourself "the great" and be canonized. Humility is a requirement for sainthood, or it should be.

We don't have to strive to be "the least." We just need to be more attentive to others than ourselves and God will take care of the rest.

Where do we need to take ourselves a little less seriously?

Tuesday of the Twenty-sixth Week in Ordinary Time

As the time approached when Jesus was to be taken from this world,
he firmly resolved to proceed toward Jerusalem,
and sent messengers on ahead of him.
These entered a Samaritan town
to prepare for his passing through,
but the Samaritans would not welcome him
because he was on his way to Jerusalem.
When his disciples James and John saw this, they said,
"Lord, would you not have us call down fire from heaven
to destroy them?"
He turned toward them only to reprimand them.
Then they set off for another town.
Lk 9: 51 – 56

One of the most difficult things we are called to do is to create a welcome space in our lives for people with whom we disagree. We tend to demonize our opposition. That way we don't have to deal with them. We give them a label, and are done with them.

It seems like every aspect of life is becoming more partisan. Politically we are practically at a standstill because there is a Democratic position on an issue and a Republican position on an issue, and never the twain shall meet. There used to be give and take and compromise, but that is but a distant memory these days. The same is true in our church. There are the liberals and the conservatives, the progressives and the traditionalists, and of late there are those who align themselves with St. John Paul II, or Benedict XVI, or Francis. This is not a new problem. Saint Paul had to address the same problem in the early church, "For it has been reported to me about you, my brothers, by Chloe's people, that there are rivalries among you. I mean that each of you is saying, 'I belong to Paul,' or 'I belong to Apollos,' or 'I belong to Cephas,' or 'I belong to Christ.' Is Christ divided? Was Paul crucified for you? Or were you baptized in the name of Paul?" (I Cor 1: 12 – 13) We are all members of one body and we need to start acting that way!

What have we let divide us as a Church?

Wednesday of the Twenty-sixth Week in Ordinary Time

> And to another he said, "Follow me."
> But he replied, "Lord, let me go first and bury my father."
> But he answered him, "Let the dead bury the dead.
> But you, go and proclaim the Kingdom of God."
> And another said, "I will follow you Lord,
> but first let me say farewell to my family at home."
> Jesus answered him, "No one who sets a hand to the plow
> and looks to what was left behind is fit for the Kingdom of God."
> Lk 9: 57 – 62

Sometimes to make a point, we say outrageous things. So did Jesus. Of course the man can bury his father. Jesus is merely trying to call attention to the excuses we come up with not to be disciples.

Jesus does not call us because we are perfect; he calls us because he needs us. We are called to bring God to a waiting world. Jesus has no hands but ours; he has no feet but ours. Are there people Jesus should call before us? Of course! Are there people who will be better disciples than we will? Of course!

Most of us are familiar with the song, "Hear I am Lord" by Dan Schutte. I am embarrassed to admit that for years I sang, "I will go Lord, if you need me" rather than the correct words, "I will go Lord, if you lead me." Subconsciously, I was giving myself a way out. Why would God need me? There are so many people who are better qualified to be disciples. Let them follow Jesus. If he gets desperate, or times are really bad, then Jesus can call me.

When I was a parish priest, I was amazed at the excuses that people could come up with not to get involved. Many people initially got involved out of guilt rather than out of faith. Fortunately, all of them grew into a faith response once they realized they were doing God's work.

Where do we need to be more enthusiastic in answering Jesus' call?

Thursday of the Twenty-sixth Week in Ordinary Time

> Jesus appointed seventy-two other disciples
> whom he sent ahead of him in pairs
> to every town and place he intended to visit.
> He said to them,
> "The harvest is abundant but the laborers are few;
> so ask the master of the harvest
> to send out laborers for his harvest."
> Lk 10: 1 – 12

Jesus was remarkably well organized for an itinerate preacher. He had twelve apostles, now he adds seventy-two disciples. We make the assumption that the disciples were all men, but nowhere is that stated. Given Jesus' unwillingness to be confined by the mores of his age, I think we can allow ourselves to believe that some of the disciples were indeed women.

When it comes to spreading the Good News, we should expect everyone to be involved. Indeed, if the laborers are few, it makes no sense to eliminate half the potential workforce. There was plenty of work to be done in Jesus' time, and there is plenty of work to be done in our time. Work is never the problem – workers are.

By Baptism we are called to be disciples. Everyone is called. Every call is different, but no call is less or more important. Someday our church will recognize this very important fact. We need to pray for all the baptized to get more involved. We need to pray for vocations in the church. Not just vocations to the priesthood or the religious life, but vocations to teach, to coach, to lead, to create beauty, to create families and friendships. When we pray for vocations to the priesthood, we need to be more open-minded. We need to pray that the church we love will soon realize that the only requirement for priestly service is baptism.

How can we answer better the call to be Jesus' disciples?

Friday of the Twenty-sixth Week in Ordinary Time

> Jesus said: "It will go ill with you, Chorazin!
> And just as ill with you, Bethsaida!
> If the miracles worked in your midst had occurred
> in Tyre and Sidon, they would long ago
> have reformed in sackcloth and ashes.
> It will go easier on the day of judgment for Tyre and Sidon
> than for you.
> Lk 10: 13 – 16

Jesus is frustrated. He has worked his signs and wonders, but the people are not responding. We know what frustration is, and we can learn from Jesus how best to deal with it.

Jesus got frustrated, but he did not give up or give in. We get frustrated, and we lash out, we curse, we give in, or give up. Getting frustrated is not the problem; letting frustration win is the problem.

There will always be obstacles in our way. Marathon runners talk about "the wall." Somewhere toward the end of the race comes that moment when their body and their mind invite them to quit. How they respond determines whether the runners experience the exultation of completion or the discouragement of failure. There is a poem by John Greenleaf Whittier entitled "Don't Quit" which opens with these words:

> "When things go wrong as they sometimes will,
> When the road you're trudging seems all up hill,
> When the funds are low and the debts are high,
> And you want to smile, but you have to sigh,
> Rest if you must, but don't you quit."

And ends with these:

> "So stick to the fight when you're hardest hit –
> It's when things seem worst that you must not quit."

No one dwells on the fact that Jesus fell three times carrying his cross; everyone celebrates that he got up each time.

What discarded dream do we need to revive?

Saturday of the Twenty-sixth Week in Ordinary Time

At that very moment he rejoiced in the Holy Spirit and said,
"I give you praise, Father, Lord of heaven and earth,
for although you have hidden these things
from the wise and the learned
you have revealed them to the childlike."
Lk 10: 17 – 24

The most important word in today's gospel passage is "childlike." Jesus wants his disciples to be childlike not childish. There is a big difference. Children have all the right instincts. Children trust others. They trust because their parents have always been there for them. God is always there for us.

Children have wonderful imaginations. They can create things to do, and have boundless energy. God wants us to be creative, and he wants us to be enthusiastic. Enthusiasm is an energy word. If we take the word apart we discover is made up of two Greek words, *en*, which means together, and *theos*, which means God. We are enthusiastic when we are together with God. It is easier to be enthusiastic when we are childlike.

A final childlike attribute is the willingness to learn by trial and error. When a child is confronted with a problem, they search for a solution. If the first solution does not work, they look for another solution. Children are not afraid of failure. They don't let themselves be defined by what they do wrong, but rather by what they finally get right. As believers, we are confronted with many problems. Too often we give up before we have found a way to let faith be our guide. Too often we learn to live with what is rather than create what ought to be.

Where have we become too sophisticated with our faith and our faith response?

Twenty-seventh Sunday in Ordinary Time (A)

> Jesus said to the chief priests and the elders of the people;
> "Hear another parable.
> There was a landowner who planted a vineyard,
> put a hedge around it, dug a wine press in it,
> and built a tower.
> Then he leased it to tenants and went on a journey.
> When vintage time drew near,
> he sent his servants to the tenants to obtain his produce.
> But the tenants seized the servants and one they beat,
> another they killed and a third they stoned.
> Again he sent other servants,
> more numerous than the first ones,
> but they treated them in the same way.
> Mt 21: 33 – 43

The spirituality of Stewardship rests on the biblical teaching that everything we have is a gift from God. More precisely, everything we have is on loan from God.

We are renters on earth, and God expects us to pay our rent, on time and in full. We have other ideas.

We fool ourselves into believing or at least acting as if we believe that everything we have is a result of our hard work. We act as if everything that is good in our lives is accomplished by us; everything that goes wrong is God's fault. It sounds both crass and foolish to write that, but to varying degrees our actions validate that false axiom.

Life is pure gift from God. The odds of being born are outrageous. God gives us life. The rent he expects is that we live honorable lives. When we fail to do so, we are no better than the tenants in today's gospel. The earth on which we live is a gift from God. We need to respect and treat the earth so that it will prosper. That is the rent we are to pay. When we pollute the earth and ravage it for profit, we are no better than the tenants in this gospel. God lavishes us with many blessings, and we are called to share those blessings in justice with others. When we hoard our blessings or let them pile up for a rainy day, we are once again the tenants who refuse to pay our rent.

Where are we bad tenants of God's many blessings?

Twenty-seventh Sunday in Ordinary Time (B)

> Some Pharisees came up to Jesus and as a test
> began to ask Jesus whether it was permissible for a
> husband to divorce his wife.
> In reply he said,
> "What command did Moses give you?"
> They answered,
> "Moses permitted divorce and the writing of a decree of divorce."
> But Jesus said to them,
> "He wrote that commandment for you
> because of your stubbornness."
> Mk 10: 2 – 16

When Jesus ended this dialogue with the Pharisees, I wonder if he knew when that dialogue would end. It certainly did not end that day. It is ongoing in our day. I doubt that Jesus could see the whole issue of divorce and remarriage that so torments our churches today. I doubt that he could foresee all the legalistic hoops his church would invent. Did Jesus really intend tribunals, judges, advocates, witnesses, oaths, procedural norms, and all that paperwork? Did Jesus have any idea what the Eucharist would become or that certain people would be barred from receiving communion because of their marital condition? I wish I knew the answers to these questions.

I recent years there have been some attempts, initiated by Pope Francis, to dial back the whole diocesan tribunal decree of nullity process, but some still cling firmly to it. I strongly believe in the ideal of a marriage being until death do us part, but perhaps we need to be a little more flexible as to what "death" means?

I, like many of you, have many more questions to which there are presently no satisfactory answers. What I do know is that too many people are hurt by our present policies. Too many people are made to feel unwelcome in our communities, and too many people are cut off from the healing and fortifying power of the sacraments because of their marital status, and that just seems wrong.

How can we make our churches more welcoming?

Twenty-seventh Sunday in Ordinary Time (C)

> The apostles said to the Lord,
> "Increase our faith," and he answered,
> "If you had faith the size of a mustard seed,
> you could say to this sycamore,
> 'Be uprooted
> and transplanted into the sea and it would obey you.'"
> Lk 17: 5 – 10

Why is it that we continue to think that if we just had more, we would do more? If God would just give us more faith, we would be better believers. Not true. If we don't use properly what we already have, why do we think that would change if we just had more? This is not just true of faith; we use this excuse in every aspect of our lives.

If we had more time, we would get more done. Not true! If we had more money; we would be more generous. Not true! If we had better teachers; we would be better students. Not true! If, if, if …

We need to learn to get the most out of what we have. We need to make the most of every opportunity. We need to respect the wisdom in the adage, "A poor workman always blames his tools."

As long as our focus is on what we don't have, we will never appreciate what we do have. And if we do not appreciate what we have, we will never have hearts filled with gratitude. If our hearts are not filled with gratitude, we will become self-centered people who are better at excuses than we are at results.

How can we use the gift of faith better?

Monday of the Twenty-seventh Week in Ordinary Time

> But because he wished to justify himself, he said to Jesus,
> "And who is my neighbor?"
> Jesus replied,

> "A man fell victim to robbers
> as he went down from Jerusalem to Jericho."
> Lk 10: 25 – 37

Even though the scholar of the law was being disingenuous when he asked the question, I am glad he asked it. If he hadn't we would never have heard the parable of the good Samaritan, and we would be diminished without it.

We can tell this story by heart. First a priest fails to act, followed by a Levite who also fails to act. Finally, a Samaritan, a member of a heretical group whom the Jewish people avoided because they were seen as inferior, comes along, and he does the right thing. He actually goes above and beyond the right thing. He treats the man's wounds, he finds him a place to stay while he recuperates, pays for his stay, and promises to pay whatever else he owes on his return trip.

Jesus tells the story and then as he so often does he flips the question around. The scholar of the law asked, "Who is my neighbor?' Jesus finished the parable and then asks, "Who was neighbor to the robber's victim?" This is a subtle, but important change in attitude. The scholar wanted a definition of neighbor; Jesus wants us to be neighbor. Jesus wants action not semantics.

With whom do we need to be a better neighbor?

Tuesday of the Twenty-seventh Week in Ordinary Time

> Jesus entered a village
> where a woman whose name was Martha welcomed him.
> She had a sister named Mary
> who sat beside the Lord at his feet listening to him speak.
> Martha, burdened with much serving, came to him and said,
> "Lord, do you not care
> that my sister has left me by myself to do the serving?
> Tell her to help me."
> Lk 10: 38 – 42

We are confronted with choices every day. There are good choices, and there are bad choices. Today's gospel makes it sound like Mary chose contemplation while Martha chose action. Would that life were that simple.

I often wonder how well Mary and Martha got along when Jesus was not around. Were their personalities as opposite as they seem in today's gospel? We don't know. What we do know is that Jesus came to visit. It sounds like he was a frequent visitor in their home. Jesus was close to Martha and Mary, and their brother Lazarus. In the Gospel of John we are told, "Jesus loved Martha and her sister, and Lazarus very much." (Jn 11: 5) When friends visit hospitality is different. There is no need to impress; there is no need to go all out. Friends understand, and do not expect special treatment. A friend can just stop by. No advance warning needed. However, Jesus was probably not alone. He would have his apostles with him, which would require more work. Obviously Martha was more worried about the extra work than Mary was, so she tried to enlist Jesus to get her some help.

We don't have the details but everything worked out in the end. Everyone got fed, and everyone got to spend some time with Jesus. Sometimes we worry more than is necessary. Sometimes we are too much like Martha and not enough like Mary.

Where do we need to worry less?

Wednesday of the Twenty-seventh Week in Ordinary Time

> One day Jesus was praying in a certain place.
> When he had finished, one of his disciples asked him,
> "Lord, teach us to pray as John taught his disciples."
> He said to them,
> "When you pray, say,
> 'Father...'"

I am not sure Jesus did what was asked of him. The disciple asked Jesus to teach them how to pray, and Jesus taught them a prayer. As we all know there is a big difference between praying and saying a prayer.

One thing is certain, Jesus knew how to pray; we are still learning.

Just about every believer I know has a favorite prayer. For some it is the rosary; for others it is a novena. For still others it is the Mass while for others it is the simplicity of the Jesus prayer.

I wonder what Jesus makes of our prayers. Does he get tired of the endless repetition of the same prayers over and over again? Does he ever wonder what we would say if we were to pray using our own words? I think he must.

Prayer is often called talking with God. Prayer assumes a relationship, an active relationship. There is an intimacy about prayer, or there should be. Nevertheless, too often we go to God with a prepared script. Formal, memorized prayer has its place, but our personal prayer should always be more.

How can we improve the personal side of our praying?

Thursday of the Twenty-seventh Week in Ordinary Time

> "And I tell you, ask and you will receive;
> seek and you will find;
> knock and the door will be opened to you.
> For everyone who asks, receives;
> the one who seeks, finds;
> and to the one who knocks, the door will be opened."
> Lk 11: 5 – 13

Too often we expect people to read our minds. Rather than ask for help, we want people to figure out we need help. We want our family and friends to be clairvoyant. We don't want to look for help; we want help to magically appear.

Whether it is asking, seeking, or knocking it all comes down to one thing. We do not want to appear needy. We always want to be in the power position. We want to be the one giving help not the one receiving it. We don't want to go seeking, we want to have all that we need at our fingertips. We want to open the door to our heart and let others in. We don't want others to welcome us into their heart.

Somewhere in our development we were told never to appear weak or needy. When we are born, we are totally dependent, and we remain dependent for a rather long time. Slowly it dawns on us that life would be better if we were independent. So we learn to distance ourselves from our parents and family. We pick and choose our friends, and we strive to be as self-sufficient as possible.

There is only one problem with this journey from dependency to independence. Independence should not be our goal; it should be a step toward our goal. Once we are independent, the next step is to willingly become interdependent. Interdependence should be our goal. There can be no team, no community, no togetherness, no belonging unless we are willing and able to be interdependent.

Where have we let independence arrest our development?

Friday of the Twenty-seventh Week in Ordinary Time

> When Jesus had driven out a demon, some of the crowd said:
> "By the power of Beelzebub, the prince of demons,
> he drives out demons."
> Others, to test him, asked him for a sign from heaven.
> But he knew their thoughts and said to them,
> "Every kingdom divided against itself will be laid waste
> and house will fall against house."
> Lk 11: 15 – 26

Christianity should be united. Christians were meant to be together not apart. The history of Christianity is a scandal. We should all be working for unity. Jesus wants us to be one.

One of the main obstacles to a united Christianity is our mistaken notion that unity requires uniformity. It does not and should not. St. Paul's wonderful image of the unity of the body shows us the way. The eye is not more important than the hand; it is just different. The head is not better than the foot; it is different. We need to rediscover the meaning of the philosophical dictum that the whole is greater than the sum of its parts. Christianity needs to be whole once again.

The other problem that keeps Christianity divided is our confusing the meaning of two different words. Those words are "agree" and "understand." It is foolish to expect that we will be able to come to agreement on everything. We need to be committed to understanding others, not agreeing with them. We need to focus on what unites us rather than what divides us.

When the Second Vatican Council referred to other Christians as separated sisters and brothers rather than heretics and schismatics, it was a step in the right direction. The ecumenical movement seems to have stalled in recent years. We need to revive it so that "all might be one."

What can we do to help Christianity be united once again?

Saturday of the Twenty-seventh Week in Ordinary Time

> While Jesus was speaking,
> a woman from the crowd called out and said to him,
> "Blessed is the womb that carried you
> and the breasts at which you nursed."
> He replied, "Rather, blessed are those
> who hear the word of God and observe it."
> Lk 11:27 – 28

I always wonder what Mary thought when someone told her about what Jesus had said. Because she was a saint, as well as a loving mother, I am sure she put it into context. Nevertheless, I hope she gave Jesus a bit of a hard time about his use of hyperbole. Jesus was making a point, but couldn't he let his mother get a little credit for the way he turned out?

No one questions the loving bond between Jesus and his mother. That is the whole point of today's gospel passage. If we listen to Jesus, if we are open to his word and his teaching, and if we put into practice what we hear and learn, then, and only then we too will have a deep personal relationship with Jesus.

Too often our relationship with Jesus is shallow. Too often we hear his word, but don't embrace it. There are times when we deliberately choose not to follow the teachings of Jesus. He tells us to be forgiving; we cling to grudges. He tells us to reach out to the needs of others; we ignore their plight. He teaches us the power of prayer; we convince ourselves that we are too busy for prayer. Sometimes we hear, but fail to observe. Sometimes we don't even hear. Other times we go through the motions of being a believer, but our hearts are divided, as is our focus.

How can Mary help us pay better attention to her son?

Twenty-eighth Sunday in Ordinary Time (A)

> Then he said to his servants, "The feast is ready,
> but those who were invited were not worthy to come.
> Go out, therefore, into the main roads
> and invite to the feast whomever you find."
> The servants went out into the streets
> and gathered all they found, bad and good alike,
> and the hall was filled with guests.
> Mt 22: 1 – 14

The invited guests decided they had better things to do than go to the wedding feast for the king's son. When they got the invitation, they accepted it. Yet, as is often the case, when the day arrived their desire to attend had waned. They did not go; they made excuses not to attend.

The king's reaction is indeed strange. First, he declares the unworthiness of those who were invited. Then he sends out his servants to invite whomever they meet, good or bad. The king would declare them worthy.

We are invited to the king's feast every week. We plan to attend, but too often as the day draws closer we find other things to do. Even so our king does not take offense. He just keeps inviting us week after week. We are not worthy of his love or unfailing patience. We do not have to earn what is freely offered. We just need to accept his invitation.

We know that attendance at Sunday Mass is anemic, and it is getting worse not better. Jesus gave the church the gift of the Eucharist with this command, "Do this to remember me." The more we ignore Christ's invitation to the Eucharist, the more we forget who he is and who he is calling us to be.

Each week we are invited to gather in faith, listen to God's word, offer our gifts, receive his presence, and go out to a waiting world to be his people.

Why are we not more faithful to Jesus' invitation to the feast of love?

Twenty-eighth Sunday in Ordinary Time (B)

As Jesus was setting out on a journey a man came running up,
knelt down before him and asked,
"Good Teacher, what must I do to share everlasting life?"
Jesus answered, "Why do you call me good?
No one is good but God alone.
You know the commandments:
You shall not kill;
you shall not commit adultery;
you shall not steal;
you shall not bear false witness;
you shall not defraud;
honor your father and your mother."
He replied, "Teacher, I have kept all these since my childhood."
Then Jesus looked on him with love and told him,
"There is one thing more you must do.
Go and sell what you have and give to the poor;
you will then have treasure in heaven.
After that come and follow me."
At these words the man's face fell.
He went away sad, for he had many possessions.
Mk 10: 17 – 30

That is a long quote from today's gospel but all of it is necessary. Notice the change from beginning to end. In the beginning the man is all business. He runs up to Jesus. He is a man with a purpose. He is clearly a Type A personality. He thinks he wants to know what he has to do to gain everlasting life. Once he gets an answer that he did not expect, he just runs out of steam. His high hopes are dashed, and he walks away sad.

He runs up; he saunters away. We are so much like this young man. We get an idea; we are fascinated by it. We can't wait to start. We are filled with enthusiasm. However, as we get into the project, we experience obstacles. For a while we fight the good fight, but all too often we just walk away when it becomes too difficult.

It is almost like the idea of a friend is preferred to an actual friend. Sometimes friends just require too much work. The same can be true of marriage, or ordination, or school, or a new job. Remember, Jesus did not abandon the young man; the young man abandoned Jesus.

Where does our faith need to be rejuvenated?

Twenty-eighth Sunday in Ordinary Time (C)

> On his journey to Jerusalem Jesus passed
> along the borders of Samaria and Galilee.
> As he was entering a village, ten lepers met him.
> Keeping their distance they raised their voices and said,
> "Jesus, Master, have pity on us!"
> When he saw them, he responded,
> "Go and show yourselves to the priests."
> On their way there they were cured.
> One of them realizing that he had been cured,
> Came back praising God in a loud voice.
> He threw himself at the feet of Jesus and spoke his praises.
> This man was a Samaritan.
> Lk 17: 11 – 19

There are two important lessons in today's gospel. We know that the Samaritans were not held in high esteem by the Jewish people. They were considered heretics; they were to be shunned by the chosen people. And yet several times in the New Testament, Jesus uses

Samaritans as the good guys in a story. One parable is even named after a Samaritan, the Good Samaritan.

We are led to believe that this group of lepers was made up of one Samaritan and nine Jews. Which means that when they were defined by a disease, the disease was more dominant than their religious differences. First lesson is we should learn to focus on what unites us not what divides us. We can always find a common denominator if we just search long enough.

The second lesson is that gratitude enriches the one who possesses it not the one who receives it. When we were young we were taught to always say "please" and to then say "thank you." If we did not say "please" our request was ignored; if we did not say "thank you" it was removed. To be kind perhaps it just took the other nine longer to realize they were cured.

Where have we neglected to thank God for all his gifts?

Monday of the Twenty-eighth Week in Ordinary Time

While still more people gathered in the crowd, Jesus said to them,
"This generation is an evil generation,
it seeks a sign, but no sign will be given it,
except the sign of Jonah
Just as Jonah became a sign to the Ninevites,
so will the Son of Man be to this generation."
Lk 11: 29 – 32

Evil is a strong word. No one wants to be called evil. Nevertheless, Jesus calls the people of his time "an evil generation." There is a very subtle point to what Jesus says. The people of his generation are not evil because they had done evil; they were evil because they would not repent. They would not give up their evil ways.

When Jonah went through the city of Nineveh proclaiming, "Forty more days and Nineveh will be destroyed," the people heard Jonah's warning and "all of them, great and small put on sack cloth and ashes." They were willing to repent.

Jesus came to his people and proclaimed, "Repent and believe the Good News!" and, except for his apostles and disciples, he was ignored. The people continued in their evil ways. They were evil because they were unwilling to repent.

Everyone, great and small, sins. Everyone is called to repentance. Unfortunately,too often we cling to our sins. We let ourselves be defined by them. We refuse to believe that we can put aside our evil ways. We get discouraged, and we give up. But Jesus does not give up on us. Every day he calls us to repent. Every day he offers his forgiveness. He is willing to forgive us, but too often we are unwilling to accept that forgiveness and believe in our goodness.

Where have we persisted in our evil ways?

Tuesday of the Twenty-eighth Week in Ordinary Time

> After Jesus had spoken,
> a Pharisee invited him to dine at his home.
> He entered and reclined at table to eat.
> The Pharisee was amazed to see
> that he did not observe the prescribed washing before the meal.
> The Lord said to him, "Oh you Pharisees!
> Although you cleanse the outside of the cup and the dish,
> inside you are filled with plunder and evil.
> You fools!"
> Lk 11: 37 – 41

Jesus set a trap, and the Pharisee walked right into it. The Pharisee was concerned with a ritual; Jesus was concerned with the truth. A Jewish person could do all the ritual washings required by law, and still not be clean.

The ritual of washing hands before eating does not make us totally clean, but it reminds us to live in the spirit of transparency. The customs we observe are a reminder; they are not the goal.

We know what perjury is. Someone puts a hand on a Bible, and swears to tell the truth and nothing but the truth. It is a very powerful ritual. We promise on the word of God to be truthful. Unfortunately, we have seen too many people perform that ritual, and then lie. The ritual does not make us tell the truth; it reminds us to tell the truth.

The Pharisee washed his hands, but he did not purify his vision. He judged Jesus for his behavior. He did not confront Jesus; he merely observed him, and added Jesus' violation of a ritual to the growing list of things Jesus was guilty of doing. Jesus never had a chance. They were out to get him, and they were going to get him.

Whom have we judged too harshly without knowing all the facts?

Wednesday of the Twenty-eighth Week in Ordinary Time

> "Woe to you Pharisees!
> You love the seat of honor in synagogues
> and greetings in marketplaces.
> Woe to you!
> You are like unseen graves over which people unknowingly walk."
> Then one of the scholars of the law said to him in reply,
> "Teacher, by saying this you are insulting us too."
> And he said, "Woe also to you scholars of the law!
> You impose on people burdens hard to carry,
> But you yourselves do not lift one finger to touch them."
> Lk 11: 42 – 46

There are not a lot of people who have the cache to say, "Woe to you." One would need to be above reproach to make such a statement. The Pharisees said it quite a lot as did the scholars of the law, but unfortunately for them, they were not above reproach. Jesus said it, and he was above reproach.

Many years ago, when I was teaching religion in a Christian Brothers High School, we used to have faculty meetings twice a month on Friday after the last class. Very few teachers enjoyed staying around after a long week of teaching, but almost everyone realized there was no other good time for faculty meetings. I remember clearly at one of my first faculty meetings, a senior member of the faculty disagreed with a suggestion from a new teacher. The veteran teacher raised his hand and was recognized. He stood solemnly and said, "You will rue the day…" He was using a word that was no longer used in common parlance. He was clinging to the old ways and old words. From that day forward, he was teased by other teachers, holding up one finger and saying, "You will rue the day." He was a respected member of the faculty so he got away with it. Other faculty members would not have gotten away with it. I wonder if the Apostles or disciples sometimes teased Jesus by saying, "Woe to you, Jesus!"

Do we sometimes take ourselves too seriously?

Thursday of the Twenty-eighth Week in Ordinary Time

> "Woe to you, scholars of the law!
> You have taken away the key of knowledge.
> You yourselves did not enter and you stopped those trying to enter."
> When Jesus left, the scribes and the Pharisees
> began to act with hostility toward him.
> and to interrogate him about many things,
> for they were plotting to catch him at something he might say.
> Lk 11: 47 – 54

When I was stationed at a university parish, there was a group of people who did not like me. (I know that is hard to believe.) A few of them began showing up at daily Mass, and were taking notes during my homilies. They were out to get me. Mostly I ignored them, but upon occasion I would chide them mildly. I would stop in the middle of my homily, and ask if I was going too quickly for them. Eventually they just stopped coming to daily Mass.

It is not a good feeling when you know that people are out to get you, and yet it happens all the time. Too often what is being said gets lost in who is saying it. Conservatives listen to conservatives; liberals listen to liberals. Never the twain shall meet. Our church and our country are racked with partisan divides.

There was a time, not that long ago, when people could have different opinions, and still be civil and respectful. There was a time when differences could be explored in the hope of finding common ground. We need to rediscover civility in our discourse, and we need to do it soon before we forget how. Partisanship has infected our politics and our religion. In our politics it is odious, in our religion it is scandalous.

Where are we guilty of not hearing what some people are trying to say?

Friday of the Twenty-eighth Week in Ordinary Time

> I tell you my friends,
> do not be afraid of those who kill the body
> but after that can do no more.
> Be afraid of the one who after killing
> has the power to cast into Gehenna;
> yes, I tell you, be afraid of that one.
> Are not five sparrows sold for two small coins?
> Yet not one of them has escaped the notice of God.
> Even the hairs of your head have all been counted.
> Do not be afraid.
> You are worth more than many sparrows.
> Lk 12: 1 – 7

God cares about us! That is a concept that is hard to wrap our arms around. I know God cares about you, but I am not sure why he would care about me. I know me from the inside out. God knows me that way as well. God should know better. God can do better. Why would God care about me?

When it comes to God we are insecure. I'm not sure why that is; I just know that it is a fact, a universal fact. We know that our parents and friends give us unconditional love. We give our families, parents, and friends unconditional love. Or at least we know we are supposed to give unconditional love.

Maybe the problem is we know that our love should be unconditional, but too often our love is fickle. In the back of our minds, we wonder about just how unconditional is the love of our friends. In the end, we trust them more than we trust ourselves.

Many years ago, a religious sister whom I knew asked me to be her confessor. I said yes. She came every other week to go to confession. We had not been working together that long when at the end of her confession, I asked her to tell me something she had done right during the past two weeks. I just had a feeling that she was more focused on her sins than her virtues. That was the beginning of the end. Shortly thereafter she told me she had found another confessor.

Why do we dwell so much on our faults, failures, and sins?

Saturday of the Twenty-eighth Week in Ordinary Time

"Everyone who speaks a word against the Son of Man will be forgiven,
but the one who blasphemes against the Holy Spirit
will not be forgiven.
When they take you before synagogues
and before rulers and authorities
do not worry about how or what your defense will be
or about what you are to say.
For the Holy Spirit will teach you at that moment
what you should say."
Lk 12: 8 – 12

There was a time in the life of our church, when the "sin against the Holy Spirit" was thought to be the sin of despair, which led our church to deny Christian burial to someone who committed suicide because suicide was considered the ultimate act of despair. Thank God that is no longer the case.

Despair is not a sin; it is a mental condition that needs to be treated. People used to come to me because they were depressed, and wanted to feel better. I would always ask them to tell me what was going on in their lives. Invariably, they would then give me a list of very sad things that had happened to them. A sick spouse, problems with a teenager, money problems, the death of a parent, loss of a job, or crushing debt. They would give me a strange look when I would say, "You are supposed to be depressed; be thankful that you are." Sad things are supposed to depress us. Despair is most often the proper attitude.

The problem is not that we are depressed; the problem is when we don't slowly recover from our depression. Today' s gospel reminds us that no matter how low we feel, we are never alone. God is always with us, and together we can face whatever life throws at us.

Where do we need God to lift us up?

Twenty-ninth Sunday in Ordinary Time (A)

> "Teacher, we know that you are a truthful man
> and that you teach the way of God in accordance with the truth.
> And you are not concerned with anyone's opinion,
> for you do not regard a person's status.
> Tell us, then, what is your opinion:
> Is it lawful to pay the census tax to Caesar or not?"
> Mt 22:15-21

At the end of today's gospel, Jesus tells the hypocrite who tried to trap him with the question about paying the census tax, "Then repay to Caesar what belongs to Caesar and to God what belongs to God." This is Jesus' version of "a place for everything and everything in its place."

If our priorities are correct, then life will run smoothly. There are myriad calls for our attention. The job calls, the family calls, friends call, the church calls, as do school and a host of other realities.

We know that family should come before our job, but is that how we allocate our time? People should come before profit, but do they? All the time? Most of the time? Some of the time?

When Sunday morning rolls around the church calls and sports call. To whom do we give allegiance? We have faith strong enough to guide our choices, but too often we mute it.

We are called to meet the needs of those on the margins of life. Jesus has told us, "Whatever you do to the least among you, you do unto me." Too often, we try to calculate what is the minimum we can give to assuage our conscience without diminishing our lifestyle.

Do our priorities need a little housekeeping?

Twenty-ninth Sunday in Ordinary Time (B)

> Jesus called them together and said to them:
> "You know how among the Gentiles those in authority
> lord it over them; their great ones make their importance felt.
> It cannot be like that with you.
> Anyone among you who aspires to greatness must serve the rest;
> whoever wants to rank first among you must serve the needs of all.
> The Son of Man has not come to be served but to serve –
> to give his life in ransom for the many.
> Mk 10: 35 – 45

"Anyone among you who aspires to greatness must serve the rest." Remember there is a difference between aspiring for greatness and aspiring for recognition. Greatness is wanting to give your very best to everything we do. Greatness means not cutting corners. Greatness means discipline and dedication. Only we know the quality of our involvement in what we do.

Recognition is another thing altogether. When we are driven by a need for recognition, we are in trouble. Do your job to the best of your ability. If we are recognized for our efforts, that is great, but not essential. Doing our best is essential; recognition is an occasional bonus.

Jesus has shown us the way we need to live. He gave his "life in ransom for the many." He served others; he put us first. Because he was not concerned with recognition, it has been lavished on him for more than two thousand years, and counting. Jesus did not seek the spotlight; the spotlight found him. That is the way it should be with us.

How can we serve the needs of others better?

Twenty-ninth Sunday in Ordinary Time (C)

> The Lord said,
> "Listen to what the corrupt judge has to say.

> Will not God then do justice to his chosen
> who call out to him day and night?
> Will he delay long over them, do you suppose?
> I tell you he will give them swift justice.
> But when the Son of Man comes,
> will he find any faith on the earth?"
> Lk 18: 1 – 8

What a great question, "When the Son of Man comes will he find any faith on the earth?" It seems to me that faith gets diminished with the passage of time. The more culture improves; the more religion is discarded.

Faith is the belief in what cannot be seen or proved scientifically. No matter how technologically advanced we become there will always be a need for faith. All that is truly important cannot be seen or proved. Have we ever seen love? No, all we have seen are what we call the signs of love. We have never seen love walking down the street. We have seen two people holding hands walking down the street, and we believe they are in love. We have never seen courage walking toward us. Yet we have seen first responders running toward danger when everyone else is running away. We say they have courage, but all we have seen are the signs of courage. We have never seen honesty, loyalty, truthfulness, or kindness. All we have seen are the signs of these virtues, and that has to be enough – faith does the rest.

No one has ever seen God, but we have seen the signs of God. The beauty and order of creation are signs of God's loving presence in our world. When people seek peace rather than revenge, when they put the needs of others before their own, when justice lifts up the lowly, we see the signs of God, and faith does the rest.

What are our special signs of God's presence in our lives?

Monday of the Twenty-ninth Week in Ordinary Time

> Someone in the crowd said to Jesus,
> "Teacher, tell my brother to share the inheritance with me."

> He replied to him,
> "Friend, who appointed me your judge and arbitrator?"
> Then he said to the crowd,
> "Take care to guard against all greed,
> for though one may be rich,
> one's life does not consist of possessions."
> Lk 12: 13 – 21

The dictionary defines greed as "a strong desire for more." There seems to be at least one flaw in the human condition – we are never satisfied with what we have! There is always something bigger, newer, and faster that will make us happy. We are told this lie over and over, and like Charlie Brown with Lucy holding the football we fall for it every time.

Jesus refutes the lie of consumerism by saying, "One's life does not consist of possessions." And yet we cling to our possessions like they are what gives us life. It is so easy to let greed rule our lives.

There was a TV show I used to watch. I think it was called Storage Wars. The show was about auctioning off the contents of abandoned storage units. Many of the people on the show were professional storage unit scavengers. They were not collectors; they were treasure hunters. As long as they made a profit on the units they bought, they were good to go for another day. One day it dawned on me just how sad the whole concept was. People paid money to store things they no longer needed. Then they stopped paying the rent. They did not collect their stored items; they abandoned them. Then others came along and tried to profit from the things that were abandoned. Watching the show was like watching a gerbil in a cage walking inside a wheel thinking it was making progress. So sad.

Where has greed taken hold in our lives?

Tuesday of the Twenty-ninth Week in Ordinary Time

> Jesus said to his disciples,
> "Gird your loins and light your lamps
> and be like servants who await their master's return from a wedding,

> ready to open immediately when he comes and knocks.
> Blessed are those servants
> Who the master finds vigilant on his arrival."
> Lk 12: 35 – 38

One day the master is going to come and knock, and when he does, ready or not, the game of life is over. Sort of like the game Hide and Seek many of us played as children. At some point, Jesus is going to say, "Ready or not, here I come." The trick is to be ready, to be vigilant.

It is hard to be vigilant. We grow tired; we grow careless. Anyone who has ever been on a diet or an exercise regime knows what I am talking about. We start off all gung ho, but then after about a week or so we begin to cut corners. We then skip a day of exercise here, or we have a few cookies there, and the next thing we know we are back to square one or worse.

If we can learn how to integrate good behavior into our daily routine, then we don't need to be vigilant. We need to live according to our values, and we will be ready for whatever comes our way. If we make prayer a regular part of every day, we will be focused on what is important. If we reach out and help others as part of our everyday living, we will always be prepared when the master comes and knocks on the door of our heart.

How can we better integrate our faith into our everyday living?

Wednesday of the Twenty-ninth Week in Ordinary Time

> Jesus said to his disciples:
> "Be sure of this:
> if the master of the house had known the hour
> when the thief was coming,
> he would not have let his house be broken into.
> You also must be prepared,
> for at an hour you do not expect, the Son of Man will come."
> Lk 12: 39 – 48

When someone goes out for a walk, and collapses and dies, it is always a shock. No one expects that to happen. We are good at fooling ourselves that we always have tomorrow. Many of us live by the procrastinator's creed, "Never do today what you can put off until tomorrow!" Eventually, we run out of tomorrows.

When someone is sick for a long period of time. When we see her slip away a little bit day after day. When we pray for recovery or a happy death. When we know death is near, it is still a shock when it comes. We are never as prepared as we think we are. No matter how long someone lives, when death comes, we always want one more minute, one more hour, one more day, one more…

I like God's system. I want to be surprised when he comes for me. The last thing I would want to know is the day and hour that would be my last. That would take all the fun out of living.

Are we prepared if today is the last day of our life?

Thursday of the Twenty-ninth Week in Ordinary Time

> "Do you think that I have come to establish peace on earth?
> No, I tell you, but rather division.
> From now on a household of five will be divided,
> three against two and two against three;
> a father will be divided against his son
> and a son against a father,
> a mother against a daughter,
> and a daughter against her mother,
> a mother-in-law against a daughter-in-law,
> and a daughter-in-law against a mother-in-law."
> Lk 12: 49 – 53

One thing is certain, none of the words above will ever be printed on a holy card or be made into a wall poster. Today's gospel is really not all that quotable. In fact, it doesn't even sound like Jesus.

Because it is Jesus, we need to struggle to figure out what point he is trying to make. Jesus wants us to be people of conviction, not people of convenience. He wants to be able to count on us, especially when the going gets tough. If we are people of conviction then there will be division. We should never set out to cause division. Never! But we need to realize that if we live our faith fully, then divisions are inevitable.

Once we start down the path of peace at any price, we know we are lost. Once we convince ourselves that we have to go along in order to get along, we are doomed.

When there are differences, we need to listen carefully and kindly. We need to struggle to understand where the other person is coming from. We need to respect differences of opinion. We need to understand the other point of view, but we don't have to agree with it.

There will always be different voices calling out to us. We need to be steadfast and always hear God's voice above all others.

Where have we failed to stand up for what we believe?

Friday of the Twenty-ninth Week in Ordinary Time

> Jesus said to the crowds,
> "When you see a cloud rising in the west,
> you say immediately that rain is coming –
> and so it does.
> When the wind blows from the south,
> you say it is going to be hot –
> and so it is.
> You hypocrites!
> If you can interpret the portents of earth and sky,
> why can you not interpret the present time?"
> Lk 12: 54 – 59

It is all about reading the signs of the times. Some people are better at it than others. God sends us signs every day. We have to be on the lookout for what God is trying to tell us.

Perhaps a story will help us understand the signs that God sends us. There was a small village built on the bank of a river. After several days of rain the river was about to flood. An elderly woman who lived along the river prayed that God would protect her. God said he would. When the river crested, a small power boat came up to her house, and offered to take her to a safe place. She refused the offer because God was going to keep her safe. The waters kept rising and now the woman was on the second floor of her house when a larger boat came to rescue her. Once again she refused. Finally, she is seated on the roof of her home when a helicopter lowers a rope to save her, but she would not grab onto the rope. Finally she drowned.

When she got to heaven, she complained to God "I asked that you would keep me safe, and you said you would. Why did you not keep me safe?" A very exasperated God said to her, "I sent a boat, a bigger boat, and finally a helicopter. What more did you want me to do?"

Where are we blind to the signs that God sends to us?

Saturday of the Twenty-ninth Week in Ordinary Time

And he told them this parable,
"There once was a person who had a fig tree planted in his orchard,
and when he came in search of fruit on it but found none,
he said to the gardener,
'For three years now I have come in search of fruit on the fig tree
but have found none.
So cut it down.
Why should it exhaust the soil?'
He said to him in reply,
'Sir, leave it for this year also,
and I shall cultivate the ground around it and fertilize it;
it may bear fruit in the future.
If not you can cut it down.'"
Lk 13: 1 – 9

The person who owned the orchard was a patient man, but his gardener was even more patient. The owner waited three years to get some figs; he was done waiting. The gardener wanted to keep trying. Perhaps a little cultivation and a good dose of manure would do the trick.

The part of the parable that I have always enjoyed is the flip-flop that takes place. The gardener says he will wait to see if the tree produces any figs. Originally, he bargains just for the rest of the growing season, "leave it for this year also." But in the very next line he just says, "it may bear fruit in the future." Then there is the ultimate flip-flop. The gardener tells the owner he may have to cut down the tree.

There are many ways to interpret this parable. In my mind the gardener is Jesus. He looks at our potential, not our results. He believes, contrary to the evidence at hand, that we will turn our lives around. He believes that we will bear good fruit in our lives. He loves us not because we deserve his love but because he knows no other way to treat us.

How can we allow Jesus' love to be the fertilizer we need to bear good fruit?

Thirtieth Sunday in Ordinary Time (A)

> When the Pharisees heard that Jesus had silenced the Saducees,
> they gathered together, and one of them,
> a scholar of the law tested him by asking,
> "Teacher which commandment in the law is the greatest?"
> Mt 22: 34 – 40

We all know Jesus' answer, which is why I did not bother to print it above. Jesus would not be controlled by the Pharisees' strictures; he would not be limited to one commandment. He gave a two-fold answer. We have to love God with all we have, and we have to love our neighbor as we love ourselves!

On the surface, the answer seems to be a contradiction. If we love God with all we have, then there should be nothing left for us to love our neighbors or ourselves. But that is not the case; love is different. The more we love, the more we are able to love. Love cannot be used up. Love is rejuvenating.

We cannot run out of love because it is a quality not a quantity. Love is a virtue not a commodity. The Bible story of Elijah and the widow of Zarephath underscores this reality. When Elijah asks for something to eat, the widow responds that she has only a handful of flour and a bit of oil. Nevertheless, she gives the prophet some water and a bit of bread. She gave to the prophet what was to be the last meal for her and her son. She responded out of love; she did not count the cost. Because of her love she was rewarded; she did not run out of flour or oil until God sent rain to end the drought. (I Kings 17: 7 – 16)

Where are we too stingy with love?

Thirtieth Sunday in Ordinary Time (B)

> Then Jesus stopped and said, "Call him over."
> So they called the blind man over, telling him as they did so,
> "You have nothing to fear from him.
> Get up! He is calling you!"
> He threw aside his cloak, jumped up and came to Jesus.
> Jesus asked him,
> "What do you want me to do for you?"
> "Rabboni," the blind man said, "I want to see."
> "Be on your way! Your faith has healed you."
> Immediately he received his sight
> and started to follow him up the road.
> Mk 10: 46 – 52

There are two events in this gospel story that always amaze me. The first is that Jesus asks the blind man, "What do you want me to do for you?" What a very sensitive question. Jesus does not assume to know what the blind man wants or needs. Remember Bartimaeus, the blind man, was a beggar; he was not used to being treated with respect. His job was to beg; to take what others wanted to give to him, and be satisfied. Jesus treated him with respect. I wonder what that must have felt like?

The second part of the gospel story that always amazes me is that when Bartimaeus jumps up he throws away his cloak. That little detail is subtle, but very important. We could easily miss its importance. His cloak did more than keep him warm; his cloak was where people would throw their donations. His cloak was his collection basket. When Andrew and

Peter were called, they abandoned their nets. They left behind what they depended on for their livelihood. James and John did the same. So did Bartimaeus. Peter and Andrew, James and John were no longer fishermen, they were Apostles; Bartimaeus was no longer a beggar, he was a disciple.

What do we need to leave behind to be better believers?

Thirtieth Sunday in Ordinary Time (C)

> Jesus spoke this parable to those who believed
> in their own self-righteousness
> while holding everyone else in contempt:
> "Two men went up to the temple to pray;
> one was a Pharisee, the other a tax collector.
> The Pharisee with head unbowed prayed in this fashion:
> 'I give you thanks, O God, that I am not
> like the rest of men – grasping, crooked, adulterous –
> or even like this tax-collector.
> I fast twice a week. I pay tithes on all I possess.'
> The other man, however, kept his distance,
> not even daring to raise his eyes to heaven.
> All he did was beat his breast and say,
> 'O God, be merciful to me a sinner,'"
> Lk 18: 9 – 14

There is a much shorter version of this parable. "Two men went up to the temple to pray. One did; one didn't." All the Pharisee did was talk about himself. He only made "I" statements. Prayer does not consist of a string of "I" statements. Prayer is not tooting our own horn. The tax collector knows what prayer is all about. Prayer is trusting in God's love, and asking for God's forgiveness.

The Pharisee was so full of himself that there was no room for God. Not only was there no room for God, truth be told, the Pharisee did not see the need for God in his life. The only thing he was able to thank God for was that he was better than everyone else.

Many years ago a friend made me a needlepoint wall hanging with this message, "God so designed the human body so that we cannot easily pat ourselves on the back or kick ourselves in the butt!"

The tax collector was not kicking himself in the butt; he was owning his failures, and asking God's help to become a better person. We should know what that feels like.

Where have we failed to make room for God in our prayers?

Monday of the Thirtieth Week in Ordinary Time

> But the leader of the synagogue,
> indignant that Jesus had cured on the Sabbath,
> said to the crowd in reply,
> "There are six days when work should be done.
> Come on those days to be cured, not on the Sabbath day."
> The Lord said to him in reply, "Hypocrites!"
> Lk 13: 10 – 17

Why is it that we think we can limit God? The synagogue leader could only see that a rule was being broken. He would not let himself dwell on the woman being healed. Rules are important, but they are a means to an end. They are not the end, and any time we lose sight of that truth we get lost in legalism.

I remember very well a theology course that I took called De Legibus (Concerning the Law). I remember clearly the day the professor dealt with the principle of "epikeia." He explained that it was never enough just to know universal law. Universal law had to be applied to the local situation. That was the blessed day that legalism died in my life.

Jesus did not disagree with Sabbath rules and regulations; he just decided that the woman had been sick for eighteen years, and it made no sense to ask her to come back tomorrow. Her healing, in his mind, was more important than the law in this very specific situation. End of story.

I remember Pope Francis' first Holy Thursday Mass. He went to a prison, and he washed the feet of women, one or two of whom were Muslims. The legal beagles went bananas. At the time universal liturgical law said that only the feet of men should be washed on Holy Thursday. Most parishes did not abide by this universal law, but a few obstinately clung to the law. On Easter Monday, Francis' press secretary was asked if the Pope had broken liturgical law. I will never forget the press secretary's answer. With a straight face he said, "The Pope did not break the law; he simply ignored it." He concluded that the universal law did not apply in his local situation. That's "epikeia" and we need more of it!

Where are we too legalistic with our faith?

Tuesday of the Thirtieth Week in Ordinary Time

> Jesus said, "What is the Kingdom of God like?
> To what can I compare it?..."
> Again he said, "To what shall I compare the Kingdom of God?
> It is like yeast that a woman took
> and mixed in with three measures of wheat flour
> until the whole batch of dough was leavened."
> Lk 13: 18 – 21

The Kingdom of God is a bit of a mystery. It is a work in process. Every believer is expected to do his or her part in building it up. We are closer to the Kingdom of God now than our parents were. And our parents were closer to the Kingdom than their parents were.

I love the image of the yeast. A little bit of yeast changes the whole batch of dough. A good deed done to a neighbor builds up the entire community. Good deeds start a chain reaction. We have no idea where our good deeds end.

Good deeds are like the pay it forward movement. Someone does something kind for us. They do not want the favor returned to them, but would rather that it be extended to someone else. And so begins a community, which will culminate someday in the Kingdom of God.

The important thing is to remember that God is in charge of his Kingdom. St. Paul speaks of the Kingdom in these words, "After all, who is Apollos? And who is Paul? Simply ministers through whom you became believers, each of them doing only what the Lord assigned to him. I planted and Apollos watered it, but God gave the growth." (I Cor 3: 5 – 6)

What piece of building up the Kingdom has God assigned to us?

Wednesday of the Thirtieth Week in Ordinary Time

> Jesus went through cities and towns teaching –
> all the while making his way toward Jerusalem.
> Someone asked him,
> "Lord, are they few in number who are to be saved?"
> He replied:
> "Try to come in through the narrow door.
> Many, I tell you, will try to enter and be unable."
> Lk 13: 22 – 30

There is something in human nature that desires exclusivity. We crave tickets to the hottest plays or concerts. Getting a ticked to World Series game or to the Super Bowl is prized. Why? Because they are so hard to get.

Gated communities are thought to be better than living without protection. Automobiles that are ridiculously expensive give their owners status.

The problem is we try to do the same thing with heaven. We try to make it exclusive, and we interpret today's gospel in that way. God has gone to a great deal of work to save us. He sent his son to be our Savior. Jesus took on flesh, and showed us how to live. He willingly gave his life on the cross that we might be saved. If God, through Jesus, went to all that effort, why would he then try to limit who will be saved?

Jesus opened his arms to everyone. He welcomed the outcasts, the sinners, the Samaritans, lepers, and tax collectors. Why then is it that we think of heaven in terms of exclusivity? Why do we think we have to earn our way to heaven? Salvation cannot be earned because it is freely given to us. God, through Jesus, has opened the gates of heaven. We are called to live our lives in ways that thank God for all his gifts, especially salvation!

Why do we think that we have to earn our salvation?

Thursday of the Thirtieth Week in Ordinary Time

> Some Pharisees came to Jesus and said,
> "Go away, leave this area because Herod wants to kill you."
> He replied, "Go and tell that fox,
> 'Behold, I cast out demons
> and I perform healings today and tomorrow.
> and on the third day I accomplish my purpose.
> Yet I must continue on my way today, tomorrow,
> and the following day,
> for it is impossible that a prophet should die
> outside of Jerusalem.'"
> Lk 13: 31 – 35

Jesus was making his way to Jerusalem. Jerusalem was his destiny. The purpose of his life always resided in Jerusalem.

In Alice in Wonderland there is a scene where Alice comes to a fork in the road. She looks one way and then the other. She looks up at the Cheshire cat seated on a tree branch and asks, "Which road should I take?" The cat says, "Where are you going?" Alice responds, "I don't know." The Cheshire cat wisely says, "Then it really doesn't matter which road you take."

Directions only work when we have a destination. We have to know where we are going. And it is not a one-time question. What do we do now that school is finished? In midlife we need to ask should I continue doing what I am doing or should I try something else? When we retire, we have to ask what now?

Things get a bit complicated when we accept the fact that God has a direction he wants us to choose. He has given us gifts, talents, and abilities, and he wants us to use them according to his plan. Jesus knew that his Father wanted him to offer his life as ransom for many; Jesus had to go to Jerusalem.

What does God want us to accomplish with our lives?

Friday of the Thirtieth Week in Ordinary Time

> On the Sabbath Jesus went to dine
> at the home of one of the leading Pharisees,
> and the people there were observing him carefully.
> In front to him there was a man suffering from dropsy.
> Jesus spoke to the scholars of the law and the Pharisees in reply, asking,
> "Is it lawful to cure on the Sabbath or not?"
> Lk 14: 1 – 6

Jesus does cure the man, and then he said to them, "Who among you, if your son or ox falls into a cistern, would not immediately pull him out on the Sabbath day?" The passage ends with, "But they were unable to answer the question." They weren't unable; they were unwilling!

They did not answer because to do so would have incriminated themselves. No one would leave a child to suffer in a ditch because it was the Sabbath. No one would let a work animal be harmed because it was the Sabbath.

The scribes and Pharisees wanted law and order. Their world was black and white. The law is the law is the law. They may have wanted that, but the world just would not fit their rigid categories.

One would think that church leaders would have learned Jesus' lessons about a black and white world a long time ago, but they haven't. The Second Vatican Council invited us to read the signs of the time. St. John XXIII in his opening message told the bishops at the Second Vatican Council that "the time had come to open the windows and let some fresh air into the church." The Council did what he asked, but ever since certain church leaders have been running around closing and nailing shut those same windows.

Where have tradition and the rules become a straightjacket on our faith?

Saturday of the Thirtieth Week in Ordinary Time

> Noticing how they were choosing
> the places of honor at the table, he said,
> "When you are invited by someone to a wedding banquet,
> do not recline at table in the place of honor.
> A more distinguished guest than you may have been invited by him,
> and the host who invited both of you may approach you and say,
> 'Give your place to this man,'
> and then you would proceed with embarrassment
> to take the lowest place.
> Lk 14: 1, 7 – 11

It is always better to be invited higher than to be directed lower. There is just no way of recovering from having too high an opinion of ourselves. Everyone enjoys seeing the high and mighty be brought down to size.

Many years ago, my father was given a pin by the Knights of Columbus for being a member in good standing for 50 years. My father bought some tickets to the dinner, and several of my brothers and I went to the dinner with him. At the door, when the ticket collector saw my Roman collar, he got all flustered. He said, "Father we will make a place for you at the head table." I said not to bother because I wanted to sit with my family. He said, "We always sit priests at the head table." I told him to relax because I had been a son a lot longer than I had been a priest, and I would sit with my family.

It is important to know where we belong. It is always more important to do what is right than to look good. When appearances are made more important than substance, we are all diminished.

How do we determine our true place in the world?

Thirty-first Sunday in Ordinary Time (A)

> Jesus told the crowds and his disciples:
> "The scribes and the Pharisees have succeeded Moses as teachers,

therefore do everything and observe everything they tell you.
But do not follow their example.
Their words are bold but their deeds are few."
Mt 23: 1 – 12

Basically, Jesus is saying respect the office they hold, but not they themselves. Jesus basically says they have forgotten what their office is all about. The scribes and the Pharisees were appointed to serve the needs of the people, but they forgot who they were supposed to be. That is easy to do; we need to be on guard.

Whenever I think of the Pharisees, both then and now, I am reminded of this story from the Native American tradition. It takes place during a time of drought. The chief called upon the medicine man to call down rain. So the medicine man banged his drum, danced wildly, and chanted his invocations. When he finished he was exhausted, but there was no rain. Someone asked the chief what he thought, and he said, "Strong wind, loud thunder. No rain!" We all know people like that – they talk a good game, but they never produce anything of substance. Jesus had the right idea, "For the Son of Man did not come to be served, but to serve, and to give his life as a ransom for many." (Mk 10: 45)

Where do our deeds not live up to our words?

Thirty-first Sunday in Ordinary Time (B)

One of the scribes came up to Jesus, and asked him,
"Which is the first of all the commandments?"
Jesus replied,
"This is the first:
'Here, O Israel! The Lord your God is Lord alone!
Therefore you shall love the Lord your God
with all your heart,
with all your soul,
with all your mind,
and with all your strength.'

> This is the second,
> 'You shall love your neighbor as yourself.'
> There is no other commandment greater than these."
> Mk 12: 28 – 34

There are two kinds of questions, questions that are honest and sincere, and questions that are not. The scribe in today's gospel is asking the latter kind of question. He is not interested in Jesus' answer; he is interested in using Jesus' answer against him. Jesus does not enter the trap.

Jesus gives a great answer. Without saying so in so many words, he rejects the question. There is no first commandment that is above all other commandments.

Without going into a long explanation Jesus, ever the teacher, reminds the scribe that love of God cannot be cut off from love of neighbor, and that love of God and neighbor is impossible unless we first love ourselves. Love is always dynamic; it is never static. Commandments seem to be static but even they are always changing. Every time we think we know how to love God we find out there is more to know about loving God. Loving God is a never-ending process. The same is true when it comes to loving ourselves and our neighbor. We can always love better.

Has our love for God and neighbor evolved or is it static?

Thirty-first Sunday in Ordinary Time (C)

> When Jesus came to the spot he looked up and said,
> "Zacchaeus, hurry down. I mean to stay in your house today."
> He quickly descended, and welcomed him with delight.
> When this was observed, everyone began to murmur,
> "He has gone to a sinner's house as a guest."
> Zacchaeus stood his ground and said to the Lord,
> "I give half my belongings, Lord, to the poor.
> If I have defrauded anyone in the least, I pay him back fourfold."
> Jesus said to him,

> "Today salvation has come to this house,
> for this is what it means to be a son of Abraham.
> The Son of Man has come to search out and save what was lost."
> Lk 19: 1 – 10

Zacchaeus' conversion began because he was curious. He wanted to see what Jesus was like. That is why he climbed the sycamore tree in the first place. Zacchaeus knew something was missing in his life. He was not satisfied with who he was. The people who were murmuring were not curious. Their worldview was fixed. They were the good folks, and Zacchaeus was a sinner. Everyone had a label, and no one was allowed to change.

Jesus abhorred labels. He came to offer forgiveness; to seek out what was lost. That was his ministry, and he perfected it. We know that the only one Jesus lost was Judas who betrayed him. In truth, Jesus did not lose Judas; Judas lost himself. Judas took his life because he had betrayed his Master. Peter denied, but he wept and let himself be forgiven. I wish Judas had trusted Jesus more. I wish he had let himself be forgiven. If he had our salvation would not be diminished; Jesus' love would only be magnified.

What label we have attached to ourselves do we need Jesus' help to erase?

Monday of the Thirty-first Week in Ordinary Time

> Jesus said to the chief of the Pharisees
> who had invited him to dinner:
> "Whenever you give a lunch or a dinner,
> do not invite your friend or brothers
> or relatives or wealthy neighbors.
> They might invite you in return and thus repay you.
> No, when you have a reception,
> Invite beggars and the crippled, the lame and the blind.
> You should be pleased that they cannot repay you,
> for you will be repaid in the resurrection of the just."
> Lk 14: 12 – 14

Let's get one thing straight. It is perfectly all right to break bread with family, friends, and neighbors. Just don't stop there. Always make sure we find ways to feed those who are without.

Most parishes are very good at having food drives for Thanksgiving and Christmas. Unfortunately, too often it stops there. We forget that people have to eat year round.

In the parish where I served before I retired, we encouraged people to bring food to church every weekend. We would store the non-perishable food in a closet, and every Monday members of the parish would take the food to our sister parish in the inner city. No one ever stopped to calculate just how much food we collected, but it was a lot. Some members of the parish who drove the food to our sister parish would go back during the week to help distribute it.

One mother who was delivering food took her three children with her. As they drove past some boarded up houses one of them said, "Do people actually live here?" Justice lived is a powerful teacher!

Where do we need to be more sensitive to the needs of our less fortunate neighbors?

Tuesday of the Thirty-first Week in Ordinary Time

> Jesus responded,
> "A man was giving a large dinner and had invited many.
> At dinner time he sent his servants to those invited,
> 'Come along everything is ready now.'
> But they began to excuse themselves one and all.
> The first said to the servant, 'I have bought some land
> and must go and inspect it.
> Please excuse me.'"
> Lk 14: 15 – 24

There were more excuses in today's gospel reading, but this first excuse is all we need. Most excuses are made up, and most of them are false. Whoever bought land without first inspecting it? No one buys land, and then goes to inspect it.

We make up excuses all the time. There is a wonderful story about a farmer who goes to his neighbor, and asks to borrow some rope. The neighbor says, "I can't let you borrow my rope because I need it to tie up my milk." Everyone knows that you can't tie up milk so the excuse is just a polite way of saying no. Polite perhaps, but definitely selfish.

The rising sun of each new day is God's invitation to be his people. Some days we accept that invitation, and live and act as God's children. On other days, we are too tired, too bored, too self-absorbed, or too unforgiving to live and act as God's people. Too often we excuse ourselves, and say we will do better tomorrow. Unfortunately, that tomorrow never comes.

What excuses do we make up so that we don't have to live our faith?

Wednesday of the Thirty-first Week in Ordinary Time

> Great crowds were travelling with Jesus,
> and he turned and addressed them,
> "If anyone comes to me without hating his father and mother,
> wife and children, brothers and sisters,
> and even his own life,
> he cannot be my disciple.
> Whoever does not carry his own cross and come after me
> cannot be my disciple."
> Lk 14: 25 – 33

Whenever I hear this gospel, I hear my mother's voice saying, "You should not hate anyone!" Growing up, I would from time to time say I hated one of my brothers. My mother would intervene, and say the words quoted above. When one of my brothers would hate me, they were reprimanded with the same words. I think all of us can relate.

I can only imagine the look on my mother's face if I told her that Jesus said I had to hate her. Trust me, my mother would have overruled what Jesus says in this gospel.

Now obviously Jesus does not want us to hate anyone. All he is doing is exaggerating to make a point. He expects his followers to be dedicated. Jesus is not interested in part-time followers. He wants all of us, not part of us. If all we are willing to give at any point is part of our dedication, Jesus will meet us there, but he will love us up to a more dedicated response. Like all good teachers, Jesus sees what we are capable of doing more than what we thus far have achieved.

Where does our faith response need to be deeper and more profound?

Thursday of the Thirty-first Week in Ordinary Time

> So Jesus addressed this parable to them.
> "What man among you having a hundred sheep
> and losing one of them
> would not leave the ninety-nine in the desert
> and go after the lost one until he finds it?
> And when he finds it,
> he sets it on his shoulders with great joy,
> and, upon his arrival home,
> he calls together his friends and neighbors and says to them,
> 'Rejoice with me because I have found my lost sheep.'
> I tell you, in just the same way
> there will be more joy in heaven over one sinner who repents
> than over ninety-nine righteous people
> who have no need of repentance."
> Lk 15: 1 – 10

In spite of the fact that Jesus is known as the Good Shepherd, today's gospel shows that he would have been a lousy one. Sometimes you have to cut your losses. Safeguard the ninety-nine and forget the one that gets lost.

As always, Jesus is making a point not writing a manual on how to be a shepherd. Jesus, the Messiah, has come to save all people. As Savior, he goes after the sinners not the saints. He rejoices that there are saints. He wants all of us to be saints, but some of us get lost along the way.

That is when Jesus seeks us out. As Francis Thompson says in his poem The Hound of Heaven, "I fled him down the labyrinthine ways." When we sin, we turn our back on God. We flee from his presence. We avoid the light of his love, and walk in the darkness of our evil deeds. But Jesus pursues us constantly until we come to our senses. No matter how often we wander from the light, he continues to let the light of his love reveal the path to find our way back to him. How fortunate are we?

Where have we turned our backs on God?

Friday of the Thirty-first Week in Ordinary Time

> Jesus said to his disciples, "A rich man had a steward.
> who was reported to him for squandering his property.
> He summoned him and said,
> 'What is this I hear about you?
> Prepare a full account of your stewardship,
> because you can no longer be my steward.'
> The steward said to himself, 'What shall I do,
> now that my master is taking the position of steward away from me?
> I am not strong enough to dig and I am ashamed to beg.'"
> Lk 16: 1 – 8

We are stewards of all that God has given us, and there will come a day when we must give an account of our stewardship. Everything we have is on loan from God.

Unlike the rich man in today's parable, God is infinitely patient with us. He refuses to believe that we will not take good care of what he has loaned to us, in spite of all the evidence to the contrary. We use the possessive pronoun far too much. This is my home, my car, my money, my reputation, etc. But deep down we know that we don't own any of those things. They are loaned to us. Jesus told them this parable, "There was a rich man who had a good harvest. 'What shall I do' he asked himself. 'I have no place to store my harvest? I know,' he said, 'I will pull down my grain bins and build larger ones'... But God said to him,

'You fool! This very night your life shall be required of you. To whom will all this piled up wealth of yours go?'" (Lk 12: 21 – 20)

A good friend of mine expresses these same thoughts more succinctly, "I have never seen a U-Haul trailer following a hearse!"

Where have we failed to be good stewards of all God's gifts?

Saturday of the Thirty-first Week in Ordinary Time

> No servant can serve two masters.
> He will either hate one and love the other,
> or be devoted to one and despise the other.
> You cannot serve God and mammon.
> Lk 16: 9 – 15

The sting of today's message is muted by the word "mammon," which is an ancient word. Webster defines "mammon" as "Riches, avarice, and worldly gain personified as a false god in the New Testament." In everyday speech today's gospel punch line is, "You cannot serve God and money."

Too often money is given a bad name in religious circles. The fact of the matter is there is nothing inherently evil about money. Money can be a very good thing if it is used correctly.

Money becomes a problem when we begin to worship it. When we become obsessed with money, we make it a false God. When I was a high school teacher and a campus minister, I used to tell students, "Never take a job because of the money it pays. Take a job that will make you happy. Take a job that you love. If you love your job, you will never have to go to work." As the old saying goes, "Money can't buy you happiness." Winning the lottery has ruined more lives than it has enriched. We need to learn how to enjoy what we have rather than always chasing after something newer, bigger, and faster.

What gifts from God do we need to appreciate more fully?

Thirty-second Sunday in Ordinary Time (A)

> "At midnight, there was a cry,
> 'Behold, the bridegroom! Come out to meet him!'
> Then all those virgins got up and trimmed their lamps.
> The foolish ones said to the wise,
> 'Give us some of your oil.'
> But the wise ones replied,
> 'No, for there may not be enough for us and you.
> Go instead to the merchants and buy some for yourselves.'
> While they went off to buy it,
> the bridegroom came
> and those who were ready went into the wedding feast with him."
> Mt 25: 1 – 13

This parable does not sound like Jesus. According to Jesus we are supposed to meet the needs of others. We are to reach out to those in need and help them. This parable is not about helping others; it is about being prepared to meet Jesus when he comes. We know this because the bridegroom comes at midnight, yet the wise virgins tell the foolish virgins to go to the merchants and buy some oil. Believe me there were no oil merchants open at one in the morning!

We are coming to the end of the liturgical year. This Sunday's readings, and next Sunday's as well, are about the end times. Jesus will come and we will be judged on how well we lived our faith. In the liturgy, the end time is scheduled; in life that is not the case. The end time will come when it comes.

Too often the end time is cloaked in fear, but no fear is necessary. Every good deed, every kindness, and every act of faith puts oil in our lamps. If we live well, we will have plenty of oil in our lamps. And the bridegroom will invite us into the celebration called heaven.

Are we on the lookout for the least among us so we can meet their needs?

Thirty-second Sunday in Ordinary Time (B)

> Taking a seat opposite the treasury,
> he observed the crowd putting money into the collection box.
> Many of the wealthy put in sizable amounts;
> But one poor widow came and put in two small copper coins
> worth about a cent.
> He called his disciples over and told them:
> "I want you to observe that this poor widow contributed
> more than all the others who donated to the treasury.
> They gave from their surplus wealth,
> but she gave from her want,
> all that she had to live on."
> Mk 12: 38 – 44

One of the amazing things about being in parish ministry is seeing up close and personal how people live out their stewardship of time, talent, and treasure.

Some people freely offer their talent for the good of the parish. They may not be the most talented, but they are the most anxious to share whatever talent they have to enrich the life of the parish. The same is true for how people share their time. It always seemed to me that it was the busiest people who were willing to share the gift of time to help the parish thrive. Whenever we needed people to help with a project, I was always amazed by both those who stepped forward and those who did not. Not always but many times it was the people with too much on their plate who stepped forward, while those who seemed available were somehow not available.

When it came to sharing treasure it was very apparent who was generous and who was not as generous. Many people would give from their surplus wealth, but it was the people who were dedicated to sacrificial giving who carried the day.

When it comes to sharing our time, talent, and treasure are we sacrificial or surplus givers?

Thirty-second Sunday in Ordinary Time (C)

Some Sadducees (the ones who claim there is no resurrection) came
forward to pose this problem to Jesus:
"Master, Moses prescribed that if a man's brother dies
leaving a wife and no child,
the brother should marry the widow
and raise posterity to his brother.
Now there were seven brothers.
The first one married and died childless.
Next, the second brother married the widow,
then the third, and so on.
All seven died without leaving her any children.
Finally the widow herself died.
At the resurrection, whose wife will she be?
Remember, seven married her."
Lk 20: 27 – 38

I can just imagine Jesus standing there, listening as if he were being asked an honest question, then realizing he was being asked a dishonest question, rolling his eyes, and deciding just how brutal he was going to be.

Jesus is actually very kind with the questioners. He reminds them that they should worry more about the here and now than the afterlife. Frequently we need the same reminder.

God is in charge of the afterlife; we need to trust him more. We are in charge of the here and now. We need to focus on our present relationships. If we have an injured or broken relationship, we need to repair it now. If someone is in need, we need to reach out now. If we take care of real problems in the here and now, we won't have time to worry about future fanciful ones.

We need to remember the wisdom of St. Matthew, "So do not worry and say, 'What are we to eat?' or 'What are we to drink?' or 'What are we to wear?' All these things the pagans seek. Your heavenly Father knows that you need them all. But seek first the kingdom and his righteousness, and all these things will be given you besides. Do not worry about tomorrow; tomorrow will take care of itself. Sufficient for a day is its own evil." (Mt 6: 31 – 34)

How can we better focus our faith on the here and now?

Monday of the Thirty-second Week in Ordinary Time

> The apostles said to the Lord,
> "Increase our faith," and he answered:
> "If you had faith the size of a mustard seed,
> you could say to this sycamore,
> 'Be uprooted and transplanted into the sea,'
> and it would obey you."
> Lk 17: 1 – 16

At our baptism the seed of faith is planted in our heart. As we grow, that seed takes root and begins to grow. That growth will proceed unabated unless we frustrate it.

We always have enough faith. What we need is to trust the faith that we have. God is our gentle teacher. All he expects is our effort; all we have to do is try. All good teachers know how to build on the effort that students put forth. Good teachers don't expect instant results, but they do expect constant effort.

Every failure in our lives is the result of our giving up. We try something new. It doesn't go as planned. Occasionally we try again, but eventually we give up. It is only when we give up that failure enters the picture.

The apostles in today's gospel are instructed to forgive those who act against them. Jesus sets the bar very high. If a brother or a sister sins against us seven times in a day, but each time says they are sorry, we are to forgive them.

I would probably throw in the towel after the third sin. How about you?

Tuesday of the Thirty-second Week in Ordinary Time

"Is he grateful to that servant because he did what was commanded?
So it should be with you.
When you have done all you have been commanded, say.
'We are unprofitable servants;
we have done what we were obliged to do.'"
Lk 17: 7 – 10

God has expectations for us. He has given us the Commandments, the Beatitudes, and the challenge of putting the needs of others ahead of our own.

Unfortunately, when we keep the Commandments and the Beatitudes we expect praise. Why? We have only done what we were supposed to do. The trick is to go beyond the minimum.

One parish director of Stewardship used to challenge the parish this way, "Do the best you can, and then some." I express that sentiment in this way. "Good is the enemy of better. Better is the enemy of best." We should never rest on our laurels. I like telling people, "This is a good parish, but it can be better. Are you willing to put in the work to make it better? Then once it becomes better are you willing to make it the best parish?" Same is true for us as individuals. We are good people, but can be better. Once we are better, will we strive to be the best? We'll never get there but we need to keep trying.

What part of our lives needs the most work at this time?

Wednesday of the Thirty-second Week in Ordinary Time

And one of them, realizing he had been healed,
returned, glorifying God in a loud voice:
and he fell at the feet of
Jesus and thanked him.
He was a Samaritan.
Jesus said in reply,
"Ten were cleansed, were they not?

> Where are the other nine?
> Has none but this foreigner returned to give thanks to God?"
> Lk 17: 11 – 19

Very early on in our lives we are taught the power of "please" and "thank you." These words never lose their power, but too often we forget to use them. We lose our manners.

When we lose our manners, we are diminished. No one gives to be thanked. We give because it is our nature to give. Unfortunately, it is not of our nature to be grateful. Too often we become insensitive to all that has been given to us.

Stop for a moment and take inventory of all we have been given. Life is a gift. No one has the right to one second of life; life is a gift from God. We are given the gift of our senses. Sight is a gift, so are hearing and feeling. That we can speak, smell, and touch are all gifts. Too often we think they are just what we deserve, but they are gifts, and we need to remember that.

Our families, children, spouse, and friends are all gifts. When the leper in today's gospel realized he had been healed, he returned to give thanks. When we realize how many gifts God lavishes upon us, we will develop the "attitude of gratitude," and we will be richer because of it.

Where have we been insensitive to God's bountiful gifts?

Thursday of the Thirty-second Week in Ordinary Time

> Asked by the Pharisees
> when the Kingdom of God would come,
> Jesus said in reply,
> "The coming of the Kingdom of God cannot be observed,
> and no one will announce, 'Look, here it is,' or, 'There it is.'
> For behold, the Kingdom of God is among you."
> Lk 17: 20 – 25

When we pray the Our Father we say, "Thy Kingdom come. Thy will be done." That is really one request said two different ways. The

Kingdom of God will come when we surrender to God's will. That is easier said than done!

We need to trust God more. With trust comes surrender. Surrender is difficult. We want to be in charge. We would never say it out loud, but deep down we think we know better than God. God invites us to be merciful; we want revenge. God want us to share what we have; we want to store what we have for a rainy day. The gospels tell us that the way we treat the least among us is what really matters. We are enthralled by status and fame. God wants us to embrace suffering; we do our best to avoid it. We are invited to take up our cross and follow him; we want to sit in an easy chair and let others sacrifice. He calls us to be holy, and we are driven to be successful. The Kingdom of God will come when we learn how to cooperate rather than compete.

What is our biggest obstacle to letting God rule our lives?

Friday of the Thirty-second Week in Ordinary Time

> Jesus said to his disciples:
> "As it was in the days of Noah,
> so it will be in the days of the Son of Man;
> they were eating and drinking.
> Marrying and giving in marriage up to the day
> that Noah entered the ark,
> and the flood came and destroyed them all."
> Lk 17: 26 – 37

All the weather person has to say is, "There's a big storm coming," and panic ensues. Everyone rushes to the market and stocks up on bread, milk, and toilet paper. We have to be ready to go into survival mode.

I have no idea what percentage of the time the weather person gets it right, but I suspect it is less than 30% of the time. Nevertheless, we still panic every time we are warned, "There is a big storm coming."

Scripture warns us often that the end is coming. There will be an end time both individually and communally, but for some reason we have learned to ignore God's warnings. God's voice is like a squeaky fan belt. We hear it, but we ignore it until it is too late. When it comes to our lives there will be no cramming for the final exam. The end will come and we will either be ready or we will fail.

Why do we put more trust in the weather person than God?

Saturday of the Thirty-second Week in Ordinary Time

> The Lord said, "Pay attention to what the dishonest judge says.
> Will not God then secure the rights of his chosen ones
> who call out to him day and night?
> Will he be slow to answer them?
> I tell you, he will see to it that justice is done for them speedily.
> But when the Son of Man comes, will he find faith on earth?"
> Lk 18: 1 – 8

"When the Son of Man comes, will he find faith on earth?" There was a time when I would not have hesitated to answer that question, but that time is gone. Less than twenty years ago, faith was a reality in most people's lives, but not any longer.

It seems that the more sophisticated we become, the more we are willing to kick God to the curb. There is even serious talk of our living in the post-Christian era. Fewer and fewer people worship regularly. Remember when Sunday was a day set aside for church? That is certainly gone. Sunday morning was reserved for worship. Not any longer. Between road races, soccer matches, and a whole variety of other sports, Sunday morning is a preferred time.

I am not sure we can restore the notion of the Sabbath, but we should not despair. We need to be like Joshua who when surrounded by people who were worshiping false gods said, "As for me and my family, we will serve the Lord." (Js 24: 15) Society may abandon faith, but we should not.

How can we worship our God more completely?

Thirty-third Sunday in Ordinary Time (A)

> Jesus told his disciples this parable:
> "A man going on a journey
> called in his servants and entrusted his possessions to them.
> To one he gave five talents; to another, two; to a third, one –
> to each according to his ability.
> Then he went away."
> Mt 25: 14 – 30

How do we measure someone's ability? Or more precisely, how do we measure someone's ability accurately? To be even more focused, if that is possible, how does God calculate our ability?

Ability is one thing; performance is another. We all know people who maximize their abilities, and people who never fully employ their gifts. I remember many report cards where my teachers wrote, "Is not living up to his potential."

We need to make the most of our opportunities, but frequently we do not. There may be a way out of this conundrum. One of the foibles of human nature is that we can see the gifts of others better than we can see our own. If we would work at building people up rather than tearing them down, the world would be a better place. We need to become better at telling others about their gifts and talents. Then once we point them out, together we can make sure those gifts and talents are properly developed and shared. It seems to me the world would be a better place quickly if we would just be more affirming.

How can we invite people to point out our gifts and talents?

Thirty-third Sunday in Ordinary Time (B)

> Then men will see the Son of Man coming in the clouds
> with great power and glory.
> He will dispatch his messengers and assemble his chosen
> from the four winds,
> from the farthest bounds of earth and sky...

> In the same way, when you see these things happening,
> you will know that he is near, even at the door...
> As to the exact day or hour, no one knows it,
> neither the angels in heaven nor even the Son,
> but only the Father.
> Mk 13: 24 – 32

There is something fascinating about "the end times." Maybe it is just the delight we take in the art of speculation. We know the world will end. Nothing that is physical lasts forever. Everything has a beginning, a middle, and an end.

Unfortunately there are good endings and bad endings. Some novels end leaving the reader unfulfilled. Some movies do the same. Today's gospel passage reminds us that the world will indeed end. What we do not know is will it be a good ending or a poor one. T. S. Eliot, the poet, takes a rather negative view of the end of the world.

> "This is the way the world ends
> This is the way the world ends
> This is the way the world ends
> Not with a bang but a whimper."

The ending I carry around in my head ends with more of a bang than a whimper. What is your image?

No matter what our image is we get to participate. We get to shape how our lives end. By our choices, by our attention to gospel values, and by our determination we get to fashion how our lives end. We do not know the day or the hour, but we know there will be a day, an hour and a last second. The only way to be prepared is to live every day as if it were our last day.

Are we properly prepared for this to be our last day?

Thirty-third Sunday in Ordinary Time (C)

> He said to them further:
> "Nation will rise against nation and kingdom against kingdom.

> There will be great earthquakes, plagues and famines
> in various places – and in the sky fearful omens and great signs.
> But before any of this, they will manhandle and persecute you,
> summoning you to synagogues and prisons,
> bringing you to trial before kings and governors,
> all because of my name.
> You will be brought to give witness on account of it…
> All will hate you because of me,
> yet not a hair of your head will be harmed.
> By patient endurance you will save your lives."
> Lk 21: 5 – 19

Apocalyptical readings are always in Technicolor never in black and white. They are full of ominous signs and warnings, and yet no one takes them seriously, because deep inside we do not believe the world is going to end. Oh, there will be difficult times. There will be wars and global pandemics, but we will always triumph, or that is what we have convinced ourselves will happen. The world will end; all material things have a beginning and an end. That is just a fact.

Rather than worry about the world ending, we need to focus on the end of our lives. It is easier to embrace the end of our life than the end of the world, so as we come to the end of another liturgical year let us focus on our end time.

We do not know when we will die, but we know that we will. Life is a gift, given to us by God. He blesses us with talents and opportunities. He wants us to make the most of life, and the most important aspect of life is the relationships that sustain us. Let us vow here and now to make the most of our relationships. If we have broken relationships, let us mend them now. If we have bruised relationships, let us heal them now. And may we strengthen our good relationships so that they become even better!

What relationships need our attention now?

Monday of the Thirty-third Week in Ordinary Time

> Then Jesus stopped and ordered that he be brought to him;
> and when he came near, Jesus asked him,
> "What do you want me to do for you?"
> He replied, "Lord, please let me see."
> Jesus told him, "Have sight; your faith has saved you."
> He immediately received his sight
> and followed him, giving glory to God.
> When they saw this, all the people gave praise to God.
> Lk 18: 35 – 43

The thing that amazed me about this gospel is that Jesus did not presume to know what the man wanted. Turns out the blind man wanted to see, but he could have had something else on his mind. He could have had a child who was sick, a wife possessed by an unclean spirit or some other malady. Jesus asked; he did not presume to know.

Too often, I think, we presume to know what others need. Or even worse, we know what they should want. Many of us have known a situation where a busy father lavished presents on his daughter. The presents pile up, but what the daughter wanted was some of the father's time. She wanted her dad to come to one of her soccer matches – to just sit in the stands and cheer for her. All the presents in the world could not satisfy her need for his presence in her life.

Too often we write a check for a worthy cause, but what the charity needs more than money is people to help serve meals, or help distribute food. It is always more important to ask what God wants us to do rather than settle for what we are comfortable doing.

Where does God want us to invest our time and our talent?

Tuesday of the Thirty-third Week in Ordinary Time

> But Zacchaeus stood there and said to the Lord,
> "Behold, half of my possessions, Lord, I shall give to the poor,
> and if I have extorted anything from anyone

> I shall repay it four times over."
> And Jesus said to him,
> "Today salvation has come to this house
> because this man too is a descendant of Abraham.
> For the Son of Man has come to seek
> and to save what was lost."
> Lk 19: 1 – 10

The people saw Zacchaeus as a sinner; Jesus saw a saint. Jesus was giving living testimony to this wise but ironic quote from Oscar Wilde, "The only difference between the saint and the sinner is that every saint has a past, and every sinner has a future."

There are none among us who have not wandered, have not sinned. Sinning is never the point; conversion is always the goal. Too often we define ourselves and others by our faults. That accomplishes nothing. We should never let the past define us.

As Natalie Snodgrass Tan of Quiet Space Ltd. notes, "Shakespeare, he knew a thing or two. People sometimes misunderstand what Antonio meant by, 'what's past is prologue', taking it in isolation to mean that the past predicts the future. The full quote, however, says quite the opposite. 'Whereof what's past is prologue; what's to come is your and my discharge.' The past is written, but the future is yours to wield, subject to the choices you decide to make. Make good ones. Each day is a new day with no mistakes in it yet."

How our lives would change and our world evolve into a better place if we could just let go of the past and realize that each day is a chance to get it right.

Where are we letting the past limit our future?

Wednesday of the Thirty-third Week in Ordinary Time

> "And to those standing by he said,
> 'Take the gold coin from him,
> and give it to the servant who has ten.'
> But they said to him,

'Sir, he has ten gold coins.'
He replied, 'I tell you,
To everyone who has, more will be given,
But from the one who has not,
even what he has will be taken away.'"
Lk 19: 11 – 28

Unless we put today's gospel into its proper context, it sounds like a certain political party has taken over scripture. In its proper context that concern disappears.

The context is "Jesus is going to Jerusalem." He is going to embrace his suffering and his death at the hands of God's chosen people. Too often, we think of parables as nice, interesting stories. But parables told by the right storyteller can cause a lot of trouble. I like to say, "Jesus told parables, and they put him to death."

In today's parable, Jesus is warning the chosen people that they have not taken proper care of God's gifts. Rather than letting faith inform more and more of their decisions, they have given in to rules and regulations. In fact they had become so lost in their man-made rules and regulations that they were missing Jesus as their Messiah. God was not going to take the gift of faith away from the chosen people. He was not going to intervene as they diluted it to the point where it disappeared.

Where have we allowed our faith to be diluted?

Thursday of the Thirty-third Week in Ordinary Time

As Jesus drew near Jerusalem,
He saw the city and wept over it, saying,
"If this day you only knew what makes for peace –
but for not it is hidden from your eyes.
For the days are coming upon you
when your enemies will raise a palisade against you;
they will encircle you and hem you in on all sides.
They will smash you to the ground and your children within you

> and they will not leave one stone upon another within you
> because you did not recognize the time of your visitation.
> Lk 19: 41 – 44

Once again remember the context. We are coming to the end of our liturgical year, and Jesus is coming to the end of his physical life. Jesus weeps for Jerusalem and the Chosen People because they have failed. They are conspiring with the enemy to get rid of Jesus.

This text is often thought of as Jesus predicting that the temple in Jerusalem will be destroyed. The enemy whom they joined in order to be rid of Jesus will never be their friend. The best they will ever be is a convenient enemy.

It is often said, "politics makes for strange bedfellows," but politics have not cornered the market in that regard. Whenever we join with others to silence or get rid of someone, it always backfires. We are not called to build fences (palisades); we are called to build bridges.

We need to better understand that there should be no enemies. And we have the power to make that happen. It takes two to make an enemy. If we can rise above the fray, there will be no enemies to turn on us.

Where have we allowed hatred to blind us to the truth?

Friday of the Thirty-third Sunday in Ordinary Time

> Jesus entered the temple area and proceeded to drive out
> those who were selling things, saying to them,
> "It is written, *My house shall be a house of prayer,
> but you have made it a den of thieves.*"
> Lk 19: 45 – 48

From time to time, I ponder what Jesus would do were he to visit one of our churches. What would he do, and what would he say?

What would he make of the custom of charging stipends for saying Masses? What would he think about bingo, raffles, and twenty-week clubs? Indeed, what would he think about all the stuff we sell at the doors of our churches? Would he treat it all the same?

Should we make a distinction between selling hand-carved ornaments that support the Christians in the Holy Land, and the unabashed gambling that we call twenty-week clubs, or the selling of Girl Scout cookies at the door?

Obviously, I don't know what Jesus would say or do, but I don't think he would be thrilled.

I do know that our churches are still supposed to be "houses of prayer" and too often they are not. We are called to gather for communal prayer as the believing community, but too often we are just individuals united by words, but not united as brothers and sisters in Christ. We are invited to go to church to pray as individuals, but often we ignore the invitation.

How can we make our churches "holy space" once again?

Saturday of the Thirty-third Week in Ordinary Time

> "Now there were seven brothers;
> the first married a woman but died childless.
> Then the second and third married her,
> and likewise all seven died childless.
> Finally the woman also died.
> Now at the resurrection whose wife will that woman be?
> For all seven had been married to her."
> Lk 29: 27 – 40

The first thing that comes to my mind is why would she want anything to do with any of them? Or for that matter, why would any of the brothers want to have anything to do with her?

The truth is that the whole conundrum is a waste of time. The Sadducees don't even believe in an afterlife so their question is obviously insincere. What they really want is to trip up Jesus for their own good. Whenever we use people to advance ourselves, we are headed down the wrong path.

People are not pawns on the chessboard of life. We should never take advantage of other people. Every individual should be treated with dignity! Always and everywhere!

We know when we are being used, and we never like it. No one deserves to be used. We need to be on our guard so that we do not manipulate, and are not manipulated as we respond to the challenges of life.

Where are we guilty of objectifying people in our life?

Monday of the Thirty-fourth Week in Ordinary Time

> When Jesus looked up he saw some wealthy people
> putting their offerings into the treasury
> and he noticed a poor widow putting in two small coins.
> He said, "I tell you truly,
> this poor widow put in more than all the rest;
> for the others have all made offerings from their surplus wealth,
> but she, from her poverty, has offered her whole livelihood.
> Lk 21: 1 – 4

I was told once that there are three kinds of givers – grudge givers, duty givers, and thanks givers. The wealthy people in today's gospel are either grudge givers or duty givers. They give because they have to give – not because they want to give. It is a duty or an obligation. They feel that they have to give so their only concern is how little can they give, and meet their obligation. There is no generosity and certainly no justice involved in their offerings.

The widow on the other hand is a thanks giver. She gives because she wants to give. There are no strings attached to her offering. She gives without calculating the cost. She gives because she knows that she has been blessed by God, and she wants to show her appreciation. She gives because she is in love with God, and lovers do foolish things. She is free to give away all that she has because she knows God will never abandon her. As scripture tell us, "Those who sow with tears will reap with cries of joy." (Ps 126: 5)

Where do we need to upgrade our reasons for giving?

Tuesday of the Thirty-fourth Week in Ordinary Time

While some people were speaking about
how the temple was adorned with costly stones and votive offerings,
Jesus said, "All that you see here –
the days will come when there will not be left
a stone upon another stone that will not be thrown down."
Then they asked him,
"Teacher, when will this happen?
And what sign will there be
when all these things are about to happen?"
Lk 21: 5 – 11

When will the end of the world come? No one knows, but that has not stopped people from predicting when it will happen. Several popes have predicted the end of the world, as did Nostradamus, John Wesley, Jim Jones, Jerry Falwell, and Pat Robertson. They all have one thing in common; they were all wrong.

Someday someone is going to be correct, but it will just be dumb luck. One thing is certain. We all have an expiration date. There is a day that will be our last day. The challenge is to live each day to the best of our ability so that when death, like a thief in the night, comes, we will not be caught unprepared.

"It is the fact that every day counts us down that makes each one such a gift. There are only two days with fewer than twenty-four hours in each life-time, sitting like bookends astride our lives: one is celebrated every year, yet it is the other that makes us see living as precious." (The Tablet, January 12, 2018, Dr. Kathryn Mannix)

Do we respect each day as a gift from God?

Wednesday of the Thirty-fourth Week in Ordinary Time

Jesus said to the crowd:
"They will seize and persecute you,
they will have you led before kings and governors because of my name.

> It will lead to your giving testimony.
> Remember, you are not to prepare your defense beforehand,
> for I myself shall give you a wisdom in speaking
> that all your adversaries will be powerless to resist or refute.
> Lk 21: 12 – 19

It is sad that this gospel does not apply to us. Our faith has been pasteurized. We have learned to blend in with the prevailing culture. Our Christianity no longer makes us stand out, but it should.

We have privatized religion. To each her own. Live and let live. That is not what Jesus intended, but it is what we have accomplished. So much of the gospel if lived properly should make us stand out.

Imagine what would happen if we learned to "love our enemies." Our world would change dramatically if we were more merciful. There is so much division and partisan behavior. If we learned "to turn the other cheek" would our world be so divided?

What would happen if we committed ourselves to living the Beatitudes?

If we would visit the sick and the imprisoned, clothe the naked, and be peacemakers, our world would be a different place.

As I think I mentioned in a previous reflection, if Christians were persecuted in our culture would there be enough evidence for us to be found guilty? Sadly for many of us the answer would be no.

What one Beatitude could we live more fully?

Thursday of the Thirty-fourth Week in Ordinary Time

> On the earth, nations will be in anguish,
> distraught at the roaring of the sea and the waves.
> Men will die of fright in anticipation
> of what is coming upon the earth.
> The powers in the heavens will be shaken.
> After that, men will see the Son of Man
> coming on a cloud with great power and glory.
> When these things begin to happen,

> stand up straight and raise your hands,
> for your ransom is near at hand.
> Lk 21: 20 – 28

Some scripture passages are black and white, while others are Technicolor. Apocalyptic passages, like today's, are always Technicolor. Anguish, distraught, heavens shaken, seas and waves pounding are action words that demand attention.

The remarkable thing is the advice that St. Luke gives. When all these frightening things happen, stand up straight and raise your hands because this is why we were born, this is why we came into the world. It is not the end times; it is the beginning time.

Some people fear dying while others embrace it. I have been fortunate to be at the bedside of several dying people. Occasionally there is a struggle, but most often the end comes peacefully. The dying person accepts the finality of life. People say their goodbyes, and the prayers of those gathered lead the dying person home, and God says, "Well done good and faithful servant, come to the Kingdom prepared for you from the beginning of time."

Life is a gift from God. How can we open the gift and live it fully?

Friday of the Thirty-fourth Week in Ordinary Time

> "Amen, I say to you, this generation will not pass away
> until all these things have taken place.
> Heaven and earth will pass away,
> But my words will not pass away."
> Lk 21: 29 – 33

"My words will not pass away." Words have staying power. Both the spoken and the written word have power that we too often overlook. Hateful words spoken in anger cannot be taken back. Even after we apologize the hurt remains. Words spoken in love never lose their power. They are treasured and get families through many difficult times.

The written word certainly has staying power. Many years ago I wrote a daily Advent reflection booklet. I got a letter that was mailed to me from Australia, where the booklet was never sold. The person writing to me was Jewish. She was having a cup of tea with her neighbor whose sister had sent her a copy of my booklet, which was on the kitchen counter while they were having tea. While her friend was making the tea, the person who wrote to me read my reflection for that day. The reflection was about the need to heal broken relationships. In her letter the neighbor told me that she had been estranged from her daughter for several years. When she got home she called her daughter, and they reconciled. She was writing to tell me the power of my written words. I was deeply appreciative, but I knew it was God's words passing through me that helped her heal. "God's words will never pass away."

Where do we need to let God's words pass through us?

Saturday of the Thirty-fourth Week in Ordinary Time

> Jesus said to his disciples:
> "Beware that your hearts do not become drowsy
> from carousing and drunkenness
> and the anxieties of daily life,
> and that day catch you by surprise like a trap.
> For that day will assault everyone
> who lives on the earth.
> Be vigilant at all times
> and pray that you have the strength
> to escape the tribulations that are imminent
> and to stand before the Son of Man.
> Lk 21: 34 – 36

We know all about "the anxieties of daily life." We are an anxious people living in an anxious time. Life is too complex. We try to control our environment, but everything moves too fast.

In one of his books, Henri Nouwen made a very helpful distinction between our occupation and our preoccupations. His point was that too often we get so lost in our preoccupations that we forget what is really important in our lives.

Everyone knows that family should come first. However too often work comes first, and our family gets our leftover time. We disguise this by calling the time we spend with family "quality time," but in our hearts we know that is a silly rationalization.

Our electronic devices can easily become our preoccupation. How many times have you seen people out to dinner with their eyes glued to their phone screen? How many times do we do the same thing? When we put our phone face up, or even face down, on a table, we say to others you don't have my undivided attention. We need to rediscover that this is rude and insulting behavior.

Where have we let insignificant things dominate our attention?

The Solemnity of Our Lord Jesus Christ, King of the Universe (A)

> Jesus said to his disciples:
> "When the Son of Man comes in his glory,
> and all the angels with him,
> he will sit upon his glorious throne,
> and all the nations will be assembled before him.
> And he will separate them one from another,
> as a shepherd separates the sheep from the goats.
> He will place the sheep on his right and the goats on his left.
> Then the King will say to those on his right.
> 'Come, you who are blessed by my father.'"
> Mt 25: 31 – 46

And so we come to the last Sunday of the liturgical year. How appropriate that the gospel is about the end of time, when Jesus will judge the world. It is the only account in all of scripture of the final judgment. This gospel is important for what it says and what it does not say.

The most striking element of the final judgment is that neither the good guys nor the bad guys recognize what is important in the eyes of

God. They are not saved by how many prayers they said, or how many times they went to Mass. There is just no mention of prayer. I think the praying part of our lives is just assumed to exist. Real prayer leads to action; it leads to justice. In the end, what matters is how we treated other people. Did we take care of the basic needs of others? Did we recognize and respond to the dignity of those on the margins of life?

Over the years, I have heard lots of confessions where the penitent confessed missing Mass or forgetting to say morning or evening prayers, but never has any one confessed that she had not visited the sick or imprisoned, or had not clothed the naked, or fed the hungry.

When will we learn to view the world as God does?

The Solemnity of Our Lord Jesus Christ, King of the Universe (B)

> Jesus answered,
> "My kingdom does not belong to this world.
> If my kingdom were of this world my subjects
> would be fighting to save me from being handed over to the Jews.
> As it is, my kingdom is not here."
> At this Pilate said to him,
> "So, then, you are a king?"
> Jesus replied:
> "It is you who say I am a king.
> The reason I was born,
> the reason why I came into the world,
> is to testify to the truth.
> Anyone committed to the truth hears my voice."
> Jn 18: 33 – 37

What is the correct title for Jesus? He used many images throughout his life. He was the shepherd; he was the gate. He was the Son of Man; he was the Son of God. Likewise, he was the Messiah or the Christ. It is only at the end of his life that Pilate comes up with the king question. Once earlier in John's gospel there is the notion of king, "So Jesus, perceiving that they were intending to come and take Him by force to make him king, withdrew again to the mountains by Himself alone." (Jn 6: 15) Jesus did not want to be a king; he wanted to be the Messiah. And yet on every crucifix there are the initials INRI (Jesus Nazarenus Rex Judaeorum – Jesus of Nazareth, King of the Jews).

In the end, titles do not matter. What matters is our dedication to Jesus. Many years ago I learned that on every helicopter there is a nut that attaches the blades to the body of the helicopter. I was amazed that it is called the "Jesus nut." The nut that holds the whole thing together, the nut that makes the helicopter work, and the nut that makes flight possible is the Jesus nut. Jesus wants to be the reality that holds us together, helps us do our best, and helps us lift up our fallen world.

Is Jesus the center of our lives?

The Solemnity of Our Lord Jesus Christ, King of the Universe (C)

> The people stood there watching,
> and the leaders kept jeering at Jesus, saying,
> "He saved others; let him save himself
> if he is the Messiah of God, the chosen one."
> The soldiers also made fun of him,
> Coming forward to offer him their sour wine and saying,
> "If you are the king of the Jews, save yourself."
> There was an inscription over his head:
> "THIS IS THE KING OF THE JEWS."
> Lk 23: 35 – 43

Kings are usually not jeered at, nor are they made fun of, but that is what we have in today's gospel. We need to remember that it is the King who makes the people not the people who make the King. Jesus is the King of creation because he does not let the crowds determine his response. He is silent before their ridicule; he is noble. It is who he is; it is who his Father calls him to be.

Today's gospel ends with the story of the two thieves who were crucified with Jesus. One of them takes the attitude of the crowd, and makes fun of Jesus. The other one realized that he and his fellow criminal are getting what they deserve, and that Jesus in innocent. He recognized Jesus' power in the midst of the crowd's mockery. He makes a profound request, "Jesus, remember me when you enter upon your reign." Jesus in all his royality says to him, "I assure you: this day you will be with me in paradise." What more can we ask from the clutter of our lives than "Jesus remember us, now and in the age to come."

Do we let Jesus rule in our hearts?

Holy Days, Solemnities and Major Feast Days

January 25 – The Conversion of St. Paul, Apostle

> Jesus appeared to the Eleven and said to them:
> "Go into the whole world and proclaim the Gospel to every creature.
> Whoever believes and is baptized will be saved;
> whoever does not believe will be condemned.
> Mk 16: 15 – 18

Paul's story is an interesting one. He started off as the Pharisee, Saul; he ended as the Apostle, Paul. At the beginning of Christianity he was dedicated to destroying those who were followers of Jesus; at the end he was the Apostle to the Gentiles.

Paul was on his way to Damascus when he got knocked off his horse, and heard a voice ask him, "Saul, Saul why are you persecuting me?" That was the beginning of his conversion experience.

All of us persecute Jesus in our own way. That is what sin is; sin is persecuting Jesus. All of us need to get knocked off our horse. We need to realize that our anger diminishes Jesus' message as does our greed, lust, gluttony, pride, envy, and laziness. To be converted we need to focus on God's mercy not our sinfulness. God's love is always greater than our sins and failures. God always sees our potential; we need to trust God's vision more than our own.

Where have we given up on our potential by settling for mediocrity?

February 2 – The Feast of the Presentation

> "Now, Master, you may let your servant go in peace,
> according to your word,
> for my eyes have seen your salvation,
> which you prepared in the sight of all the peoples:
> a light for revelation to the Gentiles,
> and the glory for your people Israel."
> Lk 2: 22 – 40

Simeon, the old man, was waiting for God to fulfill his word, his promise. He saw a child, and that was enough. We sometimes behave in the same way. What does it take for us to trust some people? For some people all they have to do is say, "Yes" and I believe them. Others say "Yes" and I know they mean "Maybe." Politicians during campaign season say all sorts of things. Only the very naive believe them. One friend tells me she will keep a confidence, and I believe. Another says the same thing, and I have my doubts.

Many years ago in philosophy class my classmates and I were taught the Scholastic adage, "Never deny, seldom affirm and always distinguish." That adage has served me well for many years. God promises to be with us. He promises that he will never abandon us. Like Simeon do we take God at his word? Or do we want more proof?

We can never say, "I love you" unless we have wrestled with the question, "Do I love you?" We can never say, "I believe" until we have wondered, "Do I believe?" Simeon got to the point of being able to say, "You have fulfilled your promise of God" because he had pondered for a long time, "Will God really be true to his promise?"

Where do we need to doubt better so that we can believe more fully?

February 22 – Feast Chair of Peter

> He said to them, "But who do you say that I am?"
> Simon Peter said in reply,
> "You are the Christ, the Son of the living God."
> Mt 16: 13 – 19

St. Peter was a fascinating guy. He was not perfect but he never gave up. In today's gospel, he correctly identifies Jesus, but just three verses later he gets it all wrong. He wants Jesus to be the Messiah but he does not want Jesus to suffer. Jesus has to reproach him. Elsewhere in the gospels Peter says he will die for Jesus and Jesus has to predict that Peter will deny him three times. Once again Jesus is right and Peter is wrong. But Peter does not give up.

He falls; he fails but he does not stay down. He picks himself up, dusts himself off, and starts over again. It is because of his tenacity that Jesus picks him as the leader of the early church.

Jesus knew the early church would get some things right but other things wrong. Jesus knew the growth of the church would be more by trial and error than by trial and success. Somewhere in her history our church forgot about the trial – error – success paradigm and opted for the dogmatic – authoritarian model from which we recently have been recovering.

Where do we need to pick ourselves up and start all over again?

March 19 – Solemnity of St. Joseph

Such was his intention when, behold, the angel of the Lord
appeared to him in a dream and said,
"Joseph, son of David,
do not be afraid to take Mary your wife into your home.
For it is through the Holy Spirit that this child
has been conceived in her.
She will bear a son and you are to name him Jesus,
because he will save his people from their sins.
Mt 1: 16, 18 – 21, 24 A

If you hear a shocking story often enough it loses its ability to shock. The story of Mary being visited by the angel Gabriel, and the scandal of a young woman being pregnant in the wrong time sequence is such a story. The reaction of her future husband plus the wagging tongues in a small town are a recipe for a disaster. Mary gets most of the headlines but Joachim and Anna need recognition for their faith response and so does St. Joseph.

God needed a deep faith response from at least four people in order to be born among us. As the old bumper sticker said, "If Mary had listened to reason there would be no season." The same is true for Mary's parents and her future husband. Today's gospel tells us that Joseph, "since he was a righteous man" was going to divorce Mary quietly. That would have saved face for Joseph but not for Mary. Mary would still be pregnant in the wrong time sequence.

So what did they do? They prayed, listened to God, got married, had the baby, called him Jesus and went about the rest of their lives.

God's plan to save us could have come crashing down except that four extraordinary people said what Jesus said in the Garden of Gethsemane, "Not my will but your will be done!"

Where do we need to be more willing to put God's will first in our lives?

March 25 – The Solemnity of the Annunciation

> And behold Elizabeth, your relative,
> has also conceived a son in her old age,
> and this is the sixth month for her who was called barren
> for nothing is impossible with God."
> Mary said, "Behold, I am the handmaid of the Lord.
> May it be done to me according to your word."
> Lk 1: 26 – 38

Mary's beautiful prayer, the Magnificat. It is so profound, and so moving. Mary is at prayer when the Angel Gabriel greets her as "full of grace", and that "the Lord is with you." Then comes "Do not be afraid, Mary, you have found favor with God." We are too familiar with the story; it has lost the power to shock us. We have lost sight of how Mary's world was turned upside down by what was announced.

Mary hears it all. She takes in as much as she can. She is riddled with questions and even raises an objection, "How can this be, since I have no relations with a man?"

Somehow the fact that her relative Elizabeth is six months pregnant gives Mary a foothold so her world will stop spinning out of control. All right if Elizabeth can get pregnant at her age, then I guess I can give birth to the Messiah. I don't get it, and I certainly don't understand it, but I will put my trust in God.

The Magnificat is Mary's way of saying what her son would say in the garden, "Not my will but your will be done!" If we are to be true believers we have to learn how to embrace God's will for us especially when it seems to make so little sense.

Where are we resisting what God is calling us to do with our lives?

April 25 – Feast of St. Mark

> Jesus appeared to the Eleven and said to them:
> "Go into the whole world
> and proclaim the Gospel to every creature.
> Whoever believes and is baptized will be saved;
> Whoever does not believe will be condemned."
> Mk 16: 15 – 20

"Jesus said to the Eleven," already there is one less voice, and Jesus needs all the voices he can get. The word "Apostle" means "one who is sent." The Eleven went and preached the Good News. Some heard, believed, and were baptized. When baptized they became apostles, and so began the spread of what we now know as Christianity.

There is of course the official list of Apostles, but there is also an unofficial list of apostles. We are on the list of lesser apostles, but that does not change the fact that every baptized person is sent into the world to announce the Good News of Jesus Christ. Does that mean we have to go door to door and try to convert people? No. Does it mean that our lives have to be so rooted in our faith in Christ Jesus that we make choices that make a difference? Yes.

St. Francis of Assisi is credited with saying, "Preach the Gospel at all times, and if necessary use words." I don't know if he actually said it, but he certainly lived it. He knew he was sent. He grew to understand that he was to rebuild the church. His efforts are still with us.

Where has God sent us to announce the Good News?

May 1 – Saint Joseph, the Worker

> Jesus went to his native place and spent his time teaching
> the people in their synagogue.
> They were filled with amazement,
> and said to one another,
> "Where did this man get such wisdom and miraculous powers?
> Isn't this the carpenter's son?
> Isn't Mary known to be his mother,
> and James, Joseph, Simon and Judas his brothers?
> Mt 13: 54 – 58

Poor Joseph just can't catch a break. His feast day, March 19, falls during Lent so it is a subdued event in the best of circumstances. So in 1955, Pius XII created this feast for Joseph, but in reality it was created to offset the Communist workers celebrations on May 1. It seems like Joseph is doomed to play second fiddle for all eternity.

Did you notice that in today's gospel everyone has a name but Joseph? He is referred to as the carpenter. We know from scripture that Joseph was known to be a just man. He was also a practical man. When it comes to doing the will of God none of us should look to be recognized. What matters is that God gets the glory. As St. Matthew tells us, "You are the light of the world. A city set on a mountain cannot be hidden…Just so, your light must shine before others, that they may see your good deeds and glorify your heavenly Father." (Mt. 5: 14 – 16)

How can we let God's light shine through us more brightly?

May 3 – Saints Philip and James, Apostles

> "I solemnly assure you,
> the man who has faith in me will do the works I do,
> and far greater than these.

> Why? Because I go to the Father,
> And whatever you ask in my name I will do,
> so as to glorify the Father in the Son.
> Anything you ask of me in my name I will do."
> Jn 14: 6 – 14

James is also known as James the Lesser so that he would not be confused with John's brother James, who is known as James the Greater. We know almost nothing about James the Lesser. Philip we know because he is the one who tells Jesus about the young boy with the five loaves and two fish that were used to feed the multitude.

These two Apostles share the same feast day not because they were particularly close. They share the same feast day because their relics were brought to Rome at the same time and there was a church dedicated to them that later became the church of the Holy Apostles.

The gospel for this feast has one of the most curious statements in the New Testament, "the man who has faith in me will do the works that I do, and far greater than these." Jesus worked miracles. He gave sight to the blind, helped the lame to walk, and the mute to speak. How can we do greater than that? Jesus is with us, and we need to trust in his ability to work through us to build his kingdom. Remember if our faith is as small as a mustard seed we can move mountains. As St. Paul tells us in Ephesians, "To him whose power now at work in us can do immeasurably more than we ask or imagine – to him be glory in the church and in Christ Jesus through all generations without end. Amen." (Acts 3: 20 – 21)

How can we trust God's transforming power more fully?

May 14 – Saint Matthias, Apostle

> You are my friends if you do what I command you.
> I no longer speak of you as slaves,
> for a slave does not know what his master is about.
> Instead, I call you friends,
> Since I have made known to you all that I heard from my Father.

> It was not you who chose me,
> it was I who chose you to go forth and bear fruit.
> Jn 15: 9 – 17

Mathias was the one who was chosen to take Judas' place. Peter called together the disciples, and directed them to pick a replacement. There were two candidates, "Joseph (called Barsabbas, also known as Justus) and Matthias." Then they prayed, "O Lord, you read the hearts of men. Make known to us which of these two you chose for the apostolic ministry, replacing Judas, who deserted the cause and went the way he was destined to go." (Acts 1: 20 – 26) Then they cast lots. Imagine that, they flipped a coin. This may seem odd, but it was not. In the bible casting lots was seen as a way to allow God to guide our choices. Everyone accepted the result of the lots to be the will of God.

Casting lots is never mentioned after the gift of the Holy Spirit at Pentecost. With the Spirit we no longer need to cast lots or flip a coin. The Holy Spirit helps us to discern the will of God. When we have a difficult decision to make, we need to pause, pray, and let the answer come to us through the power of the Holy Spirit.

Do we trust sufficiently that the Spirit we lead us to do the right thing?

May 31 – The Visitation

> Mary set out, proceeding in haste into the hill country to a town of
> Judah, where she entered Zachariah's house and greeted Elizabeth.
> When Elizabeth heard Mary's greeting,
> the baby stirred in her womb.
> Elizabeth was filled with the Holy Spirit and cried out in a loud voice:
> "Blessed are you among women and blessed is the fruit of your womb.
> But who am I that the mother of my Lord should come to me?
> Lk 1: 39 – 56

I have always been impressed that Mary, filled with her own confusing good news, nevertheless went to visit Elizabeth, her aunt. She accepted her miraculous pregnancy by going to help her mother's sister through her miraculous pregnancy. I can only imagine the conversations they had.

Mary's visit was not only a corporal work of mercy, it was also a very convenient excuse to get out of town. Mary's pregnancy was sure to set tongues wagging in Nazareth. Mary stayed with Elizabeth for three months until John was born.

Too often we get so wrapped up in our own issues and problems that we fail to see the problems of others. Mary did not let that happen to her, and she did not waste any time doing it. The gospel tells us, "She set out in haste…", and her haste was rewarded. When Mary greeted her aunt Elizabeth, her child, John the Baptist, stirred in her womb. Thus Jesus and John were connected before either of them was born.

Who needs a caring visit from us?

Immaculate Heart of Mary
(Saturday after Corpus Christi)

When his parents saw him,
they were astonished, and his mother said to him,
"Son, why have you done this to us?
Your father and I have been looking for you with great anxiety."
And he said to them,
"Why were you looking for me?
Did you not know that I must be in my Father's house?"
But they did not understand what he said to them.
Lk 2: 41 – 51

All parents can identify with this gospel scene. For years I have been saying, "Adolescence is God's one mistake." And as the saying goes, "There is some truth in all humor." What is taking place in today's gospel is that a boy and his parents are not on the same page. The boy is ahead of himself; his parents are in no hurry to catch up with him. It happens over and over again. It proves that Jesus really did take on our human condition.

What needs to be our focus point is not the disagreement or confusion that existed between Jesus and his parents but the way everyone responded to the challenge. No one understood what was going on. Mary and Joseph were filled with anxiety. Jesus was focused on his needs, and not the needs of his parents. That is not a sin; it is just part of the human condition.

In the end, Jesus went back home and was obedient to them. He got back into the right order of things. Mary, for her part, was left to ponder what all of this meant. The gospel story ends with the statement that Mary "kept all these things in her heart." Joseph's response is not recorded, but we can be sure that Mary was the bridge between father and son.

We need to ask Mary to teach us how to ponder what we do not understand.

Feast of the Sacred Heart of Jesus

> "Come to me, all you who labor and are burdened,
> and I will give you rest.
> Take my yoke upon you and learn from me,
> for I am meek and humble of heart;
> and you will find rest for yourselves.
> For my yoke is easy, and my burden light."
> Mt 11: 25 – 30

Surprisingly, the most important part of today's gospel is, "Learn from me." Jesus is the supreme teacher who is always present to help us learn. In order to appreciate Jesus as the supreme teacher, we need to think of the gifted teachers we have had in life, the teachers who made a real difference in who we are, and who we have become.

We have all had good teachers, but that is not where we need to focus right now. We need to think of the great teachers we have had. We don't need to stop and think of who they are. We know who they are, and they are with us in a special way. Great teachers have some common traits.

Great teachers see our potential. They do not get distracted by our quirks; they accept and encourage them. They care about their students in a visceral way. Great teachers love their specialty, and they let that love teach us. The great teachers encourage us to do our best. Just think of Robin Williams' portrayal of Mr. Keating in the movie The Dead Poets Society, and you will know what a great teacher is all about. Jesus was a great teacher because he loved us, respected us, guided us, and was thrilled when we overcame the obstacles that could prevent us from being the best version of ourselves.

Where is Jesus still calling us to grow?

June 24 – Solemnity of Nativity of John the Baptist

> Then fear came upon all their neighbors,
> and all these matters were discussed
> throughout the hill country of Judea.
> All who hear these things took them to heart, saying,
> "What, then, will this child be?"
> For surely the hand of the Lord was with him.
> Lk 1: 57 – 66, 80

Every parent, looking at a newborn child asks the exact same question, "What will this child be? So much is unknown; so much is envisioned. Will the child be healthy, live a long life, be happy, invent the cure for cancer, or become world famous? So many questions; so few answers. I remember reading once that every newborn baby is a sign that God has not yet given up on our world.

There is a wonderful story about a couple visiting a little town in the Midwest. At the General Store, there was an elderly gentleman sitting in a rocking chair. The couple asked him, "Any famous people born in this town?" He kept rocking, thought for a few moments and said, "Nope, just babies." Except for nobility, no one is born famous. We become famous, locally, nationally, or internationally, because of what we do with the precious gift of life.

More important than the question, "What will this child be?", is the next sentence: "For surely, the hand of the Lord was with him."

Our God is with us throughout our lives. He is there to love us, guide us, and protect us. From the moment we are born, especially from the moment we are Baptized, God says, "This is my beloved, son or daughter, on whom my favor rests." It was true of Jesus, John the Baptist, and you and me. God is with us so that we can become the people he wants us to be. Now that is a pedigree that cannot be beaten.

Who does God want us to become?

June 29 – Peter and Paul, Apostles

> When Jesus came to the neighborhood of Caesarea Philippi,
> he asked his disciples this question,
> "Who do people say that the Son of Man is?"
> They replied,
> "Some say John the Baptist, others Elijah,
> still others Jeremiah or one of the prophets."
> "And you," he said to them,
> "who do you say that I am?"
> "You are the Messiah," Simon Peter answered,
> "the Son of the living God!"
> Mt 16: 13 – 19

Some people point to today's gospel as the day the church was born; others think it is the preamble to the beginning of the church. Either way this feast teaches a very important lesson. There is more than one way to be a believer. Two people could not be more different than Peter and Paul.

Peter was impetuous to say the least. He said the first thing that came to mind. Reflection was not his strong suit. He was as quick to predict that he would never deny Jesus as he was to deny him. He got out of the boat without a lot of reflection; when he did reflect he began to sink. In spite of his faults and failings Jesus picked him to be the leader of the apostles.

Paul on the other hand was a bit of a brooder. It is clear from some of the beautiful scripture passages he wrote that he was a thinker. He had the soul of a poet, and the vision of an explorer. He was zealous, perhaps overzealous. He was capable of confrontation, and enjoyed a good debate. He was well educated. God chose him to bring the Good News to the Gentiles.

God needs each and every one of us to be his messengers. Each one of us has a special skill set that helps us speak to the full spectrum of humanity so that the Good News can reach the ends of the earth.

Where do we need to use our gifts to help spread the faith?

July 25 – Feast of St. Thomas, Apostle

Then he said to Thomas, "Put your finger here and see my hands,
and bring your hand and put in into my side,
and do not be unbelieving, but believe."
Thomas answered and said to him, "My Lord and my God!"
Jesus said to him, "Have you come to believe because you have seen me?
Blessed are those who have not seen and have believed."
Jn 20: 24 – 29

Thomas gets a lot of bad press. He is called "doubting Thomas" and "unbelieving Thomas." Thomas has other moments, better moments, which are seldom mentioned. When Jesus announced that he was going to Bethany because his friend Lazarus was dying, it was Thomas who said, "Let us also go, that we might die with him." (Jn 11:16) At the Last Supper, when Jesus announced to the disciples that "Where I am going, you know the way." It was Thomas who said, "Lord, we don't know where you are going; how can we know the way?" Which led to Jesus saying, "I am the way, the truth and the life." (Jn 14: 6) Obviously, Thomas needs a new press agent.

He is also known as the "twin" although his twin is never mentioned. We do not know if "twin" was a nickname or if he was actually a twin, but that doesn't really matter. Thomas is our twin. In his life of faith there were ups and downs; the same is true in our lives of faith. Thomas did memorable deeds of faith, and so do we. He was never afraid of sharing his doubts, which led to faith spurts. Perhaps we need to follow that trait better.

Most of all, when Thomas encountered his Savior, he proudly said, "My Lord and my God." May we grow to do the same.

Where do we need to wrestle more honestly with doubts in our faith?

August 6 – Transfiguration of the Lord

> Jesus took Peter, James, and his brother, John,
> and led them up a high mountain by themselves.
> And he was transfigured before them;
> his face shone like the sun and his clothes were as white as light.
> And behold, Moses and Elijah appeared to them,
> conversing with him.
> Then Peter said to Jesus in reply,
> "Lord, it is good that we are here.
> If you wish, I will make three tents here.
> one for you, one for Moses, and one for Elijah."
> Mt 17: 1 – 9

It is hard to say what actually happened on that mountain, but it was life changing for Jesus, and for Peter, James, and John. There are moments, perhaps not as dramatic, in every life. A time, a moment when the pieces all fit together, when the focus is clear, when we realize we have been called.

Dag Hammarskjold, in his book Markings, expresses it this way, "I don't know Who – or what – put the question. I don't know when it was put. I don't even remember answering. But at some moment I did answer Yes to Someone – or something – and from that hour I was certain that existence is meaningful and that, therefore, my life, in self-surrender had a goal." His experience was not as focused as what Peter, James, and John had, but it had the same result.

Emma McLaughlin, in The Turning Point, expresses it thusly: "It happens to all men and women the time when scattered pieces come together to form a whole, and if they are aware, forever after they can name the hour, the day, the special nuances of light and shade that shaped the miracle. Whenever it happens, you will be aware of seeing visions that others do not see, and hearing music others have not heard. The distant blur will fade and all things come sharply clear, henceforth and for all time, you will be different and you will know the shining difference."

What was your shining moment? If it has not yet come, do you believe it will?

August 10 – Saint Lawrence, Deacon and Martyr

> Jesus said to his disciples:
> "Amen, amen, I say to you,
> Unless a grain of wheat falls to the ground and dies,
> It remains but a grain of wheat;
> but if it dies, it produces much fruit."
> Jn 12: 24 – 26

Back in the days when I was a campus minister, I remember going to a workshop for youth ministers. On the first night of the workshop, the speaker was a mime. He was a Jesuit by the name of Kent Fife, who always wrote IF after his name rather than the more traditional SJ. Since he was a mime it was impossible to ask him the meaning of IF, and why he used that rather than SJ. Since this workshop took place in the era before cell phones and Siri, I had to wait until I got home to discover that he considered himself, Kent Fife, Itinerant Fool.

He led the first session. He came out with a battered old suitcase. He opened it and began to take things out and put them on the floor in front of him. There was a colorful square cloth, a candle, a metal container that rattled when he shook it, matches and a large spoon. Slowly he arranged everything; then he put the large spoon over the flame of the candle. All this was done in silence. Suddenly there was a pop, and a kernel of popcorn landed in front of him. Several more followed. Slowly he put everything back in the suitcase and left the room; facilitators guided us from there.

It took a while, but finally we realized that the kernels of popping corn had to be buried in the oil, suffer the pain of the oil in order to resurrect as something special that brought people joy. It was all about Eucharist, and in today's gospel Jesus had to suffer and die for us in order to be raised up and give us salvation.

What in our lives needs to die so that we can produce much fruit?

August 15 – Feast of the Assumption

> And Mary said,
> "My soul proclaims the greatness of the Lord;
> my spirit rejoices in God my Savior
> for he has looked with favor on his lowly servant.
> From this day all generations will call me blessed:
> the Almighty has done great things for me
> and holy is his name.
> Lk 1: 39 – 56

The old translation of the Magnificat was, "My being proclaims the greatness of the Lord." I like that translation better. "My soul" sounds like only part of Mary proclaims the greatness of the Lord. "My being" says that Mary was all in.

What an audacious thing it is to say! Mary's being does not give God greatness; she just proclaims it. That is what she did when she said, "Yes" to the angel Gabriel. She gave her life in humble obedience to God, and Jesus was born. It was Mary's great faith that proclaimed God's greatness.

We, each in our own unique way, are called to proclaim the greatness of the Lord. How can we do that? Several years ago, I was visiting with a friend I met years ago when we were studying theology. My friend never got ordained; he became a social worker. After he retired, the woman who was his secretary for many years entered the RCIA process and became a Catholic. She told him she became a Catholic because of him. She watched how he treated people. She observed his gentle, sensitive way of dealing with people in a way that respected their dignity. He never touted his faith, or talked about being a Catholic. He just proclaimed the greatness of the Lord in his everyday living. We are called to do the same.

How do we proclaim the greatness of the Lord in our everyday living?

August 24 – Feast of St. Bartholomew, Apostle

> Philip found Nathanael and told him.
> "We have found the one about whom Moses wrote in the law,
> and also the prophets, Jesus son of Joseph, from Nazareth."
> But Nathanael said to him,
> "Can anything good come from Nazareth?"
> Philip said to him,
> "Come and see."
> Jesus saw Nathanael coming toward him and said of him,
> "Here is a true child of Israel.
> There is no duplicity in him."
> Jn 1: 45 – 51

You might be wondering why if it is the feast of St. Bartholomew is the gospel about Philip and Nathanael. Matthew, Mark, and Luke call him Bartholomew; John calls him Nathanael although this is not universally agreed upon.

In the New American Bible translation Jesus says, "This man is a true Israelite. There is no guile in him." Today we would probably say, "He tells it like it is." The gospel even gives proof of his lack of guile or duplicity when he questions whether Nazareth can produce anything good. Even though Nazareth was not on anyone's "A" list of cities and towns, many would have refrained from such a disparaging remark. Not Bartholomew, he just says what he thinks; in spite of that, or is it because of that, they made him a saint. There is hope for us all.

Jesus also was without guile or duplicity. He called out the scribes and the Pharisees. He cleaned the moneychangers out of the temple. He was not afraid to confront the men who dragged before him the woman caught in adultery. He did not play any word games with either Pilate or Herod. Our world would be a better place if more people would just say what needs to be said rather than hiding behind vague words and phrases.

Where do we need to be more straightforward in the words we speak?

September 8 – Birth of Mary

> "Joseph, son of David,
> do not be afraid to take Mary your wife into your home.
> For it is through the Holy Spirit
> that this child has been conceived in her.
> She will bear a son and you are to name him, Jesus,
> because he will save his people from their sins."
> All this took place to fulfill
> what the Lord had said through the prophet:
> *Behold, the virgin shall be with child and bear a son,*
> *and they shall name him Emmanuel,*
> which means *"God is with us."*
> Mt 1: 18 – 23

I just love when the church gives us a feast day for which there is no appropriate gospel passage because it helps us focus on what is really important in our faith. Catholics are comfortable with a faith that is built on the Bible and tradition. Some of our Christian sisters and brothers do not agree with us. They want their faith built only on the Bible. I wonder if that divide will ever be healed.

Today we celebrate Mary's, the mother of Jesus, birthday. How did the church come up with Mary's birthday as September 8? The easiest answer is that September 8 is exactly nine months after the Feast of the Immaculate Conception, which raises the question why is the Feast of the Immaculate Conception celebrated on December 8. Who really cares?

What we need to celebrate is the birth of Joachim and Anne's only child, Mary. Usually the church celebrated saints on the day they died. We celebrate both the birth and death of Jesus. Only Mary and John the Baptist have their feast days on their birthdays. Mary was chosen from the moment of her conception to be the mother of Jesus. She was chosen, but she was not forced. The thing that we too easily forget is that Mary could have said "No" to the angel Gabriel. She could have put her will ahead of God's will, but she did not. She trusted God. She let faith be her guide. When faced with questions, doubts, and insecurity, she found a way to say, "Be it done to me according to your word."

Where do we need Mary to help us be better believers?

September 14 – Triumph of the Cross

> For God has so loved the world that he gave his only Son,
> so that everyone who believes in him might not perish but might have eternal life.
> For God did not send his Son into the world to condemn the world.
> But that the world might be saved through him.
> Jn 3: 13 – 17

We have forgotten the scandal of the cross. Familiarity has dulled our senses. Imagine if next week we entered church and instead of a cross or a crucifix hanging on the back wall there was a guillotine or a noose – that would get our attention.

We have decorative crosses, we have crosses made of gold that we hang around our necks, and we have crosses embossed on our stationery. We have the Jerusalem cross, the Celtic cross, the Greek cross, the Maltese cross, the cross of St. Andrew, the Latin cross, the Byzantine cross, the Papal cross, and the cross of St. Brigid to name but a few. Bishops wear pectoral crosses as a sign of their office.

Too often the cross is a decoration; too infrequently it is a call to faith. Jesus died on the cross for us. He was willing to suffer so that we might be set free from our sins. The only cross we need is the sign of the cross we make whenever we enter a church, or whenever we begin our prayers.

The Trappists have many wonderful customs. One that we could all follow is to put a simple cross over our bed as a reminder that we all need to climb on that cross and join our sacrifices with his.

How can we make sure that the cross does not lose its power to motivate us?

September 21 – Feast of St. Matthew

> As Jesus passed by,
> he saw a man named Matthew sitting at the customs post.
> He said to him, "Follow me."
> And he got up and followed him.
> Mt 9: 9 – 13

The gospel accounts of Jesus calling the Apostles have been cleaned up to say the least. We are led to believe that the first time Jesus met James and John or Peter and Andrew he said, "Follow me" and they did. Highly unlikely.

They no doubt met Jesus on several occasions, heard him teach with parables, were fascinated, and then Jesus called them. Even then, it is unlikely that they dropped everything and followed him. They went through a discernment process. They were ambivalent. Part of them wanted to follow him, and part of them wanted to keep fishing. The same is true for Matthew. To follow Jesus meant giving up a very lucrative career.

The same is true for us. Jesus calls up at Baptism, but we don't realize that until much later on. Each new day is a call from Jesus to be his disciples. Every time we see someone in need, every time we encounter an injustice, and every time forgiveness is required, Jesus is calling us.

We need to remember that the call of faith is a process. We have to work at it every day. We may never have our own feast day like the Apostles, but we must remember that Jesus needs our yes every bit as much as he needed the yes of Matthew and the other Apostles.

How can we respond to Jesus' call in a more vibrant way?

October 18 – Saint Luke, Evangelist

> The Lord appointed a further seventy-two and
> sent them in pairs to every town and place he intended to visit.
> He said to them:
> "The harvest is rich but the workers are few,
> therefore ask the harvest-master to send workers to his harvest.
> Be on your way, and remember:
> I am sending you as lambs in the midst of wolves."
> Lk 10: 1 – 9

Luke is the author of both the gospel that bears his name and the Acts of the Apostles, which makes him the most prolific author in the New Testament. Paul refers to him as a physician, and he is considered a disciple of Paul. He is the patron saint of artists, physicians, bachelors, surgeons, students, and butchers, which is a strange mix indeed.

In today's gospel, we have Jesus sending out his disciples to prepare folks for his visit. Jesus gives them very specific instructions. They are to go with just the basics – no walking stick, no travel bag, and no sandals.

Their first instruction is to keep their eye on the prize; they are not to get distracted by greeting folks along the way. When they get to their destination extend peace to whatever house they enter. Do not expect special treatment. Eat whatever they put before you, and then heal the sick and announce, "The reign of God is at hand!"

In what simple ways can we announce God's kingdom is at hand?

Oct 28 – Saints Simon and Jude, Apostles

> Jesus went out to the mountain to pray,
> spending the night in communion with God.
> At daybreak he called his disciples,
> and selected twelve of them to be his apostles:
> Simon, to whom he gave the name Peter,
> and Andrew his brother, James and John,
> Philip and Bartholomew, Matthew and Thomas,

> James son of Alphaeus, and Simon called the Zealot,
> Judas son of James, and Judas, Iscariot,
> Who turned traitor.
> Lk 6: 12 – 16

With the exception of Peter James, John, and Matthew we know very little about the Apostles. Today's feast bears this out. Simon we know only because he is listed whenever the Apostles are listed. I do not think he is the patron saint of anything. Jude is mentioned only twice in the lists of the Apostles; in the other two lists he is called Thaddeus. Why he has two different names is unknown. His actual name was Judas but for obvious reasons that was shortened, which may explain why Jude is the patron saint of hopeless causes.

The Apostles are made up of two sets of brothers, Peter and Andrew, and James and John. A tax collector and what else? Eight of the Apostles labored in relative obscurity, but labor they did.

At Mass today we will use the Preface of the Apostles I in which we will pray, "You are the eternal Shepherd who never leaves his flock untended. Through the apostles you watch over us and protect us always. You made them shepherds of the flock to share in the work of your Son and from their place in heaven they guide us still." (old translation) It seems like their job is never finished. Good thing because we can use all the help we can get.

How often have you prayed to St. Jude?

November 1 – All Saints

> "How blest are the poor in spirit: the reign of God is theirs.
> Blest too are the sorrowing; they shall be consoled.
> Blessed are they who hunger and thirst for holiness,
> they shall have their fill."
> Mt 5: 1 – 12

Our liturgical year is full of recognized saints. Some are very popular; some are practically unknown. Most of us have a patron saint. In my family of origin, I always felt left out when it came to my patron saint. One of my brothers had John the Baptist, another had St. Matthew, and the third brother had Albert the Great. Me, I had St. John Eudes, whom, I am pretty sure, you know nothing about.

Today we have a feast day for all those saints the church never recognized because she knows nothing about them. All of us have personal saints who have enriched our lives. It might be a grandmother who had great devotion to the Blessed Mother, or a grandfather who was always helping someone in need. Some of us are blessed to have parents who are saintly. Then there is the coach who gave so freely of his time to makes sure that his players learned to embrace the value of fairness, and that winning was not the most important lesson in sports. Most of us had a teacher who was a saint blessed with unlimited patience and a keen eye for hidden talent. Maybe there was that certain priest who just made God real, or the religious sister or brother whose life glowed with the divine presence. Today we are invited to celebrate these saints and thank God for their presence in our lives.

How are we doing on our journey to become one of God's holy ones?

November 2 – All Souls

> Jesus said to his disciples:
> "Do not let your hearts be troubled.
> Have faith in God and faith in me.
> In my father's house there are many dwelling places;
> Otherwise, how could I have told you
> that I was going to prepare a place for you?"
> Jn 14: 1 – 6

How can a death denying people pay their respects to the dead? I am an avid reader of obituaries. Over time there has been a devolution of that art form. Wakes used to be two days long, and sometimes you would go to both days and to the funeral Mass. There was no formula to determine what your level of respect should be. Some people got both days of the wake, others just one day. Seldom if ever would you go to a funeral Mass unless you had been to the wake.

Today things are completely different. Wakes are shorter and shorter. They used to be two days long with calling hours in both the afternoon and evening. Now the calling hours are late afternoon into early evening and just one day. There is a growing trend of having calling hours on the morning of the funeral Mass. Still worse is when calling hours are omitted, and the funeral is private. I am sure that sometimes this needs to be, but less frequently, I suspect, than it is happening.

The wake and the funeral are for the living not the deceased. We need this day so that we can respectfully remember our faithfully departed. The longer we live the longer the list gets until the day comes that we are among the remembered and not among the remembering.

May their souls and the souls of all the faithfully departed rest in peace. Amen.

November 9 – Dedication of St. John Lateran

> Jesus said to his disciples:
> "If you bring your gift to the altar
> and there recall that your brother has anything against you,
> leave your gift at the altar,
> go first to be reconciled with your brother,
> and then come and offer your gift."
> Mt 5: 23 – 24

You have to be very good at Catholic trivia to know why the Basilica of St. John Lateran is a first class feast. It is the oldest church in the world built when Melchiade (311 – 314) was the Pope. During its long history it has been desecrated, sacked, and set on fire. It is where all popes were enthroned up until 1870. The Archbasilica of St. John Lateran is the mother church of the Catholic world. Although we are much more familiar with St. Peter's Basilica, which is a magnificent structure, it is outranked by St. John Lateran because it is the cathedral for the diocese of Rome, and as we know the proper title for the Pope is the Bishop of Rome. Thus today's feast day.

Church buildings are an important part of our faith. Many of us have visited some of the major churches in the world. All of us have "our parish church." That special place where our faith is nurtured, the sacraments are celebrated, and we bury our dead. The place where we can sit in quiet reflection, and know that we belong. We all have our spiritual home. Today we get to thank God for that gift.

In quiet reverie let us be connected with our spiritual home.

Thanksgiving Day

> As Jesus continued his journey to Jerusalem,
> He travelled through Samaria and Galilee.
> As he was entering a village, ten persons with leprosy met him.
> They stood at a distance from him, raised their voices, saying,
> "Jesus, Master! Have pity on us!"
> And when he saw them, he said,
> "Go show yourselves to the priests."
> As they were going they were cleansed.
> And one of them, realizing he had been healed,
> returned, glorifying God in a loud voice,
> and he fell at the feet of Jesus and thanked him.
> Lk 17: 11 – 19

Today is a holiday that truly is a holyday. A day set aside to thank God for all his gifts and blessings. Of course, it is impossible to have a day for thanksgiving. Every day needs to be a day of thanksgiving. If we don't set aside a bit of time every day to appreciate God's lavish bounty in our lives, we, not God, are diminished.

One of the first lessons we were all taught was to always say "please" when we ask for something, and always say "thank you" when your request is granted. We need frequent reminders of the importance of this primal couplet.

People will frequently say to me, "There is no need for a thank you note." I just smile and ignore them. There is a need because that is what my mother taught me to do. We need to restore the written thank you note. It seems to be falling by the wayside. A text thank you is better than nothing; the same is true for an email one. There is something special about receiving a thoughtful hand-written thank you note.

Sometime today between the football and the turkey sit down and write a thank you note to God. No postage will be required.

November 30 – Saint Andrew, Apostle

As Jesus was walking along the Sea of Galilee he watched two brothers,
    Simon now known as Peter, and his brother, Andrew,
        Casting a net into the sea. They were fishermen.
He said to them, "Come after me and I will make you fishers of men."
    They immediately abandoned their nets and became his followers.
               Mt 4: 18 – 22

Andrew was the one who introduced his brother, Peter, to Jesus. In the Orthodox Church, Andrew is considered the first disciple to be called. I have always found it strange that the group of Peter, James, and John who were present at the Transfiguration and at the Agony in the Garden did not include Andrew. I wonder was it Peter who did not get along with his brother, or was it Jesus who excluded Andrew. I'll never know.

Andrew is the patron saint of Barbados, Romania, Russia, Ukraine, and Scotland, where there is a city, a university, and a famous golf course named after him.

Andrew and his brother, Peter, and their fishing partners, James and John, have a very important lesson to teach us. In order to be a follower of Jesus you have to give up your security. Imagine what it must feel like when you abandon your nets and leave the security of your former way of life. But that is what they did. Jesus calls us every day, and if we are going to be his disciples we have to abandon our selfishness, our greed, our revenge, and anything else that prevents us from giving our lives more fully to him.

What is Jesus calling us to abandon in order to follow him more fully?

December 8 – Immaculate Conception

> Mary said: "I am the maidservant of the Lord.
> Let it be done to me as you say."
> With that the angel left her.
> Lk 1: 26 – 38

The United States of America is dedicated to the Immaculate Conception of Mary. In Washington, DC, there is a magnificent basilica of the Immaculate Conception. Today's feast always causes confusion because of the gospel. The gospel is of the Annunciation not the Immaculate Conception. Why? Because there is no scripture for the Immaculate Conception. It is part of our tradition.

The feast celebrates that we believe that when Mary was conceived in her mother, Anne's, womb she was conceived without sin because she was to be the mother of Jesus. Pius IX proclaimed the Immaculate Conception a dogma of the Catholic Church on December 8, 1854. This made formal what everyone already believed, that Mary had to be a proper vessel for the savior.

Without Mary's yes to the angel Gabriel none of this would have happened. God had his plan; Mary had her free will. God could only ask through Gabriel, and even God had to hold his breath while waiting for her answer. Although Mary was filled with questions and doubts, she trusted God and said, "Let it be done to me as you say." Today we need to ask Mary to help us say yes as she did.

How can we more fully embrace God's will in our lives?

Lectio Divina

1. Read the scripture for the day slowly and prayerfully.
2. Ponder what the scripture passage is trying to say to you.
3. Thank God in prayer for speaking to you through his word.

Pope Francis in Evangelii Gaudium (The Joy Of The Gospel) offers a series of questions that we could ask during our pondering of the daily scripture passage: "In the presence of God, during a recollected reading of the text it is good to ask, for example: 'Lord, what does this text say to me? What is it about my life that you want to change by this text? Why am I not interested in this? Or Perhaps, What do I fine pleasant in this text? What is it about this word that moves me? What attracts me" Why does it attract me?' When we make an effort to listen to the Lord temptations usually arise. One of them is simply to feel troubled or burdened, and to turn away. Another common temptation is to think about what the text means for other people, and so avoid applying it to our own life. It can also happen that we look for excuses to water down the clear meaning of the text. Or we can wonder if God is demanding too much of us, asking for a decision which we are not yet prepared to make. This leads many people to stop taking pleasure in the encounter with God's word; but this would mean forgetting that no one is more patient than God our Father, that no one is more understanding and wiling to wait. He always invites us to take a step forward, but does not demand a full response if we are not yet ready. He simply asks that we sincerely look at our life and present ourselves honestly before him, and that we be willing to continue to grow asking from him what we ourselves cannot as yet achieve." (EG #153)

Made in United States
North Haven, CT
21 September 2022

24394098R00264